THE THEORY OF INVESTMENT VALUE

THE THEORY OF INVESTMENT VALUE

By John Burr Williams

FRASER PUBLISHING COMPANY

To

MY WIFE

PREFACE

To OUTLINE a new sub-science that shall be known as the Theory of Investment Value and that shall comprise a coherent body of principles like the Theory of Monopoly, the Theory of Money, and the Theory of International Trade, all branches of the larger science of Economics, is the first aim of this book. To relate the abstract principles of Economics to the practical problems of investment, and to show how the theories of interest, rent, wages, and profits, taxes, and money, can be applied to the evaluation of stocks and bonds, is another aim of this book. To examine certain economic consequences of the New Deal so far as the investor is concerned, and to determine the most important questions on which investment policy today must rest, is a third aim of this book. These last two aims, however, are but incidental to the primary purpose of codifying the Theory of Investment Value and making it into a department of Economics as a whole.

While this book is addressed primarily to the intelligent investor and the professional investment analyst, it is hoped, nevertheless, that it will be of interest to the economic theorist also, because of what it has to offer on long- and short-term interest rates, liquidity preference, uncertainty and risk, the future of interest rates, the likelihood of inflation, the proper response of stock and bond prices thereto, the behavior of markets, the formation of stock prices, the liaison between speculative commodity and security prices, the incidence of various taxes, and other questions of theory.

Investment Value, defined as the present worth of future

dividends, or of future coupons and principal, is of practical importance to every investor because it is the *critical* value above which he cannot go in buying or holding, without added risk. If a man buys a security *below* its investment value he need never lose, even if its price should fall at once, because he can still hold for income and get a return above normal on his cost price; but if he buys it above its investment value his only hope of avoiding a loss is to sell to someone else who must in turn take the loss in the form of insufficient income. Therefore all those who do not feel able to foresee the swings of the market and do not wish to speculate on mere changes in price must have recourse to estimates of investment value to guide them in their buying and selling.

Dedicated as it is by its very title to the intrinsic or ultimate worth of investments, this book cannot help but imply as a corollary, however, a Theory of Speculation also. If marginal opinion, not intrinsic value, determines market price, as claimed in this book, and if changes in opinion, but nothing else, cause changes in price, then those who trade in the market for a living will find herein a philosophy of their work. Nevertheless, the book is not a manual of rules for speculators, nor are the estimates of investment value reached in its Case Studies intended as forecasts of the next move in stock prices.

A pioneer step in the measurement of intrinsic value was taken several years ago in a book entitled *Stock Growth and Discount Tables* by S. E. Guild, R. G. Wiese, Stephen Heard, T. H. Brown, and other collaborators. A further step was taken recently by G. A. D. Preinreich, in the mathematical appendix to his book, *The Nature of Dividends*. The present book follows the same trail still further, and shows in particular how the dividends a company will pay in the future can be forecast, either by "algebraic budgets" using estimates concerning the future growth, earnings, and capital structure of a company, or by other methods.

Although the book makes frequent use of simple algebra, facility with this subject is needed only by those specialists who focus their attention on Part II; all others can read the rest of the book without knowledge of mathematics. Any symbols that are likely to trouble the non-technical reader are carefully explained when first introduced. The mathematics is not to be considered as a drawback to the analysis, however, nor as a method of reasoning which serious students can afford to neglect. Quite the contrary! The truth is that the mathematical method is a new tool of great power, whose use promises to lead to notable advances in Investment Analysis. Always it has been the rule in the history of science that the invention of new tools and new methods is the key to new discoveries, and we may expect the same rule to hold true in this branch of Economics as well.

That investment analysis until now has been altogether unequal to the demands put upon it should be clear from the tremendous fluctuations in stock prices that have occurred in recent years. As will be shown in the "Post Mortems" in Book II, proper canons of evaluation, generally accepted as authoritative, should have helped to check these price swings somewhat, and thereby reduce in some degree the violence of the business cycle, to the benefit of all the world.

J. B. W.

OCTOBER 1, 1937

ACKNOWLEDGMENTS

I WISH to express my gratitude to Professors Joseph A. Schumpeter, Wassily W. Leontief, and Shaw Livermore for criticisms of the entire manuscript; and to Mr. C. L. Weaver for a final check of the mathematics. Others who have read various chapters and offered helpful comments include Mr. J. L. Holley, Mr. A. C. Patton, Mr. Gustav Burke, Mr. Gladden W. Baker, Mr. Edward Milligan, and Mr. George C. Long, Jr. Miss Pearl Cohen has prepared the index. To Harcourt, Brace and Company, Inc., Professor Edwin W. Kemmerer, The Macmillan Company, Dr. Gabriel A. D. Preinreich, and *The Spectator*, I am indebted for permission to quote from copyright material.

J. B. W.

CONTENTS

BOOK I
INVESTMENT VALUE AND MARKET PRICE

PART I
SPECULATION IN THE STOCK MARKET

PART II
THE PURE THEORY OF INVESTMENT VALUE

BOOK II

CASE STUDIES IN INVESTMENT VALUE

PART I

CURRENT STUDIES

PART II

POST MORTEMS

SYMBOLS AND ABBREVIATIONS

ALTHOUGH every symbol is defined in the text when first introduced, the following table is inserted here for easy reference.

GREEK LETTERS

α = alpha = aggregate earnings on assets, per share of common stock

β = beta = bond interest and preferred dividends, per share of common stock

γ = gamma = earnings per share, after interest and preferred dividends

ρ = rho = reinvestment requirement per share

π = pi = pure or net dividend per share, after any assessment or subscription

κ = kappa = actual dividend per share

σ = sigma = subscription for new stock, or assessment, per share

λ = lambda = *rate* of earnings on common (special case in Chapter XIII)

ϵ = epsilon = error of approximation (special case in Chapter X)

CAPITAL LETTERS

A = assets per share of common stock, net after depreciation, etc.

B = bonds and preferred stock, per share of common stock

C = common stock's book value per share

D = depreciation, etc., per share

N = number of shares

M = market price per share

V = investment value per share

Q = quick assets per share, excess thereof over normal requirements

H = height of commodity prices, i.e., index number for the price level of goods and services

SMALL LETTERS

a = rate of earnings on assets

b = rate of bond interest and preferred dividends, i.e., the "bond rate"

c = rate of earnings on common ⎫

r = reinvestment rate

p = pure dividend rate   ⎬ based on *book value* of common stock

k = actual dividend rate

s = subscription rate ⎭

g = rate of growth

h = rate of inflation

$\hat{\imath}$ = rate of interest on riskless investments

x = premium for risk

i = rate of interest proper for the security in question

$j_{(2)}$ = annual rate of interest equivalent to twice the semi-annual rate i (special case in Chapters X and XX)

l = leverage

q = distribution rate

e = price-earnings ratio

m = market-price to book-value ratio

y = yield

t = time

n = number of years, or interest periods

VARIATIONS OF THE FOREGOING SYMBOLS

$\hat{M}$ = M-cap = market price per share ⎫

$\hat{V}$ = V-cap = investment value per share ⎬ after recapitalization in the manner specified

$\hat{B}$ = B-cap = bonds and preferred stock

$\hat{l}$ = l-cap = leverage ⎭

$\bar{V}$ = V-bar = mean of the various investment values given by the probability curve for V

$\bar{q}$ = q-bar = ratio of taxes, interest, and dividends to quasi-rent (Chapter XXII, § 12)

$M_c = m$ sub C = market price of common stock
$M_w = M$ sub W = market price of option warrant
$N_c = N$ sub C = number of shares of common stock
$N_w = N$ sub W = number of option warrants
ΔC = delta C = small increment in the quantity C (Chapter XIII, § 2)
Δt = delta t = small increment in the time t (Chapter XIII, § 2)
Δq = delta q = small increment in the quantity q (Chapter XVII, § 9)

ABBREVIATIONS

(14a) $\quad u = 1 + g$

(14d) $\quad u = \dfrac{1}{1+h}$

(2) $\quad v = \dfrac{1}{1+i}$

(15) $\quad w = uv$

(35) $\quad j_{(2)} = 2i$

(120) $\quad z = \dfrac{A_n}{A_o}$

(106) $\quad G = \sum_{t=1}^{t=n} \gamma_t$

(100) $\quad K = \sum_{t=1}^{t=n} \kappa_t$

(101) $\quad S = \sum_{t=1}^{t=n} \sigma_t$

(105) $\quad P = \sum_{t=1}^{t=n} \pi_t$

(107) $$R = \sum_{t=1}^{t=n} \rho_t$$

(30a) $$a_{\overline{n}|} = \sum_{t=1}^{t=n} v^t = \frac{1}{i}(1 - v^n)$$

(103) $$s_{\overline{n}|} = \sum_{t=1}^{t=n} (1 + i)^{n-t} = \frac{1}{i}\left[(1 + i)^n - 1\right]$$

RELATIONS IMPLICIT IN THE DEFINITIONS

(38b) $a = aA$

(41b) $\beta = bB$

(47b) $\gamma = cC$

(48b) $\rho = rC$

(28b) $\pi = pC$

        $\kappa = kC$

        $\sigma = sC$

(11b) $a = \beta + \gamma$

(39a) $A \rightleftharpoons B + C$

(3a) $\pi = \kappa - \sigma$

(10a) $\pi = \gamma - \rho$

        $g = \dfrac{A_1 - A_0}{A_0}$

(31a) $h = \dfrac{H_1 - H_0}{H_0}$

(40a) $l = \dfrac{A}{C} = \dfrac{B + C}{C}$

(82) $q = \dfrac{\beta + \pi}{a}$

(7b) $\qquad i = \hat{\imath} + x$

(76a) $\qquad e = \dfrac{M}{\gamma}$

(68a) $\qquad m = \dfrac{M}{C}$

(80a) $\qquad y = \dfrac{\kappa}{M}$

BOOK I

INVESTMENT VALUE AND MARKET PRICE

———

PART I

SPECULATION IN THE STOCK MARKET

CHAPTER I

THE DIFFERENCE BETWEEN SPECULATION AND INVESTMENT

I. REAL WORTH AND MARKET PRICE

Separate and distinct things not to be confused, as every thoughtful investor knows, are real worth and market price. No buyer considers all securities equally attractive at their present market prices whatever these prices happen to be; on the contrary, he seeks "the best at the price." He picks and chooses among all the stocks and bonds in the market until he finds the cheapest issues. Even then he may not buy at all, for fear that everything is too high and nothing will give him his money's worth. If he does buy, and buy as an investor, he holds for income; if as a speculator, for profit. But speculators as a class can profit only by trading with investors,[1] to whom they can sell only for income; therefore in the end all prices depend on someone's estimate of future income.[2] Of investment value in this sense some men will make one estimate, others another, and of all these estimates only one will coincide with the actual price, and only one with the true worth.

Our problem, therefore, is twofold: to explain the price as it is, and to show what price would be right. Part I of this book will deal with the first question, Part II with the second.

2. DEFINITION OF AN INVESTOR

As will be shown later, the longer a buyer holds a stock or bond, the more important are the dividends or coupons

[1] Cf. Chapter III, § 4.
[2] A full discussion of the question of whether earnings or dividends determine the value of stocks will be found in Chapter V, § 2.

while he owns it and the less important is the price when he sells it. In the extreme case where the security is held by the same family for generations, a practice by no means uncommon, the selling price in the end is a minor matter. For this reason we shall define an investor as a buyer interested in dividends, or coupons and principal, and a speculator as a buyer interested in the resale price.[3] Thus the usual buyer is a hybrid, being partly investor and partly speculator. Clearly the pure investor must hold his security for long periods, while the pure speculator must sell promptly, if each is to get what he seeks.

If the investor chooses his holdings wisely, he can make quite as much money as the speculator. In fact, he can probably make more, or so it would seem from the history of great fortunes. But to buy when a security goes below its true worth, and to sell when it goes above it, is not enough to constitute wise investment, for such a policy would put the buying and selling points very close together, and in the end would yield no more than pure interest on the fund so invested. Wise investment requires that only such issues as are selling far below their true worth should be bought; then, as large income payments are received in subsequent years because things turn out better for the security than most people expected, a handsome return on the principal can be enjoyed.[4]

[3] For the traditional view on this point, see Benjamin Graham and David L. Dodd, *Security Analysis* (New York and London: McGraw-Hill Book Company, Inc., 1934), chap. IV, "Distinction between Investment and Speculation."

[4] It would be misleading to leave the reader with the impression that speculation and investment together exhaust the subject of security profits. Not all fortunes founded on stock-market operations are obtained by either skillful investment or adroit speculation, for other procedures of a less defensible sort, which fall outside the range of our discussion, are resorted to sometimes. For instance, promoters at times succeed in erecting some sort of monopoly that will stand for a while, and then they proceed to capitalize the high earnings that result, and sell huge issues of bonds and stocks to savings banks, insurance companies, employees, customers, and the general public. In this way the original owners of the monopoly "get out from under." By shifting the load to

Nowadays rich men are being forced by the income-tax laws to be investors instead of speculators. So heavy now are the surtaxes on stock profits that wealthy men often will not run the risks entailed in speculating for quick gains, with most of the profit in good years going to the government, but all of the loss in bad years falling on themselves. To avoid such unfair odds, rich men are being forced to hold their stocks for five or ten years, so as to bring their taxable gains down to 40 or 30 per cent of their total gains.[5] Seeing that taxes load the dice against quick profits and make speculation a losing game, these men are falling back on investment. As investors they are looking to dividends during a long period to bring them their profits, because profits of this kind come in small installments and are not caught in the net of high surtaxes. As a result of the Federal Income Tax Law, therefore, rich men, in a purely practical way, are finding themselves confronted with precisely the problem which we ourselves have set out to investigate entirely as a question of economic theory; namely, "What is the *investment value* of a given security?"

In any science the choice of definitions is a matter of convenience. For reasons that will be given in due course,

---

a big group of innocent security holders, they so strengthen the monopoly politically that it is in no danger of falling down on anyone. As a result, the innocent buyers do not find themselves defrauded, and the promoters need not reproach themselves for selling bad securities, for such securities are not bad. They are just as good as any others, and their owners are not cheated. It is only the customers who suffer, for it is they who have had a monopoly foisted upon them so skillfully that they cannot get rid of it. In practice it is very hard to pick out these monopolies with certainty. The mere fact that insiders have sold out to the general public is, of course, no proof that they have sold out a monopoly. This particular stock-market procedure is mentioned only in passing, however, and will not occupy us henceforth, since it stands apart from our own inquiry. (For an account of an actual monopoly of this sort, see Eliot Jones, *The Anthracite Coal Combination in the United States*, Cambridge, Mass., 1914.)

[5] For details concerning these provisions of the Federal Income Tax Law, see the instruction sheet of the personal income-tax blank.

we shall see fit to define Investment Value, therefore, as the present worth of the future dividends in the case of a stock, or of the future coupons and principal in the case of a bond.

The definition for investment value which we have chosen is in harmony with the time-honored method of economic theory, which always begins its investigations by asking, "What would men do if they were perfectly rational and self-seeking?" The answer is that rational men, when they buy stocks and bonds, would never pay more than the present worth of the expected future dividends, or of the expected future coupons and principal; nor could they pay less, assuming perfect competition, with all traders equally well informed.[6] Such a price is what we have already defined as the *investment value* of a security. In thus choosing a definition in harmony with standard economic methodology, we have cleared the way for the same sort of deductive reasoning in this new branch of economics as has proved so successful in the older branches like the Theory of International Trade, the Theory of Value, and the Theory of Distribution.

Before taking up the main thesis of this book, let us pause, however, to clear the ground of certain troublesome misconceptions, and let us digress to discuss the question of speculation in the stock market first. In other words, before asking what the price for a given security *should be*, let us stop to explain how the price comes to be what it *is*. In this way the reader will become more familiar with the distinction between investment value and market price, and will find it easier to accept the premises of Part II, dealing with the Pure Theory of Investment Value.

[6] See Chapter III for a discussion of differences of opinion concerning the future.

CHAPTER II

DOES THE STOCK MARKET PREDICT THE FUTURE?

I. THE ALLEGED "MIND" OF THE MARKET

Like a ghost in a haunted house, the notion of a soul possessing the market and sending it up or down, with a shrewdness uncanny and superhuman, keeps ever reappearing. In the field of financial speculation more than anywhere else, people seem to believe in a "social mind," or "collective intelligence" — a mind above and apart from the minds of individual traders, and greater than the mind of any one of them in the range of its knowledge and the sureness of its judgment.[1] Although this animistic notion of a "market mind" is seldom set forth explicitly, it is often met with implicitly in theories to explain the lead and lag of different indices of the business cycle. People say that, since speculative prices move first, business volumes second, and interest rates third, the reason why speculation precedes everything else must be that speculators as a class can foretell, even though speculators as individuals cannot, the course of business months ahead. Let us see if this collective power of divination actually exists.

Unless it can be proved that stock prices turn up or down before any other business index, it cannot be maintained that the stock market foresees the future of business with the help of nothing but its own supernatural intuition; while if something else can be found that moves as soon as stocks, or even sooner, then this soothsayer will stand

[1] Cf. Floyd H. Allport, *Social Psychology* (Boston and New York: Houghton Mifflin Company, c. 1934), p. 4, section entitled "Psychological Forms of the Group Fallacy."

convicted of quackery, and the trick of its prophecies will be seen to be simple enough for anyone to use. This last is in fact the case; there does exist a business series, to be described below, that moves as soon as, or even sooner than, stocks, and one which any novice can follow if he can only get access to it. Hence we must conclude that the speculative fraternity as a class has no greater ability to foresee business conditions than have well-informed traders as individuals.

2. BOOKINGS AND STOCK PRICES

The business series referred to above, which moves even sooner than stocks, and which displays even longer forecasting power, is called "Orders Received," or "Bookings." It leads all other series in the business cycle. Why should it not? Orders must be booked by the salesmen before goods can be made in the factories, or receivables financed by the banks. Naturally, orders move first, business volumes next, and interest rates last. Stock prices only do their best to keep up with orders. If everyone, from customer to salesman and from sales-manager to president, is looking for a chance to make money in the stock market, then enough stock may be bought or sold today for the ticker to disclose now the change that took place in bookings yesterday. If not, and if insiders are lethargic, then several weeks may have to pass before word will circulate that business is going to be better or worse, and several weeks, therefore, may elapse before stock prices turn up or down.

Chart No. I [2] compares the price of Steel common with the bookings [3] of the Steel Corporation. It shows that

[2] The data used in drawing this chart are given in Appendix I at the end of this volume.

[3] The figure for bookings is derived from two other series; namely, unfilled orders and shipments, as follows:

CHART I

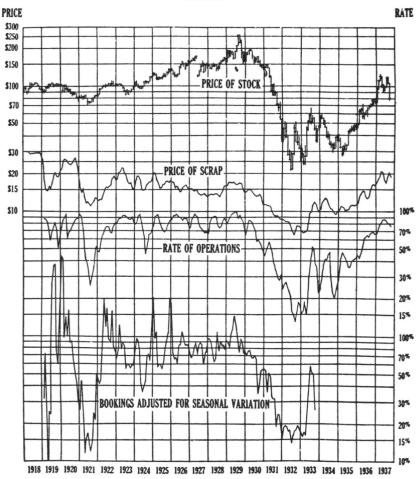

PRICE   RATE

PRICE OF STOCK

PRICE OF SCRAP

RATE OF OPERATIONS

BOOKINGS ADJUSTED FOR SEASONAL VARIATION

FORECASTERS FOR THE PRICE OF STEEL COMMON

bookings more often lead than follow stock prices,[4] and that bookings are a better forecaster of stock prices than are either the rate of operations or the price of scrap, two other well-regarded business indices. The rate of operations never precedes stock prices, and scrap prices seldom do, but bookings often do, as the chart shows. From this we may conclude that it is bookings, or new orders, that is the principal force at work to turn stock prices up or down, and that it is access to information on bookings that causes an important group of individuals to buy and sell. It is clear, therefore, that a satisfactory explanation of the apparent forecasting powers of the stock market with regard to general business conditions can easily be made without recourse to any occult theories of social psychology that ascribe the market's power of prophecy to some superhuman intuitive faculty of the "group mind."

(1) Unfilled orders at start of month	xxxx	tons
(2) Plus unknown bookings	+ xxxx	tons
(3) Less known shipments	− xxxx	tons
(4) Unfilled orders at end of month	xxxx	tons

The foregoing "order book" is solved for item (2). To eliminate the trend in unfilled orders, they are reduced to a percentage of monthly capacity, a step which also facilitates comparison with shipments, likewise reported as a percentage of capacity. The monthly shipment figures are reached by averaging the weekly estimates of output published by the Dow-Jones Co. Unfortunately for the development of business cycle theory, the U. S. Steel Corporation stopped publishing its unfilled orders upon the adoption of the NRA code for the steel industry, which required that orders be canceled automatically at the end of three months. Output and shipments may differ slightly if inventories are undergoing liquidation.

[4] An earlier study of price forecasters for the steel stocks appears in H. B. Vanderblue and W. L. Crum, *The Iron Industry in Prosperity and Depression* (Chicago and New York: A. W. Shaw Co., 1927), pp. 126–128. The use of bookings as a forecaster of stock prices seems to have been discovered at about the same time by several of Vanderblue's students who exchanged views as they worked on the problem. Credit should be given to Charles Pierson of the State Street Management Corporation in particular.

CHAPTER III

MARGINAL OPINION AND MARKET PRICE

The price of a stock as it is, not as it should be, was discussed in a very practical way in the preceding chapter, where it was shown that new business booked was the main cause of the ups and downs of prices in the market. In the present chapter, let us continue to discuss the price as it is, but let us now drop the exclusively practical tone of the preceding chapter, and proceed to deduce a logical theory of market prices and changes therein.

I. THE MARKET FOR A SINGLE STOCK

Let us assume for the moment that the market contains only a single stock, and that none but investors buy and sell shares of this issue. Concerning its true worth, every man will cherish his own opinion; as to what price really is right, time only will tell. Time will not give its answer all at once, though, but only slowly, word by word, as the years go by; nor will the last word be spoken till the corporation shall have closed its books for ever and ever. Those who bought their stock long ago will know their answer in the main by now, but those who buy now will hear theirs only in the future. Most of their answer will be given in the near future, to be sure, by their earlier dividends,[1] for the present worth of near-by is greater than of far-off payments. But right now, in advance of any dividends at all to buyers of today — now, when all investors can merely estimate, and none can surely know, what their stock will prove to be worth in the end — the

[1] As to whether dividends or earnings determine the true value of a stock, see Chapter V, § 2.

market can only be an expression of opinion, not a statement of fact. Today's opinion will make today's price; tomorrow's opinion, tomorrow's price; and seldom if ever will any price be exactly right as proved by the event.

Both wise men and foolish will trade in the market, but no one group by itself will set the price. Nor will it matter what the majority, however overwhelming, may think; for the last owner, and he alone, will set the price. Thus *marginal* opinion will determine market price. Always some would-be buyers will be excluded from ownership because to them the price will seem more than expected dividends can justify. These buyers will stand with cash in hand, waiting for some present owner to change his mind and sell out to them at their price. If this happens, then the quotation will fall to their figure, but if they change their own minds, then the price will rise to whatever they must bid to dislodge stock from the least optimistic present owner. The bid and asked quotations will reflect the opinions of the most optimistic non-owner and the least optimistic owner. The margin will fall between owners and non-owners, the ins and the outs, the ayes and the nays; and, at this margin, opinion, mere opinion, will determine actual price, even to the extent of values running into billions of dollars.

If each man's opinion be given a weight corresponding to the number of shares he owns or could buy with his uninvested cash at the value he ascribes to the stock, then the *distribution of opinion* can be shown by a frequency curve like that shown in Diagram 1, in which V represents the true value as estimated by each investor, and N' represents the number of shares to which this value is ascribed.

For the stock shown in this diagram, the range of opinion is from 20 to 100, with the mode at 40; no one thinks the stock worth less than 20, no one more than 100, while the most common estimate is 40. Like as not this modal estimate is far wide of the truth, and certainly it is based on no such refined methods of evaluation as we shall develop in Part II of this book.

Even though 40 is the most common estimate of V, 40 will not be the actual market price, M, for 40 is not the *marginal*, but only the *modal*, estimate. To find the mar-

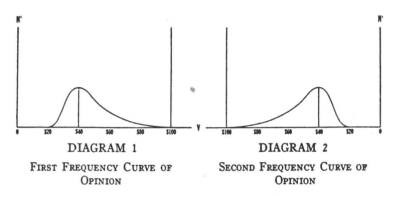

DIAGRAM 1

FIRST FREQUENCY CURVE OF
OPINION

DIAGRAM 2

SECOND FREQUENCY CURVE OF
OPINION

ginal estimate, first reverse the curve in Diagram 1 and make it look like that in Diagram 2.

This second curve shows how many shares are thought by their owners to be worth exactly 100, exactly 80, exactly 60, etc., but what we need is a different curve, a curve that will show how many shares are esteemed to be worth 100 or more, 80 or more, 60 or more, etc. To draw such a curve, one should begin by noting that no shares are considered worth 100 or more, because none are considered worth exactly 100. Hence the new curve must start at zero for 100. To show how many shares are thought to be worth 80 or more, note how many are considered worth 99, 98, 97, and so forth, down to 80, and plot the sum. To show how many are thought to be worth 60 or more, note again how many are considered worth 99, 98, 97, and so forth, down to 60 this time, and plot this larger sum. In this way a 'cumulative frequency curve, or ogive, can be constructed from the same data as yielded the original curve for the distribution of opinion. The resulting ogive [2] will be as shown in Diagram 3. This diagram should now be rotated clockwise 90°, as shown in Diagram 4. (The

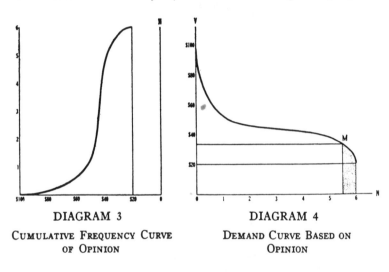

DIAGRAM 3

CUMULATIVE FREQUENCY CURVE OF OPINION

DIAGRAM 4

DEMAND CURVE BASED ON OPINION

shaded area which is introduced into the new diagram will be explained presently.) This last curve looks like a demand curve, and is one. To find the actual market price, M, lay off on the horizontal axis a distance equal to the total number of shares outstanding, and erect a perpendicu-

[2] *Note for the non-technical reader.* For the convenience of non-technical readers, a few footnotes specially labeled will be introduced here and there; these will contain certain mathematical information that may prove helpful, such as the following: The ogive corresponds to the definite integral of the function $N' = f(V)$, of Diagram 2, and represents the area under the curve. (The integral is written $\int_{100}^{V} N' dV$, and is read "integral from 100 to V, of N prime dV.")

lar from this point, cutting the curve $V = f(N)$ in the point M. This point represents the market price of the given unalterable supply, and corresponds to the *marginal opinion* regarding the worth of the stock.

It is evident from the foregoing description of how the demand curve is formed that the shape of the curve at any moment depends upon the state of opinion at that moment; hence, the publication of any news that changes opinion likewise changes the shape of the demand curve and the height of the curve at the margin, and thus the price of the stock in the market.

The demand curve for shares as thus drawn differs in certain ways from that for a consumer's good like clothing. In the first place, each and every share owned by any one man retains the same value in his estimation; no matter how large his holdings become, there is no decline in value to him such as would occur with clothing, for instance, the marginal utility of which would become less and less the more completely his needs were satisfied.[3] In the second place, the inner reaches of the demand curve are never called into play to determine the price, because the number of shares outstanding is fixed once and for all, and no such changes in quantity occur from time to time as take place with a commodity like wheat or cotton. When the price of a stock moves, it moves because the demand curve itself moves, not because the quantity changes. In general it is true that stock prices are altered by a change in the business outlook, causing a *shift* in the demand curve,

[3] Even if the theory is expanded to take account of *uncertainty* in estimates (see Chapter V, § 8), still it does not follow that each investor should have his own separate sloping demand curve, for it is not a sound application of the laws of probability for a man to put a little of his money into a stock because he thinks there is a slight chance it may be worth the high price asked. A man should not buy until the price falls to the *mean* of his probability curve for estimated value; after that, he should invest all his cash, lest a competing investor get the stock and leave him with nothing to buy.

while commodity prices are altered by a change in the quantity supplied, causing a movement of price along an *unshifting* demand curve.[4]

The chart for stocks as drawn in Diagram 4 depicts a case where 5,500,000 shares are outstanding and held by owners, while non-owners stand with cash in hand waiting to buy 500,000 shares more at lower prices. The amount of uninvested cash is shown by the area of the shaded strip. According to the diagram, in this case liquidation by owners seeking cash could proceed in an orderly manner until 500,000 shares had been disposed of, and the price had declined along the demand curve to 20; after that "the bottom would fall out of the market" unless other present owners borrowed money to buy stock on margin — something we have not provided for in our assumptions up to this point.

2. MARGINAL OPINION AND BOND PRICES

With bonds, as with stocks, prices are determined by marginal opinion, but with bonds, if they are good bonds, no question regarding the size of future payments can arise, and investors can therefore confine their attention to the question of the interest rate to use in discounting the known future payments. Concerning the right and proper interest rate, however, opinions can easily differ, and differ widely. Some investors will believe that a low rate will equate the supply and demand for savings; others, a high rate. As to who is right, time only will tell. Hence those who believe in a low rate will consent to pay high prices for bonds, and will promptly invest their cash as

---

[4] Commodities, to be sure, are also affected by the business outlook, for a change in the outlook causes a shift of the demand curve to a degree that depends on the nature of the commodity. See Part II of my article entitled "Speculation and the Carryover," in the *Quarterly Journal of Economics*, May 1936.

soon as it is saved, while those who believe in a high rate will insist on low prices, and will persistently hoard their savings in cash, unless prices already are low. Thus investors will be bullish or bearish on bonds according to whether they believe low or high interest rates to be suitable under prevailing economic conditions. As a result, the actual price of bonds, and the level of interest rates implied thereby, will represent, not the true equilibrium between the supply and demand for savings, but only the supposed equilibrium. The market rate will thus be only an expression of opinion, not a statement of fact. Today's opinion will make today's rate; tomorrow's opinion, tomorrow's rate; and seldom if ever will any rate be exactly right as proved by the event.[5]

Keynes, taking note of this very diversity and spread of opinion, seeks in his latest book [6] to overthrow the orthodox theory of interest invoked above and replace it with an entirely new theory of his own. This new theory of his uses the term *liquidity-preference* to describe the attitude of those investors who are bearish and expect to see bonds decline because of a future increase in the rate of interest. Keynes argues that the rate of interest must always be low enough and the price of bonds high enough to make some investors bearish, and make them willing, therefore, to hold cash instead of bonds. The more the bank deposits of the nation are increased by the central banking authorities, says Keynes, the more the rate of interest must fall and the more the price of bonds must rise to create enough bears to absorb the redundant deposits outstanding. Hence, to Keynes's mind, the rate of

[5] In this respect interest rates and bond prices are like any other speculative prices, such as the prices of wheat or cotton, which latter prices represent merely the *supposed* equilibrium and not the true equilibrium.

[6] J. M. Keynes, *The General Theory of Employment, Interest and Money* (New York: Harcourt, Brace and Co., 1936).

interest prevailing, both long- and short-term, is mainly
dependent on the quantity of idle money outstanding.

Translating his argument into our own terms, we should
say that an increase in the quantity of money necessitates
the redrawing of the frequency curve showing the distribution of opinion concerning bonds, because this curve, as
defined above, must always represent the opinion of all
those who either (1) own bonds already or (2) have cash
available for their purchase, with the result that any increase in the quantity of idle money tends to increase the
number and importance of those investors who belong to
the second class above. If the frequency curve is redrawn
as required by the new distribution of opinion among investors, the ogive will change as a result, and so will the
demand curve. Then, when the fixed supply is measured
off as before, the position of the margin will be found to
have shifted, with marginal opinion giving a higher price
for bonds of the same quality. Thus Keynes is quite right
in saying that the quantity of idle money affects the market rate of interest. But it should be remembered that the
quantity of idle money is only one of several factors at
work; and it is by no means the main factor. As always,
the frequency curve of opinion will reflect the beliefs
of various investors as to what is the equilibrium rate
of interest that will succeed in equating the demand and
supply of new savings. Every man will have his own opinion
on this question; the quantity of money will only determine whose opinion will be the *marginal* opinion. The
quantity of money in itself cannot set the rate of interest,
therefore, because there must be a frequency curve of
opinion in the first place for the quantity of money to
modify. Hence we are forced to conclude that Keynes
does not disprove the classical theory of the rate of interest,
but only perfects it.

3. BROKERS' LOANS AND STOCK PRICES

Let us now introduce the further assumption that buying may take place with borrowed money, and let us make at the same time certain other changes in our description of the group of non-owners who are potential buyers at a lower price. Let us assume that in the beginning no one has any cash for investment, and that the universe of those who cherish an opinion about the stock in question comprises none but owners; then the demand curve as drawn would come to an abrupt end at $N = 5,500,000$, and no one could liquidate his stock and get cash for it if he wanted to, because there would be no cash buyers. Then let us further assume that the practice of making brokers' loans "for the account of others" is now introduced,[7] so that some of the present owners can buy more stock by giving interest-bearing promissory notes to such of the other owners as will sell out to them. Then parts of the intra-marginal sections of the demand curve will be enlarged, and a new curve will emerge, as shown in Diagram 5. In this diagram, the solid curve is the old demand curve, the dotted one, the new.[8] The right-hand shaded area is the amount of promissory notes accepted by the sellers, while the left-hand shaded area is the amount of loans contracted by the buyers. Both areas are equal, of course, because both stand for the same debt; the right-hand area being the asset, and the left-hand the liability, aspect of the debt. Not alone on the bullishness of the buyers, however, but also on the bearishness of the sellers, does the total amount of the debt depend; for sellers will demand an adequate

[7] The fact that loans "for the account of others" are now prohibited in the United States is discussed in § 4 below, and it is shown there that this does not alter the present analysis.

[8] Restriction of security loans by the government nowadays is tending to keep the new demand curve for stocks closer to the old than was formerly the case.

margin on their loans. If the market price after accumulation by the bulls is $38, then the sellers will grant loans of $20 a share, let us say, with this stock, which they consider

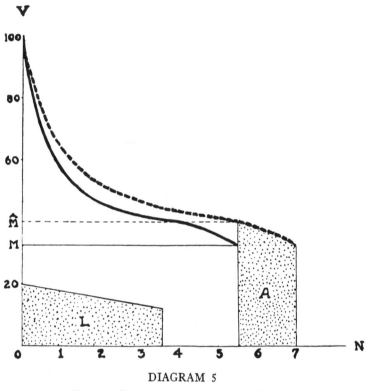

DIAGRAM 5

DEMAND CURVE ALTERED BY BROKERS' LOANS

to be selling rather high, as collateral. Some bulls may not care to risk borrowing the full amount allowable, because they may fear intermediate declines in the stock, and hence the loan area on the left will exhibit a sloping top as shown, with the largest loans being asked as a rule only by the most rampant bulls.

To the marginal investor, it will be indifferent whether he invests in stock or in promissory notes, for in his opinion each will yield him the same return over a period of years. Intra-marginal investors, however, will prefer stock to notes, while extra-marginal investors will have the opposite preference, the preference for the one or the other being founded on each man's view of the dividends to be paid by the stock. The rate of interest used in discounting these dividends will be the rate obtainable on the promissory notes, since the interest rate, exclusive of risk,[9] must be uniform throughout the investment market. If the interest rate on notes is expected to vary over time, then the annuity of dividends will be discounted at a variable rate.[10]

In the equilibrium just described, the location of the margin between those who own stock and those who own notes will determine the market price of the stock. In Diagram 5, this margin is depicted by the vertical line running through the point $N = 5,500,000$. This line cuts the demand curve at a level which gives the new price of $38 a share, as shown by the dotted horizontal line.

Except in one particular, the location of this margin depends only on the opinion held by investors concerning the ultimate worth of the stock, which particular is the risk of short-term declines in the stock. If a bull thinks the stock is worth 60 but may easily fall from 38 to 25 before going up to stay, he will not dare borrow $20 on the stock now, regardless of how sure he is of its ultimate worth. If the speculative outlook changes, however, so that he becomes convinced that recessions in price are unlikely, then he will borrow heavily to buy, even though he may not have changed his opinion at all as to the true worth of the stock in the end. In borrowing to buy, he will

[9] See comments on risk, in Chapter V, § 8.
[10] See discussion of compound interest at a changing rate, in Chapter V, § 4. See also Chapter X.

alter the shape of the demand curve in the way already described, and will change the location of the margin. Market price will then still be determined by marginal opinion concerning ultimate value, but the location of the margin will be affected by further opinions, on the part of certain intra-marginal owners, concerning the risk of intermediate price declines. Thus it is possible for an accession of confidence regarding the immediate future to cause a rise in prices, or a loss of confidence a fall in prices, even though people may in no way alter their views concerning value as such in the long run.

Throughout all of the present discussion it is never assumed that bears sit with mere cash in hand waiting to repurchase at their own lower prices. To keep the proceeds of their sales in cash would entail the loss of interest on their money, since demand deposits now receive no interest. Therefore bears may be expected to invest their cash in loans of some sort. Even in 1929, when interest on demand deposits was still being paid, it was more profitable to reinvest the proceeds of stock sales in call loans, commercial paper, or other short-term securities free from price fluctuation, than to leave the money in cash. And nowadays, when no interest at all is allowed on demand deposits, only those bears who are bearish for a few days only, who are mere in-and-out traders, may be expected to refrain from buying interest-bearing paper of some sort, and only they will immobilize bank deposits by their actions.

In the discussion to follow, the term "bank assets" will be used to mean commercial paper, collateral loans, and short-term government bonds, such as would thus be bought by all investors who feared a decline in stock prices, and such as can be sold back and forth between banks and individuals without capital gains or losses to either party.

4. BROKERS' LOANS AND INTEREST RATES

In the United States, where loans for "the account of others" are prohibited, the investor cannot exchange stock for promissory notes, or vice versa, with other investors, and get the same rate of interest [11] at the margin on the one or the other. If a bull borrows and buys from a marginal investor, the seller cannot turn around and loan directly to the buyer; but he can do so indirectly, by using the proceeds of his sale to buy bank assets like acceptances, commercial paper, Treasury bills and notes, and so forth. Sale of these assets by the bank enables and impels it to invest in brokers' loans instead, and through the brokers the funds reach the original bullish buyer of stock.

The interest rate which the banks will charge on brokers' loans can hardly be less than what they received on their assets just sold, else they would not have sold; it can hardly be more, unless the clearing house can maintain a monopoly price. [12]

The amount of money the bulls will borrow depends in no wise on the price they must pay for it. Strange, but true, however contrary to the general rule in economics. For the bulls, since they consider their stock worth more (in terms of future dividends) than its present market price, will feel they can afford to pay for their borrowed money an interest rate in excess of the market rate. But why, one may ask, does not their bidding for funds drive up the market rate to some point of equilibrium where they will feel it is no longer worth their while to borrow any

[11] Subject to the usual adjustment between long- and short-term rates discussed in Chapters X and XX.

[12] See the item in the *New York Times* for April 21, 1935, section 3, p. 1, entitled "Another Peg Broken," which says, "To the wreckage of 'pegging' agreements which broke down in the course of the depression there was added last week the agreement of the big Wall Street banks to peg Stock Exchange call money at 1 per cent. . . ."

more? The attainment of equilibrium in such a way is what ordinarily happens in the economic world. In this case, however, it does not happen. There are two reasons why it does not happen, either of which by itself would be quite sufficient to keep the rate down. These reasons are as follows:

First, lenders do not dare loan the bulls too much money; they dare loan only a modest fraction of the market price.[13] The bulls likewise do not dare borrow too much. Most bulls will not borrow at all, but prefer to own their stock outright. Even in the boom of 1929, brokers' loans did not quite reach 10 per cent of the market value of all listed stocks. Because collateral loans if thinly margined are dangerous for lender and borrower alike, the amount so lent is kept down, and therefore the demand for collateral loans cannot reach sufficient proportions to draw all interest rates up to an equilibrium point where the bulls will not wish to borrow any further, because the rate in itself is too high.

Second, no matter if the bulls did borrow all they would like to borrow, regardless of risk, still they would not ordinarily force up interest rates in general, because money loaned in the stock market goes right through the stock market, and cannot stick there.[14] If a bull borrows and buys, then a bear must sell and receive payment in cash to the full extent of the bull's loan. This cash the seller ordinarily invests in bank assets, and the banking system by selling some of its assets to depositors thus reverts to the same reserve ratio which it had prior to making the

[13] In 1929 many brokers actually reduced their lending ratios for the express reason that high prices for stocks made former margin requirements inadequate and unsafe.

[14] Except to the extent that bulls may hold funds idle between trades or may fail to keep 100 per cent invested. Likewise bears may be slow in using the proceeds of their stock sales for the purchase of bank assets.

brokers' loan.[15] The entire process, therefore, in no wise diverts savings from borrowers seeking funds wherewith to build new capital goods, and so interest rates are in no wise affected at the crucial place where the level for the money market as a whole is set.[16] Only to the extent that sellers refrain from reinvesting the proceeds of their sales, and divert the cash to other uses, does borrowing to buy stocks tend sometimes to send the rate of interest up. If sellers mistake their capital gains for true income,[17] and proceed to spend their profits on luxuries, then the demand for consumers' goods throughout the country will come to exceed the true income of the nation, prices will be inflated, and a boom financed by brokers' loans may get under way. The same result can be brought about by borrowing by bulls who remain non-sellers, if these latter mistake their paper profits for true income and proceed to spend these profits on goods and services paid for with borrowed money. Such borrowing, however, "diverts capital from legitimate industry" only to the extent that the banks themselves fight the increase in brokers' loans by asking high interest rates and forcing borrowers who are living beyond their true income to go directly to savers as such for their loans. If this latter happens, then the inflationary aspect of the boom is curtailed, but an equally unsound condition of another sort develops, in which one group of citizens lends its savings to another group to permit the latter to live beyond its

[15] Stock exchange loans thus differ from loans to business in that the proceeds do not have to circulate slowly, going out as wage payments and coming back as sales of product. Cf. Chapter IV, § 3.
[16] Cf. Chapter XVIII. Concerning the effect of excess reserves see Chapter XIX, § 10.
[17] True income for the investor does not arise until the actual dividends are received from his stocks. If prices go up, an increase in dividends is prophesied thereby, but no increase truly materializes until the hoped-for higher dividends are actually received. Cf. Chapter V, § 6.

means. Economically the process has many analogies to the current practice of taxing away the savings of the rich in order to finance doles to the poor, for both processes divert savings from the capital market, and thus tend to raise the rate of interest. The process also resembles the extraction of cash profits from the market by speculators, for speculators can acquire such profits only by trading with investors and by winning some of the current savings of the community that otherwise would have been applied to the construction of new capital goods. Extravagant living by speculators, therefore, is a form of national dissaving.

If brokers' loans increase, it is sometimes a bad sign, therefore, in that it may indicate that savings are being diverted from productive enterprise. But it is also a bad sign for another reason — quite another reason — for it always indicates that someone is selling out, someone is bearish, someone thinks prices too high, and someone expects them to fall before they rise any higher. The size of brokers' loans thus measures the size of the bear party in the market.[18] By bears is meant not simply the few who actually go short, but also the many who just sell out, yet who may be quite as firmly convinced of the unreasonableness of prices.

It would be an interesting question to investigate, whether buyers on margin or "sellers out" are the better informed, the more level-headed, withal the wiser, sample of investors as a whole. May it not be that the man who owns a stock when low, sees it rise, and has the thrill of a paper profit, but still knows enough about general business and his own company to persuade himself that things are going to take a turn for the worse, is more likely to be

---

[18] Cf. J. M. Keynes, *A Treatise on Money*, 2 vols. (New York: Harcourt, Brace and Company, 1930), II, 195.

right than the average margin buyer? If so, large brokers'
loans are a sinister index of expert opinion.

5. MULTIPLE STOCK MARKETS

The marginal opinion concerning, and hence the market
price of, any given stock is affected by opinion regarding
other stocks too. If John Doe owns American Telephone,
but holds an opinion concerning United States Steel as
well, then he will own whichever stock he considers the
cheaper — in this case American Telephone, let us say.
If now some news comes out on United States Steel, such
as an increase in its rate of operations, he may decide that
Steel is the cheaper, and wish to switch his investment.
John Doe then sells Telephone to a marginal non-owner,
Mr. Wiseman, and uses the cash thus obtained to buy
Steel from a marginal owner, Richard Roe. Richard Roe
then becomes a marginal non-owner of Steel, replacing the
original marginal non-owner of Telephone, Mr. Wiseman,
and invests the proceeds of his sale in the same bank assets
that the other non-owner, Mr. Wiseman, once held. The
switching sends Telephone down and Steel up; it causes
two transactions to occur, and two sales to be recorded on
the ticker tape.

Sometimes the switching is even more complete, for
John Doe and Richard Roe may exchange Telephone and
Steel with each other, and in this case neither changes
from being an owner to being a non-owner. Without doubt
the vast majority of the sales reported each day represent
switching transactions, and very few represent either outright accumulation by optimistic buyers and liquidation
by pessimistic sellers on the one hand, or outright liquidation by marginal holders and accumulation by erstwhile
bears on the other hand.

Switching operations throughout the market represent

a change of places among various buyers and sellers along several hundred demand curves for individual stocks. Heavy trading indicates widespread changing of opinion. Usually the day's news is reflected in switching operations, and seldom in outright accumulation or liquidation. It is wrong, therefore, to say of a market rising on heavy volume that it shows the inrush of new money seeking investment, or of a falling market that it shows capital scurrying to safety. Such statements as these,[19] all too common, are naïve in the extreme. The correct view is that rising and falling markets show changing marginal opinion, while heavy volume shows much switching.

In multiple stock markets, each stock will be held only by those who like that particular issue better than any other, and those who prefer some other stock will not be owners of that particular stock, even though they may entertain an opinion on that one along with opinions on all others. Hence in a multiple stock market when the curve of opinion is drawn up for any given stock, and the mode and the margin are located as already described, if the views of the holders of all other stocks are included, the margin will be found to lie to the left of the mode, rather than to the right as in the case of a market containing only a single issue. In other words, in a multiple

[19] For example, note the following sentence from such an otherwise able source as the weekly *Bulletin of the American Institute of Finance*: "*Buying power* in the week ended March 28, 1936, from a general market standpoint, has diminished, with current average daily volumes of less than 2,000,000 shares compared with around 3,000,000 shares a month ago...." (Italics mine.) One might just as well say that selling power has diminished.

Another example of the same error is to be seen in the following statement in an article in the *New York Times*, April 5, 1936, section 3, p. 1, col. 1: "Only a tremendous volume of cash buying could account for the difference between the trend of stock values [which rose from 31 to 52 billion] and loans [which rose only 193 million] during the last year...." Surely the writer did not mean to imply that 21 billion dollars of cash were absorbed by the rise. If the figures show anything, they show that 193 millions were taken out by investors selling to margin buyers.

stock market there is a tendency for most people to think all stocks but their own too high. If most people are right in their opinion of the other fellow's investments, then it would follow that stocks in general have a tendency to sell too high, because almost every stock will enjoy some distinction of its own, and will tend to gather around itself its own special group of enthusiasts who will bid its price up too high. If every stock is somebody's favorite, then every price should be viewed with skepticism.

6. THE BEHAVIOR OF MARKETS

The reason why volume tends to increase in bull markets when stocks go up is simple enough. Most people prefer to switch when they have a profit rather than a loss on what they are selling. If they discover some stock that seems more likely to go up than what they already hold, they will nevertheless postpone buying it until they can show a profit on their first transaction. If they have a small paper loss at present, they will not say, "I can make up my loss quicker in this other issue." Instead they will wait till all prices rise, and then will make their switch, proudly proclaiming, "You'll never go broke taking profits." Such behavior is illogical, of course, but it explains most of the increase in activity that occurs on the top of each rally in the general market.

The same sort of illogical behavior explains the existence of so-called "resistance levels" in the stock market.[20] If for some time stocks sell at a certain price, and many people buy or sell at this price, a so-called "resistance level" will be created, with the result that the reaction from any subsequent advance or the rally from any subsequent decline will tend to stop when this level is reached again. Thus

[20] Cf. R. A. Schabacker, *Stock Market Theory and Practice* (New York: B. C. Forbes Publishing Company, 1930), pp. 565-567.

if a great many people buy General Motors, for instance, at 57, a resistance level will be formed at this figure, and any reaction after an advance above this level will tend to stop at 57. Likewise if the stock goes down from 57, any rally thereafter will tend to halt at 57. The reason for this peculiar behavior of prices is the reluctance of traders to take losses. The man who bought at 57 and saw his stock rise 10 or 20 points may decide to take his profit at almost any price on the way down so long as this price is above 57, but under that figure he is reluctant to admit his mistake and take his loss; hence offers to sell become scarce below 57. Likewise the man who sold out at 57, but saw his stock advance 10 or 20 points to the benefit of someone else, may regret his mistake (unless he has switched into something still better) and may decide to repurchase his holdings as soon as he can do so without loss; hence offers to buy become numerous under 57. The decrease in offers and the increase in bids when the reaction reaches 57 thus tend to absorb whatever forced liquidation is under way and bring the decline in prices to an end. A similar explanation will account for the behavior of the market when it meets a resistance level on the up side. The reason why old resistance levels slowly lose their holding power as time goes on is that people slowly become reconciled to their losses and become willing to buy and sell stocks on intrinsic merit instead of original cost. When enough buyers and sellers at the old resistance level come to realize the truth of the maxim that "the market doesn't care what you paid for your stock," the resistance level fades out of existence altogether.

Unwillingness to take losses also explains the market's habit of declining no more than 50 per cent of the previous advance when traders become engaged in a temporary scramble to take profits during a bull market. Followers

of the "Dow Theory" maintain that a bull market is liable
to undergo a reaction of 50 per cent of the previous advance
at any time, and that such a reaction by itself does not
indicate the end of the bull movement.[21] These "Dow
theorists" offer no reason, however, why the reaction
should be limited to 50 per cent, and so the following explanation is put forward as a suggestion:

The average bull, if he is neither keener nor duller than
the rank and file whose trading is causing the advance in
prices, will make his first purchase at 144, let us say, his
next at 149, his third at 154, and so on every 5 points up,
till the very top of the rise is reached. If the top is at 194,
for instance, his average cost will be 169. Under these circumstances he can sell out his entire commitment with a
profit at any price above 169, but at any price below 169
he must take a loss. If a profit-taking stampede should be
touched off by a sudden shock to confidence, therefore, it
could run from the peak at 194 down to the midpoint at
169 before the average trader would show a loss.[22] And
just so long as traders have a paper profit, they are likely
to be frightened into selling by the declining trend of the
market once it starts to fall; but just as soon as they have
a paper loss, they will become stubborn and refuse to sell.
Hence any reaction that is spectacular at the start is likely
to carry the full distance, and then come to an end of its
own accord when 50 per cent of the previous advance has
been canceled.

Even if the reaction represents the beginning of a bear

[21] Cf. Charles J. Collins, "Calling the Turns in the Stock Market," *Barron's*,
September 13, 1937, p. 18. See also William Peter Hamilton, *The Stock Market
Barometer* (New York and London: Harper and Brothers, 1922), and Robert
Rhea, *The Dow Theory* (New York: Barron's, 1932).

[22] These particular figures were chosen for illustration because they correspond
to the Dow-Jones averages for the 1936–37 advance and the March–June 1937
reaction, for which the actual low was 165.51.

market, it may still run for no more than 50 per cent of the previous advance, because bear markets and depressions are often calamities that are long overdue and are merely touched off by the profit-taking stampede.

The subsequent rally after the decline requires no fresh "purchasing power" to bring it about, for, as already explained, prices can rise or fall in a bull or bear market merely by the "swapping" of securities between traders, and without the use of any cash at all, provided each trader merely switches his holding from one stock to another. If the market is beset by forced liquidation to satisfy margin calls, the buying by those who sold out earlier at higher prices when their stop-loss orders were executed will usually suffice to stem the tide, once the stampede to salvage paper profits has subsided. Therefore forced selling need not carry the reaction below the critical point where the average trader begins to show a loss instead of a profit.

In a bear market, the tendency of rallies to equal 50 per cent of the preceding decline may be explained again by the unwillingness of investors to take a loss. But this time investors reckon their loss or gain from a different point of view. The investor in a bear market usually considers the decline only temporary, and sells out only with the idea of repurchasing at a lower price; therefore he considers it a gain if he can buy his stock back lower down and have money left over. The typical investor liquidates bit by bit all the way down to the very bottom, with the result that his average selling price is halfway between the high and the low. If a repurchasing stampede should be touched off by a sudden piece of good news, the rally would be likely to run to the point where the average trader could no longer cover his previous sales without the help of additional cash; the rally, in other words, would be likely to run to 50 per cent of the previous decline, and beyond that it would not go unless the news was of far-reaching importance, because the average trader hates to admit he has made a mistake.

7. INVESTORS AND SPECULATORS

So far we have discussed a stock market for investors only. Bull or bear a man may be, and still be an investor rather than a speculator, so long as he looks to dividends rather than to price changes to justify the cost of his stock. There exists another large class of traders, however, made up of speculators, whose business it is to buy and sell for changes in price alone. To these speculators dividends are inconsequential because they hold for too short a time to receive many dividends.

To gain by speculation, a speculator must be able to foresee price changes. Since price changes coincide with changes of marginal opinion, he must in the last analysis be able to foresee *changes in opinion.* Successful speculation [23] consists in just this. It requires no knowledge of intrinsic value as such, but only of what people are going to *believe* intrinsic value to be. Now opinion, when it changes, need not change for the right; it may change for the wrong, and the probability of a change for the wrong is about as great as of a change for the right. If opinion were not founded in part on current dividends and changes therein, there would be nothing to prevent price and value from drifting miles apart. That opinion may change for the wrong, many a speculator learned to his sorrow when he sold short too soon in 1929, or went long too soon in 1932. Hence some old traders think it a handicap, a real handicap, to let themselves reach any conclusion what-

---

[23] Cf. Keynes, *General Theory*, p. 158. "If I may be allowed to appropriate the term *speculation* for the activity of forecasting the psychology of the market...."

soever as to the true worth of the stocks they speculate in.[24]

How to foretell changes in *opinion* is the heart of the
problem of speculation, just as how to foretell changes in
dividends is the heart of the problem of investment.

Since opinion is made by the news, the task of forecasting opinion resolves itself into the task of forecasting
the news. There are two ways to do this: either to cheat
in the matter, or to study the forces at work.

Cheating has been outlawed, so far as can be, by the
Securities Act of 1934, which tries to prevent insiders
from gaining by foreknowledge of dividend changes, earnings statements, contracts let, etc., and requires these
insiders to refund all short-term profits in their own stock
to the treasury of their company. Certainly the old situation was scandalous, but the new law overcomes it only
in part, for an officer of International Harvester, let us
say, if he sees his own sales shoot ahead, *could* make use
of this inside knowledge to the detriment of the small
stockholder by buying shares of Deere & Co., for instance,
whose business, he can feel sure, is enjoying the same
gains, and whose earnings, when published at the end of
the year, should prove a surprise to outsiders. In having
access to this inside information, officers and directors
have a most unfair advantage over the host of ordinary
stockholders. Only stupidity or indifference, on the one
hand, or great scrupulousness or recklessness on the other
hand, can prevent insiders from getting rich in the market,
and all that the law itself can really do is to advertise
the ethics of the problem.[25]

[24] Such famous traders as Bernard M. Baruch, Arthur W. Cutten, and John
W. Pope, however, are reputed to have been profound students of intrinsic
value.

[25] A notable instance of the recent improvement in ethical standards among
insiders is the case of Alfred P. Sloan, President of the General Motors Corpora-

Just because there exists a large group of traders-on-inside-information, many outsiders base their own speculative operations on guesses as to what the insiders are doing. They watch the tape and study the chart of the market. Any slight rise in a stock, therefore, tends to provoke a further rise as outsiders rush in to buy, believing they are imitating the insiders. To this procedure there is much logic, and in the great boom ending in 1929 it proved highly successful as a rule.[26]

The other way to forecast the news, and thus the change of opinion and the movement of prices, is to study the forces at work, in the belief that "coming events cast their shadows before." In this spirit of prophecy Keynes wrote his *Economic Consequences of the Peace*. If an economist is good for anything, he ought to be able to foresee the consequences of the NRA, the AAA, and the CIO, for instance, in our time, just as he should have been able to foresee the consequences of the wartime rise in gold prices, or of reparations, or of mounting tariffs, ten or twenty years ago. But rare is the man so sagacious as to foresee, so certain as to believe, and so steadfast as to remember; he who is makes a good speculator.

---

tion, who delayed his purchase of 30,000 shares of the company's stock in the summer of 1935 until August 6, after the publication of the good earnings for the second quarter. Cf. *New York Times*, November 22, 1935, p. 31, and November 23, 1935, p. 23. This delay cost him three points a share, the stock closing that day at 41¼.

Over a year later, on November 9, 1936, the stock reached a high of 77, and in this month Sloan sold 6,430 shares, according to the routine report on such transactions made public by the Securities Exchange Commission and summarized in the *New York Times*, December 31, 1936, p. 23, col. 7.

[26] Evans and Roos, observing this behavior of prices, have gone so far as to found a theory of dynamic economics on it, and have sought to define demand curves involving the derivatives and integrals of price movements, but there would seem to be room for argument concerning the correctness of these theories. Cf. G. C. Evans, "The Dynamics of Monopoly," *American Mathematical Monthly*, February 1924, and D. J. Roos, "A Dynamic Theory of Economics," *Journal of Political Economy*, October 1927.

Long and detailed observation of the market in its response to news will convince one how much wiser the market as a whole usually is than the average participant in it, for the market, whatever the news it is trying to discount, always includes among its members some traders who are experts in the particular subject at issue. Thus a few traders may be experts on moving pictures, for instance, and may exert their influence on the market once in a lifetime, when a successful process for making talking pictures is finally perfected. To the outsider, strength in a certain moving picture stock may seem wholly inexplicable until months later when it becomes known that pictures using this new process have met with public acclaim.[27] Other traders may be experts in German politics, and foresee the final triumph of Hitler, with the consequent persecution of the Jews, foreign boycotts, shrinkage of exports, and fall of German bonds. And so it goes. No one man can hope to be an expert in everything, and if he ventures to speculate outside his own special field he takes the chance of finding that he has bet not with but against the experts, for which impudence he must pay dearly.

Because experts see the truth first, and are few in number, big price changes do not occur instantaneously, but only over a period of days or weeks, during which time a large volume of trading takes place. Not until the price stops changing after a piece of news has appeared can one say that this news has been thoroughly disseminated among and interpreted by investors. If the news is good, those who understand it first buy from the marginal owners, who are caught napping and who sell out, much to their own future chagrin, because they do not know enough at the time to remove their standing offers, or refrain from selling their stock when they see it go up. If the news is

[27] Cf. the rise of Warner Bros. Pictures in 1928.

bad, the alert traders take advantage this time of the standing bids in the market. The preoccupied investor is often outsmarted, therefore, if he persists in placing standing orders close to the market in the hope of taking advantage of some minor dip or rally in his direction, for such standing orders are sure to be filled whenever he has guessed wrong, but are by no means sure to be filled when he is right. The policy of placing limited orders loads the dice against the non-professional trader.

Every speculator's life is strewn with regrets, vain regrets for the news he did not understand until it was too late. That "time and tide wait for no man" he knows full well; opportunity, like a bird on the wing, must be shot in a jiffy, or she flies out of range forever. Hence the first speculative opinions are usually snap judgments, often wide of the mark, and as such they usually need to be revised by the later trading of those who have had time to take a sober second thought.

8. TEMPORARY PRICE CHANGES

While market price is ordinarily determined by marginal opinion, it may happen at certain times that prices break away from marginal opinion temporarily, or rather, that prices reflect for the time being the marginal opinion of an unduly restricted group of buyers or sellers. During sudden liquidation, or during a panic or a corner, prices for a few hours or a day may fail to reflect the marginal opinion of any large group of stockholders or potential stockholders, because many would-be buyers and sellers may fail to have any bids or offers resting on the specialists' books awaiting execution, or may fail to react promptly and enter market orders as soon as the wave of concentrated buying or selling gets under way. Consequently it is possible for prices to be temporarily set awry by an emergency. In the old days before the SEC, big operators, knowing this, used to "raid the market," hoping to "turn around" before the general public could rescue the situation. Nowadays a startling piece of news can produce a similar temporary displacement of prices, because nowadays markets are very thin, and few standing orders are to be found on the specialists' books.

To illustrate this point, we might consider what would happen in the hypothetical case that a great war in Europe suddenly became imminent, with the result that everyone became afraid that the English and French governments would commandeer the American securities held by their citizens, and would force the sale of these stocks and bonds on the New York market in order to pay for supplies and munitions.[28] While under the new margin rules the selling would not of necessity grow more intensive the more prices declined,[29] as once it would have done, nevertheless the sudden impact of the selling would almost certainly depress prices temporarily far more than would be warranted by the mere change in marginal opinion among *all* investors, including those whose response to lower prices is very

[28] Because England and France, whose war debts are still in default, could not, under the Johnson Act, issue new bonds of their own and sell them in this country, they would be all the more under the necessity of commandeering such existing securities as they could still sell here. Even if our neutrality laws stayed in force and prevented England and France from buying munitions *per se* in this country, still these nations would find it imperative to buy huge quantities of other things, such as cotton, copper, steel, and motor trucks; and they might even buy clothing for their civilians in order to release their own factories for making uniforms for their soldiers.

[29] The new margin rules of the Federal Reserve Board, although they require new purchases to be paid for in cash to the extent of 55 per cent at least, do not require, as did the old rules, that this high margin should be kept good if the stock should later decline; hence no new money has to be put up during a break until the buyer's equity has declined far enough to call the Stock Exchange's own margin rules into play, and the latter rules require only that the equity shall be at least 30 per cent of the debit balance. Thus the new rules create a cushion, and help to prevent cumulative liquidation. It is hard to understand why such a wise arrangement was not adopted years ago.

leisurely. Doubtless the sudden liquidation would prove so severe that the Exchange would have to be closed very soon, as it was in 1914.

Sudden buying or selling in smaller amounts occurs in everyday trading, and if it.takes the market unawares will produce results of the same sort as those just described but of much less spectacular proportions. The minor fluctuations that occur in prices from hour to hour are probably caused more by imperfections of this sort in the response of the market to price changes than by actual shifts in marginal opinion throughout the entire country.

9.   UNANIMITY AMONG MARKETS

The various speculative markets do not contradict each other. The stock market does not forecast inflation, for instance, at the same time that the bond market forecasts deflation. Therefore those who think that stocks were high late in 1936 because inflation was feared by the stock market must be wrong, for bonds were not low at this same time as they should have been if inflation were simultaneously feared by the bond market.[30] While it is true that at such a time all the pessimists would hold stocks (provided stocks were legal investments for them), and all the optimists would hold bonds, nevertheless the two markets could not disagree unless there were exactly the right amounts of stocks and bonds to satisfy each group of investors. If there were too few stocks to go around, those investors who could not buy stocks would be forced to hold bonds, and would become the marginal holders thereof. Since market price is made by marginal opinion, these disgruntled bondholders, trading among themselves, would

[30] Concerning the argument that stocks do not deserve to rise before inflation begins, see Chapter IX, § 1. Concerning the likelihood of inflation occurring, see Chapter XIX.

establish quotations for bonds that would reflect the fear of inflation to the same extent as the quotations for stocks reflected it. In this way the two markets would be brought into agreement, and the Law of the Unanimity of Markets would be fulfilled.

The various speculative markets tend to go up and down together, with the same news being reflected at the same time in all markets. Thus the markets for steel shares and steel scrap tend to turn up or down at the same time, for the same news is relevant to values in both markets. Since stock traders and scrap dealers both read the same newspapers, ordinarily they both decide at the same time that steel operations are going to increase or decrease. Moreover, each group of speculators is free to trade in the other's market if it wishes; and scrap dealers and scrap users in particular are quick to seize upon any opportunity that may present itself for speculating in the stock market. Outright arbitrage may even be resorted to. Therefore it is not to be expected that scrap prices should move in advance of share prices, or vice versa. Instead, the two markets are normally synchronized, with prices in both markets always in the same phase.

What is true in the steel business for scrap and shares is true in the oil business for crude and shares, in the farm implement business for wheat and shares, and in the banking business for interest rates and shares. The same news is reflected at the same time in all markets; hence it is unlikely that any scheme could be devised for forecasting the stock market by the prior movements of some other speculative market.

The prices of speculative commodities, like wheat and copper, tend to move in phase with the prices of common stocks. It is only non-speculative commodities, like automobiles and clothing, whose prices move later in the business cycle. What distinguishes a speculative from a non-speculative commodity is the existence of a carryover or an inventory that can be bought by traders in slack times for resale in boom times. If such a carryover exists, its value will be determined in part by expected changes in demand during the business cycle, and so the same news that is relevant to speculative stocks will be relevant to speculative commodities. Therefore, in the absence of changes in supply (caused by the weather, for instance), wheat, cotton, wool, copper, scrap, and other speculative commodities will move with common stocks, and will not wait for changes in employment, wage rates, and non-speculative commodity prices, which latter normally move later in the business cycle.

PART II

THE PURE THEORY OF INVESTMENT VALUE

CHAPTER IV

DOES THE QUANTITY THEORY OF MONEY APPLY TO STOCK PRICES?

I. FISHER'S EQUATION

The simplest explanation of the effect of money on price is given by the so-called quantity theory of money, usually expressed by Fisher's well-known "equation of exchange" [1]

$$MV = PT$$

where

M = quantity of money
V = velocity of circulation
P = price level
T = volume of trade

Fisher includes in the volume of trade all sales of consumer's goods to the public, all sales of raw materials to manufacturers, all payments for wages, interest, rent, and profits, all taxes, all dealings in real estate and securities, in short, all cash transactions of any kind whatsoever. Fisher says that, other things being equal, an increase in the quantity of money will cause a rise in the general price level, and that the increase in money and in prices will be exactly proportionate.[2] Hence, if certain prices refuse to

---

[1] See Irving Fisher, assisted by Harry G. Brown, *The Purchasing Power of Money* (New York: Macmillan, 1911 and 1922). A more elaborate form of the same equation distinguishes between hand-to-hand money M and bank deposits M', and reads as follows: $MV + M'V' = PT$. See also Edwin W. Kemmerer, *Money and Credit Instruments in Their Relation to General Prices* (New York: Henry Holt & Co., 1907); also Kemmerer, *Money* (New York: Macmillan, 1935).

[2] Fisher says prices may also rise because of an increase in the velocity of circulation of money, but it would seem that, in the absence of hoarding or the reverse, the velocity of circulation remains constant, being fixed by the tech-

rise, others must rise all the more, in order that the *average* of all prices shall rise in the required proportion.

Although in some quarters it is the fashion nowadays to pooh-pooh the quantity theory, the fact remains that the modern theories of Keynes, Hawtrey, and many others are only revisions of the original quantity theory, whose beginning goes back almost as far as economics itself. Because all these versions of the quantity theory inevitably raise the question of the extent to which security values are affected by the quantity of money, no outline of the Theory of Investment Value would be complete without an inquiry into the way in which stocks and bonds are dependent on the present and prospective purchasing power of money. This chapter and also Chapters VIII and IX will be devoted to this subject.

2.   CAN INFLATION STRIKE ANYWHERE?

Because Fisher said that real estate and securities, as well as finished and unfinished goods, must be included in the equation of exchange, and because he seemed to imply that if one price does not rise in response to an increase in the quantity of money, another must, and must rise all the more,[3] there is a notion abroad in the land, a false and misleading notion, to the effect that inflation is capricious, that it may strike here, there, or anywhere, that it may cause a rise either in commodity prices, as in this country in 1915–1920, or in real estate, as in Florida in 1925, or in stocks, as in Wall Street in 1928 and 1929,[4]

nique of production, by the customary frequency of pay days, rent days, etc., and by other mores. If so, prices are determined simply by the quantity of money and the quantity of goods. See § 3 of this chapter.

[3] Fisher himself did not say this in so many words and might well take the position that the failure of any one group of prices to rise in response to an increase in the quantity of money would be offset, not by a greater rise in other prices, but by a fall in the velocity of circulation of money.

[4] Cf. Benjamin M. Anderson, "Eating the Seed Corn," *The Chase Economic Bulletin*, May 12, 1936, p. 37: "The primary cause of the great capital gains [attendant on the rise in stocks] was excessive bank expansion...."

but that it is in any event a mechanical result of the increase in the quantity of money. Although this view is not accepted by all writers on monetary theory, it is widely held in financial circles, where the opinion is frequently expressed that inflation in this country, as a result of our huge excess reserves, is likely soon to take the form of a wild speculative boom in the stock market. In a speech on October 9, 1935 Charles R. Gay, President of the New York Stock Exchange, said:

> The position today is entirely sound, from the standpoint of credit directly employed in the security markets. It should be kept so. I am not an alarmist, but we should not close our eyes to the inflammability of the material we are dealing with and to the fact that inflation, if it should once get started, might sweep through the markets as a fire sweeps through a city of wooden houses.[5]

This passage has been widely quoted by financial commentators, and has been interpreted as meaning that inflation the next time may well manifest itself primarily in the stock market.[6]

3. THE QUANTITY OF MONEY AND THE PRICE OF STOCKS

With the notion that the present excess reserves of the banking system cause low interest rates and tend to make stocks sell high no one should quarrel, but with the notion that these same excess reserves portend an increase in the quantity of money soon, which increase will act upon stocks according to a quantity theory of money and prices, we should disagree. When Mr. Gay says, "Given a sufficient degree of confidence, or perhaps of desperation, or even

[5] *New York Times*, October 10, 1935, p. 43.
[6] A more recent expression of the same opinion is to be found in a speech by Orrin G. Wood, president of the Investment Bankers Association of America, who said: "A second lane [to inflation] is speculation.... [From] the recent action of the Federal Reserve Board in raising the margin requirements [however] ... it seems that the Federal Reserve Board does not intend that inflation shall enter by the lane of stock speculation." — *New York Times*, April 15, 1936, p. 33, col. 1.

of reckless boredom over the prolonged idleness of money, a situation could develop which would threaten the gravest consequences through an upward flight of security prices," he seems to imply that excess reserves might breed excess bank deposits which would flow into the stock market and cause inflation in stock prices.[7] That *stock* prices would rise merely because of an increase in the quantity of money, we should deny; for we maintain that stock prices will rise only because people think stocks are worth more. The quantity of money, as we shall show, has nothing to do with the price of stocks. Thus stocks are different from goods and services, for the price of goods and services is proportional to the quantity of money in circulation between producers and consumers.

An increase in the quantity of money is neither a necessary nor a sufficient condition for a rise in the price of stocks. It is not necessary, because stock prices can rise by sales that involve no use of money — by sales between traders using only bookkeeping entries on brokers' books. Thus if John Doe owns American Telephone, now quoted at 160, and Richard Roe owns Allied Chemical, now quoted at the same price, there is nothing to prevent them from exchanging these stocks at 180 next month without the use of any money at all, if each buys and sells within the same trading day. If investors generally trade back and forth with each other, continually becoming more optimistic, just such a rise as this will occur. In fact, this is just what took place during most of the 1935–36 bull movement. Stock prices in general rose without the use of any new credit to finance the rise.

Clearly an increase in the quantity of money is not a necessary condition for a rise in stock prices.[8] Neither is it

---

[7] Care should be taken not to form a final opinion from the quotation given as to Mr. Gay's views on the mechanism of inflation as it affects stock prices, for he was not discussing precisely the point at issue here.

[8] While cash is not needed to finance a rise in the price of stocks, it may be

a sufficient condition. No matter if bank deposits increased, stocks would not go up if people become more pessimistic. Payment of the soldiers' bonus, for instance, might increase the quantity of money, but stock prices might still go down — if the bonus bill carried a heavy tax on dividends, for example. Evidently the quantity of money does not determine the price of stocks.

This is not to say that the making or calling of loans on stocks does not affect their price. But loans on stocks are not money, being neither currency nor bank deposits. Loans are bank assets, while currency and deposits are bank liabilities. Loans on stocks, moreover, can be made, directly or indirectly, by investors, savings banks, insurance companies, and other non-banking lenders; and in this case no increase in demand deposits results, and no change in the quantity of money occurs. Even if loans are made by commercial banks, the proceeds of the loans will be used to pay off the seller of the stocks, who will then use his receipts either to pay off his own bank loans, in which case no effect on the general price level will occur, or to buy goods and services, in which case the loan is like any other bank loan in causing commodity prices, rather than stocks, to rise. In short, stocks rise because people think they are worth more, but commodities rise because buyers have more money wherewith to buy them. For stocks, the quantity theory does not apply; for goods and services it does, at least to some extent.

In this respect stocks are like real estate, whose price is also independent of the quantity of money, save indirectly as this quantity determines the money incomes of consumers and thus the earning power of land and buildings. So rapid can be the velocity of circulation of money

---

needed to finance an increase in the *volume* of speculative trading, for in-and-out traders often tie up large sums temporarily. See Chapter III, § 4, footnote 14.

in both the stock market and the real-estate market that
neither stocks nor real estate need ever wait for an increase in the quantity of money in order to rise in price,[9]
and no shortage of money need ever keep prices down in
these markets.

Inflation, therefore, can occur only in the prices of goods
and services. But inflation so occurring will affect stock
prices *indirectly*. It will make the selling price of manufactured goods rise, and will force up wages and other
expenses. In the end it will increase profits and dividends
in terms of depreciated money. Hence stocks will rise in
price because they are worth more in terms of depreciated
money. But they will rise because they are worth [10] more,
not because there is more money wherewith to buy them;
and inflation outside the stock market, not within it, will
make them rise. Furthermore, the rise should occur
largely *step by step* with, and not in anticipation of, inflation in the prices of goods and services, as will be shown
in a later chapter.[11]

The market for consumers' goods, or for the machines
and raw materials that are used in making them, is quite
different from the market for stocks and real estate, because the production and consumption of goods, unlike the
purchase and sale of stocks and real estate, is a *time-consuming* process, and as a result the circulation of money
to finance this process is also a time-consuming process in
the same degree. In this process, both producer and consumer are obliged to restrict the velocity of circulation of
money coming into their hands, and neither can spend

[9] This statement refers especially to business property; private homes built
for sale to individual families for their own occupancy may be an exception to
the rule, because such pieces of real estate partake more of the nature of consumers' goods than of producers' goods.

[10] In the sense that the present value of their expected future dividends is
greater. Cf. Chapter V, § 1.   [11] See Chapter IX, § 1.

his income with indiscriminate speed. The producer, on his part, when he collects his receivables, must hold the proceeds in cash in order to meet his pay roll at the end of the week or month; if he should chance to collect his money one day earlier or later, he must then hold on to it one day more or less, because always he must pay his wages on the same day of the week or month; hence the process of meeting the pay roll, which is one of the most important uses for money, becomes at the same time a process for stabilizing the velocity of circulation of money. The consumer, on his part also, when he receives his wages, must hold the proceeds in cash at first and must spend the money only a little at a time, in order to make sure that it shall last until the next pay day, so that his family shall not have to go hungry for the last day or so; if he spends rapidly at first, he must spend all the more slowly later; hence the process of buying the family supplies, which, like that of meeting the pay roll, is one of the most important uses for money, becomes at the same time a process for stabilizing the velocity of circulation of money.

The economic mechanism may be likened to a watch that keeps time properly because it contains a balance wheel and hairspring, actuated by an escapement, which together prevent the mainspring from unwinding more than just so fast. In the economic mechanism the pay-roll envelope and the housewife's purse are the two pallets on the escapement lever.

With both producers and consumers, it should be clearly noted, the amount of money which is kept on hand in any particular day of the week or month, whether to meet the coming pay roll or to buy tomorrow's food and clothing, is determined not by considerations of *convenience*, but of *necessity*. It is only the exceptional producer [12] or con-

---

[12] The exceptions among producers comprise mainly the large corporations;

sumer who is not pressed for cash and who does not live from hand to mouth financially; rare indeed are those who, in Marshall's words, are thrifty enough to be able to say that

a large command of resources in the form of currency renders business easy and smooth, and puts them at an advantage in bargaining; but, on the other hand, it locks up in a barren form resources that might yield an income of gratification if invested, say, in furniture; or a money income, if invested in extra machinery or cattle.[13]

To say that the cash balances held by producers and consumers are a matter of convenience, or to imply that most people have any choice in these matters, is utterly to miss the point.[14] Whatever cash most people have in their purses or their checking accounts they are *compelled* to have there in order to pay their bills when the time comes. In consequence it may be said that the velocity of circulation of most cash balances is habitually kept at the maximum figure that the ingenuity of producers and consumers can devise under the existing customs of the country concerning the frequency of pay days, salary days, rent days, and settlement days for charge accounts, and that nothing could substantially increase the velocity of circulation of such cash and deposits as actually do circulate at all in the proper meaning of the term [15] except to make pay days

---

other producers, like farmers, storekeepers, and small manufacturers, usually are pressed for ready cash, as are most consumers.

[13] Alfred Marshall, *Money, Credit, & Commerce* (London: Macmillan, 1923), vol. I, chap. IV, § 3, p. 45.

[14] The same error seems to be continued by the later proponents of the "Cambridge quantity equation." Cf. Keynes, *Treatise*, I, 229–233. Petty avoided this error, but made another one when he asked how much money was sufficient for transacting the business of the nation, and spoke as though the volume of trade and the price level were the independent variables, with the quantity of money the dependent variable, whereas the truth would seem to be that the volume of trade and the quantity of money are the independent variables, with the price level the dependent variable.

[15] Cf. Keynes, *Treatise*, II, 20–21: "Thus it has been usual to limit the 'velocity of circulation,' so far as practicable, to the effective money or money

come daily instead of weekly, salary and rent days weekly
instead of monthly, and tax days monthly instead of yearly.
Nothing else would really alter the velocity of circulation
of money appreciably; but even then, what could be done
about the farmers, whose crops mature but once a year
and who could hardly be paid more often than that?

Seldom is money withdrawn from circulation in the ordinary processes of production and consumption, saving and
investment, except for one single reason, *speculation*. If
people are speculating on the bear side, as during deflation,
they withdraw part of their cash receipts from circulation
while they wait for lower prices on stocks, bonds, real
estate, and speculative commodities. But if people are
speculating on the bull side, as during inflation and a
flight from the currency, they likewise withdraw part of
their cash receipts from circulation in productive channels
and use the money for buying existing supplies of land,
machinery, raw materials, and finished goods. In either
case, cash receipts are withdrawn from production and consumption, with the result that the real income of the community tends to shrink.

Since the velocity of circulation of non-hoarded money
within the productive process is substantially constant,[16]
it follows that the price level for goods and services produced by this process is independent of the *velocity* of

---

in active circulation, and not to stultify the conception by watering down the
velocity of the money in circulation by including money which was not in
circulation at all, but was being used as a 'store of value' and therefore had *no*
velocity...."

[16] Cf. James W. Angell, "The Components of the Circular Velocity of
Money," *Quarterly Journal of Economics*, February 1937. See also his book
The Behavior of Money (New York and London: McGraw-Hill Book Company, Inc., 1936), chap. V. Marshall hints at the same idea when he says:
"Every change in the rapidity of circulation of goods tends to cause a corresponding change in the rapidity of circulation of currency, and substitutes for
currency"; but does not go on to develop his point. *Money, Credit, & Commerce*, p. 43. See also Keynes, *Treatise*, chap. XXIV.

circulation of money; hence this price level must be determined only by the *quantity* of money as compared with the volume of goods and services. In other words, the price level for consumers' goods depends only on the money income of consumers used to buy these goods. Likewise, the price level for producers' goods depends only on the money incomes of producers, which in turn are derived mainly [17] from their sales of finished goods to consumers. As a result, the entire price level for all goods and services is determined almost wholly by the quantity of money in circulation and the volume of production.

The price level for stocks and bonds and real estate, however, which are not produced and consumed, and are not bought out of income, and do not require time for passing from one purchaser to the next as goods in process of manufacture do, and which can even be "swapped" back and forth between traders at rising prices without the use of any cash at all; the price level for these things, to repeat, which represent mere claims to future money payments, does not depend on the quantity of money in circulation. For such things as stocks and bonds, therefore, with which we are primarily concerned in this book, it may correctly be said that no such thing as the quantity theory of money applies.[18]

[17] Some slight alteration in the money outlays of producers may arise from bank borrowing in response to changes in the interest rate or the outlook for profits, and this borrowing gives rise partly to fluctuations of price and partly to fluctuations of volume during the business cycle, as described by Hawtrey, Keynes, and others.

[18] In the very short run the same thing is true of speculative commodities like wheat and cotton, copper and wool, for traders in these commodities can put the price up or down temporarily by "swapping" these things among themselves; but in the less short run it is not true even of speculative commodities, for the quantities produced and consumed during a year are so much larger than the "open interest," or quantity held by speculators, that consumers rather than speculators prove to be the dominating factor in determining price over a period of months, and all that speculators can do is to guess as closely as possible what the actual volume of supplies and force of demand will turn out to be.

CHAPTER V

EVALUATION BY THE RULE OF PRESENT WORTH

I. FUTURE DIVIDENDS, COUPONS, AND PRINCIPAL

Now that we have disposed of the troublesome misconception that stock prices are somehow determined in accordance with a quantity theory of money, we are at last ready to take up the main thesis of this book.

Let us define the investment value of a stock as the present worth of all the dividends [1] to be paid upon it. Likewise let us define the investment value of a bond as the present worth of its future coupons and principal. In both cases, dividends, or coupons and principal, must be adjusted for expected changes in the purchasing power of money. The purchase of a stock or bond, like other transactions which give rise to the phenomenon of interest, represents the exchange of present goods for future goods — dividends, or coupons and principal, in this case being the claim on future goods. To appraise the investment value, then, it is necessary to estimate the future payments. The annuity of payments, adjusted for changes in the value of money itself, may then be discounted at the pure interest rate demanded by the investor. This definition of investment value can be expressed by the following equations: [2]

---

[1] Cf. Robert F. Wiese, "Investing for True Values," *Barron's*, September 8, 1930, p. 5: "*The proper price of any security, whether a stock or bond, is the sum of all future income payments discounted at the current rate of interest in order to arrive at the present value.*" See also Chapter I, § 2.

[2] *Note for the non-technical reader:* It is not necessary to master all of the algebra in the following chapters to understand the rest of this book, for the text between the equations has been so written as to summarize the argument and make it possible to take the derivation of the formulas for granted. The symbols used in the formulas are defined one by one when first introduced, but for

For stocks —

(1a) $$V_o = \sum_{t=1}^{t=\infty} \pi_t v^t = \pi_1 v + \pi_2 v^2 + \pi_3 v^3 + \cdots\cdot$$

where V_o = investment value at start

π_t = dividend in year t

(2) $v = \dfrac{1}{1+i}$, by definition

i = interest rate sought by the investor

For bonds —

(1b) $$V_o = \sum_{t=1}^{t=n} \pi_t v^t + C v^n$$

where π_t = coupon in year t

C = face value, or principal, of bond

n = number of years to maturity

---

easy reference they are reprinted with explanations in a systematic "Table of Symbols" at the end of the book.

The subscripts 1, 2, 3, etc., attached to the Greek letter π in the equations below signify the first, second, third, etc., value of the variable π. Thus π_1 is the amount of the dividend in the first year, π_2 in the second year, π_3 in the third, etc., and π_t in the tth year, where t means time.

The series of terms $\pi_1 v + \pi_2 v^2 + \pi_3 v^3 + \cdots\cdot$ is called an infinite series because there is no end to the number of terms. In this particular series each term is constructed according to the rule that the exponent of the factor v shall be the same as the subscript of the factor π, thus $\pi_3 v^3$, $\pi_t v^t$, etc. In certain special cases the sum of all the terms in an infinite series is a finite number, and not infinity, even though the number of terms is infinite; under these circumstances, the series is said to be convergent. Suffice it to say that a series will often be convergent if each additional term is smaller than the preceding one; any further discussion of convergency would take us too far into higher mathematics.

Two ways of denoting an infinite series are as follows:

$$\pi_1 v + \pi_2 v^2 + \pi_3 v^3 + \cdots\cdots$$

and

$$\sum_{t=1}^{t=\infty} \pi_t v^t$$

The second notation, using the Greek letter Σ, means exactly the same as the first, but is briefer. This notation is read "Summation from t equals one, to

The way in which dividends, or coupons and principal, should be adjusted for changes in the value of money in future years will be discussed later.[3]

2. FUTURE EARNINGS OF STOCKS

Most people will object at once to the foregoing formula for stocks by saying that it should use the present worth of future *earnings*, not future *dividends*.[4] But should not earnings and dividends both give the same answer under the implicit assumptions of our critics? If earnings not paid out in dividends are all successfully reinvested at compound interest for the benefit of the stockholder, as the critics imply, then these earnings should produce dividends later; if not, then they are money lost. Furthermore, if these reinvested earnings will produce dividends, then our formula will take account of them when it takes account of all future dividends; but if they will not, then our formula will rightly refrain from including them in any discounted annuity of benefits.

Earnings are only a means to an end, and the means should not be mistaken for the end. Therefore we must say that a stock derives its value from its dividends, not its earnings. In short, a stock is worth only *what you can get out of it*. Even so spoke the old farmer to his son:

---

t equals infinity, of pi sub t, times v to the tth power." It should be noted that

$$\sum_{t=1}^{t=\infty}$$

is not a factor to be multiplied by the other factors π_t and v^t, but is an operational sign applied to these two factors taken together.

If the series runs from $t = 1$ to $t = n$, as in formula (1b) applying to bonds, the series is a finite series instead of an infinite series, because the number of terms is limited and is given in this case by the number of coupons payable during the life of the bond.

A series of the kind under discussion here, whether finite or infinite, is known as a geometric progression if π_t is constant.

[3] See Chapter VIII, § 2, and Chapter IX.

[4] See also Chapter XXII, "U. S. Steel," especially § 13.

A cow for her milk,
A hen for her eggs,
And a stock, by heck,
For her dividends.

An orchard for fruit
Bees for their honey,
And stocks, besides,
For their dividends.

The old man knew where milk and honey came from, but he made no such mistake as to tell his son to buy a cow for her cud or bees for their buzz.

In saying that dividends, not earnings, determine value, we seem to be reversing the usual rule that is drilled into every beginner's head when he starts to trade in the market; namely, that earnings, not dividends, make prices. The apparent contradiction is easily explained, however, for we are discussing permanent investment, not speculative trading, and dividends for years to come, not income for the moment only. Of course it is true that low earnings together with a high dividend for the time being should be looked at askance, but likewise it is true that these low earnings mean low dividends *in the long run*. On analysis, therefore, it will be seen that no contradiction really exists between our formula using dividends and the common precept regarding earnings.

How to estimate the future dividends for use in our formula is, of course, the difficulty. In later chapters ways of making an estimate will be given for such stocks as we now know how to deal with. In so doing, this book seeks to make its most important contribution to Investment Analysis.

3. PERSONAL VS. MARKET RATE OF INTEREST

In applying the foregoing formulas, each investor should use his own personal rate of interest. If one investor de-

mands 10 per cent and another 2 per cent as minimum
wages of abstinence, then the same stock or bond will be
accorded a lower value by the one than by the other.

The only case in which the market rate of interest should
be applied is when the analyst is speaking not for himself
personally but for investors in general. Then he should
use the pure interest rate as it is expected to be found in
the open market in the years to come.[5]

4.   COMPOUND INTEREST AT A CHANGING RATE

In the usual discussion of compound interest, it is always
assumed that the rate of interest stays the same throughout the period in question. The assumption of a changing
rate is never met with, and apparently the possibility of
such a thing is not even considered.[6] Yet in theory a changing rate is easily conceivable, and so provision for it, when
it occurs, should be made in our formula, thus:

(1c)
$$V_o = \sum_{t=1}^{t=\infty} \pi_t v_1 v_2 \cdots v_t$$

where

(2)
$$v_1 = \frac{1}{1+i_1}; \; v_2 = \frac{1}{1+i_2}; \text{ etc.}$$

and

i_1 = interest rate in first year
i_2 = interest rate in second year
i_t = interest rate in tth year

The interest rate i_t in every case is that for one-year loans
made at the beginning of the year t, and paid at the end
of it.

[5] See Chapter XX, § 21.
[6] An exceptional case in which the possibility of changing interest rates is
in fact considered occurs in life insurance, where actuaries of non-participating
companies occasionally use a split rate in computing premiums and making other
calculations.

The meaning of the equation can be shown by an example. Suppose that investors think that the interest rate for one-year loans, as determined by the equilibrium of the demand and supply for new savings, will be

$$
\begin{aligned}
i_1 &= \tfrac{1}{2}\% \ \text{ in } 1937 \\
i_2 &= 1\% \ \text{ in } 1938 \\
i_3 &= 1\tfrac{1}{2}\% \ \text{ in } 1939 \\
i_4 &= 2\% \ \text{ in } 1940 \\
i_5 &= 2\tfrac{1}{2}\% \ \text{ in } 1941 \\
i_6 &= 3\% \ \text{ in } 1942
\end{aligned}
$$

Then the present worth of π dollars payable

at the end of 1937 will be $\dfrac{\pi}{(100\tfrac{1}{2}\%)}$

at the end of 1938 will be $\dfrac{\pi}{(100\tfrac{1}{2}\%)\ (101\%)}$

at the end of 1939 will be $\dfrac{\pi}{(100\tfrac{1}{2}\%)\ (101\%)\ (101\tfrac{1}{2}\%)}$

and at the end of t years will be $\pi v_1 v_2 \cdots v_t$

Long-term interest rates are not a genus wholly distinct from short-term interest rates, and they are not determined separately from short-term rates by independent considerations. Rather, long-term rates are only a thing derived, an average of a special kind, a mere figure of substitution that can be used in place of the series of short-term rates for the years covered. This average is not an ordinary arithmetic average, nor even a geometric average, but is a more complicated average whose formula is given implicitly by the formula for the value of the bond or stock under consideration.[7]

[7] For a further discussion of this point, see Chapter X, "Bonds with Interest Rates Changing."

5. RIGHTS AND ASSESSMENTS

In the case of growing companies,[8] rights to subscribe to additional shares may be offered from time to time, and this will affect the annuity of payments received by the stockholder. Such an issue of rights is equivalent to a stock dividend paid to the stockholder together with an assessment levied on him. Since it is well recognized that a stock dividend, like a split-up, does not change the values behind a given percentage of a company's stock, it follows that an offering of "rights," in so far as it increases the number of shares outstanding but leaves unchanged the percentage owned by each stockholder, adds nothing to the value of the stockholder's equity. And in so far as the offering brings new money into the company's treasury, it is like any other assessment in building up the stockholder's equity. But in so far as the offering draws this money out of the stockholder's pocket, it increases the total cost of his commitment. This latter fact is clearly reflected by the change in the market worth of an issue of stock when it goes ex-rights. Then the new value of the entire issue becomes greater than that of the old by exactly the amount of new money paid in, and the stockholders' bank accounts become less by the same amount. The operation is thus exactly the opposite of the payment of a cash dividend, in that the payment of dividends re-

[8] Cf. Gabriel A. D. Preinreich, *The Nature of Dividends* (New York: Lancaster Press, Inc., 1935), p. 9: "There are various kinds of corporations. Some are unable to reinvest their earnings, others can do so only in part, still others can use every cent they earn and there are cases where the retention of the entire earnings is insufficient to provide for expansion. It is an important duty of the corporate management to formulate dividend policies which conform to these conditions. A company which can not reinvest its earnings must distribute them; slowly expanding companies will distribute the difference between the total earnings and that portion which can be reinvested, while rapidly expanding companies will not only endeavor to retain all earnings but must in addition attract new capital."

duces the value of the stockholders' investment and increases the value of their bank accounts, while the exercise of rights does the reverse.

But, it may be asked, will not the new money collected by the company be invested at a good profit, and so will not the stock rise as the profits accrue in the future? No, it may be answered, the rise will not occur in the future, because it has already occurred in the past. The price does not ordinarily wait for the profits to accrue, or even for the funds to be collected, but responds as soon as the investment opportunity appears, because usually there is no question as to the power of a company to secure such new money as may be needed to enable it to exploit any new opportunities that may arise. For established companies, the mechanism of issuing rights to take advantage of recognized opportunities for profit is known to be so sure that when the feat is successfully accomplished each time, the market sees no cause for surprised elation. The assessment is viewed as merely a routine operation in the company's growth.

That the word "assessment" used above carries an invidious connotation is true. The word "contribution" could have been used instead, but such a choice of terms would have been less challenging to old views. Just because my opponents call the contribution a "right," I shall retort by calling it an "assessment." [9] In either case, however, innuendo obscures the real facts. Assessments and dividends are opposite aspects of the same thing, differing only with respect to the direction in which the money flows. A company which pays liberal cash dividends and offers frequent rights should not be considered doubly

[9] Cf. Stephen Heard, in *Stock Growth and Discount Tables*, by S. E. Guild (Boston: Financial Publishing Company, 1931). Heard says on page 293, in an appendix written by him for that book, "If, therefore, a stockholder wishes to maintain his position, rights are in reality an assessment."

generous — the usual interpretation of such a policy — but rather as taking back with one hand what it doles out with the other. Its *gross* dividend is offset by an assessment which often makes its *net* dividend very small, or even negative. Nevertheless, such a course does not affect the intrinsic, long-run value of the stock, for, be it remembered, the investment value of a common stock is the present worth of its *net* dividends to perpetuity.

"Rights" should not be treated as income. Methods of evaluation based on such a treatment involve endless difficulties and often certain bad errors. A method which assumes, for instance, that the investor is to sell some of his rights to provide cash for subscribing with the rest makes it necessary to know the price at which these rights can be sold, and thus also the price of the stock at intervals during the period treated. If the past is drawn upon, as is sometimes done, to provide a figure for the worth of rights, then the answer becomes dependent on the general level of stock prices prevailing in the past, with the result that this method of evaluation becomes of no use in estimating the price which should prevail in the future. Not what has been but what should be the price of a given stock is our problem; and we must not use the widely fluctuating and hence mostly incorrect prices of the past as data in our calculations.[10]

The relation which exists between gross dividends, subscriptions, and net dividends may be expressed by the following equation:

(3a) $$\pi = \kappa - \sigma$$

where

π = pure, or net, dividend in any given year — per share
κ = actual, or gross, dividend in any given year — of original
σ = subscription, or assessment in any given year — stock

[10] Heard's method of adjusting for rights (Guild, *Stock Growth and Discount Tables*, pp. 296–297) would seem to be open to this objection.

If no rights are issued in a particular year, then the assessment, or subscription, in that year will be nil, and $\sigma = 0$. It usually happens that assessments are large but infrequent, hence in the years when they do occur, σ exceeds κ and π becomes temporarily negative. Even though the assessments do not come every year, however, and even though they are spaced at irregular intervals, we may still treat them as items in an annuity (a negative one this time), and then find their present worth, and deduct this sum from the present worth of the gross dividends, to get a figure for the fair value of a stock, thus:

$$(\text{1d}) \qquad V_o = \sum_{t=1}^{t=\infty} \kappa_t v^t - \sum_{t=1}^{t=\infty} \sigma_t v^t$$

From the foregoing discussion of the place of rights in the evaluation of common stocks, it should be clear that nothing but *cash* dividends ought to be included in the formulas for appraisal,[11] and that neither rights nor stock dividends nor option warrants nor any other form of distribution should be considered except in terms of the cash payments to which it may later give rise.

6. THE FORMATION POINT FOR INCOME

If, as argued above, assessments add to the value of one's stockholdings only so much as they subtract from one's bank account, and if dividends do only the opposite, how can either operation add to one's wealth, and how can anyone get rich from his stockholdings? Surely income accrues sometime, somewhere. The behavior of stock prices indicates, and reason confirms, the conclusion that a man's income arises and his wealth increases at that point in the chain between customer and stockholder where

[11] Cf. Chapter XXIV, § 2, dealing with the rights offered on American Telephone.

a company's earnings reach its cash account. When a corporation, after making and paying for its wares and selling them at a profit, finally collects the cash due on them, then at last it realizes its profit. From that moment on, shareholders may take their money at will.[12] The date of distribution does not matter. But when the dividend is once allotted, on that day the stock goes ex-dividend by the amount of the payment, and then what a man gains in cash assets he loses in invested assets.

The reason for drawing the line at the time when profits reach the cash account instead of earlier in their development is because at the cash stage they are no longer among the earning assets of a business. Plant, inventories, receivables, all in their proper proportions, make up a going concern, and are expected to earn a higher return than cash assets. Cash assets, however, if loaned in the money market, yield the same return to all companies, just as they would to their individual stockholders; but invested assets yield varying returns to different companies. A stockholder does not give his cash to a corporation to be lent for him, but to be invested in bricks and mortar, or in current assets. He can do his own lending. When profits are still in the form of invested assets, their final cash equivalent is uncertain, but when they reach the cash account, their exact amount is known, and no variation results from the mere processes of distribution or contribution. Hence the place to draw the line is between cash and other assets.

Of course if cash piles up in a company's treasury, and is then spent again, unwisely this time, that is another story, and the stockholders' wealth decreases when the unwise expenditure is made. It still remains true, nevertheless, that the stockholders' wealth had previously increased when operations succeeded in yielding a cash profit.

[12] Cf. Schabacker, *Stock Market*, p. 348, section entitled "Dividends not a Fundamental Benefit."

7. THE VALUE OF A RIGHT

After each assessment, or offering of new stock, the old shares go ex-rights, and change their value because the number of shares and the cash assets of the company have increased. The value of a right is derived as follows:

Let

M = market price rights-on

$\hat{M}$ = market price ex-rights [13]

M_w = market price of right, or subscription warrant

S = subscription price of new stock offered

N = number of rights required for subscription to one new share

Since

N = total number of shares held before subscription to one new share

NM = total value of shares held before subscription to one new share

and

$N + 1$ = total number of shares held after subscription

$NM + S$ = total value of holdings after subscription

and

$\hat{M}(N + 1)$ = total value of shares held after subscription

therefore

(4a) $\hat{M}(N + 1) = NM + S$

and

(4b) $\hat{M} = \dfrac{NM + S}{N + 1}$, the price of the stock ex-rights [14]

and

(5) $M_w = M - \hat{M}$, the price of a right

---

[13] The symbol $\hat{M}$ is read "M-cap," and may be thought of as meaning "M after recapitalization in the manner specified."

[14] The application of this formula is illustrated in Chapter XXIV, § 8, dealing with American Telephone.

8. UNCERTAINTY AND THE PREMIUM FOR RISK

If the investor is uncertain about the future, he cannot tell for sure just what is the present worth of the dividends or of the interest and principal he will receive. He can only say that under one set of possible circumstances it will have one value and under another, another. Each of these possible values will have a different probability, however, and so the investor may draw a probability curve to express the likelihood that any given value, V, will prove to be the true value. Thus, if he is appraising a risky twenty-year bond bearing a 4 per cent coupon and selling at 40 to yield 12 per cent to maturity, even though the pure interest seems to be only 4 per cent, he may conclude that the probabilities are as shown in Diagram 6.

The various possible values, V, of the bond, from zero to par, are shown by the abscissae of the curve, while the likelihood, $f(V)$, that any given value will prove to be the true value, is shown by the ordinates. A uni-modal curve, of the form usual for probability curves, could not be used in this case, because it would fail to show the relatively high chances of receiving all or none of the interest and principal.

Whenever the value of a security is uncertain and has to be expressed in terms of probability, the correct value to choose is the mean value,[15]

(6)
$$\overline{V} = \frac{\int_0^\infty V \; f(V)dV}{\int_0^\infty f(V)dV}$$

The customary way to find the value of a risky security has always been to add a "premium for risk" to the pure interest rate, and then use the sum as the interest rate for

[15] The value of the denominator is always unity because the sum of all the separate probabilities is necessarily one. For values of V above the maximum, $f(V) = 0$.

discounting future receipts. In the case of the bond under discussion, which at 40 would yield 12 per cent to matu-

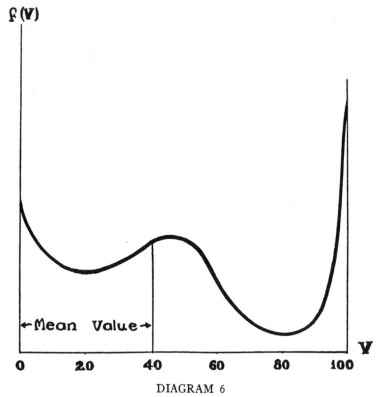

DIAGRAM 6

PROBABILITY CURVE FOR TRUE VALUE

rity,[16] the "premium for risk" is 8 per cent when the pure interest rate is 4 per cent.

Strictly speaking, however, there is no risk in buying the bond in question if its price is right. Given adequate diversification, gains on such purchases will offset losses,

[16] See, for instance, *High Yield Tables of Bond Values* (Boston: Financial Publishing Co., and London: George Rutledge and Sons, Ltd., 1919), p. 83.

and a return at the pure interest rate will be obtained. Thus the *net risk* turns out to be nil. To say that a "premium for risk" is needed is really an elliptical way of saying that payment of the full face value of interest and principal is not to be expected on the average. This leads to the mathematical definition of the "premium for risk" as the value of x that will satisfy the following two equations:

(7) $$x = i - \hat{i}$$

(1e) $$\bar{V} = \sum_{t=1}^{t=n} \frac{\pi_t}{(1+i)^t} + \frac{C}{(1+i)^n}$$

where

x = premium for risk
i = yield, at face value of interest and principal
$\hat{i}$ = pure interest rate [17]
$\bar{V}$ = mean of all possible values of bond, as defined in equation (6)
π = face value of coupons
C = face value of principal
n = number of years to maturity of bond

If the mean value, $\bar{V}$, is known, equation (1e) can be solved for i, the proper yield. Or, if i is known, the same equation can be solved for $\bar{V}$. The problem can be approached in either way. Most people are used to going about it in the latter way, however, and find it easier to think in terms of interest and principal at face value heavily discounted than in terms of interest and principal at reduced value lightly discounted. They think they can make a better estimate of the proper rate of discount in

[17] Although it would make a more consistent notation to use $\hat{i}$ instead of i for the risk-inclusive rate, so as to correspond with $\bar{V}$ for the risk-inclusive value, the more common symbol was made the simpler, and i was used for the risk-inclusive, $\hat{i}$ for the riskless, rate of interest.

The economic "premium for risk" is not to be confused with the accounting "premium" on a bond bought above par.

any given situation than of the various possibilities of partial or complete default. If they can, their method has the advantage of being quicker and easier, because it requires the calculation of the present worth of one simple, instead of many varied, annuities. The final choice depends on whether the element of uncertainty in forecasts can be handled by the mind more easily in the one way or the other. Usually the method of using an enlarged discount rate will prove to be the simpler to think of, and so we shall generally employ it in the pages to follow.[18]

9.   SENIOR AND JUNIOR ISSUES OF THE SAME CONCERN

As everyone knows, the risk factor varies between the several securities of the same company. Usually the bonds are considered safer than the shares, with the underlying bonds having a better rating than the junior bonds, and the preferred stock than the common stock. Sometimes, however, this rule appears to be refuted by actual market prices, especially in the case of overcapitalized enterprises that nevertheless enjoy good speculative prospects. With such enterprises, the senior securities usually sell to give a high yield, the common stock a low yield. Yet the market is quite right in thus reversing the usual rule, for if the venture should fail, the bondholders would lose much; but if it should succeed, they would gain little, since all the profits in excess of stipulated interest would go to the common stockholders, who have but little to lose and much to gain. A notable instance of the foregoing was the United States Steel Corporation at the beginning of its career. As discussed in a later chapter,[19] its senior securities sold to yield 6.5 per cent on the average soon after it was

---

[18] See also the discussion of risk and uncertainty in connection with option warrants and convertible bonds in Chapter XIV, and in connection with government bonds during inflation in Chapter XIX, § 20.

[19] Chapter XXII, § 17, Table 25.

formed, while its stock sold at a high price-earnings ratio, because the success of the new trust was then still in doubt, although the company was thought to have great speculative possibilities.

The proper yield on the *common* stock of such an enterprise is fixed and determined, after the manner of a dependent variable, once the proper yield on the *senior* securities and on the enterprise as a whole are agreed upon, as the following algebraic analysis shows. (For simplicity a horizontal trend of earnings is assumed.)

Let

V_b = investment value of bonds, per share of common
V_c = investment value of stock, per share of common
V_a = investment value of entire enterprise, per share of common

Then

(18a) $\qquad V_a = V_b + V_c$

Likewise let

β = bond interest, per share of common
π = pure dividend, per share of common
i_b = fair interest rate for bonds
i_c = fair interest rate for common stock
i_a = fair interest rate for entire enterprise

Then

(8c) $\qquad V_b = \dfrac{\beta}{i_b}$ (see Chapter VI, § 2. For simplicity, the bonds are assumed to be perpetual bonds.)

(8a) $\qquad V_c = \dfrac{\pi}{i_c}$

(8b) $\qquad V_a = \dfrac{\beta + \pi}{i_a}$

Combining (18a) and (8b), we get

(8d) $\qquad V_b + V_c = \dfrac{\beta + \pi}{i_a}$

and combining (8c) and (8a) with (8d), we get

$$\frac{\beta}{i_b} + \frac{\pi}{i_c} = \frac{\beta + \pi}{i_a}$$

$$\frac{\pi}{i_c} = \frac{\beta + \pi}{i_a} - \frac{\beta}{i_b}$$

whence

(8e)
$$i_c = \frac{\pi}{\dfrac{\beta + \pi}{i_a} - \dfrac{\beta}{i_b}}$$

Q. E. F.

The foregoing formula [20] shows the proper yield for a common stock once the fair yield for the senior securities and the enterprise as a whole have been decided upon.

10. THE LAW OF THE CONSERVATION OF INVESTMENT VALUE

If the investment value of an enterprise as a whole is by definition the present worth of all its future distributions to security holders, whether on interest or dividend account, then this value in no wise depends on what the company's capitalization is. Clearly if a single individual or a single institutional investor owned all the bonds, stocks, and warrants issued by a corporation, it would not matter to this investor what the company's capitalization was.[21] Any earnings collected as interest could not be collected as dividends. To such an individual it would be perfectly obvious that total interest- and dividend-paying power was in no wise dependent on the kind of securities issued to the company's owner. Furthermore, no *change* in the investment value of the enterprise as a whole would

---

[20] The application of this formula is illustrated in Chapter XXII, § 17, dealing with U. S. Steel.

[21] Except for details concerning the income tax.

result from a *change* in its capitalization. Bonds could be retired with stock issues, or two classes of junior securities (i.e., common stock and warrants) could be combined into one, without changing the investment value of the company as a whole. Such constancy of investment value is analogous to the indestructibility of matter or energy; it leads us to speak of the Law of the Conservation of Investment Value, just as physicists speak of the Law of the Conservation of Matter, or the Law of the Conservation of Energy.

Since market value does not usually conform exactly to investment value, no "conservation of market value" is to be found in general. Only to a rough extent do total market values remain the same regardless of capitalization. The exceptions in practice are important enough to afford many opportunities for profit by promoters and investment bankers.[22]

11. REFUNDING OPERATIONS

If a bond issue matures, or if general interest rates decline enough to allow the replacement of a callable issue with another bearing a lower interest rate, a refunding operation may be undertaken that will alter the corporation's interest charges and change the investment value of its common stock. Since the distributable fraction of a company's quasi-rents is independent of its capital structure and is entirely available for taxes, interest, and dividends, any saving in interest can be used for dividends, and any increase in interest must come out of dividends. Hence the resulting increment or decrement in earnings per share must be capitalized at a different rate from the original earnings per share. If by refunding its bonds at a lower rate and replacing its preferred stock with low-coupon

[22] See discussion of United Corporation in Chapter XXV.

notes, for instance, a company saves a dollar a share in senior charges, then — assuming that dividends are capitalized at 5 per cent, and earnings at 10 per cent (the usual rule of thumb) — it adds twenty dollars a share, and not ten, to the value of its common stock. If, on the other hand, a company is forced to refund a maturing issue at a higher rate, as might happen if its bonds came due during a banking crisis, then the decrease in earnings per share, resulting from the higher interest charges, would have to be capitalized at twenty times, and not at ten as would an ordinary change in earnings.

12.   MARKETABILITY

Marketability, or salability, or liquidity, is an attribute of an investment to which many buyers of necessity attach great importance. Yet it would not be helpful to amend our definition of investment value in such a way as to make it take cognizance of marketability. Risk, to be sure, should be covered by the definition, as done above, but not marketability, for the inclusion of marketability would only lead to confusion. Better to treat intrinsic value as one thing, salability as another. Then we can say, for instance, that a given investment is both cheap and liquid, not that it is cheap partly because it is liquid; the latter phraseology would only raise the question of how much of the cheapness was due to liquidity and how much to other factors. To divorce liquidity, or salability, or marketability, from the concept of investment value is in conformity, moreover, with accepted usage outside the field of investment. In speaking of goods and services, for instance, one does not say that a pound of sugar is cheap at six cents because it is so "salable." Nothing of the sort; for the sugar is bought for consumption and not for resale. By the same token, why should one say that a bond is cheap because it is so salable? For if the bond is bought for investment, as by a life insurance company, it is not intended for resale at all, but for holding to maturity. Of course, if the buyer is a speculator, that is another matter, since investment value is only one of several things considered by a speculator. But even a speculator should not confuse salability with cheapness, any more than he should confuse popularity with cheapness.[23] Just as market price determined by marginal opinion is one thing, and investment value determined by future dividends is another, so also salability is one thing and cheapness another.

Likewise *stability* is a thing distinct from investment value, and from marketability as well. While the expected stability of the price of a security in future years is a consideration of great importance to some investors, particularly banks, yet it is not a component of investment value as the latter term ought to be defined. Many individual investors who buy and hold for income do not need to concern themselves with stability any more than with liquidity; hence to include the concept of stability in the definition of investment value would only make investment value mean something different for each and every investor, according to his own personal need for stability as compared with other things.

In conclusion, therefore, it may be said that neither marketability nor stability should be permitted to enter into the meaning of the term *investment value*.

[23] Cf. Chapter III, § 7.

CHAPTER VI

STOCKS WITH GROWTH COMPLETED

I. STOCKS WITH DECLINING DIVIDENDS

It is approximately correct to consider that the dividends on all stocks with declining dividends continue for a limited period of time only, after which the stocks become worthless. In this case the value of each share is given by the following equation:

$$(1f) \qquad V_0 = \sum_{t=1}^{t=n} \pi_t v^t = \pi_1 v + \pi_2 v^2 + \cdots + \pi_n v^n$$

where

$V_0 =$ investment value per share
$\pi_t =$ dividend in any given year, t, per share
$i =$ interest rate

$$(2) \qquad v = \frac{1}{1 + i}, \text{ by definition}$$

$n =$ number of years dividends are paid

This formula is a special case of (1a) where $t = n$ as a maximum. The formula states that the stock is worth the present value of the annuity of dividends to be paid per share. Successive annual dividends need not be equal, of course. Mining shares often belong to the class of stocks characterized by dividends for a limited period only; for mining shares future dividends can be inferred from estimates of costs, selling prices, and the life of ore reserves.[1]

When bonds go through an inflation, their coupons lose real value in much the same way that the dividends of

---

[1] Cf. J. A. Grimes and W. H. Craigue. *Principles of Valuation* (New York: Prentice-Hall, Inc., 1928).

declining enterprises shrink. We shall not consider the problem of bond values at this point, however, because the formulas used can more easily be developed later; since the bond formulas for a period of inflation turn out to be much like the stock formulas for growing companies, it seems best to cover the subject in a later chapter.

2. STOCKS WITH CONSTANT DIVIDENDS

Preferred stocks, and common stocks of mature companies, which neither wax nor wane in dividend-paying power, may be evaluated by the following formula: [2]

$$(8a) \qquad V_0 = \frac{\pi}{i}$$

where

$V_0 =$ investment value
$\pi =$ real dividend per year
$i =$ rate of interest on investment

This formula states that the investment value of a stock whose dividends are constant is equal to a single year's dividend divided by the rate of interest sought on the investment.

To prove this theorem by algebra, one must make use of a well-known device for finding the value of an infinite series; this device will be used again and again in the pages to follow, and its use is shown below:

To prove:

$$(8a) \qquad V_0 = \frac{\pi}{i}$$

Given:

$$(1a) \qquad V_0 = \sum_{t=1}^{t=\infty} \pi_t v^t$$

[2] The application of this formula is illustrated in Chapter XXI, § 1, dealing with General Motors.

(1aa)
$$= \pi \sum_{t=1}^{t=\infty} v^t, \text{ since } \pi \text{ is constant}$$

(1aa)
$$= \pi(v + v^2 + v^3 + \cdots + v^{t=\infty})$$

(1ab)
$$= \pi v(1 + v + v^2 + \cdots + v^{t-1=\infty})$$

The first part of the device is to divide by v as shown above. The second part of the device is to reduce the infinite series $(1 + v + v^2 + \cdots)$ to a finite number by means of the further expedient of multiplying it by $\dfrac{1-v}{1-v}$, which is equal to one; this second expedient gives a value of $\dfrac{1-v^t}{1-v}$ for the infinite series in equation (1ab), and a value of $v\,\dfrac{1-v^t}{1-v}$ for the infinite series in equation (1aa).[3]

It may be noted that in these infinite series

(2)
$$v = \frac{1}{1+i}, \text{ where } i > 0,$$

with the result that

$$v < 1$$
(9a)
$$\lim_{t \to \infty} v^t = 0, \text{ if } i > 0,$$

[3] *Note for the non-technical reader:* If the reader will perform the actual multiplication for himself, he will see at a glance why all but the first and last terms of the infinite series drop out, thus:

$$
\begin{array}{l}
1 + v + v^2 + \cdots + v^{t-1} \\
1 - v \\
\hline
1 + v + v^2 + \cdots + v^{t-1} \\
\quad - v - v^2 - \cdots - v^{t-1} - v^t \\
\hline
1 \qquad\qquad\qquad\qquad\quad - v^t
\end{array}
$$

The symbol lim appearing on this page is read "limit as t approaches infinity." See also Chapter VII, § 1, footnote 3.

and

(9b) $$\lim_{t \to \infty} v \frac{1 - v^t}{1 - v} = \frac{v}{1 - v}, \text{ if } i > 0$$

Hence the expression for V_o in formula (1aa) may be written as follows:

$$V_o = \frac{\pi v}{1 - v}$$

$$= \frac{\pi}{\dfrac{1}{v} - 1}$$

$$= \frac{\pi}{1 + i - 1} \quad \text{since } \frac{1}{v} = 1 + i, \text{ by definition } (2)$$

(8a) $$= \frac{\pi}{i}$$

Q. E. D.

The net or pure dividend, π, of the preceding equations has already been defined thus:

(3a) $$\pi = \kappa - \sigma$$

In practice, however, this definition does not enable us to determine π, and so we must look for aid to other equations, such as

(10a) $$\pi = \gamma - \rho, \text{ by definition}$$

where

$\gamma = $ total earnings per share

$\rho = $ reinvestment required per share

or

(10b) $$\pi = \alpha - \beta - \rho$$

where

(11a) $$\gamma = \alpha - \beta, \text{ by definition}$$

and

α = earnings on invested assets, after reserves and taxes, per share of common

β = bond interest and preferred dividends, per share of common

It is often said that earnings, not dividends, determine the value of a stock. This statement is partly true when it refers to actual dividends currently paid, as is usually meant, but it is false as a rejoinder to the foregoing analysis, where the symbol π refers to pure dividends as determined by reinvestment needs.

To conclude, a stock is worth the present value of all the dividends ever to be paid upon it, no more, no less. The purchase of a stock represents the exchange of present goods for future goods, just as in other cases where interest arises. Dividends are the claim on future goods. Present earnings, outlook, financial condition, and capitalization should bear upon the price of a stock only as they assist buyers and sellers in estimating future dividends.

3.   THE REINVESTMENT OF EARNINGS

Experience shows that a certain portion of earnings must be reinvested to enable a company to maintain its competitive position and keep abreast of the times.[4] That the reinvested earnings of mature companies do not increase dividend-paying power, but merely maintain it, is clear from the failure of such mature enterprises as the steel and railroad companies to pay dividends in keeping with the large book values they have built up during a long period of years. The reason is probably that ordinary

---

[4] See Chapter XXII, on the U. S. Steel Corporation.

accounting practice does not make adequate charges for obsolescence, and thus overstates earnings. In a static world, earnings and charges for depreciation, as commonly figured, would be correct; but in a dynamic one the mere replacement of out-worn machinery with replicas does not suffice. Provision for cost reduction to meet competition is essential to the maintenance of earnings in the mere *status quo*. A charge for this purpose may properly be made against the earnings of a mature company, therefore, before arriving at net or distributable profits.

The customary arrangement of income accounts does not bring out the real priorities that govern the distribution of profits. Since reinvestment is necessary for maintaining earning power, income accounts might well be set up as shown on the right-hand side of the following comparison:

	CUSTOMARY ORDER		PRIORITY ORDER
Profit after taxes	$1,000,000	Profit after taxes	$1,000,000
Interest and pre-ferred dividends	−200,000	Reinvestment require-ment	−200,000
Net income	$ 800,000	Balance for dis-tribution	$ 800,000
Common dividends	−600,000	Interest and pre-ferred dividends	−200,000
Surplus for reinvest-ment	$ 200,000	Balance for common dividends	$ 600,000

In practice the *dividend* policy of a company, after allowing for rights as explained in Chapter V, § 5, is a thing not within the discretion of the management once policies regarding *reinvestment* have been laid down.

It will now be of interest to see whether the correct price-earnings ratio to use in evaluating the stock of the company whose income account is shown above is the familiar "ten times earnings," [5] or some other figure. To begin with, let us note that the value of the company's stock is given by the following formula:

$$(8a) \qquad V = \frac{\pi}{i}$$

The price-earnings ratio for any stock is defined as

$$(12a) \qquad e = \frac{V}{\gamma}$$

$$(12b) \qquad V = e\gamma$$

where

$$\gamma = \text{earnings per share of common}$$

Substituting (12b) in (8a), we get

$$(13a) \qquad e\gamma = \frac{\pi}{i}$$

$$(13b) \qquad e = \frac{\pi}{i\gamma}$$

and multiplying by N, we get

$$(13c) \qquad e = \frac{N\pi}{iN\gamma}$$

In the company under discussion

$$N = \text{number of shares of common}$$
$$N\gamma = \text{total earnings on common}$$
$$= \$800,000$$
$$N\pi = \text{total dividend on common}$$
$$= \$600,000$$

If it be assumed that 5 per cent is the proper rate of interest to use for discounting the dividends, then

$$i = 5 \text{ per cent}$$

[5] Cf. Schabacker, *Stock Market*, pp. 409–410.

When the foregoing data are put into equation (13c) above, it becomes

(13c)

$$e = \frac{N\pi}{iN\gamma}$$

$$= \frac{(\$600,000)}{(.05)\ (\$800,000)}$$

$$= 15 \qquad \text{Q. E. F.}$$

Evidently the correct price-earnings ratio for this particular stock is 15 instead of 10. Such a price-earnings ratio is high for a company that is not growing, but it results from the fact that both reinvestment needs and prior charges are low. If there had been no senior securities at all in the company's capitalization, a still higher price-earnings ratio would have been justified.

Suppose that competition makes for such a large reinvestment requirement that a company has to reinvest 40 per cent of its earnings. Suppose, moreover, that the ·company has a large bonded debt, with the result that bond interest requires 60 per cent of earnings. Then interest and reinvestment requirements between them will exhaust all of the company's earnings, and leave nothing whatsoever for common dividends. Under these circumstances the investment value of the common stock will be zero. Even though the stock may have large assets behind it and may enjoy regular earnings, it will still be worthless because it can never pay a dividend.[6] If the number of shares of stock is small, earnings may reach

[6] Concerning stocks of this kind there is an old joke to the effect that every newcomer on the Stock Exchange must learn two things: first, that the hours of business are from ten to three, and second, that Erie will never pay a dividend.

Erie, to be sure, has never yet paid a dividend, but, to judge by its market price (as of June 15, 1937) of 14⅞, it is expected to do so sometime, directly or indirectly.

$5, $10, or even $100 a share without giving the stock any investment value, so long as it can never pay a dividend.[7]

In practice, however, the facts are seldom as simple as here assumed, because, as discussed in the chapter on option warrants,[8] the market must take account of the entire range of possibilities for dividends, and give consideration to the possibility that earnings may be unexpectedly large or unexpectedly small. To reflect these extreme possibilities, the common stock in the case here discussed would sell *above* zero, and the bonds *below* par.

4.   THE EVALUATION OF NET QUICK ASSETS

A word as to financial position and its bearing on the price of a company's stock may be added here. If a company has cash holdings, for instance, in excess of what are needed to maintain its earning power, it is in a position to pay an extra, non-recurrent dividend, equal in amount to the excess cash per share. Likewise, if its receivables, inventories, or other quick assets are redundant, an extra dividend can be paid whose amount will depend upon what the excess of net quick assets can be liquidated for. On the other hand, if net quick assets are too small, either because of low cash, inventories, or receivables, or high bank loans, the company will have a deficiency in net quick assets that will curtail dividends while current assets are being built up out of earnings. With this in mind, we may rewrite equation (8a) thus:

$$(8k) \qquad V = \frac{\pi}{i} + Q$$

[7] Texas and Pacific Land Trust pays no dividends of the ordinary sort, yet its stock sells far above zero because it pays a virtual dividend in liquidation when it buys in its own shares for cancellation.

[8] Chapter XIV, § 3.

where

$$Q = \text{excess of net quick assets per share}$$

or

$$-Q = \text{deficiency of net quick assets per share}$$

and

$$\pi = \text{dividend-paying power except for excess or deficiency of net quick assets}$$

In this connection the effect of inventory profits or losses should be noted. A fall in raw material quotations, for instance, necessitating as it does a credit to Inventory and a debit to Earnings, does not directly reduce dividends, and so should not hurt the price of a stock, however much it may hurt earnings reported. Even though selling prices of finished goods fall equally with those of raw materials, the smaller receipts from sales will still suffice to replenish inventories with an equal tonnage — though lower value — of raw materials for the next manufacturing cycle. In the same way, inventory profits do not add to the real value of a stock, because the extra proceeds of sales at higher prices are needed to replenish raw materials at higher prices.[9] The observed fact that stock prices

[9] A notable case where the accounts are designed especially to reflect this fact is that of the American Smelting and Refining Co., whose inventory of work-in-process is subject to wide changes in market value. This company has given a clear explanation of its accounting practice in its *Annual Report for 1930*, where it says (p. 4):

"To avoid such excess losses and to enable it to carry on its smelting and refining operations, your Company accumulated the amount of each metal it must have in process under normally prosperous conditions, thus forming a reservoir. It endeavors to sell each day from the outgoing end of the reservoir the amount equal to that taken in at the incoming end. The metal content of the reservoir is known as normal stock. Variations in the price of the normal stock are as immaterial from year to year as are variations in the price of the land upon which a plant is situated, for the reason that it will only be at the end of the Company's activities that such variation will be of any practical consequence. To prevent the trend of our current business from being clouded by immaterial ups and downs in the value of the normal stock from year to year, your Company has heretofore taken from surplus and set up, as a metal

change with raw-material prices must be explained then in some other way. To the extent that the change is justified, it is caused by the fact that business conditions affect dividend-paying power and the demand for raw materials at the same time, while secondary effects are produced in bad times by distress sales on the part of those who used their inventories as collateral; but to the extent that the change is not justified, it is caused by false ideas regarding stock values, whereby appraisals are based too largely on a single financial statement covering only the present year.

Many companies whose inventory values are unstable belong also to the general class of "prince and pauper" companies, the secular trend of whose earnings is hard to estimate because of their extreme fluctuation from year to year. If it is necessary to find the investment value of stocks of these companies, they should usually be treated as belonging to the class of stocks without growth, to which the formulas of the present chapter apply; but in practice it is often wiser to speculate on their cyclical swings than to hold them for permanent investment.

If dividends are in arrears on the preferred stock of a company, as sometimes happens with companies whose earning power is unstable, allowance should be made for this fact in computing the investment value of the common stock of the company, and the total accumulation should be treated as a deficiency in net quick assets.[10]

---

stock reserve, an amount which was believed to be sufficient to protect the normal stock against any abnormal fall in prices.

"At the close of each calendar year, the normal stock is valued at cost or market, whichever is lower, and the metal stock reserve account debited or credited with the difference between the so adjusted inventory value and the value as per books before adjustment. This debit or credit is not taken into account in calculating current or yearly earnings." See also this same company's *Annual Report for 1936*, p. 13.

[10] Cf. Chapter XXII, § 20, on U. S. Steel's arrears.

CHAPTER VII

STOCKS WITH GROWTH EXPECTED

More important than stocks with declining or constant dividends, already discussed, are stocks with increasing dividends, now to be considered.[1]

I. DIVIDENDS INCREASING FOREVER — A HYPOTHETICAL CASE

At the outset it is obvious that no stock exists whose dividends will increase without limit, for no company can continue to grow in dividend-paying power forever, even at 1 per cent or 2 per cent per annum; in other words, infinite dividends are impossible in a finite world. But in spite of the non-existence of this type, it is nevertheless instructive to study the mathematical laws that would determine the value of stocks belonging to it, which laws may be set down as follows:

If

$$\pi_1 = \text{dividend paid during the first year}$$
$$g = \text{annual growth of dividend-paying power}$$
(14a) $$u = 1 + g, \text{ by definition}$$

and if the growth of dividends proceeds thus:

$$\pi_1 = \pi_0 u$$
$$\pi_2 = \pi_1 u = \pi_0 u^2$$

or

(16a) $$\pi_t = \pi_0 u^t$$

then the value of a stock whose dividends grow in this way is found by substituting (16a) in the general equation (1a), as shown on the next page.

---

[1] See Chapters XI and XII for methods of estimating the size of the dividends themselves.

(1a)
$$V_o = \sum_{t=1}^{t=\infty} \pi_t v^t$$

$$= \sum_{t=1}^{t=\infty} \pi_o u^t v^t$$

(1ac)
$$= \pi_o \sum_{t=1}^{t=\infty} w^t$$

where

(15) $w = uv$, by definition

By the method used for stocks in an earlier chapter,[2] we can find the limit [3] of the foregoing infinite series thus:

(1ad)
$$\pi_o \sum_{t=1}^{t=\infty} w^t = \pi_o w \, (1 + w + w^2 + w^3 + \cdots)$$

(1ae)
$$= \frac{\pi_o w}{1 - w} \lim_{t \to \infty} (1 - w^t)$$

The dependence of V_o on w is as follows:
If $w < 1$, then V_o is finite, for

$$\lim_{n \to \infty} \pi_o \sum_{t=1}^{t=n} w^t = \frac{\pi_o w \, (1 - 0)}{1 - w}$$

(17a)
$$= \frac{\pi_o w}{1 - w}$$

If $w = 1$, V_o is infinite, for

$$\lim_{n \to \infty} \pi_o \sum_{t=1}^{t=n} w^t = \pi_o w \, \frac{1 - 1}{1 - 1}$$

(17b)
$$= \pi_o w \, \frac{0}{0}$$

---

[2] See Chapter VI, § 2.

[3] *Note to the non-technical reader:* The limit of an infinite series is the value which that series approaches as the number of its terms is allowed to increase

Although the expression $\dfrac{0}{0}$ found in the foregoing equation has no meaning, it can be shown that V_o increases without limit as w increases to 1 as a limit.[4]

If $w > 1$, V_o is infinite, for

$$\lim_{n \to \infty} \pi_0 \sum_{t=1}^{t=n} w^t = \frac{\pi_0 w}{1 - w} (1 - \infty)$$

$$= \frac{\pi_0 w}{w - 1} (\infty - 1)$$

(17c) $= \infty$

In order to interpret this dependence of V_o on w, it should be remembered that

If $g < i$, then $\dfrac{1 + g}{1 + i} < 1$ and $w = uv < 1$, and V_o is finite.

If $g = i$, then $\dfrac{1 + g}{1 + i} = 1$ and $w = uv = 1$, and V_o is infinite.

If $g > i$, then $\dfrac{1 + g}{1 + i} > 1$ and $w = uv > 1$, and V_o is infinite.

The foregoing analysis shows that if the rate of growth (of dividend-paying power) is less than the rate of interest (used for discounting dividends), the stock has a finite value, even though growth continue without limit.

2. DIVIDENDS INCREASING RAPIDLY, THEN SLOWLY

The growth of a company often corresponds to the curve shown in Diagram 7. For a while such a company

---

without limit; thus 1 is the limit of the infinite series $\frac{1}{2} + \frac{1}{4} + \frac{1}{8} + \frac{1}{16} + \frac{1}{32}$, etc., or, in symbols,

$$\lim_{n \to \infty} (1 + \tfrac{1}{2} + \tfrac{1}{4} + \cdots) = 1$$

[4] See the last section of this chapter (§ 3).

grows at a constant rate, and dividends increase according to a compound interest law; the period when this happens may be called the growing period, and be represented by the section of the graph to the left of the ordinate n. Later

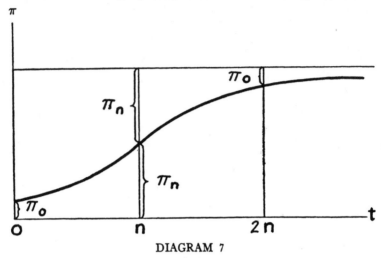

DIAGRAM 7

S–CURVE OF GROWTH OF DIVIDENDS

the rate of growth slows down, and dividends continue to increase, but at an ever slower rate; this second period may be called the maturing period, and be represented by the section of the graph to the right of the ordinate n. To make the curve $\pi = f(t)$ symmetrical, use an asymptote equal to $2\pi_n$ and place the point of inflection at (n, π_n), then, for the first part of the curve, representing the growing period, set

(16a) $$\pi_t = \pi_0 u^t \text{ when } t \leqq n$$

and for the second part, representing the maturing period,

(19) $$\pi_t = 2\pi_n - \pi_0 u^{2n-t} \text{ when } t \geqq n$$

The process of evaluating a stock whose dividends increase in this way may be divided into two parts corresponding to the two periods of growth. If V_o is the investment value at the start, and V_n at the time when growth begins to slacken, then the following two equations hold true:

$$(20) \qquad V_o = \sum_{t=1}^{t=n} \pi_t v^t + V_n v^n$$

$$(21) \qquad V_n v^n = \sum_{t=n+1}^{t=\infty} \pi_t v^t$$

whence

$$V_o = \sum_{t=1}^{t=n} \pi_t v^t + \sum_{t=n+1}^{t=\infty} \pi_t v^t$$

By our usual method of casting the expression $\sum \pi_t v^t$ into the form of a geometric progression, we can show that equation (20) can be reduced to the following:

$$(22a) \qquad V_o = \pi_0 w \cdot \frac{1 - w^n}{1 - w} + V_n v^n$$

or

$$(22b) \qquad \quad = \pi_0 w \cdot \frac{w^n - 1}{w - 1} + V_n v^n$$

Likewise, equation (21) can be reduced in a similar manner, using equation (19), as follows:

$$(21) \qquad V_n v^n = \sum_{t=n+1}^{t=\infty} \pi_t v^t$$

$$= \sum_{t=n+1}^{t=\infty} (2\pi_n - \pi_0 u^{2n-t}) v^t$$

$$(23) \qquad = \sum_{t=n+1}^{t=\infty} 2\pi_n v^t - \sum_{t=n+1}^{t=\infty} \pi_0 u^{2n-t} v^t$$

The first term in (23) may be evaluated by methods used in the preceding chapter, as follows:

(24a)
$$\sum_{t=n+1}^{t=\infty} 2\pi_n v^t = 2\pi_n \sum_{t=n+1}^{t=\infty} v^t$$

$$= 2\pi_n(v^{n+1} + v^{n+2} + v^{n+3} + \cdots)$$

$$= 2\pi_n v^{n+1}(1 + v + v^2 + \cdots)$$

This has been shown, for $v < 1$, to reduce to

$$\frac{2\pi_n v^{n+1}}{1 - v} = \frac{2\pi_n v^n}{\dfrac{1}{v} - 1}$$

$$= \frac{2\pi_n v^n}{1 + i - 1}$$

$$= \frac{2\pi_n v^n}{i}$$

$$= 2\pi_0 \frac{u^n v^n}{i}, \text{ since } \pi_n = \pi_0 u^n, \text{ by equation (13)}$$

(24b)
$$= \left(\frac{2\pi_0}{i}\right) w^n, \text{ since } uv = w, \text{ by definition (15)}$$

By the use of a geometric progression again, we can likewise evaluate the second term in (23) thus:

(25a)
$$\sum_{t=n+1}^{t=\infty} \pi_0 u^{2n-t} v^t = u^{2n}\pi_0 \lim_{t \to \infty} \sum_{t=n+1}^{t=t} \left(\frac{v}{u}\right)^t$$

$$= u^{2n}\pi_0 \lim_{t \to \infty} \left[\left(\frac{v}{u}\right)^{n+1} + \left(\frac{v}{u}\right)^{n+2}\right.$$

$$\left. + \cdots + \left(\frac{v}{u}\right)^t\right]$$

$$= u^{2n}\pi_0 \left(\frac{v}{u}\right)^{n+1} \lim_{t \to \infty} \left[1 + \left(\frac{v}{u}\right)\right.$$

$$\left. + \cdots + \left(\frac{v}{u}\right)^{t-(n+1)}\right]$$

$$(25b) \qquad = \pi_0 u^{n-1} v^{n+1} \lim_{t \to \infty} \left[\frac{1 - \left(\dfrac{v}{u} \right)^{t-(n+1)}}{1 - \dfrac{v}{u}} \right]$$

But $v < 1$ and $u > 1$, therefore $\dfrac{v}{u} < 1$

Consequently the infinite series in (25b) may be reduced as follows:

$$\lim_{t \to \infty} \left(\frac{v}{u} \right)^{t-(n+1)} = \left(\frac{u}{v} \right)^{n+1} \lim_{t \to \infty} \left(\frac{v}{u} \right)^t$$

$$= 0$$

Therefore

$$\lim_{t \to \infty} \sum_{t=n+1}^{t=t} \pi_0 u^{2n-t} v^t = \pi_0 u^{n-1} v^{n+1} \left(\frac{1}{1 - \dfrac{v}{u}} \right)$$

$$= \pi_0 u^n v^n \cdot \frac{v}{u} \left(\frac{1}{1 - \dfrac{v}{u}} \right)$$

$$(25c) \qquad = \pi_0 w^n \cdot \frac{1}{\dfrac{u}{v} - 1}$$

Substituting the values we have just obtained in (24b) and (25c) for the first and second terms in (23), we get

$$(26) \qquad V_n v^n = \frac{2\pi_0}{i} w^n - \frac{\pi_0}{\dfrac{u}{v} - 1} w^n$$

We have already shown that

$$(22b) \qquad V_0 = \pi_0 w \cdot \frac{w^n - 1}{w - 1} + V_n v^n$$

If equation (26) is combined with equation (22b) above, it gives

$$V_o = \pi_o w \cdot \frac{w^n - 1}{w - 1} + \pi_o w^n \left(\frac{2}{i} - \frac{1}{\dfrac{u}{v} - 1} \right)$$

(27a)
$$= \pi_o \left[w \left(\frac{w^n - 1}{w - 1} \right) + w^n \left(\frac{2}{i} - \frac{1}{\dfrac{u}{v} - 1} \right) \right]$$

The logistic curve employed above is not the only one that may be used to represent the course of dividend payments on the stock of a company passing through stages of rapid and then slower expansion. Any other function that lends itself to convenient mathematical treatment may be used, so long as the general premise that stocks derive their value from their future dividends is adhered to. In order to make practical use of the foregoing mathematical analysis, the student of investments must turn to economics for his data. Economic facts, interpreted with his best judgment, must tell him what the probable curve of a company's growth is, and how far along this curve the company has progressed.

3.   SPECIAL CASE WHERE $w = 1$

In the special case where $w = 1$, formulas (22b) and (27a), just given, will not work, because the first term becomes meaningless, thus:

$$w \left(\frac{w^n - 1}{w - 1} \right) = (1) \left(\frac{1 - 1}{1 - 1} \right) = (1) \left(\frac{0}{0} \right), \text{ if } w = 1$$

To find the value of this term in this case, one must go back to the beginning and deduce the formula all over again, thus:

(20)
$$V_o = \sum_{t=1}^{t=n} \pi_t v^t + V_n v^n$$

But

(16a) $$\pi_t = \pi_0 u^t$$

therefore

(16b) $$\pi_t v^t = \pi_0 u^t v^t = \pi_0 w^t = \pi_0, \text{ when } w = 1$$

and so

(1af) $$\sum_{t=1}^{t=n} \pi_t v^t = \sum_{t=1}^{t=n} \pi_0 = n\pi_0, \text{ when } w = 1$$

Hence

(22c) $$V_o = n\pi_0 + V_n v^n, \text{ if } w = 1$$

Likewise formula (27a) becomes

(27b) $$V_o = \pi_0 \left(n + \frac{2}{i} - \frac{1}{\frac{u}{v} - 1} \right), \text{ if } w = 1$$

A special case under formula (22c) is found when dividends after growth ceases continue to be paid at the same rate as in the last year of growth. This assumption may be stated algebraically thus:
Let

$$\pi_n = \pi_{n+1} = \pi_{n+2}, \text{ etc.}$$

In general this assumption would be reasonable for an industrial stock (e.g. Woolworth), but not for a utility stock (e.g. Telephone), because when a utility company stops growing it ordinarily ceases to issue rights, and its net dividend, therefore, undergoes a sudden increase. For industrials, however, this is not usually true, and so a new formula can be developed for them, as follows:

(22c) $$V_o = n\pi_0 + V_n v^n$$

where

(8a) $$V_n = \frac{\pi_n}{i} = \frac{1}{i} \pi_n$$

and

(16a) $$\pi_n = \pi_0 u^n$$

with the result that

(55a) $$V_n v^n = \left(\frac{1}{i} \right) (\pi_0 u^n v^n) = \frac{1}{i} (\pi_0 w^n)$$

But

$$w = 1, \text{ by hypothesis}$$

and so

$$w^n = 1$$

Therefore equation (55a) becomes

(55b) $$V_n v^n = \frac{\pi_0}{i}, \text{ if } w = 1$$

and equation (22c) becomes

$$V_0 = n\pi_0 + \frac{\pi_0}{i}$$

(22d) $$= \pi_0 \left(n + \frac{1}{i} \right), \text{ if } w = 1$$

CHAPTER VIII

BONDS AND THE PRICE LEVEL

I. BONDS WITH GENERAL PRICES HOLDING STEADY

Whenever the general price level promises to remain steady, all good bonds can be treated like stocks paying a series of uniform dividends, with a big final dividend in liquidation at the end. In this case, the value of the bond can be found thus:

(1b)
$$V_o = \sum_{t=1}^{t=n} \pi_t v^t + Cv^n$$

where

π = worth of each coupon
C = principal of bond
n = number of interest periods to maturity

If we sum the geometric progression, and set

(28b) $\qquad \pi = pC$, by definition

we get

$$V_o = C\left[pv\left(\frac{1-v^n}{1-v} \right) + v^n \right]$$

(29a)
$$= C\left[\frac{p}{i}(1-v^n) + v^n \right], \text{ since } v = \frac{1}{1+i}$$

or

(29b)
$$= \pi\left(\frac{1-v^n}{i} \right) + Cv^n$$

Such a formula as this is what is used in constructing the ordinary bond table.[1] Generally the abbreviation

---

[1] Cf. C. N. Hulvey, *The Mathematics of Finance: Principles and Problems* (New York: Macmillan, 1934), p. 96, or H. L. Rietz, A. R. Crathorne, & J. C. Rietz, *Mathematics of Finance* (New York: H. Holt and Co., 1932), p. 96. Hulvey uses the symbol *r* instead of *p*, and Rietz *g* instead of *p*.

(30a) $$a_{\overline{n}|} = \frac{1 - v^n}{i}, \text{ by definition}$$

is used, making the formula read

(29c) $$V_o = C(pa_{\overline{n}|} + v^n)$$

or

(29d) $$V_o = \pi a_{\overline{n}|} + Cv^n$$

2.   BONDS WITH INFLATION OR DEFLATION IMPENDING

Whenever the general price level seems likely to fall or rise rather than hold steady, then bonds must be valued as though they were common stocks paying an annuity of increasing or decreasing dividends. If the real purchasing power of the coupons and of the principal, too, when repaid in the end, is expected to be greater or less than now, then the bond itself should be valued accordingly, as was so clearly brought out by Irving Fisher in his *Appreciation and Interest*, written years ago. During all the shifting of the general price level, however, the real rate of interest in commodities may be considered as invariant, although the money rate of interest will appear high when rising commodity prices or inflation are foreseen, and low when declining prices or deflation are foreseen.[2]

A convenient way to untangle the many factors involved is to reduce both coupons and principal to their real values by means of an index number for the general price level, and then find the present worth of the annuity resulting. To do this, it is necessary to start by forecasting the movement of general prices, using a chart like that shown in Diagram 8 for the case where inflation is expected. On this chart the zigzag line represents the actual movement of prices, while the heavy black line represents their trend. Fortunately for the simplicity of our formulas, a compound

[2] Cf. Chapter XIX, § 1, dealing with inflation and government bonds.

interest curve for the interval from $t = 0$ to $t = n$ usually gives a good fit for the period during which inflation is under way.

To derive the law of growth (or shrinkage) of the coupon

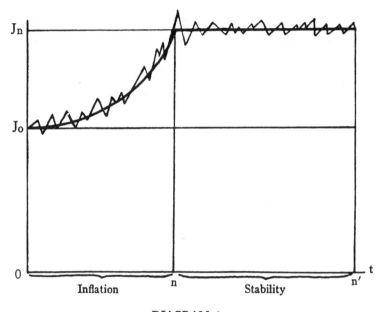

DIAGRAM 8

<small>MOVEMENT OF THE PRICE LEVEL DURING INFLATION</small>

annuity in terms of purchasing power, proceed as follows: Let

$$H_t = \text{general price level at any time } t,$$
$$h = \text{annual rate of inflation or deflation.}$$

Then, if inflation proceeds steadily year after year, we may write

(31a) $$h = \frac{H_1 - H_o}{H_o} = \frac{H_2 - H_1}{H_1}, \text{ etc.,}$$

$$(31b) \qquad H_1 = H_0(1 + h), \ H_2 = H_1(1 + h), \text{ etc.}$$

$$(31c) \qquad H_t = H_0(1 + h)^t$$

If $\dfrac{H_1}{H_0}$ is the ratio representing the change in the price level

in the first year, then its reciprocal, $\dfrac{H_0}{H_1}$, is the ratio repre-

senting the change in the purchasing power of money in

this same year. By the use of the latter ratio, $\dfrac{H_0}{H_t}$, there-

fore, we can show the purchasing power π_t of the original
coupon π_0 in the year t, as follows:

$$\pi_t = \frac{\pi_0 H_0}{H_t}, \text{ where } \pi_0 = \text{face value of coupon}$$

$$= \frac{\pi_0 H_0}{H_0(1 + h)^t}$$

$$(16c) \qquad\qquad = \frac{\pi_0}{(1 + h)^t}$$

In the foregoing equation, let

$$(14c) \qquad 1 + h = \frac{1}{1 + g}, \text{ by definition}$$

$$= \frac{1}{u}$$

where

$$(14a) \qquad\qquad u = 1 + g, \text{ by definition}$$

Then

$$(14d) \qquad\qquad u = \frac{1}{1 + h}$$

and as a result equation (16c) becomes

$$(16a) \qquad\qquad \pi_t = \pi_0 u^t$$

In this way we may translate changes in the value of money into terms of changes in the value of the coupons themselves and get a formula analogous to that for a stock with rising dividends, thus:

(32)
$$V_0 = \sum_{t=1}^{t=n} \pi_0(uv)^t + \sum_{t=n+1}^{t=n'} \pi_0 u^n v^t + C_0 u^n v^{n'}$$

in which

C_0 = principal of bond
n = number of years of inflation
n' = number of years to maturity of bond

In this formula the first term represents the present worth of the annuity of coupons to be paid during the period of inflation. The second term covers the period of stability after inflation and until the date of maturity; it shows the purchasing power of these coupons, reduced by the constant factor u^n, and discounted by the variable factor v^t. The last term shows the present worth of the principal itself, likewise reduced and discounted.

The formula can be simplified by remembering that

(28b) $\pi_0 = pC_0$, by definition

and

(15) $w = uv$, by definition

and

$$\sum_{t=n+1}^{t=n'} v^t = \sum_{t=1}^{t=n'} v^t - \sum_{t=1}^{t=n} v^t$$

By means of these equations, formula (32) above can be converted into

$$V_0 = pC_0 \left\{ \sum_{t=1}^{t=n} w^t + u^n \left[\sum_{t=1}^{t=n'} v^t - \sum_{t=1}^{t=n} v^t \right] + \frac{u^n v^{n'}}{p} \right\}$$

When the geometric progressions are summed, this gives

$$V_0 = pC_0 \left\{ w \left(\frac{1 - w^n}{1 - w} \right) + \frac{u^n v}{(1 - v)} \left[(1 - v^{n'}) - (1 - v^n) \right] + \frac{u^n v^{n'}}{p} \right\}$$

$$(33) \qquad = pC_0 \left\{ w \cdot \frac{1 - w^n}{1 - w} + \frac{u^n}{i} \left[v^n - v^{n'} (1 - \frac{i}{p}) \right] \right\}$$

This last formula represents the investment value of a bond when inflation or deflation impends.[3]

[3] The application of this formula is illustrated in Chapter XIX, § 2, dealing with long-term Treasury bonds.

CHAPTER IX

STOCKS AND THE PRICE LEVEL

I. SHOULD STOCKS RISÉ BEFORE INFLATION BEGINS?

Because inflation itself makes stocks go up, most people think that the mere prospect of inflation should do so too. Yet this is not true, as we shall now show. Let the prospect of inflation be ever so sure, still no rise in stocks is warranted except when the factor of leverage is involved. No common stock in a company free from debt is worth more today merely because the price level is going to go up tomorrow.

Reconsideration of the argument on bonds when inflation impends, given in the preceding chapter, will make this assertion seem more plausible. If bonds are worth less because inflation reduces the purchasing power of future coupons, then stocks also are worth less to the extent that inflation reduces the purchasing power of future dividends. But to the extent that inflation increases these very dividends, stocks are worth more. The two effects cancel. In the absence of leverage, the loss in purchasing power of future dividends will be just offset by the increase in the *paper* value of these same dividends, so that the *real* value of the future dividends will remain unaffected by inflation. The prospect of inflation, therefore, may be disregarded in estimating the investment value of a common stock without leverage.[1] After all, why should an investor pay more in sound money today simply because a stock is going to

---

[1] Contrast the views of Keynes (*General Theory*, pp. 141-142), who says, "The expectation of a fall in the value of money stimulates investment, and hence employment generally, because it raises the schedule of the marginal efficiency of capital, *i.e.* the investment demand-schedule; and the expectation of a rise in the value of money is depressing, because it lowers the schedule of the marginal efficiency of capital."

be quoted higher in depreciated money tomorrow? Furthermore, how can stocks be a hedge against inflation, protecting their owners during inflation, if they go up before inflation? They cannot discount the same event twice. No, they should respond but once to inflation, and that *during* inflation, step by step, dollar for dollar, with the rise in general prices.

In order for stocks to rise, and deserve to rise, before inflation begins, it is necessary that there should be some prospect of making a genuine profit by using sound money now for buying something that will be worth more in depreciated money later. But wherein does it profit a man to forego the good things of life this year, such as his vacation in Europe, let us say, in order to buy today shares which, if they double in price during inflation, will still be worth only one trip to Europe after inflation? If there is no profit in such postponed consumption, why should marginal opinion deem stocks to be worth more now and send them up in price?

By the same token, why should one buy speculative commodities out of additional savings merely because he expects inflation? What would a man gain by economizing and buying 10,000 pounds of copper at 14¢ today merely because he thinks he could sell it for 28¢ five years from now when each dollar received [2] from the sale of the copper would buy only half as much in goods and services as it will now?

Even those who do not need to economize in order to save, and who are so rich that they continually come into possession of cash that must be invested sooner or later

[2] A man who expects inflation should go *short* of cash by borrowing money; if the loan is secured by a pledge of commodities owned, the ownership of the commodities is only incidental to the speculative contract for the future delivery of money, and it is the successful speculation in money, not in commodities, that will yield the trader his profit.

because it cannot be used for living expenses — even these people do not need to go into the stock market and force up the prices of existing stocks, for by no means is the purchase of existing stocks the only outlet available for their savings when the threat of inflation makes them afraid to buy bonds. Nothing of the sort. If these fortunate people do not want to buy bonds, they can use their money to erect new buildings, for instance, or otherwise to improve real estate. Or they can buy *newly issued* shares of stock, since corporations will be seeking to finance with stocks if investors are distrustful of bonds. Indeed, the more that savers dislike bonds, the more will corporations be forced to offer rights, and the more will original stockholders be obliged to shift the growing burden to outsiders by selling their rights in the open market. Clearly there is nothing, therefore, in the logic of impending inflation that need compel people to use their savings for bidding up the price of existing shares to a point where inflation will be completely discounted in advance of the event. Yet those who think stocks should rise before inflation begins imply just such a foolish pattern of behavior on the part of investors.

Or, to put the argument another way, let us see if it is true that widespread fear of inflation, and widespread desire to move from bonds into stocks, should put stocks up. The attempt to switch from bonds into stocks should certainly put bonds down — of that there can be no doubt, but should it also put stocks up? In answer, it may be observed that no investor can buy stocks without cash, hence everyone must sell his bonds before he can buy his stocks. But if everyone fears inflation, who will be willing to buy the bonds offered for sale? (Let us assume for the moment that we are discussing an economic system in which the banks have already made loans to the extent of their capacity, and are unable, therefore, to add to their holdings of bonds.) And if no one will buy bonds, then will they not simply fall in price, and keep on falling until they have gone so low that they discount the impending inflation completely? At this low price, bondholders will be dissuaded from selling, and the result will be that no one will carry out his plans to switch from bonds into stocks; then no one will bid eagerly for stocks, and no one will drive up their prices. Hence the result of a widespread fear of inflation will be merely a fall in bond prices that will leave the unfortunate bondholders "locked in."

Or, to put the argument still another way, one may ask why, if inflation hurts bonds, should it help stocks? Bad news on the rails, for instance, would not send the industrials up, bad news on wheat would not send cotton up, and why should bad news on bonds send stocks up?

If the market behaved toward inflation in a completely rational way — which it does not do — it would respond to the first prospects of inflation by letting bonds drop violently at the start; later bonds and stocks would both rise together. Under these circumstances the speculator who was keen enough to see inflation coming before everyone else saw it coming would go first into *cash*, or better still, would go short of bonds, and then, after the initial drop in bonds, he would go long of either stocks or bonds.

By the time everyone sees inflation coming, no one will any longer be able to benefit himself by moving out of bonds into stocks; for bonds will be quoted at prices so low that nothing will remain to be gained by exchanging the one for the other. The only investors who will be able to help themselves by moves at this late date will be the holders of uninvested cash; for them the purchase of either stocks or bonds will serve equally well as a way of protecting their wealth from inflation.

What stocks should do in anticipation of inflation, and

what they will do, are, of course, two different questions. Here we are concerned only with the former, the question of investment value, and make no attempt to answer the latter, concerning market price. Were we practical speculators, however, instead of scientists, we should bother with nothing but forecasting the follies of a hapless public at its wit's end to preserve its savings.

Only for equities without leverage, however, does the rule that stocks should not rise in anticipation of inflation hold true. If senior issues are outstanding, then stocks should respond twice, or rather in two steps, to inflation; first on the promise, and second during the fulfillment, of inflation. The first response should be abrupt, and should reflect the gain by stockholders of the prospective loss by bondholders, while the second should be gradual, and should reflect the change in the purchasing power of money from month to month.

The amount of the first response for stocks is determined by the amount of this same response for bonds. In the preceding chapter we have shown how much a bond should fall in response to any particular degree of expected inflation. To show how much the stock of the same company should advance in response to the same expectation, we must remember that the threatened inflation or deflation should have no effect on the present investment value of the enterprise as a whole, and that if a single family, for instance, owned all the senior and junior securities, it would neither gain nor lose by the mere prospect of inflation, no matter how certain. Whatever loss was shown on the bonds should be offset by an equal gain on the stock. Thus if

V_b = investment value of bonds and preferred stock before inflation threatens

$\hat{V}_b$ = investment value of bonds and preferred stock after inflation threatens

V_o = investment value of common stock before inflation
    threatens

$\hat{V}_o$ = investment value of common stock after inflation
    threatens

then

(18b) $V_b + V_o = $ a constant $= \hat{V}_b + \hat{V}_o$

The new investment value, $\hat{V}_b$, of the senior securities is found as described in § 2 of the preceding chapter entitled "Bonds with Inflation or Deflation Impending." [3] In computing the new investment value for the bonds, some decrease in the interest rate used would be justified by the prospective change in the price level, because the real burden of the debt would be reduced and the security of the debt increased by inflation. In other words, the premium for risk would fall.

Once the new investment value, $\hat{V}_b$, for the bonds has been computed, the new investment value, $\hat{V}_o$, for the common stock may then be found by transposing equation (18b) above, so as to make it read

(18c) $\hat{V}_o = (V_b + V_c) - \hat{V}_b$

When inflation first threatens, a company's bonds should drop and its stock should rise at once, but only by the amount specified above. Such is the first response to inflation. Then, after inflation really begins, the bonds and stock should both start to rise in investment value expressed in depreciated money, and should both continue to advance until the inflation is over, at which time the bonds should be back to par, as explained in the preceding chapter, and the stock should be up to the new level warranted by its increased dividend in depreciated money. Such is the second response to inflation. Thus if

$(1 + h) = $ change in price level, i.e., ratio of new to
    old price index

[3] The symbol $\hat{V}$ may be read as "V-cap."

and if

V_b = investment value of senior issues per share before inflation threatens

V'_b = investment value of senior issues per share after inflation has occurred

V_c = investment value of common stock per share before inflation threatens

V'_c = investment value of common stock per share after inflation has occurred

then

(18d) $$(1 + h) (V_b + V_c) = (V'_b + V'_c)$$

According to this equation, the investment value in sound money of the enterprise as a whole before inflation, multiplied by the change in the price level, equals the investment value of the whole in depreciated money after inflation.[4]

All of the foregoing statements about inflation assume a uniform, thoroughgoing inflation, in which all selling prices, wages, taxes, rentals, and raw material costs rise by exactly the same percentage at exactly the same time. In practice, of course, this never happens. Yet for many industrial enterprises it may happen approximately; for an automobile company, as an example, it might happen.[5] For railroads and public utilities it probably would not happen; the New York traction companies are a notorious example of the failure of selling prices to move up with costs during the wartime inflation.

It would not be hard to imagine a case in which moderate

[4] Application of the foregoing principles may be found in the case study on U. S. Steel, Chapter XXII.

[5] As a hedge against inflation, the motors would not seem to be the best choice, however, for if people had to economize during inflation because of the high cost of living, they might postpone their replacement of automobiles. But on gasoline and cigarettes, for instance, people would economize scarcely at all; hence the oil and the tobacco stocks would make good inflation hedges, provided no fixing of retail prices occurred, no taxes on inventory profits were levied, and (for the oils) no big new oil fields were opened up.

inflation produced, not a bull market in stocks, but a bear market, at least during the period when wages and the cost of living were rising fastest and before stabilization and readjustment at the new and higher level had been attained. For instance, if general inflation should be provoked by unwarranted increases in money wages,[6] with the increased labor costs being passed on to consumers and added to the cost of living, a bear market might result at first. The railroads and public utilities would be strangled by higher costs and would have to reduce their outlays for maintenance and improvements; the steel mills and electrical-equipment factories would shut down, and railroad, utility, steel, and electrical stocks and bonds would certainly be in a bear market. Even government bonds would depreciate, because as explained in Chapter XIX, investors, fearing a further rise in the cost of living, would demand compensation in terms of better yields. The rise in *nominal*[7] long-term interest rates might tend to stifle borrowing for plant expansion, and this would produce still further stagnation in the capital-goods industries. Fear for the safety of the dollar, moreover, would cause a withdrawal of foreign capital and a flight of domestic capital, and gold exports would tend to tighten short-term interest rates. Even some commodities might fall in price despite the inflation; pig iron, lumber, and many other raw materials might suffer more from the shrinkage of demand in the capital-goods industries than they would benefit from the greater purchasing power of those consumers who still held their jobs. Thus it might be possible for an unwarranted and continuous increase in money wages to produce the anomalous combination of inflation in general prices and a bear market in most of the securities listed on the Stock Ex-

[6] Cf. Chapter XIX, § 16, entitled "The Thirty-Hour Week."
[7] As contrasted with *real* long-term interest rates.

change.[8] When the inflation was over, of course, and when all other prices had finally adjusted themselves to the increased wage-rates, a bull market in stocks would be able to proceed unhindered, as it did in 1922–1929 after the wartime inflation, and then at last the common stockholder would gain the protection from his ownership of equities which he had expected in the beginning. But until then it might turn out that mere sterile cash would prove a better investment for the time being than a diversified list of common stocks.

In conclusion, then, it may be said first that stocks ought not to rise *before* inflation, because the mere prospect of inflation does not increase their investment value; second, that stocks often do not rise *during* inflation, because the actuality of inflation often hurts corporate earnings temporarily; and third, that stocks will almost surely[9] rise *after* inflation, because the capital goods they represent are then possessed of greater earning power in terms of depreciated money.

2.   THE CHANGE IN PRICE WARRANTED DURING INFLATION

The effect of inflation or deflation on the investment value of a common stock is magnified by the presence of any bonds standing ahead of the shares. If the enterprise as a whole has a horizontal trend of earnings, a given change in the price level will affect the stock in the degree deduced below:

$$V_c = \text{investment value of common}$$
$$i_c = \text{fair interest rate for common stock}$$
$$i_b = \text{fair interest rate for senior securities}$$

[8] A violent inflation like the one in Germany in 1923 would not, of course, produce any such results. But in the German inflation, wages, instead of leading other prices, lagged behind. Perhaps the rule is that inflation causes depression if wages lead, prosperity if they lag, in the general advance of prices.

[9] With the exception of the rails and utilities, whose rates may never be increased enough fully to offset inflation.

i_a = fair interest rate for entire enterprise

β = bond interest plus preferred dividends, per share of common

π = pure dividend, per share of common

$(1 + h)$ = ratio of level of commodity prices at end to level at start

Then

$\beta + \pi$ = total disbursements, per share of common

Values at the start will be represented as above, thus, V_c

Values at the end will be represented with a prime sign, thus, V'_c

The effect of inflation will be to increase total disbursements to the same degree as the value of money changes, thus:

(34a) $$(1 + h)(\beta + \pi) = (\beta' + \pi')$$

or

(34b) $$\pi' = (1 + h)(\beta + \pi) - \beta'$$

For a stock whose dividends have a horizontal trend [10] and tend to be the same year after year except for the business cycle, the investment value is given by the following formula:

(8a) $$V_o = \frac{\pi}{i_o}$$

Likewise for the senior securities

(8c) $$V_b = \frac{\beta}{i_b} \quad \text{(assuming the bonds to be perpetual)}$$

and for the enterprise as a whole

(18a, 8d) $$V_a = V_b + V_c = \frac{\beta + \pi}{i_a}$$

We wish to see how the value V_c of a stock is affected by changes in the various known quantities, and so we proceed as follows to find the ratio $\dfrac{V'_c}{V_c}$

[10] Cf. Chapter XXII, § 2.

Transposing in (8d), we get

(8f) $$V_o = \frac{\beta + \pi}{i_a} - V_b$$

Substituting (8c) in (8f), we get

(8g) $$V_o = \frac{\beta + \pi}{i_a} - \frac{\beta}{i_b}$$

Likewise:

(8h) $$V'_c = \frac{\beta' + \pi'}{i'_a} - \frac{\beta'}{i'_b}$$

Substituting (34a) into the first term on the right-hand side of (8h), we get

(8i) $$V'_c = \frac{(1 + h)(\beta + \pi)}{i''_a} - \frac{\beta'}{i'_b}$$

Dividing (8i) by (8g), we get

(8j) $$\frac{V'_c}{V_c} = \frac{\dfrac{(1 + h)(\beta + \pi)}{i'_a} - \dfrac{\beta'}{i_b}}{\dfrac{(\beta + \pi)}{i_a} - \dfrac{\beta}{i_b}}$$

Q. E. F.

The foregoing equation [11] shows how the price of a common stock is affected by changes in (1) the purchasing power of money, (2) the interest rate for the entire enterprise, and (3) the interest rate for the senior securities.

The factors listed above, rather than the growth of the country and the profitable reinvestment of earnings, largely account for the persistent rise of stocks found by Edgar Lawrence Smith and Dwight C. Rose [12] in their studies cov-

[11] The application of this formula is illustrated in Chapter XXII, § 22, where the rise in price of U. S. Steel from 1901 to 1929 is discussed.

[12] Dwight C. Rose, *A Scientific Approach to Investment Management* (New York and London: Harper and Brothers, 1928).

ering various periods from 1860 to 1929, as anyone who will apply the foregoing equation can see for himself. This fact greatly weakens their whole claim that the growth of the country tends to make stocks in general go up year after year indefinitely, save for temporary reactions. Unfortunately, during the great bull market of the 1920's the real explanation of the past advances in stocks was never pointed out to the many readers of Smith's *Common Stocks as Long Term Investments*, and this book, therefore, achieved such an influence as to entitle it to be listed among the causes of the speculative mania of 1929.

CHAPTER X

BONDS WITH INTEREST RATES CHANGING

I. LONG— AND SHORT—TERM INTEREST RATES

Whenever the interest rate is expected to change [1] during the life of a bond, the simple method of evaluation given in an earlier chapter [2] will need to be amplified as follows:

Let

i_1 = short-term interest rate during first year

i_2 = short term interest rate during second year, etc.

(2)
$$v_1 = \frac{1}{1 + i_1} = \text{discount factor for first year}$$

(2)
$$v_2 = \frac{1}{1 + i_2} = \text{discount factor for second year, etc.}$$

Then the present worth of a coupon π due in one year will be πv_1, in two years $\pi v_1 v_2$, in three years $\pi v_1 v_2 v_3$, etc.; and the present worth of the principal C will be $C v_1 v_2 \ldots v_n$, where n is the number of years to maturity. Therefore we may define the investment value V of such a bond as follows:

(1g)
$$V = \pi v_1 + \pi v_1 v_2 + \pi v_1 v_2 v_3 + \cdots + \pi v_1 v_2 \cdots v_n \\ + C v_1 v_2 \cdots v_n$$

The long-term interest rate may now be defined as an average interest rate $\bar{i}$ based on an average discount factor $\bar{v}$, the value of the latter being such that it may be substituted for v_1, v_2, v_3, etc. in equation (1g) in a way that will satisfy the following condition:

[1] Cf. Chapter V, § 4.
[2] Chapter VIII, § 1.

(1b) $V_o = \pi \bar{v} + \pi \bar{v}^2 + \pi \bar{v}^3 + \cdots + \pi \bar{v}^n + C\bar{v}^n$

(1g) $= \pi v_1 + \pi v_1 v_2 + \pi v_1 v_2 v_3 + \cdots + \pi v_1 v_2 \cdots v_n$
                    $+ C v_1 v_2 \cdots v_n$

If there were no coupons π but only the principal C to be considered, then the average discount factor $\bar{v}$ would be the *geometric* mean of the successive discount factors v_1, v_2, v_3, etc., as is shown by the following equations:

$$V_o = C\bar{v}^n = C v_1 v_2 \cdots v_n, \text{ if } \pi = 0$$

whence

(37a) $\bar{v}^n = v_1 v_2 \cdots v_n$

and

(37b) $\bar{v} = \sqrt[n]{v_1 v_2 \cdots v_n}, \text{ if } \pi = 0$

This last equation is the ordinary formula for the geometric mean. But since there are usually coupons as well as principal to be considered, the long-term discount factor is not usually a simple geometric average of the successive short-term discount factors.

The "yield to maturity" of a bond, it may be mentioned in passing, is the long-term interest rate $\bar{i}$ that results from equating the actual market price M to the sum of the present worths of the coupons and principal, in the manner of equation (1g), thus:

(1b) $M = \pi \bar{v} + \pi \bar{v}^2 + \cdots + \pi \bar{v}^n + C\bar{v}^n$

where

(2) $\bar{v} = \dfrac{1}{1 + \bar{i}}, \text{ or } \bar{i} = \dfrac{1}{\bar{v}} - 1$

2.   COMPETITION BETWEEN LONG– AND SHORT–TERM LOANS

It is not possible, as claimed by some writers, for long- and short-term rates to be brought into approximate equality by the operations of intermediaries who borrow short and lend long, or vice versa. A little consideration will show why this is so. Suppose, for instance, that short-term rates are low [3] and a profit might seem to be obtainable by borrowing short and lending long. If an intermediary tried to do this, he would find later, when he had to renew his short borrowings, that short-term rates were rising; and finally he would find that short-term rates had become even higher than his original long-term rate, with the result that when he had finished it would turn out that no profit at all had emerged from his operations. Likewise, if he tried to borrow long when short-term rates were high, he would find, if everything worked out as was expected by the market when the disparity between short- and long-term rates arose in the first place, that short-term rates would soon fall, and that eventually the time would come when he could not place his long-term money in short-term loans at rates as high as he had committed himself to pay on his original borrowings; thus in this case also no profit, and no loss either, could rightly be expected.

The same reasoning applies to borrowers; a businessman cannot expect to take advantage of temporarily favorable short-term rates to build a plant that ought to be financed with long-term money, because if he does try to do this he may reasonably expect to find the short-term rate moving against him so severely in the end that nothing will be gained by his unorthodox procedure. Likewise it is of no use for the businessman to finance a short-term investment, like a seasonal or cyclical increase in inventory

[3] The particular reasons why short-term rates were lower than long-term rates in 1937 are given in Chapter XIX, § 10. There is no reason to think that short-term notes are normally lower than long-term notes. In 1929, for instance, the relation between long- and short-term rates was reversed, for at that time Treasury Notes and Certificates gave a higher yield than Treasury Bonds. Cf., however, "A Note on the Government Bond Market, 1919–1930," by Charles C. Abbott, in the *Review of Economic Statistics*, January 1935, where a somewhat different view is expressed.

and receivables, by long-term loans when long-term money is cheaper than short-term, because later he will probably find that short-term rates have fallen below his long-term rate.

All of the foregoing discussion assumes for the sake of argument that long- and short-term rates are in proper conformity with each other,[4] and that the market exhibits no inconsistencies and implies no improbabilities. So long as the borrower and lender, or the saver and investor, do not know of an inconsistency in prices or of any inaccuracy in expectations, they have no choice but to accept the verdict of the market and assume that it is a matter of indifference whether one borrows on short or long term.[5] Should anyone, however, whether he is a regular borrower or lender, or an outside speculator, believe he has superior information, then of course he may seek to profit by his advantage, and may choose one or the other sort of borrowing or lending in the hope of gaining something thereby.[6]

3.   THE YIELD TO PERPETUITY

Just as one may speak of the "yield to maturity" of a bond, one might speak of the "yield to perpetuity" of a stock, especially a preferred stock, because a stock is like a perpetual bond in having no maturity date. It would be convenient to coin such a phrase and give it an exact definition, for any calculation of the yield to maturity of a bond

---

[4] The greater cost of servicing short-term loans, however, would make short-term rates average slightly higher than long-term rates.

[5] For a further discussion of the pros and cons of long- or short-term borrowing, see Chapter XX, § 3.

[6] In expectation, apparently, of a greater rise in short-term rates than the market itself expects, the General Motors Acceptance Corporation has thought it shrewd business to fund its floating debt by selling $100,000,000 of long-term debentures bearing 3 and 3¼ per cent coupons, even though the money was currently being borrowed on short term at a much lower rate of interest than this. For the terms of the new issue, see the *New York Times*, August 20, 1936, p. 27, col. 8, and advertisement, p. 29.

when interest rates are changing during its life at once raises the question of what yield to perpetuity for a preferred stock would be implied by the same series of interest rates. For example, if a five-year bond yields 1 per cent to maturity, a ten-year bond 2 per cent, and a fifteen-year bond $2\frac{1}{2}$ per cent, and if it be assumed that the interest rate implied for the last five years is to continue in force thenceforth to perpetuity, what should a perpetual bond yield to be consistent with the given yields on the five-, ten-, and fifteen-year bonds? In other words, what yield $\bar{v}$ to perpetuity would correspond with the given yields v_1, v_2, etc., before maturity?

For the general case the formulas would be as follows:

(1h) $\pi(\bar{v} + \bar{v}^2 + \cdots + \bar{v}^{n'}) = \pi\,[v_1 + v_1 v_2 + \cdots$
$$+ v_1 v_2 \cdots v_n\,(1 + v_n + v_n^2 + \cdots + v_n^{n'-n})]$$

Summing the series, we get

$$\frac{\bar{v}}{1 - \bar{v}}\,(1 - \bar{v}^{n'}) = v_1 + v_1 v_2 + \cdots$$
$$+ v_1 v_2 \cdots v_n\left[1 + \left(\frac{v_n}{1 - v_n}\right)(1 - v_n^{n'-n})\right]$$

If we now let n' increase without limit, the terms $\bar{v}^{n'}$ and $v_n^{n'-n}$ vanish, and we get

$$\frac{\bar{v}}{1 - \bar{v}} = v_1 + v_1 v_2 + \cdots + v_1 v_2 \cdots v_n\left(1 + \frac{v_n}{1 - v_n}\right)$$

By equation (2), this gives

(1i) $$\frac{1}{\bar{i}} = v_1 + v_1 v_2 + \cdots + v_1 v_2 \cdots v_n\left(1 + \frac{1}{i_n}\right)$$

If the various temporary interest rates that apply to the early years of a perpetual bond in the foregoing formula persist for several years at a time, the formula may be abbreviated by using the symbol for the present worth of an annuity, thus:

(30b) $$a_{\overline{n}|} = v + v^2 + \cdots + v^n$$

For example, if one interest rate prevails for the first five years, another for the second, and a third for the third, and if this third rate is then assumed to continue to perpetuity, the formula for the yield to perpetuity $\bar{\imath}$ will appear as follows:

(1j) $$\frac{1}{\bar{\imath}} = a_{\overline{5}|i_1} + v_1{}^5 a_{\overline{5}|i_2} + \frac{v_1{}^5 v_2{}^5}{i_3}$$

4.   CALCULATION OF IMPLIED FUTURE INTEREST RATES

By the inverse use of formula (1g), it is possible to see what the bond market expects the short-term interest rate to be in various future years, for these expected future rates are necessarily implicit in the prices of any series of bonds of like security and unlike maturity. Thus if the price of a bond due in one year is related to its yield by the formula

(1b) $$M_1 = \pi v_1 + C v_1$$

and of another bond due in two years by the formula

(1g) $$M_2 = \pi v_1 + \pi v_1 v_2 + C v_1 v_2$$

then, if the prices M_1 and M_2 are known, the short-term discount factors v_1 and v_2 can be inferred. To find the first discount factor, transform the first equation into the form

(1kb) $$v_1 = \frac{M_1}{\pi + C}$$

and solve for v_1. Then insert this value of v_1 into the second equation, and transpose it into the form

(1kg) $$v_2 = \frac{M_2 - \pi v_1}{(\pi + C) v_1}$$

The discount factors v_1 and v_2 obtained in this way yield the short-term interest rates i_1 and i_2 implied for the first and second years.

In a similar way, the short-term interest rate i_n implied for any other year n may be obtained by transposing an appropriate equation involving v_n, as follows:

$$(1g) \qquad \begin{aligned} M_n &= \pi v_1 + \pi v_1 v_2 + \cdots + \pi v_1 v_2 \cdots v_n \\ &\quad + C v_1 v_2 \cdots v_n \\ &= \pi (v_1 + v_1 v_2 + \cdots + v_1 v_2 \cdots v_{n-1}) \\ &\quad + v_1 v_2 \cdots v_{n-1}(\pi + C) v_n \end{aligned}$$

whence

$$v_1 v_2 \cdots v_{n-1}(\pi + C) v_n = M_n - \pi(v_1 + v_1 v_2 + \cdots + v_1 v_2 \cdots v_{n-1})$$

and

$$(1l) \qquad v_n = \frac{M_n - \pi(v_1 + v_1 v_2 + \cdots + v_1 v_2 \cdots v_{n-1})}{(\pi + C) v_1 v_2 \cdots v_{n-1}}$$

If the two bonds used for comparison have maturities more than a year apart, the separate interest rates for the earlier and later years of the entire period covered can be found by an obvious modification of the preceding formula.

Likewise, if the coupons are payable semi-annually, as is usually the case, instead of annually, the various interest rates can be found in the same way, with n standing for the number of *half*-years, π for *half* the stated coupon rate, v for the *semi*-annual discount factor, and i for *half* the nominal yield. The formula for a one-year bond would then be

$$(1b) \qquad M_1 = \pi_1 v_1 + \pi_1 v_1{}^2 + C v_1{}^2$$

To find the value of v_1 and thus of i_1, the simplest procedure is to look up the price M_1 and the coupon rate $2\pi_1$ in an ordinary book of bond tables, which will give the nominal yield [7]

$$(35) \qquad j_{(2)} = 2i$$

[7] Ordinarily the symbol i is used to mean the annual rather than the semi-annual rate. The ordinary bond table is so constructed that it gives the annual

for a one-year bond of this description. The value for the
semi-annual discount factor

$$(2) \qquad\qquad v_1 = \frac{1}{1 + i_1}$$

so obtained may now be inserted in the formula for the
longer bond, whose formula, if it is a two-year bond, would
be as follows:

$$(1g) \qquad\qquad M_2 = \pi_2 v_1 + \pi_2 v_1{}^2 + \pi_2 v_1{}^2 v_2 \\ + \pi_2 v_1{}^2 v_2{}^2 + C v_1{}^2 v_2{}^2$$

Transposing, we get

$$v_1{}^2 (\pi_2 v_2 + \pi_2 v_2{}^2 + C v_2{}^2) = M_2 - (\pi_2 v_1 + \pi_2 v_1{}^2)$$

$$(1b, 1m) \quad V_2 = \pi_2 v_2 + \pi_2 v_2{}^2 + C v_2{}^2 = \frac{M_2 - (\pi_2 v_1 + \pi_2 v_1{}^2)}{v_1{}^2}$$

The center member of the last pair of equations is the ordinary formula for the value V_2 of a bond bearing a semi-
annual coupon π_2, yielding a semi-annual return i_2, and
maturing in two interest periods. The fair price for such
a bond is given by the right-hand member of the equations,
which represents what the price of the longer bond, now
worth M_2, should be a year from now. Since every variable
on the right-hand side is known, V_2 is likewise known. To
find the value of i_2, refer to the bond tables as before, looking up a bond whose price is V_2, whose annual coupon is
$2\pi_2$, and whose maturity is one year. The annual yield
shown by the tables will be the nominal yield $j_{(2)} = 2i$.

A more general form of equation (1m) is derived as fol-

---

yield as exactly *twice* the semi-annual yield; in other words, the yield shown in
the tables is the nominal rate

$$(35) \qquad\qquad j_{(2)} = 2i, \text{ if } i \text{ is the } \textit{semi-annual} \text{ yield}$$

rather than the effective rate

$$(1 + \tfrac{1}{2} j_{(2)})^2 - 1$$

Cf. Rietz, Crathorne, and Rietz, *Mathematics of Finance*, pp. 23 and 110.

lows for a pair of bonds having respectively n and n' interest periods to run:

(1b) $M_1 = \pi_1(v_1 + v_1{}^2 + \cdots + v_1{}^n) + Cv_1{}^n$

(1g) $M_2 = \pi_2(v_1 + v_1{}^2 + \cdots + v_1{}^n)$
$$+ v_1{}^n [\pi_2(v_2 + v_2{}^2 + \cdots + v_2{}^{n'-n}) + Cv_2{}^{n'-n}]$$

By analogy with equation (1m) we may write

(1b, 1n) $V_n = \pi_2(v_2 + v_2{}^2 + \cdots + v_2{}^{n'-n}) + Cv_2{}^{n'-n}$

$$= \frac{M_2 - \pi_2(v_1 + v_1{}^2 + \cdots + v_1{}^n)}{v_1{}^n}$$

If

(30b) $$a_{\overline{n}|} = v + v^2 + \cdots + v^n$$

then

(29d, 1p) $$V_n = \pi_2 a_{\overline{n'-n}|i_2} + Cv_2{}^{n'-n} = \frac{M_2 - \pi a_{\overline{n}|i_1}}{v_1{}^n}$$

Here [8]

(29e) $$j_{(2)} = 2i = f [V_n, \tfrac{1}{2}(n'-n), 2\pi_2]$$

If the foregoing method [9] of isolating the individual short-term interest rates apparently expected for future years is applied to serial bonds, a whole series of such implicit rates, covering a long period of years in the future, can be inferred. It is not maintained, of course, that the future rates so calculated will necessarily come to pass; it is merely asserted that such rates are implicitly forecast by the bond prices in question, and that such a forecast by the market is an interesting fact in itself, worthy of criti-

---

[8] *Note for the non-technical reader:* The notation $j_{(2)} = f [V_n, \tfrac{1}{2}(n'-n), 2\pi_2]$ in equation (29e) is read "$j_{(2)}$ is a function of V_n, etc.," and in this notation the brackets do not signify multiplication, as they would in simple algebra. This notation affords a brief way of saying that $j_{(2)}$ depends upon the quantities within the brackets according to some implied rule that need not be stated precisely for the time being.

[9] The application of these formulas is illustrated in Chapter XX, § 8, dealing with Treasury bonds of various maturities.

cism as to its plausibility like any other forecast made by the securities market.

For those readers who question whether the market as a whole displays enough rationality to *forecast* the short-term interest rate, the argument stated above may be reworded as follows: The foregoing method of comparing bond prices shows what future short-term interest rates would be *consistent with* present prices for bonds.

But whether or not the market actually makes a forecast of interest rates, the investor himself cannot escape doing so, if he is to appraise security values intelligently. And once he has done so, he is faced with the necessity of finding out how his own forecast compares with the implications of the market. To facilitate such a comparison, the foregoing method is offered.

5.   APPROXIMATE METHODS OF CALCULATION

The foregoing method of inferring expected future interest rates is the only method that gives exact results. Two other methods that give approximate results, however, can be deduced from it, as will be shown. Both of these approximate methods make use of the *yield to maturity*, a figure conveniently obtainable for any given issue by reference to a bond table.

The first method is based on the following reasoning:

Let

n = number of interest periods to maturity of shorter bond
n' = number of interest periods to maturity of longer bond
i_1 = yield to maturity of shorter bond
i_2 = short-term interest rate for intervening period
i = yield to maturity of longer bond
M_2 = market price of longer bond

Then, using the two separate discount factors, v_1 and v_2, we may write

(1g) $M_2 = \pi \left[(v_1 + v_1{}^2 + \cdots + v_1{}^n) + v_1{}^n (v_2 + v_2{}^2 + \cdots + v_2{}^{n'-n}) \right] + C v_1{}^n v_2{}^{n'-n}$

(29g) $= \pi \left[\left(\dfrac{1 - v_1{}^n}{i_1} \right) + v_1{}^n \left(\dfrac{1 - v_2{}^{n'-n}}{i_2} \right) \right] + C v_1{}^n v_2{}^{n'-n}$

Likewise, using the single interest rate i that covers the entire n' years, we may write

(1b) $M_2 = \pi (v + v^2 + \cdots + v^{n'}) + C v^{n'}$

(29b) $= \pi \left(\dfrac{1 - v^{n'}}{i} \right) + C v^{n'}$

Equating the two values for M_2, given by (29g) and (29b) above, we have

$$\pi \left[\left(\frac{1 - v_1{}^n}{i_1} \right) + v_1{}^n \left(\frac{1 - v_2{}^{n'-n}}{i_2} \right) \right] + C v_1{}^n v_2{}^{n'-n}$$

$$= \pi \left(\frac{1 - v^{n'}}{i} \right) + C v^{n'}$$

whence

$$C v_1{}^n v_2{}^{n'-n} - C v^{n'} = \pi \left[\left(\frac{1 - v^{n'}}{i} \right) - \left(\frac{1 - v_1{}^n}{i_1} \right) \right.$$

$$\left. - v_1{}^n \left(\frac{1 - v_2{}^{n'-n}}{i_2} \right) \right]$$

(36) $$v_1{}^n v_2{}^{n'-n} - v^{n'} = \frac{\pi}{C} \left[\left(\frac{1 - v^{n'}}{i} \right) - \left(\frac{1 - v_1{}^n}{i_1} \right) \right.$$

$$\left. - v_1{}^n \left(\frac{1 - v_2{}^{n'-n}}{i_2} \right) \right]$$

Let us call the right-hand member of the foregoing equation the error of approximation, ϵ. Since its value is small, as can be seen by inspection, we may say that it is approximately zero, and write the following approximate equations:

$$v_1{}^n v_2{}^{n'-n} - v^{n'} = \epsilon \doteq 0$$

(37c)
$$v_1{}^n v_2{}^{n'-n} \doteq v^{n'}$$

$$\frac{1}{v_2{}^{n'-n}} \doteq \frac{v_1{}^n}{v^{n'}}$$

(37d)
$$(1 + i_2)^{n'-n} \doteq \frac{(1 + i)^{n'}}{(1 + i_1)^n}$$

(37e) [10]
$$1 + i_2 \doteq \sqrt[n'-n]{\frac{(1 + i)^{n'}}{(1 + i_1)^n}}$$

It will be noticed that the formula given above

(37c)
$$v_1{}^n v_2{}^{n'-n} \doteq v^{n'}$$

is the same as would be obtained from using bonds without any coupons at all, for which we would write the two formulas

(1g)
$$M_2 = C v_1{}^n v_2{}^{n'-n} \quad , \text{ if } \pi = 0$$

and

(1b)
$$M_2 = C v^{n'} \quad , \text{ if } \pi = 0$$

whence

$$C v_1{}^n v_2{}^{n'-n} = C v^{n'}$$

and

(37c)
$$v_1{}^n v_2{}^{n'-n} = v^{n'}$$

which is the same result we have already obtained above. Evidently if the number of coupons is few and their value is small the approximate formula derived above will be very nearly exact.

This first approximate formula lends itself to still further approximation, as follows:

(37d)
$$(1 + i_2)^{n'-n} = \frac{(1 + i)^{n'}}{(1 + i_1)^n}$$

whence

$$(1 + i_1)^n (1 + i_2)^{n'-n} = (1 + i)^{n'}$$

[10] The application of this formula is illustrated in Chapter XX, § 7, Table 7, dealing with Treasury bonds of various maturities.

By use of the binomial theorem, the foregoing expressions may be expanded thus:

$$1 + ni_1 + \cdots + (n' - n)i_2 + \cdots = 1 + n'i + \cdots$$

$$(37f) \qquad\qquad (n' - n)i_2 = n'i - ni_1 + \cdots$$

This formula [11] gives us our second approximation. By neglecting all the higher terms, it is tantamount to finding the answer in terms of simple interest instead of compound interest, with coupons neglected as before.

[11] The application of this formula is illustrated in Chapter XX, § 7, Tables 4, 5, and 6, dealing with Treasury bonds of various maturities.

CHAPTER XI

ALGEBRAIC BUDGETING

[NOTE: The next four chapters (XI to XIV) prepare the way for the case studies on Phoenix Insurance, American Telephone, Consolidated Gas, and American and Foreign Power, and can be passed over for the time being by readers who wish to give their attention at once to the chapters on the Economics of Interest and Dividends and the Outlook for Interest Rates and the Price Level.]

The formulas for the investment value of common stocks given in earlier chapters would be of little use unless some way could be found to estimate the size of the dividends whose present worth it was there proposed to take. How to estimate these future dividends is the heart of the problem, and in helping to solve this problem, the present book hopes to make a significant contribution to the art of Investment Analysis.[1]

The solution to be proposed is straightforward; it consists in making a budget showing the company's growth in assets, debt, earnings, and dividends during the years to come. This budget is not drawn up with debit and credit, however, using a journal and ledger as an accountant would do, but is put into algebraic form in a way that is altogether new to the accountant's art. Then, by the manipulation of algebraic symbols, the warp of development is traced through the woof of time with an ease unknown to ordinary accounting. Such a procedure we shall call "algebraic budgeting." It can best be explained by illustration with particular cases.

---

[1] These formulas were first derived in May 1930.

1. THE PROPERTIES OF A UTILITY COMPANY WITH CONSTANT LEVERAGE

Let us consider first the case of a utility company whose earnings, because it is a monopoly, are fixed by law at a specified rate [2] on its investment. Let us assume that the company has already adopted the capital structure most favorable to its stockholders, and that it therefore maintains a constant ratio of bonds to stocks as it continues to grow. This policy would make it a "utility with constant leverage." Let us further assume that the interest rate on its borrowed capital is kept the same throughout the period of growth, additional loans being negotiated at the same rate as that on the bonds already outstanding. Likewise let us assume that its growth in assets continues at compound interest at a uniform rate year after year until the point of inflection in its growth is reached.

The foregoing assumptions can be set down mathematically in the form of seven constant characteristics of such a company, as follows:

(i)   *The return on invested assets stays the same, so that*

$$a_t = \text{a constant}$$

where

(38) $$a_t = \frac{\alpha_t}{A_t}, \text{ by definition}$$

and

a_t = rate of return on invested assets in year t

α_t = profits after taxes ⎫

A_t = net investment, after deducting reserves for depreciation, etc., and current liabilities ⎬ per share of common stock at end of year t.

(39a) $$= B_t + C_t, \text{ by definition}$$ ⎭

[2] In the 1920's a return of 8 per cent was considered fair, but by 1937 this rate had fallen as low as 5 per cent in some states, particularly Pennsylvania. See also Chapter XXV, § 5.

(ii)   *The ratio of stocks to bonds in its capitalization stays the same, so that the leverage*

$$l_t = \text{a constant}$$

where

(40a) $l_t = \dfrac{A_t}{C_t}$, by definition

and

l_t = leverage at end of year t

C_t = common stock's book value per share at end of year t.

(iii)   *The rate of interest paid on bonded debt and other senior securities stays the same, so that*

$$b_t = \text{a constant}$$

where

(41a) $b_t = \dfrac{\beta_t}{B_t}$, by definition

and

b_t = rate of interest on bonds and preferred

β_t = bond interest and preferred dividends, per share of common, paid in year t

B_t = senior securities per share of common at end of year t.

(iv)   *The rate of growth of invested assets stays the same, so that*

$$u = \text{a constant}$$

where

(42a) $u = \dfrac{A_1}{A_0}$, by definition

and

$$A_2 = A_1 u = A_0 u^2, \text{ etc.}$$

(43) $A_t = A_0 u^t$

where

(14a) $u = 1 + g$, by definition

g = growth in assets in per cent per year

We wish to prove that the following proposition (v, below) holds true for a company with these properties until the point of slackening growth arrives:

(v) *The rate of net dividend, expressed as a ratio to book value, stays the same, so that*

(44) $\qquad p_t = $ a constant

where

(28a) $\qquad p_t = \dfrac{\pi_t}{C_t},$ by definition

and

$\qquad p = $ pure dividend rate, expressed as per cent of book value

$\qquad \pi_t = $ pure dividend per share paid in year t

Dividing equation (10a) by C, we get

(45) $\qquad \dfrac{\pi}{C} = \dfrac{\gamma}{C} - \dfrac{\rho}{C}$

or

(46a) $\qquad p = c - r$

where

(28a) $\qquad p = \dfrac{\pi}{C},$ by definition

(47a) $\qquad c = \dfrac{\gamma}{C},$ by definition

(48a) $\qquad r = \dfrac{\rho}{C},$ by definition

and

$\qquad c = $ rate of earnings on *book* value of common

$\qquad r = $ reinvestment rate, expressed as a ratio to *book* value

To prove that p is constant in (46a), it must be shown that c and r are constant.

For c the procedure is as follows:

(11a) $\gamma = a - \beta$

whence

(49a) $cC = aA - bB$

Since

(40b) $A = lC$

therefore

(49b) $cC = alC - bB$

By definition,

(40a) $l = \dfrac{A}{C}$

and

(39a) $A = B + C$

Therefore

(50a) $l = \dfrac{B + C}{C}$

and so

(50b) $B + C = lC$

(50c) $B = C(l - 1)$

or

(50d) $\dfrac{B}{C} = l - 1$

Inserting (50c) in (49b), we get

$$cC = alC - b(l - 1)C = alC - blC + bC$$

whence

(52a) $c = l(a - b) + b$

or

(52b) $c = l\left(a - b + \dfrac{b}{l}\right)$

(vi)   *Since all the terms on the right-hand side of these last equations, (52a) and (52b), are constant, according to characteristics (i) to (iii) set forth above, it follows that* c *is also constant under these conditions.*

To prove r constant like c, the procedure is as follows:

(48a) $r_1 = \dfrac{\rho_1}{C_o}$, by definition

(48b, 53a) $\rho_1 = r_1 C_o = C_1 - C_o$, by definition

whence

$$r_1 = \frac{C_1 - C_o}{C_o}$$

$$= \frac{C_1}{C_o} - 1$$

$$= \frac{A_1}{l_1} \cdot \frac{l_o}{A_o} - 1 \text{, since } C_t = \frac{A_t}{l_t} \text{, by equation (40)}$$

$$= \frac{A_1}{A_o} - 1 \text{, since } l_o = l_1 = \text{a constant, by hypothesis}$$

$$= \frac{A_o u}{A_o} - 1 \text{, since } A_1 = A_o u \text{ by equation (42)}$$

whence

(54) $r_1 = u - 1 = g = $ a constant by hypothesis

Likewise for r_2, r_3, etc.   Q. E. D.

(vii)   *Since* g *is constant by hypothesis it follows that* r, *the reinvestment rate, is also constant in* (54).

Having proved in equations (52) and (54) that both c and r are constant, we can now see that p is also constant in equation (46a), under conditions (i) to (iv), as we set out to show.

The properties of such a company as we have been discussing, up to the point of inflection, may now be summarized as follows:

(i) $a = $ a constant, by hypothesis

(ii) $l = $ a constant, by hypothesis

(iii) $b = $ a constant, by hypothesis

(14a) (iv) $u = 1 + g = $ a constant, by hypothesis

(46a) (v) $p = c - r = $ a constant, in consequence

(52b) (vi) $c = l\left(a - b + \dfrac{b}{l}\right) = $ a constant, in consequence

(54)   (vii) $r = g = $ a constant, in consequence

We can now show that the dividends themselves follow a compound interest law till the point of inflection is reached, for

(40c) $$C_o = \frac{A_o}{l}$$

$$C_t = \frac{A_o u^t}{l}, \text{ by equation (43)}$$

$$pC_t = p\,\frac{A_o u^t}{l}$$

where

(28b) $$pC_t = \pi_t$$

so that

$$\pi_t = p\,\frac{A_o u^t}{l}$$

Since

(40c) $$\frac{A_o}{l} = C_o$$

therefore

$$\pi_t = pC_o u^t$$

(16a) $= \pi_o u^t$, a compound-interest function

Q. E. D.

Since dividends thus increase according to a compound-interest law up to the point of inflection in the company's growth, the value of its stock may be found by one of the formulas already worked out in Chapter VII, § 2, which is as follows:

$$(22b) \qquad V_0 = \pi_0 w \cdot \frac{w^n - 1}{w - 1} + V_n v^n$$

2. ITS DIVIDENDS BEYOND THE POINT OF INFLECTION

The algebraic analysis in the section to follow is difficult, and may be passed over by the general reader. The specialist, however, will find it of interest because it shows how dividends behave in the latter portion of a company's growth, a period seldom examined in detail.

In the foregoing formula $V_n v^n$ represents the present worth of the dividend annuity beyond the point of inflection. It is very doubtful if a company engaged in competitive business could in practice keep up its return on invested assets after the point of inflection in its growth was passed, but the legal guarantee now given the monopolistic utilities makes such an achievement easier for them. Accordingly we shall assume, for the sake of argument, such persistence of earnings for them; and proceed to deduce the law of their dividends after the point of inflection, on the following assumptions:

(i) a = a constant

(ii) l = a constant

(iii) b = a constant

(iv) u = a constant

where

(14a) $u = 1 + g$, by definition

and

g = rate of growth in assets before point of inflection is reached

The growth of the assets of such a company after the point of inflection is reached is defined by the following equation:

$$(56) \qquad \frac{2A_n - A_{n+1}}{A_n} = \frac{1}{u} = u^{-1}, \text{ etc.}$$

A glance at Diagram 9 will make this clear.

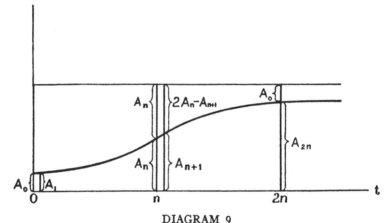

DIAGRAM 9

RATE OF GROWTH OF ASSETS

Just as

$$(42a) \qquad \frac{A_1}{A_0} = u = \frac{A_2}{A_1},$$ etc., because the left-hand side of the curve is a compound interest curve concave up, with

and

$$(42b) \qquad \frac{A_0}{A_1} = \frac{1}{u}$$ the horizontal axis as its asymptote,

so

$$(42c) \qquad \frac{A_n}{2A_n - A_{n+1}} = u,$$ because the right-hand side of the curve is a compound interest curve concave down, with a horizontal

and

$$(42d) \qquad \frac{2A_n - A_{n+1}}{A_n} = \frac{1}{u}$$ line through $A_t = 2A_n$ as its asymptote.

In general

(42e) $$\frac{A_n}{2A_n - A_t} = u^{t-n}$$

$$u^{n-t} = \frac{2A_n - A_t}{A_n}$$

$$= \frac{2\dfrac{A_n}{l} - \dfrac{A_t}{l}}{\dfrac{A_n}{l}}$$

$$= \frac{2C_n - C_t}{C_n}, \text{ since } C_t = \frac{A_t}{l}, \text{ and } l \text{ is constant}$$

whence

(58a) $$C_t = (2 - u^{n-t})C_n$$

It has already been shown that dividends are determined by the following general law:

(10a) $$\pi_t = \gamma_t - \rho_t$$

The first term on the right-hand side may be found thus:

(47b) $$\gamma_t = c_t C_t$$

where

(58a) $$C_t = C_n(2 - u^{n-t})$$

$$= C_o u^n(2 - u^{n-t}), \text{ from equations (40) and (43)}$$

with the result that

$$\gamma_t = c_t C_o u^n(2 - u^{n-t})$$

(59a) $$= C_o u^n(2c_t - c_t u^{n-t})$$

In this equation, $c_t = c_o$, as shown below:

(52a) $$c_t = l_t(a_t - b_t) + b_t$$

and

$$a_t = a_o = \text{a constant, by hypothesis}$$
$$b_t = b_o = \text{a constant, by hypothesis}$$
$$l_t = l_o = \text{a constant, by hypothesis}$$

with the result that

(52a) $$c_t = l_0(a_0 - b_0) + b_0 = c_0$$

Q. E. D.

Therefore equation (59a) becomes

(59b) $$\gamma_t = C_0 u^n (2c_0 - c_0 u^{n-t})$$

The second term on the right-hand side of (10a) may be found thus:

(53b) $$\rho_t = \Delta C_t = C_t - C_{t-1}, \text{ by definition}$$
where
(58a) $$C_t = [2 - u^{n-t}] C_n$$
and
(58b) $$C_{t-1} = [2 - u^{n-(t-1)}] C_n = [2 - u^{n-t+1}] C_n$$
with the result that
(53c) $$\rho_t = [(2 - u^{n-t}) - (2 - u^{n-t+1})] C_n$$
$$= [u^{n-t+1} - u^{n-t}] C_n$$
(53d) $$= u^{n-t} (u - 1) C_n$$

But
(14b) $$u - 1 = g, \text{ by definition}$$
and
(71) $$C_n = C_0 u^n, \text{ by equations (40) and (43) }[3]$$

Therefore equation (53d) becomes

(60) $$\rho_t = C_0 u^n g u^{n-t}$$

Combining these two expressions, (59b) and (60), for the first and second terms, we get

$$\pi_t = \gamma_t - \rho_t = C_0 u^n (2c - c u^{n-t} - g u^{n-t})$$
(61) $$= C_0 u^n [2c - (c + g) u^{n-t}]$$

By means of equation (61) we are at last in a position to evaluate the second term of equation (22b) when it applies to companies whose growth conforms to the curve

---

[3] Cf. proposition iv above.

in Diagram 9. The evaluation of the second term in (22b) then proceeds as follows:

$$(21) \qquad V_n v^n = \sum_{t=n+1}^{t=\infty} \pi_t v^t$$

$$= \sum_{t=n+1}^{t=\infty} C_0 u^n \left[2c - (c+g)\, u^{n-t}\right] v^t, \text{ by equa-}$$
$$\text{tion (61)}$$

$$= \sum_{t=n+1}^{t=\infty} C_0 u^n v^n \left[2cv^{t-n} - (c+g)\, u^{n-t} v^{t-n}\right]$$

$$(62) \qquad = C_0 w^n \left[\, 2c \sum_{t=n+1}^{t=\infty} v^{t-n} \right.$$

$$\left. - (c+g) \sum_{t=n+1}^{t=\infty} \left(\frac{v}{u}\right)^{t-n} \right]$$

To find the sums of these two series from $t = n + 1$ to $t = \infty$, let

$$(63) \qquad t' = t - n$$

or

$$n = t - t'$$

Then, if the sums of these infinite series are to be taken from

$$t = n + 1$$

to

$$t = \infty$$

this procedure is equivalent to taking these same sums from

$$t' = 1$$

to

$$t' = \infty$$

The first series in (62) can be developed as follows:

$$\sum_{t=n+1}^{t=\infty} v^{t-n} = \sum_{t'=1}^{t'=\infty} v^{t'}$$

$$= \frac{v}{1-v} \lim_{t' \to \infty} (1 - v^{t'})$$

$$= \frac{v}{1-v}, \text{ since } v < 1, \text{ and (9a) } \lim_{t' \to \infty} v^{t'} = 0$$

$$= \frac{1}{\dfrac{1}{v} - 1} = \frac{1}{1 - i - 1}$$

(64)
$$= \frac{1}{i}$$

In the same way it can be shown that

$$\sum_{t=n+1}^{t=\infty} \left(\frac{v}{u}\right)^{t-n} = \frac{1}{\dfrac{u}{v} - 1}$$

(65)
$$= \frac{1}{u(1 + i) - 1}$$

Insertion of these values for the sums in (62) gives

(66)
$$V_n v^n = C_0 w^n \left[\frac{2c}{i} - \frac{c+g}{u(1+i)-1} \right]$$

whence (22b) becomes in this case

(67a) [4]
$$V_0 = C_0 \left\{ pw \cdot \frac{w^n - 1}{w - 1} + \left[\frac{2c}{i} - \frac{c+g}{u(1+i)-1} \right] w^n \right\}$$

[4] The application of this formula is illustrated in Chapter XXV, § 10, dealing with Consolidated Gas.

It should be borne in mind that this formula applies only to those companies who are able to reinvest all their reported surplus earnings in such an effective way that profits do not fall in relation to assets. Such effective reinvestment seems impossible in competitive industry beyond the point of uniformly rapid growth, but in the utility business, where the law fixes the relation between profits and assets, such an achievement is within the realm of possibility. Its probability, however, is a matter that can only be decided after a detailed study of political and engineering considerations such as fall outside the scope of this part of the analysis.[5] The foregoing equation, therefore, is only to be regarded as defining the *maximum* possible value for a utility stock.

In case it is felt that reinvested earnings in the period of slackening growth will be subject to the law of diminishing returns as far as profits go, then equation (67a) will not apply, and the value for $V_n v^n$ must be found in some other way. As a matter of fact, the cases where equation (67a) holds good are so few that the only reasons for including it in this study are to make clear the limit of value for any stock and to show the adaptability of the algebraic method of evaluation.

Fortunately, the alternative formulas for the stocks of growing companies are simpler than equation (67a). They are developed from equation (22b) by defining $V_n v^n$ in terms of some one of the following three quantities:

(i) m_n = ratio of market price to book value at end of year n
(ii) e_n = price-earnings ratio at end of year n
(iii) y_n = yield at end of year n

It will be seen that these quantities, by their very nature, are things concerning which the investor may reasonably be expected to form some fairly definite opinion, especially

[5] For a discussion of these considerations, see Chapter XXV, §§ 2–6.

if the company is expected to take on the character of a stable, non-growing enterprise at the end of the period in question. The three formulas which make use of the three measures listed above are derived in Sections 3, 4, and 5 to follow.

3.   ITS BOOK VALUE AT THE POINT OF INFLECTION

If the investor, measuring the terminal value $V_n v^n$ in the first way, expects to see his stock when growth is over sell at some specified ratio to book value, defined as

$$(68a) \qquad m_n = \frac{V_n}{C_n}$$

then his stock should be worth, at the end of the year n,

$$(68b) \qquad V_n = m_n C_n$$

and the present worth of this future selling price should be

$$(69) \qquad V_n v^n = m_n C_n v^n$$

To evaluate the stock, we now need only to find the book value, C_n, at the end of the period of uniform growth in total assets at the rate g, thus:

$$(70) \qquad A_n = A_0(1 + g)^n$$
$$= A_0 u^n, \text{ by equation (14a)}$$
$$\frac{1}{l} A_n = \frac{1}{l} A_0 u^n$$

or

$$(71) \qquad C_n = C_0 u^n, \text{ since } C_t = \frac{A_t}{l_t}, \text{ and } l_t \text{ is constant by}$$
$$\text{hypothesis}$$

When this value for C_n is put into equation (69) above, it gives

$$(72a) \qquad V_n v^n = m_n (C_0 u^n) v^n,$$

and since

$$(15) \qquad w = uv,$$

equation (72a) becomes

$$(73) \qquad V_n v^n = m_n C_o w^n$$

Hence equation (22b) itself becomes

$$(74) \qquad V_o = \pi_o \left(w \cdot \frac{w^n - 1}{w - 1} \right) + m_n C_o w^n$$

Here

$$(28b) \qquad \pi_o = p C_o, \text{ by definition}$$

and so equation [6] (74) becomes

$$(75a) \qquad V_o = C_o \left(pw \cdot \frac{w^n - 1}{w - 1} + m_n w^n \right) \qquad \text{Q. E. F.}$$

This last equation is the most useful of all formulas for evaluating public utilities whose growth is not affected by mergers. It is a simple matter, moreover, to apply this formula to the stock of any given company. The balance sheet gives C_o. Income account and balance sheet together give a, b, and l, for use in computing p by means of equations (40a), (46a), (52b), and (54). Comparison of several balance sheets assists in estimating the annual growth, g, of total assets. Judgment is needed for determining i, n, and m_n. From i and g are derived u, v, and w, by means of equations (2), (14a), and (15).

4. ITS PRICE–EARNINGS RATIO AT THE POINT OF INFLECTION

If the investor, measuring terminal value in the second way, expects to see his stock when growth is over sell at some specified price-earnings ratio, defined as

$$(76a) \qquad e_n = \frac{V_n}{\gamma_n}$$

---

[6] The application of this formula is illustrated in Chapter XXIV, § 6, dealing with American Telephone, and in Chapter XXV, §§ 10 and 14, dealing with Consolidated Gas.

then his stock should be worth, at the end of the year n,

(76b) $$V_n = e_n \gamma_n$$

and the present worth of this future selling price should be

(77) $$V_n v^n = e_n \gamma_n v^n$$

To evaluate the stock we now need to find only the earnings per share, γ_n, in the year n, thus:

(47b, 71) $$\gamma_n = c_n C_n = c C_0 u^n$$

where c is a constant, as shown in § 1, (vi), equation (52b). When this value for γ_n in (47b) is put into equation (77) above, it gives

$$V_n v^n = e_n\, c C_0 u^n v^n$$

(78a) $$= C_0 e_n c w^n$$

This value should now be inserted in equation (22b) to give a second formula [7] for the present worth of shares in a company growing like this, as follows:

(79a) $$V_0 = C_0 \left(pw \frac{w^n - 1}{w - 1} + e_n c w^n \right)$$

5.   ITS YIELD AT THE POINT OF INFLECTION

If the investor, measuring terminal value in the third way, expects to see his stock when growth is over sell at some specified yield, defined as

(80a) $$y_n = \frac{\pi_n}{V_n}$$

then his stock should be worth, at the end of the year n,

(80b) $$V_n = \frac{\pi_n}{y_n}$$

---

[7] The application of this formula is illustrated in Chapter XXV, §§ 10 and 11, dealing with Consolidated Gas.

and the present value of this future selling price should be

$$(81a) \qquad V_n v^n = \frac{\pi_n}{y_n} \cdot v^n$$

To evaluate the stock, we now need to find only the pure dividend π_n, in the year n. This pure dividend will depend, however, on the distribution rate q_n which the company is expected to achieve on its bonds and stocks as a whole. If the company when it becomes mature is expected to be able to pay out in bond interest β, and in common dividends π, a certain fraction q of its total earnings-on-investment a, then its distribution rate will be [8]

$$(82, 83a) \qquad q = \frac{\beta + \pi}{a} = \frac{\beta + \pi}{\beta + \gamma}, \text{ by definition}$$

From this it follows that

$$(83b) \qquad q(\beta + \gamma) = (\beta + \pi)$$

$$(83c) \qquad \pi = q\beta + q\gamma - \beta$$

$$(83d) \qquad = (q - 1)\beta + q\gamma$$

Since

$$(41b) \qquad \beta = bB, \text{ by definition}$$

and

$$(47b) \qquad \gamma = cC, \text{ by definition}$$

equation (83d) becomes

$$(85) \qquad \pi = (q - 1)bB + qcC$$

Dividing by C, this gives

$$(86) \qquad \frac{\pi}{C} = (q - 1)b\left(\frac{B}{C}\right) + qc$$

Since

$$(28a) \qquad \frac{\pi}{C} = p,$$

[8] The application of these formulas is illustrated in Chapter XXI, Table 17, dealing with General Motors, and Chapter XXV, § 10, dealing with Consolidated Gas.

and

(50d) $$\frac{B}{C} = l - 1,$$

it follows that equation (86) becomes

(87)
$$\begin{aligned} p_n &= (q_n - 1)(l - 1)b + q_n c \\ &= (1 - l)(1 - q_n)b + q_n c \end{aligned}$$

In the case now under discussion, where the company, to finance its growth, issues new senior and junior securities in such a way as to keep their ratio always the same, l is constant by hypothesis, as are a and b also, and so c is a constant too, according to equation (52b). The real dividend, π_n, in the year n, will then be found by combining (28b) and (87), thus:

(28b)
$$\begin{aligned} \pi_n &= p_n C_n \\ &= C_n \left[(1 - l)(1 - q_n)b + q_n c \right] \end{aligned}$$

Here

(71) $$C_n = C_o u^n$$

and so

(88) $$\pi_n = C_o u^n \left[(1 - l)(1 - q_n)b + q_n c \right]$$

The foregoing value for π_n, when put into equation (81a) above, gives the following value for the present worth of a future selling price based on yield:

(89) $$V_n v^n = C_o \frac{w^n}{y_n} \left[(1 - l)(1 - q_n)b + q_n c \right], \text{ where}$$

$$uv = w$$

This value should now be inserted in equation (22b) to give a third formula [9] for the present worth of shares in a company growing like this, as follows:

(90a) $$V_o = C_o \left\{ pw \frac{w^n - 1}{w - 1} + \frac{w^n}{y_n} \left[(1 - l)(1 - q_n)b + q_n c \right] \right\}$$

[9] The application of this formula is illustrated in Chapter XXV, § 10, dealing with Consolidated Gas.

6. SUMMARY

To summarize our results so far, we may list four different formulas for use in evaluating a growing company with a constant leverage, as follows:

Logistic Growth:

$$(67a) \qquad V_o = C_o \left\{ pw \cdot \frac{w^n - 1}{w - 1} + \left[\frac{2c}{i} - \frac{c + g}{u(1 + i) - 1} \right] w^n \right\}$$

Book Value at End:

$$(75a) \qquad V_o = C_o \left(pw \cdot \frac{w^n - 1}{w - 1} + m_n w^n \right)$$

Price-Earnings Ratio at End:

$$(79a) \qquad V_o = C_o \left(pw \cdot \frac{w^n - 1}{w - 1} + e_n c w^n \right)$$

Yield at End:

$$(90a)$$

$$V_o = C_o \left\{ pw \cdot \frac{w^n - 1}{w - 1} + \frac{w^n}{y_n} \left[(q_n - 1)(l - 1) b + q_n c \right] \right\}$$

7. SPECIAL CASE WHERE $w = 1$

In one special case, namely when $w = 1$, the foregoing formulas will not work, because a value of unity for w will make the first term in each formula become meaningless. In this special case, however, it can be shown, as has been done in Chapter VII, § 3, that

$$(84) \qquad pw \frac{w^n - 1}{w - 1} \text{ may be replaced by } np, \text{ if } w = 1$$

with the result that the foregoing formulas reduce to the following simpler ones:

Logistic Growth:

$$(67b) \qquad V_0 = C_0 \left[np + \frac{2c}{i} - \frac{c+g}{u(1+i)-1} \right]$$

Book Value at End:

$$(75b) \qquad V_0 = C_0 \, (np + m_n)$$

or

$$(75c) \qquad V_0 = n\pi_0 + m_n C_0$$

or

$$(75d) \text{ [10]} \qquad V_0 = n\pi_0 + C_0, \text{ if } m_n = 1$$

Price-Earnings Ratio at End:

$$(79b) \qquad V_0 = C_0 \, (np + e_n c)$$

or

$$(79c) \qquad V_0 = n\pi_0 + e_n \gamma_0$$

Yield at End:

$$(90b) \qquad V_0 = C_0 \left\{ np + \frac{1}{y_n} \left[(q_n - 1)(l - 1) + q_n c \right] \right\}$$

In certain special cases, notably in the case of a fire insurance company at the end of its growth,

$$q_n = 1$$

with the result that

$$(90c) \qquad V_0 = C_0 \left(np + \frac{c}{y_n} \right)$$

or

$$(90d) \qquad V_0 = n\pi_0 + \frac{\gamma_0}{y_n}$$

or

$$(90e) \text{ [11]} \qquad V_0 = n\pi_0 + \frac{\gamma_0}{i}, \text{ if } y_n = i$$

[10] The application of this formula is illustrated in Chapter XXIII, § 14, dealing with Phoenix Insurance.

[11] The application of this formula is illustrated in Chapter XXIII, § 13, dealing with Phoenix Insurance.

Since in practice it often happens that companies grow at the same rate as the rate of interest, in other words, that

$$g = 6\%, \text{ for instance,}$$

and

$$i = 6\%, \text{ also}$$

it often happens that

(14a) $\quad u = 1 + g = 1.06, \text{ for instance}$

and

(2). $\qquad \dfrac{1}{v} = 1 + i = 1.06$

with the result that

(15, 2) $\qquad w = uv = \dfrac{u}{1+i} = \dfrac{1.06}{1.06} = 1$

Such a value for w is a common occurrence; when met with, it permits the use of the foregoing simpler formulas.

These formulas are very convenient for the hasty appraisal of growing companies. In appraising such companies, it is often enlightening to pose the question, How far ahead is the market discounting a progressive increase in dividends?

To answer this question, an inverted form of equation (75c) may be used, derived as follows:

Let

$$M_0 = \text{actual market price now}$$

then

(75c) $\qquad M_0 = V_0 = n\pi_0 + m_n C_0$

or

$$n\pi_0 = M_0 - m_n C_0$$

whence

(75e) $\qquad n = \dfrac{M_0 - m_n C_0}{\pi_0}$

In many rough calculations, we can let

$$m_n = 1$$

and get

(75f) $$n = \frac{M_0 - C_0}{\pi_0}, \text{ if } m_n = 1$$

A similar transformation of (79c) gives

(79c) $$M_0 = n\pi_0 + e_n\gamma_0$$

(79d) $$n = \frac{M_0 - e_n\gamma_0}{\pi_0}$$

Instead of transforming (90b) likewise, it is usually better to transform (22c), thus:

Let

(57) $$V_n = \frac{\pi_0 u^n}{i}, \text{ by assumption, as in (80b)}$$

and

(22c) $$V_0 = n\pi_0 + V_n v^n$$

whence

$$V_0 = n\pi_0 + \frac{\pi_0}{i} u^n v^n$$

$$= n\pi_0 + \frac{\pi_0}{i} w^n$$

$$= n\pi_0 + \frac{\pi_0}{i}, \text{ if } w = 1$$

(22d) $$V_0 = \pi_0\left(n + \frac{1}{i} \right), \text{ when } w = 1$$

If we now let

$$M_0 = V_0$$

then

(22e) $$n = \frac{M_0}{\pi_0} - \frac{1}{i}$$

CHAPTER XII

ALGEBRAIC BUDGETING (cont.)

I. THE PROPERTIES OF A UTILITY COMPANY WITH LEVERAGE INCREASING

If growth is attended by a change in leverage, so that the ratio of bonds to stock is altered, then the dividends to be paid by a company will increase at a different rate from its assets, and allowance for this irregularity must be made in evaluating the company's stock. In particular, if the leverage is progressively changed so as to increase the ratio of bonds to stock, then dividends can be raised faster than otherwise, and the stock can thus be made more valuable.

Advantageous to stockholders is a capitalization top-heavy with bonds if the interest rate on the bonds is low, as can be made obvious by comparing the utility business with the banking business and the insurance business. In the banking business, every effort is made to secure deposits, and the money so obtained is invested in assets yielding 4 to 6 per cent (in normal times), while nothing is paid for the deposits except the cost of bookkeeping. The difference between the interest rate on loans granted and the handling cost on deposits accepted gives rise to the profits of the stockholders. Likewise, in the fire insurance business, funds to invest are secured by inducing people to deposit premiums with the company without payment of any interest at all.[1] If the business can be conducted without underwriting loss, as some of the most careful companies succeed in doing year after year, then the company becomes equivalent to a bank which secures its deposits for nothing, and the entire interest income from its invest-

---

[1] Cf. Chapter XXIII on the Phoenix Insurance Co.

ments will accrue to its stockholders. These deposits in the fire insurance business go under the name of "Reserve for Unearned Premiums" and "Reserve for Unpaid Losses." In the life insurance business, as contrasted with the fire insurance business, the situation is somewhat less favorable to stockholders in that interest must be paid on the "deposits," so to speak, at 3 or $3\frac{1}{2}$ per cent, the usual rates for compounding reserves; but the thinner equity for the common stock in the life insurance business gives stockholders a larger fund to work with in proportion to their own investment, and as a result both life insurance and fire insurance, like banking, offer the chance of large profits, honestly got, from the investment of other people's money. All banks and insurance companies, therefore, normally try to build up their "deposits," call them by whatever name you will, to the highest figure allowed by law.

The same business principle governs the utilities. In the 1920's they were practically guaranteed 8 per cent on their investment by the courts,[2] and so the more "deposits" they could secure, in the form of bonded debt at 5 per cent or thereabouts, the more profit for their stockholders. In states where utility regulation is most intelligent, capital expenditures are supervised to prevent extravagance in building up the rate base, and it seems as though this aspect of regulation must eventually become coördinate in importance with the question of the rate of return, if the present rule of a "fair return on a fair value" is to be carried to its logical conclusion.

It follows from the banking analogy, therefore, that the future of the utilities is to be appraised in terms of growth in *assets*, rather than in terms of growth in electrical output and gross revenues or improvement in operating ratios.

---

[2] At a later date the courts began to waver and to pare down the rate thought fair.

However much output, revenues, or operating ratios may gain, earnings themselves will always be subject to such an adjustment through taxes or rate changes as to bring net income after taxes down to a specified return on property value.

From the stockholder's point of view, therefore, things which reduce investment needs are bearish. Reductions in the cost of equipment, or increases in its capacity, are of themselves unfavorable except to the extent that they permit rate reductions that cause a demand for greater output and larger investment in the end.

The greater the percentage of borrowed money, the higher the rate of earnings on stockholders' capital, as may be seen by reference to equation (52a), which reads

(52a) $$c = l(a - b) + b$$

where

(50e) $$l = \left(\frac{B}{C} + 1 \right)$$

whence

(52c) $$c = \left(\frac{B}{C} + 1 \right)(a - b) + b$$

The larger B is in relation to C, therefore, the larger c will be. It follows from this that the possibility of financing future growth largely with borrowed money ought to be reflected in the market price of a company's stock.

2. FORMULA FOR ITS FUTURE DIVIDENDS

The extreme case of a company with leverage increasing would be one which reinvested none of its earnings on the common stock, but disbursed all of them in dividends and secured all of its funds for expansion from the sale of new bonds or preferred stock. Let us deduce the law of dividends for such a company, assuming at the same time that it retains certain properties already met with in the preceding chapter, with the result that its characteristics may be summarized as follows:

(i) $$r = 0$$
instead of l = a constant
(ii) $$a = \text{a constant}$$
(iii) $$b = \text{a constant}$$
(iv) $$u = 1 + g = \text{a constant}$$

Dividends for such a company would be determined by the usual rule:

(10b) $$\pi = a - \beta - \rho$$
where
(48b) $$\rho = rc = 0, \text{ by hypothesis}$$
with the result that
$$\pi = a - \beta$$
$$= aA - bB$$
Here
(39b) $$B = A - C$$
and so
$$\pi_t = aA_t - b(A_t - C_t)$$
Since
(43) $$A_t = A_o u^t$$
and
$$C_t = C_o, \text{ by hypothesis}$$
therefore
$$\pi_t = aA_o u^t - b(A_o u^t - C_o)$$
Since
(40b) $$A_o = l_o C_o$$
therefore
$$\pi_t = al_o C_o u^t - b(l_o C_o u^t - C_o)$$
$$= (a - b) l_o C_o u^t + bC_o$$
$$= C_o [(a - b) l_o u^t + b]$$

The present worth of the annuity of dividends to be paid by such a company during n years of growth at a uniform rate would be as follows:

$$\sum_{t=1}^{t=n} \pi_t v^t = \sum_{t=1}^{t=n} u^t v^t (a - b) C_o l_o + \sum_{t=1}^{t=n} b v^t C_o$$

$$= (a - b) C_o l_o \sum_{t=1}^{t=n} w^t + b C_o \sum_{t=1}^{t=n} v^t$$

(91)
$$= \left[(a - b) \cdot \frac{w^n - 1}{w - 1} \cdot w l_o \right.$$
$$\left. + \frac{b}{i} (1 - v^n) \right] C_o$$

according to Chapter VI, § 2.

This value for

$$\sum_{t=1}^{t=n} \pi_t v^t$$

may now be inserted in (20) to give

(92) $\quad V_o = C_o \left[(a - b) \cdot \dfrac{w^n - 1}{w - 1} \cdot w l_o + \dfrac{b}{i} (1 - v^n) \right] + V_n v^n$

In the foregoing equation, $V_n v^n$ is the present worth of the future selling price in the year n. Because in this case where the leverage is increasing,

$$l_o \neq l_n$$

it is impossible to use the values for $V_n v^n$ employed in the previous chapter. Instead it is necessary to deduce three entirely new values for $V_n v^n$, depending on whether this expression is defined in terms of book value, price-earnings ratio, or yield. The deductions for each of these definitions follow below:

3. ITS BOOK VALUE AT THE END

If the final selling price, V_n, is defined in terms of final book value, C_n, then

(68b) $$V_n = m_n C_n$$

the same as in the case of constant leverage, and so the present worth, $V_n v^n$ of this future selling price is

(69) $$V_n v^n = m_n C_n v^n$$

the same as in the case of constant leverage. Since the company in this case of increasing leverage is assumed to pay out all of its earnings in dividends, and to reinvest none of them, it adds nothing to the book value of its stock during the n years in question, and so

$$C_n = C_o, \text{ by hypothesis}$$

in the present case of increasing leverage. When this latter figure for the future book value, C_n, is put in equation (69) above, it gives

(72b) $$V_n v^n = m_n C_o v^n$$

The resulting formula for the value of the shares of such a growing company, if it pays out all of its earnings in dividends, is obtained from equation (92), and is as follows:

(93) $$V_o = C_o \left[(a - b) \frac{w^n - 1}{w - 1} w l_o + \frac{b}{i} (1 - v^n) + m_n v^n \right]$$

4. ITS PRICE–EARNINGS RATIO AT THE END

If the final selling price, V_n, is defined in terms of the final price-earnings ratio, e_n, then

(76b) $$V_n = e_n \gamma_n$$

the same as in the case of constant leverage; whence

$$V_n = e_n c_n C_n, \text{ by equation (47)}$$
(76c) $$= C_o e_n c_n, \text{ since } C_o = C_n, \text{ by hypothesis,}$$

and so the present worth of the future selling price is

(78b) $$V_n v^n = C_o e_n c_n v^n$$

Since

(52b) $$c_n = l_n \left(a - b + \frac{b}{l_n} \right)$$

therefore

(94) $$V_n v^n = C_o e_n l_n \left(a - b + \frac{b}{l_n} \right) v^n$$

Now

(40a) $$l_n = \frac{A_n}{C_n}, \text{ by definition}$$

$$= \frac{A_o u^n}{C_o}, \text{ where } \frac{A_o}{C_o} = l_o$$

and so

(95) $$l_n = l_o u^n, \text{ and } \frac{1}{l_n} = \frac{1}{l_o u^n}$$

If this value for l_n is now inserted in equation (94) above, it gives

(96) $$V_n v^n = C_o e_n l_o w^n \left(a - b + \frac{b}{l_o u^n} \right),$$
$$\text{where } w^n = u^n v^n$$

This value should now be inserted in equation (92) to give a second formula for a growing company with capitalization changing like this, as follows:

(97) $$V_o = C_o \left[(a - b) \cdot \frac{w^n - 1}{w - 1} \cdot w l_o + \frac{b}{i} (1 - v^n) \right.$$
$$\left. + e_n l_o w^n \left(a - b + \frac{b}{l_o u^n} \right) \right]$$

5. ITS YIELD AT THE END

If the final selling price, V_n, is defined in terms of the final yield, y_n, then

(80a) $$y_n = \frac{\pi_n}{V_n}$$

or

(80b)
$$V_n = \frac{\pi_n}{y_n}$$

the same as in the case of constant leverage; and so the present worth of this future selling price is

(81a)
$$V_n v^n = \frac{\pi_n v^n}{y_n}$$

the same as in the case of constant leverage. The final pure dividend, π_n, will be

(28b)
$$\pi_n = p_n C_n$$

Since in this case

$$C_n = C_o, \text{ by hypothesis}$$

it follows that

$$\pi_n = p_n C_o$$

and so equation (81a) becomes

(81b)
$$V_n v^n = C_o \frac{p_n v^n}{y_n}, \text{ if } C_n = C_o$$

The final dividend rate, p_n, can be estimated only if some final distribution rate, q_n, is assumed. Then the dividend rate will be

(87)
$$p_n = (1 - l_n)(1 - q_n) b + q_n c_n$$

Moreover, the final rate of earnings-on-common, c_n, will be

(52b)
$$c_n = l_n \left(a - b + \frac{b}{l_n} \right)$$

From this it follows that

$$p_n = (1 - l_n)(1 - q_n) b + l_n q_n \left(a - b + \frac{b}{l_n} \right)$$

The final leverage, l_n, will be

(95)
$$l_n = l_o u^n$$

Hence

$$p_n = (1 - l_0 u^n)(1 - q_n) b + l_0 u^n q_n \left(a - b + \frac{b}{l_0 u^n} \right)$$

$$= b - b l_0 u^n - b q_n + b l_0 u^n q_n + a l_0 u^n q_n - b l_0 u^n q_n + b q_n$$

The third and seventh terms in the right-hand side of the equation above cancel, as do the fourth and sixth, with the result that

$$p_n = b - b l_0 u^n + a l_0 u^n q_n$$

$$= l_0 u^n \left[a q_n - b + \frac{b}{l_0 u^n} \right]$$

$$= l_0 u^n \left[a q_n - b \left(1 - \frac{1}{l_0 u^n} \right) \right]$$

If this value for p_n is now put into the equation (81b), it gives

(98)
$$V_n v^n = C_0 \frac{w^n l_0}{y_n} \left[a q_n - b \left(1 - \frac{1}{l_0 u^n} \right) \right],$$

where $w = uv$

This value should now be inserted in equation (92) to give a third formula for a growing company with capitalization changing like this, as follows:

(99)
$$V_0 = C_0 \left\{ (a - b) \cdot \frac{w^n - 1}{w - 1} \cdot w l_0 + \frac{b}{i} (1 - v^n) \right.$$

$$\left. + \frac{w^n l_0}{y_n} \left[a q_n - b \left(1 - \frac{1}{l_0 u^n} \right) \right] \right\}$$

6. SUMMARY

To summarize the results of this chapter, which treats of companies that arrange their borrowing and dividend policies in such a way as to reshape their leverages more and more in favor of their stockholders, the following formulas [3] should be listed:

---

[3] The application of these formulas is illustrated in Chapter XXV, § 10, dealing with Consolidated Gas.

Book Value at End:

$$(93) \qquad V_o = C_o \left[(a - b) \cdot \frac{w^n - 1}{w - 1} \cdot wl_o + \frac{b}{i} (1 - v^n) \right. $$
$$\left. + m_n v^n \right]$$

Price-Earnings Ratio at End:

$$(97) \qquad V_o = C_o \left[(a - b) \cdot \frac{w^n - 1}{w - 1} \cdot wl_o + \frac{b}{i} (1 - v^n) \right.$$
$$\left. + e_n l_o w^n \left(a - b + \frac{b}{l_o u^n} \right) \right]$$

Yield at End:

$$(99) \qquad V_o = C_o \left\{ (a - b) \cdot \frac{w^n - 1}{w - 1} \cdot wl_o + \frac{b}{i} (1 - v^n) \right.$$
$$\left. + \frac{w^n l_o}{y_n} \left[aq_n - b \left(1 - \frac{1}{l_o u^n} \right) \right] \right\}$$

The foregoing equations for the value V of a company's stock can also be used to find the number of years n that it would take for the company to reshape its capitalization to any specified leverage. We have simply to treat V_o as a known quantity, setting it equal to the present market price M_o, and solve the equation for n by a method of successive approximations.

CHAPTER XIII

GROWTH BY MERGER OR SUDDEN EXPANSION

When companies grow by merger or sudden expansion, rather than by slow development as has been discussed heretofore, then their dividends may be affected by a change in several factors at once, for their invested assets, their return on investment, their ratio of stocks to bonds, and so forth, may all undergo a change at the same time. Such a multitudinous change in characteristics would be in contrast to the cases discussed so far, which have all had the following properties:

$$a = \text{a constant}$$
$$b = \text{a constant}$$
$$u = \text{a constant}$$
$$\text{Either } l = \text{a constant}$$
$$\text{or } r = 0$$

For companies not having the foregoing properties, methods of evaluation quite different from any yet discussed are needed. One of these other methods will be discussed in this chapter; this method would apply to a company which was buying many new properties and building up the earning power of its old ones, for instance,[1] or which was making a huge new addition to plant, as for natural gas lines.[2]

I. KNOWNS AND UNKNOWNS

In describing such a company's condition at the start, its development during the period of growth, and its condition at the end, one would need to list eighteen charac-

---

[1] E.g., American and Foreign Power Co., Inc., in 1929.
[2] E.g., Columbia Gas and Electric Co., in 1929.

teristics in all, of which any eleven might be taken as known (or assumed for the sake of argument) and seven might be treated as unknown. A convenient way to group these characteristics into knowns and unknowns is as follows:

Knowns

A_0 = assets per share at start

C_0 = book value of common at start

M_0 = market price of common at start

K = actual dividends paid during growth (assuming continuance of present dividend rate)

n = time involved in period of growth (assumed)

l_n = leverage to be attained at end (assumed)

c_0 = rate of earnings on common at start

$c_{n'}$ = rate of earnings on common at end (assumed)

e_n = price-earnings ratio at end (assumed)

i = rate of interest

$s_{\overline{n}|}$ = amount of an annuity of \$1 at the rate i

Unknowns

A_n = assets per share at end

C_n = book value of common at end

M_n = market price at end

S = subscriptions to new stock during growth

R = reinvested earnings during growth

G = earnings on common during growth

z = increase in size of company, in per cent

It would be possible to change the foregoing assortment, and, by assuming a plausible value for the expected growth z, put it among the knowns in place of the initial price of the stock M_0, with the result that we could solve for the investment value V_0 of the stock instead of for the expected growth z. In the way the problem usually presents itself in practice, however, it is more convenient to include z among the unknowns and M_o among the knowns as done above, because usually it is a question of finding what conditions are necessary to justify the market price actually prevailing. Once we know these necessary conditions, we are in a position to inquire as to their plausibility.

Since the unknowns are seven in number, seven equations are needed to find their value. Let us proceed to formulate these seven equations; such of the foregoing symbols as are new can be defined as they are referred to in the analysis. The first step will be to derive the formula for C_n, after which it will be easy to find the rest of the unknowns.

2.   THE BOOK VALUE ON COMPLETION OF GROWTH

In the case of companies with sudden growth ahead of them, just as in the case of other companies, we may write

$$(20a) \qquad V_o = \sum_{t=1}^{t=n} \pi_t v^t + M_n v^n$$

Since sudden growth such as we are now considering usually takes place in a short period of from two to five years, the interest on any dividends received from or assessments paid to the company during the period in question is a relatively unimportant item. In particular, it would not make much difference in the value of the stock whether the larger dividends and assessments came in the earlier or the later years of the period in question; therefore it is permissible to simplify the problem by assuming that the net dividend

$$(3a) \qquad \pi = \kappa - \sigma$$

is the same in each of the n years of rapid growth, or in other words, that

$$\pi = \text{a constant}$$

This assumption permits us to change equation (20a) to

$$(20b) \qquad V_o = \pi \sum_{t=1}^{t=n} v^t + M_n v^n$$

Since we know that

$$(3b) \qquad \sum_{t=1}^{t=n} \pi = \sum_{t=1}^{t=n} \kappa - \sum_{t=1}^{t=n} \sigma$$

we may write, if we assume π to be constant, that

$$(3c) \qquad n\pi = \sum_{t=1}^{t=n} \kappa - \sum_{t=1}^{t=n} \sigma$$

For convenience, we may use a simpler notation, and set

$$(100) \qquad K = \sum_{t=1}^{t=n} \kappa$$

and

$$(101) \qquad S = \sum_{t=1}^{t=n} \sigma$$

Then equation (3c) can be rewritten as

$$(3d) \qquad n\pi = K - S$$

$$(3e) \qquad \pi = \frac{1}{n}(K - S)$$

If the foregoing value of π is put into equation (20b), it gives

$$(102a) \qquad V_o = \frac{1}{n}(K - S)\sum_{t=1}^{t=n} v^t + M_n v^n$$

This equation can be made more convenient to work with by dividing it by v^n, thus:

$$(102b) \qquad V_o (1 + i)^n = \frac{1}{n}(K - S)\sum_{t=1}^{t=n} (1 + i)^{n-t} + M_n,$$

$$\text{where } \left(\frac{1}{v}\right)^n = \left(1 + i\right)^n$$

To simplify the notation, reverse the order of the terms in the series, and write

$$(103) \qquad s_{\overline{n}|} = \sum_{t=1}^{t=n} (1+i)^{n-t} = \sum_{t=0}^{t=n-1} (1+i)^t$$

It will be seen that $s_{\overline{n}|}$ as defined by the middle member of equation (103) is the *amount* of an annuity at the rate i for n years.[3] Its value can be computed, or obtained from published tables compiled for actuaries, accountants, and engineers.[4] The use of $s_{\overline{n}|}$ in (102b) gives

$$(102c) \qquad V_o (1+i)^n = \frac{1}{n} (K-S) s_{\overline{n}|} + M_n$$

Since we are using the market price at the start as one of the knowns of the problem, and are seeking the implications of this known price, we can put M_o in place of V_o in (102c), and make it read

$$(102d) \qquad M_o (1+i)^n = \frac{1}{n} (K-S) s_{\overline{n}|} + M_n$$

As in the case of other companies, we may define the market price at the end in terms of the price-earnings ratio then, and write

$$(78c) \qquad M_n = e_n c_{n'} C_n$$

where

$\qquad c_{n'}$ = rate of earnings in the first year n' after growth ends.

When this expression is inserted in (102d) it gives

$$(104) \qquad M_o (1+i)^n = \frac{1}{n} (K-S) s_{\overline{n}|} + e_n c_{n'} C_n$$

[3] Cf. Rietz, Crathorne, and Rietz, *Mathematics of Finance*, pp. 40–41.
[4] Cf. J. W. Glover, *Tables of Applied Mathematics in Finance, Insurance, Statistics* (Ann Arbor, Mich.: G. Wahr, 1923), pp. 104 ff., or E. V. Huntington, *Handbook of Mathematics for Engineers* (New York: McGraw-Hill Book Company, Inc., 1918), p. 65.

In the foregoing equation, the expression $(K-S)$ is the aggregate amount paid out in dividends during the period in question, that is,

(3d) $$n\pi = K - S$$

Just as it is true that for any one year

(10a) $$\pi = \gamma - \rho$$

so also it is true that for n years

(10c) $$\sum_{t=1}^{t=n} \pi_t = \sum_{t=1}^{t=n} \gamma_t - \sum_{t=1}^{t=n} \rho_t$$

or

(10d) $$P = G - R$$

where the symbols P, G, and R are defined as follows:

(105) $$P = \sum_{t=1}^{t=n} \pi_t = n\pi, \text{ since } \pi \text{ is assumed to be constant.}$$

(106) $$G = \sum_{t=1}^{t=n} \gamma_t$$

(107) $$R = \sum_{t=1}^{t=n} \rho_t$$

By equations (3d) and (10d), we have

$$K - S = n\pi = P = G - R$$

or, in other words

(108a) $$(G - R) = (K - S)$$

If this value of $(K-S)$ is put into (104) it gives

(109) $$M_o (1 + i)^n = \frac{1}{n} (G - R)s_{\overline{n}|} + e_n c_n{}' C_n$$

By definition

(110) $$C_n = C_o + \Delta C$$

and

(111) $$\Delta C = R$$

Hence

(112a) $$C_n = C_o + R$$

In other words, the increase in the book value of the common stock is obtained by the reinvestment of any earnings not paid out in dividends. Transposing in (112a), we get

(112b) $$R = C_n - C_o$$

If this value of R is now inserted in (109), it gives

(113) $$M_o (1 + i)^n = \frac{1}{n} (G - C_n + C_o) s_{\overline{n|}} + e_n c_{n'} C_n$$

As already pointed out

(106) $$G = \sum_{t=1}^{t=n} \gamma_t = \gamma_1 + \gamma_2 + \cdots + \gamma_n$$

The subscripts refer to the first, second, and nth year of the period in question. If it be assumed that the growth in earnings during the period treated is at an approximately constant rate, then the graph of earnings will be as shown in Diagram 10.

To find the total earnings per share, G, for the period of n years between the last year, $t = o$, before growth begins, and the first year, $t = n + 1 = n'$, after growth is completed, obtain the area of the trapezoid underneath the straight line $L_o L_n$ in Diagram 10, thus:

Let

λ_o = rate of earnings in dollars per share at start

$\lambda_{n'}$ = rate of earnings in dollars per share at end

Δt = an interval of time, namely, one year

n = number of years during which earnings increase

The base of the trapezoid is then $n \, \Delta t$, and its area

(114) $$G = \frac{1}{2} \left(\lambda_0 + \lambda_{n'} \right) n \Delta t$$

(115) $$= \frac{1}{2} n \left(\lambda_0 \Delta t + \lambda_{n'} \Delta t \right)$$

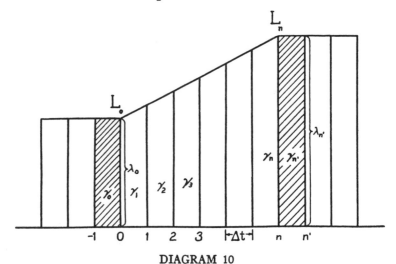

DIAGRAM 10

RATE OF GROWTH OF EARNINGS

A glance at the diagram will show that

$$\lambda_0 \Delta t = \gamma_0$$

and

$$\lambda_{n'} \Delta t = \gamma_{n'}$$

Therefore equation (115) becomes

(116) $$G = \frac{1}{2} n \left(\gamma_0 + \gamma_{n'} \right)$$

Since

(47b) $$\gamma_0 = c_0 C_0$$
$$\gamma_{n'} = c_{n'} C_{n'}$$
$$= c_{n'} C_n, \text{ where } C_n = C_{n'}$$

therefore equation (116) becomes

$$(117) \qquad G = \frac{1}{2}\, n \,(c_0 C_0 + c_{n'} C_n)$$

If this value for G is now put into equation (113), it gives

$$(118a) \qquad M_0 \,(1+i)^n = \frac{1}{n}\, (\tfrac{1}{2} n c_0 C_0 + \tfrac{1}{2} n c_{n'} C_n - C_n + C_0)\, s_{\overline{n|}}$$
$$+ e_n c_{n'} C_n$$

$$(118b) \qquad M_0 \,(1+i)^n = \left(\tfrac{1}{2} c_0 + \frac{1}{n} \right) s_{\overline{n|}} C_0 + \left[\left(\tfrac{1}{2} c_{n'} - \frac{1}{n} \right) s_{\overline{n|}} \right.$$
$$\left. + e_n c_{n'} \right] C_n$$

$$M_0 \,(1+i)^n - \left(\tfrac{1}{2} c_0 + \frac{1}{n} \right) s_{\overline{n|}} C_0 = C_n \left[\left(\tfrac{1}{2} c_{n'} - \frac{1}{n} \right) s_{\overline{n|}} \right.$$
$$\left. + e_n c_{n'} \right]$$

whence

$$(119) \qquad C_n = \frac{M_0 \,(1+i)^n - \left(\tfrac{1}{2} c_0 + \dfrac{1}{n} \right) s_{\overline{n|}} C_0}{e_n c_{n'} + \left(\tfrac{1}{2} c_{n'} - \dfrac{1}{n} \right) s_{\overline{n|}}}$$

Q. E. F.

3.   THE DETERMINATION OF THE OTHER UNKNOWNS

Having obtained the value for C_n, one of the seven unknowns listed above, we can now proceed to find the other six unknowns easily by the use of the following six equations in the order given:

(40b) $\qquad A_n = l_n C_n$, by definition, where l_n is given to start with

(120) $\qquad z = \dfrac{A_n}{A_0}$, by definition, where A_n is given by equation
(40b) above

(78c) $\qquad M_n = e_n c_{n'} C_n$, by the definition of e_n, where e_n and $c_{n'}$
are given to start with

(112b) $\qquad R = C_n - C_0$, by definition, where C_n is given by equation (119) above

(117) $G = \frac{1}{2}n(c_0 C_0 + c_n \cdot C_n)$, as shown in § 2 above

(108b) $S = K + R - G$, as shown in § 2 above

Of the seven unknowns listed above, one in particular, z, is always of interest, because it represents the amount of growth in the specified number of years n required to justify the present price M_0. The formula [5] for z in terms of the original knowns works out to be as follows:

(120)
$$z = \frac{A_n}{A_0} = \frac{l_n C_n}{A_0}, \text{ by equation (40)}$$

(121)
$$= \frac{l_n}{A_0} \cdot \frac{M_0 (1 + i)^n - \left(\frac{1}{2}c_0 + \frac{1}{n} \right) s_{\overline{n}|} C_0}{e_n c_{n'} + \left(\frac{1}{2}c_{n'} - \frac{1}{n} \right) s_{\overline{n}|}}$$

If the value for z is assumed at the start, and its place among the seven unknowns is taken by V_0 instead — a procedure discussed at the end of § 1 — then the value of V_0 can be deduced in the following way:

(118b)
$$M_0 (1 + i)^n = (\frac{1}{2}c_0 + \frac{1}{n}) s_{\overline{n}|} C_0 + \left[\left(\frac{1}{2}c_{n'} - \frac{1}{n} \right) s_{\overline{n}|} + e_n c_{n'} \right] C_n$$

Let
$$V_0 = M_0$$

and multiply by

(2)
$$\frac{1}{(1 + i)^n} = v^n$$

to get

(118c)
$$V_0 = v^n \left\{ \left(\frac{1}{2}c_0 + \frac{1}{n} \right) s_{\overline{n}|} C_0 + \left[\left(\frac{1}{2}c_{n'} - \frac{1}{n} \right) s_{\overline{n}|} + e_n c_{n'} \right] C_n \right\}$$

[5] The application of these formulas is illustrated in Chapter XXVI, § 2, dealing with American and Foreign Power.

In the foregoing equation, C_n needs to be expressed in terms of C_o, thus:

$$(120) \qquad z = \frac{A_n}{A_o}$$

$$= \frac{l_n C_n}{l_o C_o}, \text{ by equation (40a)}$$

$$(122) \qquad C_n = z C_o \frac{l_o}{l_n}$$

Substituting the foregoing value for C_n in (118c), we get

$$(123)$$
$$V_o = C_o v^n \left\{ s_{\overline{n}|} \left(\tfrac{1}{2} c_o + \frac{1}{n} \right) + z \frac{l_o}{l_n} \left[s_{\overline{n}|} \left(\tfrac{1}{2} c_{n'} - \frac{1}{n} \right) + e_n c_{n'} \right] \right\}$$

CHAPTER XIV

OPTION WARRANTS AND CONVERTIBLE ISSUES

I.   OPTION WARRANTS

Option warrants and conversion privileges affect the value of stocks of growing companies because they result in the assignment of a portion of future dividends to security holders other than those now owning the common shares. These privileges add nothing to the investment value of an enterprise as a whole, of course, and likewise they subtract nothing, for, according to the Law of the Conservation of Investment Value, cited in Chapter V, § 10, no change merely in the capitalization of a company can alter the intrinsic value of all its securities added together. Hence whatever value passes to the option warrants or the conversion privilege must come out of the common stock.

The relation between the prices of option warrants and common shares is complicated, and the amount of money required to exercise the warrant is by no means the only variable that determines the spread between them. The size of the present dividend on the common stock, the current rate of interest, and the length of time that is expected to elapse before the dividend increases to a specified figure (to be defined below) are other variables also to be considered, as the following analysis shows:

Let

S = subscription price at which option-warrant holders may buy new stock

M_c = market price of common already outstanding

M_w = market price of warrants

$(M_c - M_w)$ = spread in price between common and warrants

n = number of years until warrants are to be exercised

κ_1 = actual dividend now

κ_n = actual dividend at time of exercise of warrant

y_s = yield on subscription price when warrant is exercised

Then

(124) $\qquad y_s = \dfrac{\kappa_n}{S}$, by definition

The spread between the price of the common and the warrants can never be *more* than the cost of exercising the warrants, for if it were, arbitragers could buy warrants, exercise them with additional cash, and sell the new shares of common at a profit. Therefore we may write

(125) $\qquad\qquad\qquad (M_c - M_w) \leqq S$

Likewise, the spread between the price of the common and the warrants can never be *less* than the sum on which the current dividend affords a fair return, for if it were, warrant holders could sell their warrants, buy the same number of shares of common stock, and receive a better-than-normal return on the additional cash invested. Therefore we may write

(126) $\qquad \dfrac{\kappa_1}{i} \leqq (M_c - M_w)$, or $\dfrac{\kappa_1}{(M_c - M_w)} \leqq i$

A combination of (125) and (126) gives the upper and lower limits for the spread between the common and the warrants, thus:

(127) $\qquad\qquad\qquad \dfrac{\kappa_1}{i} \leqq (M_c - M_w) \leqq S$

To determine the exact size of the spread, one more datum is needed, namely, the length of time that is expected to elapse before the dividend becomes large enough to justify exercise of the option warrant. In other words, in order to determine $(M_c - M_w)$ it is necessary to specify a value for the variable n, as well as for the variables κ_1, i, and S. If n is now given, we may take note of the fact that anyone who holds the common shares for n years and receives dividends from them ought to fare the same, no better and no worse, as one who holds the warrants for n years and at the same time keeps enough money invested elsewhere at compound interest to amount to the full subscription price by the time the exercise of the option warrant is finally justified. In other words,

$$(128a) \qquad M_w + Sv^n = M_c - \sum_{t=1}^{t=n} \pi_t v^t$$

Thus the total outlay of the warrant buyer will be the cost of his warrant *plus* the present worth of his future subscription, while the total outlay of the stock buyer will be the cost of his common *less* the present worth of his dividends during the interval of n years.

Transposing in (128a), we get the following formula for the difference in price, or the spread, between the common and the warrants:

$$(128b) \qquad (M_c - M_w) = Sv^n + \sum_{t=1}^{t=n} \pi_t v^t$$

If no dividends are expected during the interval of n years, (128b) becomes

$$(128c) \qquad (M_c - M_w) = Sv^n, \text{ if } \sum_{t=1}^{t=n} \pi_t = 0$$

The foregoing formula gives us a substitute value to insert in (127) in case $\kappa_1 = 0$.

When the general problem of warrants and share prices

presents itself in another way, with $(M_c - M_w)$ appearing as a known instead of an unknown, it is necessary to use equation (128b) differently, and solve it for n instead of for $(M_c - M_w)$. In this way it is possible to determine the number of years which the market expects to elapse before exercise of the warrants becomes justified. In order to transpose equation (128b) in such a way as to make it an explicit formula for n, proceed as follows:

(128b) $$(M_c - M_w) = Sv^n + \sum_{t=1}^{t=n} \pi_t v^t$$

$$Sv^n = M_c - M_w - \sum_{t=1}^{t=n} \pi_t v^t$$

$$v^n = \frac{M_c - M_w - \sum_{t=1}^{t=n} \pi_t v^t}{S}$$

$$n \log v = \log\left(M_c - M_w - \sum_{t=1}^{t=n} \pi_t v^t \right) - \log S$$

(128d) $$n = \frac{\log\left(M_c - M_w - \sum_{t=1}^{t=n} \pi_t v^t \right) - \log S}{\log v}$$

Q. E. F.

Whenever no dividends are expected from the common stock before the warrants are exercised, equation (128d) takes on the simpler form [1]

(128e) $$n = \frac{\log (M_c - M_w) - \log S,}{\log v} \text{ when } \pi_t \underset{t=n}{\overset{t=n}{}} = 0$$

[1] Application of this formula is illustrated in Chapter XXV, § 12, dealing with United Corporation warrants.

Equation (128b) may also be transposed in such a way as to show the fair value of the warrants when the price of common itself is given, thus:

(128f) $$M_w = M_c - \sum_{t=1}^{t=n} \pi_t v^t - Sv^n$$

Examination of this equation shows, just as one would expect, that the warrants would be worth nothing if their exercise price was too high. It also shows that a liberal dividend policy makes the warrants worth less, so long as the dividend does not reach the critical size where it justifies the exercise of the warrants because

(129) $$\frac{\kappa}{S} \geqq i$$

Equation (128f) also shows that the more distant the time when the warrant is to be exercised, the greater its value; and the higher the rate of interest, the greater its value; in other words the larger n or i is, or the smaller v is, the larger M_w will be.

A company can injure its warrant holders by giving frequent rights to stockholders, because rights have somewhat the same effect as stock dividends in depressing the price of a stock. Unless warrant holders are protected by contract against the effects of such a policy, they are likely to find their options turning out to be worthless. A company cannot hurt its warrant holders by any cash-dividend policy used alone, however; for if an effort is continually made to keep the book value of the common down by means of large cash disbursements, the resulting high dividend rate will cause the stock to sell at a price where the warrants can be exercised at a profit. The critical value of this dividend is given in equation (129) above.

When warrants are outstanding and threaten to dilute

the equity of the common stockholder eventually, the common stock itself may be evaluated by means of the following device:

Let

$$N_c = \text{number of shares of common}$$
$$N_w = \text{number of warrants}$$

(130) $M_c + \dfrac{N_w}{N_c} M_w = M_o = \text{market price of one "unit"}$

This amounts to saying that if a "unit" is taken consisting of one share of common and a proportionate number of warrants, the company may be treated as though the warrants had never been issued; and then the value of the "unit" may be found by our usual methods, just as though it were an ordinary common share. This done, the values of M_c and M_w may next be found by solving (128b) and (130) as simultaneous equations.

An incorrect method of appraisal is used by some investment analysts· in dealing with warrants; their method consists in assuming that all the warrants are exercised for the cash *at the start*, and that total earnings are increased by the amount of interest that could be earned on this cash, while earnings per share are reduced at the same time through the increase in the number of shares. The incorrectness of this method lies in its failure to recognize that investors purposely *postpone* the exercise of warrants, and increase thereby the dividends payable to present stockholders in the interim.

Now that the question of the receipt of cash by a company when its warrants are exercised has been raised, the reader may well ask what disposition of the cash by the company is contemplated under our own assumptions. The answer is that this cash is to be paid out again at once by the corporation as an extra dividend, with the result that the holder of one unit as defined above will receive back exactly what he paid in. No well-managed company would wait on the caprice of its warrant holders to put its financial house in order;[2] any well-managed company would already have the right amount of cash on hand, and the optimum funded debt outstanding. Hence further cash would be of more use to its stockholders than to itself,[3] and would be paid out again in dividends.

The foregoing remarks on warrants apply to perpetual options with unchanging subscription prices, and must be modified for options of limited life or for scale options.

2. CONVERSION PRIVILEGES

The conversion point for a convertible bond or preferred stock is found in much the same way as the exercise point for an option warrant. Following the method of the preceding section, let

$$(131) \qquad y_b = \frac{\beta}{M_b}$$

where

$$y_b = \text{yield of a bond}^{4}$$
$$\beta = \text{bond coupon per annum}$$
$$M_b = \text{market price of the bond}$$

For the sake of simplicity, let us assume that conversion is permitted perpetually, and on a "share for share" basis. Then the bondholder may at any time exchange his coupon annuity, $\sum_{t=1}^{t=\infty} \beta$, for a dividend annuity, $\sum_{t=1}^{t=\infty} \pi_t$. Whenever

---

[2] Cf. Chapter XXV, § 12, dealing with the option warrants issued by the United Corporation.

[3] Except perhaps in the case of an investment trust.

[4] The income yield is here meant, not the yield to maturity. Strictly speaking, the analysis applies only to a perpetual bond or a preferred stock.

the common dividend exceeds the bond coupon, conversion may be justified. Thus if

$$\pi_t > \beta$$

with the result that

$$(132) \qquad \frac{\pi_t}{M_b} > \frac{\beta}{M_b} = y_b$$

then the alternative yield, $\dfrac{\pi_t}{M_b}$, exceeds y_b, and conversion is justified if the difference in yield is enough to compensate for the increase in risk.

Arbitrage will always prevent the bonds from selling *below* the stock, because it is always possible to buy bonds and convert them for delivery against stock sold short. Likewise, other considerations will sometimes prevent the bonds from selling *above* the stock, for if dividends are safe and exceed coupons by a large amount, the lower yield afforded by the bonds will then tend to keep the bonds down to a parity with the stock.[5]

To find the value of any given convertible bond we must ascertain the law of its dividends. For the sake of simplicity let us assume that the bond and the stock into which it is convertible are each of $100 par, that conversion is on a dollar-for-dollar basis, and that the number of bonds is the same as the number of shares of stock. Diagram 11 shows the facts to be represented.

Here

π = dividend which could be paid if no bonds at all were outstanding

π_b = dividend (coupon) actually to be paid on bonds until conversion takes place

π_c = dividend to be paid on stock

[5] As illustrated by the market action of American Rolling Mill convertible 4½'s in the early months of 1930, when the high for the bonds was 134⅝ and for

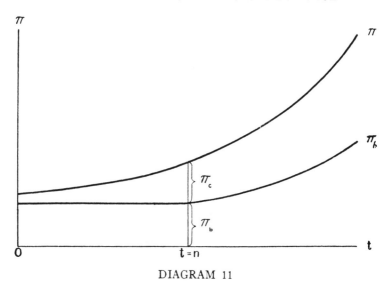

DIAGRAM 11

THE ANNUITY OF PAYMENTS FROM THE CONVERTIBLE BONDS OF A
GROWING COMPANY

The following equation will hold true:

(133) $\pi = \pi_b + \pi_c$, or $\pi_c = \pi - \pi_b$

The law of coupons and dividends for the convertible bond
is then as follows:

For the interval $t \leqq n$,

(134) $\pi_b = \beta = $ a constant

and for the interval $t \geqq n$

$\pi_b = \pi_c = \frac{1}{2}\pi$

It is here assumed that the bondholder does not delay in
converting for fear that the stock is not as safe as the bonds.

Once the annuity of coupons or dividends on the bonds
has been determined as above it becomes a simple matter

the stock 34, equivalent to 136 for the bonds. (Unless the two sales were made
at exactly the same time, the year's high for the two related issues would not be
expected to be exactly the same.)

to set down the equations for the value of the bonds and stock. The equations are as follows:

$$(135) \qquad V_b = \sum_{t=1}^{t=n} \beta v^t + \sum_{t=n+1}^{t=\infty} \tfrac{1}{2}\pi_t v^t$$

$$(136) \qquad V_c = \sum_{t=1}^{t=n} (\pi_t - \beta) v^t + \sum_{t=n+1}^{t=\infty} \tfrac{1}{2}\pi_t v^t$$

The conversion of a convertible bond, unlike the exercise of an option warrant, never proves inconvenient to the issuing company, because the conversion of a bond, unlike the subscription to new stock, never brings new money into a company. In practice, moreover, the company can often take the initiative away from its own security-holders, provided its convertible bonds are callable. If the company wishes to force conversion, it can call its bonds in small installments, provided its stock is selling high enough to put the market price of its bonds above their redemption price. To finance this forced conversion, only a small revolving fund — to guard against the possibility of a break in the stock market — is needed, because all bondholders will prefer to convert their bonds into stock rather than take cash for less than the market value of their holdings. And to avoid the need of any cash at all, the company can have the operation underwritten by investment bankers. The issuance of convertible bonds, therefore, is a good way for a company to go about getting rid of its funded debt.[6] Since such bonds go up as high as the stock, but do not go

[6] A good example of a company which in 1936 was reducing its funded debt with very little cash outlay, merely by calling its convertible bonds in small installments, is the American Rolling Mill Co., which called $1,000,000 of its convertible 4½'s of 1945 on December 23, 1935, $1,500,000 on February 10, 1936, and $5,000,000 on March 30, 1936. Although the total issue amounted to $25,000,000, almost no cash at all would be required for its elimination if the market price of the common stayed above 25⅝, with the call price at 102½, and the conversion rate at 40 shares of stock for each $1000 bond.

down below par as easily, they are attractive to investors seeking a speculative security involving little risk. The common stockholders, however, if they wish to avoid the dilution of their equity when such bonds are issued, should insist on the right to subscribe to the new issue before it is sold to the public.

3.   OPTIONS AS AFFECTED BY UNCERTAINTY

In the foregoing discussion of option warrants and convertible bonds, no mention has been made of the important factor of uncertainty, yet uncertainty is always present in any forecast of a company's future growth and dividend-paying power. Hence it is not strictly correct to use a *single* dividend annuity, instead of a *variety* of possible dividend annuities, in appraising the value of a convertible bond, an option warrant, or a common stock outstanding in the presence of such a bond or warrant. To explain the significance of uncertainty as such, there is needed a probability curve showing the estimated likelihood of all the various possible dividend annuities; a curve of this sort is shown in Diagram 12.

On this probability curve, the present worth V_o of the future dividends payable on a "unit" of common stock and option warrants, or common stock and convertible bonds, is given by the abscissa, while the likelihood $f(V_o)$ of such a present worth is given by the ordinate. In general

$$(1a) \qquad V_o = \sum_{t=1}^{t=\infty} \pi_t v^t = \text{investment value of one "unit."}$$

Let us use the symbol $\bar{V}_o$ to represent the mean value of V_o; the vertical line through $\bar{V}_o$ on the diagram will then divide the area under the curve in half. Whatever the capitalization of the particular company whose possibilities of growth are under consideration, and whatever the exercise price of its warrants or the conversion price of its bonds, there will always be some critical value of V_o which will just barely make it worth while to exercise the warrants or convert the bonds; let us call this critical value V_o'. The vertical line through V_o' will then divide the area under

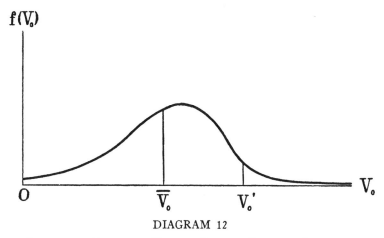

DIAGRAM 12

the curve into two parts, and the ratio of one part to the other will give the likelihood of recapitalization. Thus the likelihood may be 1 to 9, for instance, or 1 out of 10, in other words. If V_o' lies to the left of $\bar{V}_o$, the chances may be said to be better than even for recapitalization; if to the right, less than even.

In the ordinary investigations of value, it is a satisfactory approximation to neglect the *range* of possible dividend annuities, and to employ instead a single annuity, usually represented [7] by $\bar{V}_o$, but when optional privileges are outstanding, such a precedure is incorrect, for the option holder always makes the choice which he thinks will

[7] Cf. Chapter V, § 8.

favor him at the expense of the common stockholder. Therefore, if a common stockholder consents to the issue of option warrants or convertible bonds by his company, he does so with the knowledge that he is letting someone else bet "heads I win much, tails I lose little," against him. For if the company turns out to be a great success, the original stockholder's equity will be diluted by an increase in the number of shares outstanding, whereas if it proves to be a disappointment, the option holders will lose only the cost of their options.

In Diagram 12, if V_o' lies to the right of $\bar{V}_o$, the exercise of the warrants will not *usually* be justified, yet the option need not always go to waste, because sometimes the unexpected may happen.[8] Hence if the value of the common stock were to be computed on the basis of $\bar{V}_o$ alone in this case, with no allowance being made for the possibility of conversions or subscriptions, too high a value for the common stock would be obtained. Likewise, if V_o' lies to the left of $\bar{V}_o$, the exercise of the warrants would usually be justified, yet the option need not always prove of value, because sometimes the unexpected may happen. Hence if the value of the common stock were to be computed on the basis of $\bar{V}_o$ alone, with no allowance for the possibility of *no* conversions or subscriptions, too low a value would be obtained. And whatever gives too low a value for the common, gives too high a value for the option, and vice versa. Consequently whatever value for $\bar{V}_o$ is used in the calculations, allowance must also be made for the favorable or unfavorable position of V_o'.

With all of these considerations the market itself has long been familiar in a general way, and none of them are

---

[8] This same argument has been applied in Chapter VI, § 3, to explain the value of a stock which could pay no dividends because all of its earnings were required for reinvestment.

here claimed to be in any sense new discoveries. Yet it should be remembered that it is quite as much the function of science to explain the familiar as to discover the unknown. Concerning this point, we are reminded of Marshall's comments on the history of the theory of capital, as follows:

The aid which economic science has given towards understanding the part played by capital in our industrial system is solid and substantial; but it has made no startling discoveries. Everything of importance which is now known to economists has long been acted upon by able business men, though they may not have been able to express their knowledge clearly, or even accurately.[9]

[9] Alfred Marshall, *Principles of Economics*, 8th ed. (London: Macmillan, 1922), p. 580.

CHAPTER XV

A CHAPTER FOR SKEPTICS

So different from the old rule-of-thumb methods are the formulas of appraisal derived in the foregoing chapters that the new methods are likely to be criticized on several grounds. In this chapter, therefore, an attempt will be made to answer some of the objections that are likely to arise.

I. ARE THE FORMULAS TOO INTRICATE?

First, it may be objected that the new formulas are much more intricate than the old. The answer to this objection is that the old-fashioned methods of appraisal in reality took cognizance of all the factors which give such intricacy to the new formulas, but the old methods did so implicitly, whereas the new methods do so explicitly. In the past, growth, leverage, and so forth, were all allowed for by a hit-or-miss adjustment of the price-earnings ratio. Now it is proposed to allow for each of these by the introduction of specific parameters in the formulas. Thus intricacy in the formulas is merely a sign of frankness in the procedure.

For computing the relative values of two or more stocks, rather than the absolute value of a single stock as heretofore, the new methods will again be found superior to the old, because the new formulas contain a separate parameter for each point of comparison, and thus allow each element of strength or weakness in every security undergoing comparison to be given its proper and logical weight in the final answer. Consequently, if one is merely asking whether a particular security is "selling out of line," there is no better way to ascertain the answer than to apply the new formulas.

In the science known as the Mathematics of Finance, it has long been the practice to employ algebra in the making of bond tables and the calculation of depreciation; now it would seem to be time greatly to enlarge the scope of that science so as to make it include methods for dealing with *all* kinds of securities, under *all* kinds of conditions. In the past this science could handle only bonds, and even bonds it could not handle if the purchasing power of money or the rate of interest was expected to change; now it is desirable to equip it to handle stocks, warrants, and convertible issues, as well as bonds, and to handle bonds also when inflation or deflation impends or when interest rates seem likely to rise or fall.

2.   ARE LONG-RANGE FORECASTS TOO UNCERTAIN?

Second, it may be objected that no one can possibly look with certainty so far into the future as the new methods require and that the new methods of appraisal must therefore be inferior to the old. But do the new methods really require any more foresight than the old? How could anyone using the old methods explain the market price of a stock except by recourse to some long-range forecast that implied either the continuation of present dividends or earnings, or an increase or decrease therein? Why should General Motors, for instance, if appraised by the old methods, deserve to sell at fourteen times current earnings, let us say, instead of at four, forty, or four hundred times these earnings, unless people expected average earnings many years hence to be much the same as now? Clearly the old methods required just as much foresight as the new.

But is good forecasting, after all, so completely impossible? Does not experience show that careful forecasting — or foresight as it is called when it turns out to be correct — is very often so nearly right as to be extremely helpful to the investor? And is not careful forecasting a practice in which prudent and successful investors habitually indulge, regardless of what methods of appraisal they employ? Therefore the difficulty of making good forecasts cannot fairly be cited as a drawback to the use of the new methods in place of the old.

Those who feel it unsound to use long-range forecasts under any circumstances may still use the new formulas in another way, a way that was almost impossible with the old methods. They may transpose the new formulas and use the actual market price as a datum, instead of seeking the theoretical investment value as an answer. Then with the transposed formulas they may deduce the particular rate of growth, the particular duration of growth, or the like, that is implied by the actual market price, and see in this way whether the prevailing price is reasonable or not. Thus the formulas become a touchstone for absurdity.[1]

But even if quantitative application of the Theory of Investment Value were impossible for lack of reliable data on the future of given corporations, the new science would still be no worse off than many other branches of Economics, such as the Theory of Value for ordinary goods and services, which lacks data on the elasticities of demand and supply but is never discarded as nonsense on that account.

In any inquiry, the correct procedure is first to form a hypothesis, then seek out the needed data. Without the hypothesis, how should we know what data to look for, what constants to determine, what properties to measure? Precisely such guidance as this is what the Theory of Investment Value offers. It shows us what is relevant and why. When in Book II such stocks as General Motors and

[1] An illustration of such an inverted use of the formulas is to be found in Chapter XXVI.

United States Steel are discussed, an attempt will be made to find the relevant data for each by making a careful forecast of the future of each corporation. But the merit of these studies will not depend primarily on the accuracy of the data, for the studies are only by way of illustration and the data are required only to pass the test of plausibility. If it should turn out in any particular case that the data were inaccurate and the estimate of the investment value of a given security was wrong, that would not disprove the Theory of Investment Value, any more than it would disprove the science of Statics if engineers used inaccurate data on the strength of materials and built a bridge that collapsed. If the practical man, whether investment analyst or engineer, fails to use the right data in his formulas, it is no one's fault but his own. And when he finds the right data, he must then use the best formulas that are known. That is what this book seeks to supply.

3. IS THE THEORY TOO IMPRACTICAL?

Third, it may be objected that the use of these formulas is not the best way to make money, and that it is more profitable to spend one's time studying the business cycle. The answer to this objection is that this book is not intended as a code of maxims for speculators, but as a treatise on economic theory for scientists. Not wealth, but understanding, is its object, not hygiene, but physiology, its subject. The Theory of Investment Value shows how traders would act in the stock market if they were perfectly rational and farseeing, just as the Theory of Monopoly shows how extortionists would act in the commodity market if in that case also men were perfectly rational and farseeing. Gradually as men do become more intelligent and better informed, market prices should draw closer to the values given by our theory. In the meantime, it will be found that this book throws much light on prices as they actually exist today. Furthermore, in the case of certain very rich investors, it will be found that their buying and selling tend to conform exactly to the Theory of Investment Value, because for them surtaxes make it less profitable to speculate on the business cycle than to hold for the long pull.

The Theory of Investment Value, like the rest of Economics, is a science that would be of interest for its own sake even if it had no practical applications. Just as it would be of interest to understand the workings of money as a medium of exchange, even if we did not wish to manipulate the price level, and just as it would be of interest to understand the balance of trade, even if we did not wish to control imports and exports, so also it would be of interest to know what determines the real worth of stocks and bonds, even if we did not wish to make money in the stock market. Hence, even if the Theory of Investment Value were wholly without commercial use — which it is not — it would still be no worse off than the Theory of Evolution, or the sciences of Philology and Astronomy.

4.   IS THE THEORY CORROBORATED BY EXPERIENCE?

Fourth, it may be asked, by those who are more hopeful than skeptical, if the true values for stocks as given by the new theory are usually verified later by the action of the market itself. The answer to this question is that such "verification" sometimes happens, sometimes not, merely according to chance. There is no theoretical reason, however, to expect corroboration or verification. After all, if the market makes a wrong estimate of true value today, why should it be expected to do better tomorrow? By tomorrow, today's facts may be more widely understood, of course; but by tomorrow new facts may be interjected into the situation, with the result that a new estimate of true worth will be needed and a further correction of price will be called for. Thus the market may find itself as far away from a logical value tomorrow as today. But even if no new facts appear, the market may still refuse to move in the right direction between today and tomorrow. Since market price depends on popular opinion, and since the public is more emotional than logical, it is foolish to expect a relentless convergence of market price toward investment value.[2] Corroboration of estimates by subsequent market action, therefore, ought not to be expected. After all, investment value and market price are two quite different things.

5. CONCLUSION

The wide changes in stock prices during the last eight years, when prices fell as much as 80 or 90 per cent from their 1929 peaks only to recover much of their decline later, are a serious indictment of past practice in Investment Analysis. Had there been any general agreement among analysts themselves concerning the proper criteria of value, such enormous fluctuations should not have occurred, because the long-run prospects for dividends have not in fact changed as much as prices have. Prices have been based too much on current earning power, too little on long-run dividend-paying power. Stock prices, in fact, have moved more violently than almost anything else in the business cycle. Is not one cause of the past volatility of stocks the lack of a sound Theory of Investment Value? Since this volatility of stocks helps in turn to make the business cycle itself more severe, may not advances in Investment Analysis prove a real help in reducing the damage done by the cycle?

[2] See also Chapter III, § 5, last paragraph.

PART III

THE ECONOMICS OF INTEREST AND DIVIDENDS

CHAPTER XVI

THE SOURCE OF INTEREST AND DIVIDENDS

If the investment value of a stock is equal by definition to the present worth of its future dividends, as developed at length in the foregoing section of this book (Part II), then the problem of evaluation reduces itself to the task of estimating future interest rates [1] on the one hand and future dividends on the other. Accordingly, the following section of this book (Part III) will be devoted to the Economics of Interest and Dividends, in the hope that the established principles of Economics may be made to throw fresh light on the forces which set the rate of interest and determine the amount of dividends.

For ease in exposition, the economic principles involved will be taken up under the following chapter headings:

> The Source of Interest and Dividends
> Taxes and Socialism
> Where Is the Interest Rate Determined?

I. INTEREST, RENT, BUSINESS PROFITS, AND MONOPOLY GAINS

Some people speak of interest and dividends as though they corresponded to the shares in distribution which the economist calls Interest and Business Profits, in the same way as ordinary wages and land rent correspond to the Wages and Rent of the economist. Such a treatment of interest and dividends would seem to be incorrect, for it is clear that stockholders in receiving dividends may get a return consisting of Interest and Rent as well as of Busi-

---

[1] The connection between *future* short-term interest rates and the *present* long-term rate has already been developed in Chapter V, § 4, and Chapter X.

ness Profits, and that part of Business Profits may be distributed to the hired managers as salaries or bonuses, or be garnered by speculators in the stock market in a commuted form when stocks rise in price.

The correct view would seem to be that a successful corporation, after paying for materials and labor, has left a gross profit in the nature of Quasi-Rent, from which it can accumulate a reserve for depreciation, depletion, and obsolescence, and from which it can pay taxes to the government, interest to its bondholders, dividends to its stockholders, and bonuses to its managers. This Quasi-Rent is likewise the income from which true Rent, Interest, and Business Profits are paid, but the division of the income by financial and by economic categories need not necessarily coincide, and hardly ever does. In particular, the amount of interest going to the bondholders depends on the specific contract made with them, and not on what the economist would call the true Interest on the total investment. If the bonded debt is small or the coupon rate low, then there remains a part of the Interest available for payment to the stockholders. Thus, in the case of the United States Steel Corporation, for instance, which in normal times pays good dividends to its shareholders, the bondholders get only a small part of the Interest on the Corporation's plant, and the stockholders get the rest. The dividend to the stockholders also includes Rent from the Corporation's land and natural resources owned, and Business Profits, if any, from its new devices and methods. An element of Monopoly Gain, in the case of this particular corporation, may also be present, but to what extent it is hard to say.

2. COMPOSITE QUASI-RENT

The Quasi-Rent earned by a corporation as a whole is derived from the many small quasi-rents of its multitudinous machines and appliances. Thus in the case of the United States Steel Corporation, for instance, each blast furnace, each coke oven, each open hearth, each rolling mill, earns a quasi-rent of its own when operating. Since some furnaces and mills are newer or better located than others, some will secure more quasi-rent than others. In boom times most of the equipment — whether efficient or inefficient — is put into operation, because prices for steel are then so high that even the oldest and most poorly located furnaces and mills can be made to yield a quasi-rent. In slack times only a part of the equipment, the more efficient part, is used. Because the demand curve at that time has fallen, prices too may be lower.

In the particular case of the iron and steel industry, however, the normal working of demand and cost is obscured, as regards pig iron, by the heavy expense of starting up a merchant furnace; and as regards steel products, by conditions of monopolistic competition.[2] Hence we should do better to turn to the textile industry, where operations are very flexible and competition is thoroughgoing, to find an illustration of our theory in its pure form. Diagram 13 shows how equilibrium is reached in the textile industry. The curve D_oD_o' represents the demand curve for the entire industry in boom times, the curve D_1D_1' in slack times. P_o is the boom price for the product, P_1 the slack price. S_oS_o' is the supply curve in boom times, S_1S_1' in slack times. In the steel industry, which digs its raw materials out of the ground,[3] the supply curve rises in good times only enough to offset whatever increase in wages is granted, but in the cotton-textile industry, which buys its raw materials in a speculative market, the supply curve reflects material as well as labor costs, and responds to the influence of the

[2] Cf. Edward Chamberlin, *The Theory of Monopolistic Competition* (Cambridge: Harvard University Press, 1933).

[3] With the principal exception of scrap.

weather on the size and price of the prospective cotton crop as well as to the influence of the amount of unemployment on the rate of wages. Each of the rectangles that together make up the area under the supply curve represents

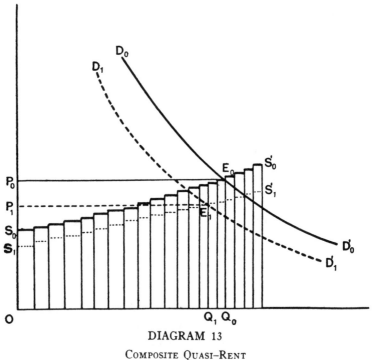

DIAGRAM 13

COMPOSITE QUASI-RENT

an individual lot of equipment, such as a group of spinning frames and looms in the case of the textile industry; the base of the rectangles is the capacity in yards per day, and the altitude the prime cost [4] per yard, for the machinery

---

[4] Prime cost includes only those outlays which are added when a new piece of business is taken on, and which cease when it is finished. Cf. Alfred Marshall, *Principles of Economics*, p. 360, where he says that prime cost includes "nothing but the [money] cost of the raw material used in making the commodity and the wages of that part of the labor spent on it which is paid by the hour or the

in question. The roughly triangular area $P_oE_oS_o$ or $P_1E_1S_1$ is the quasi-rent received by the industry as a whole at any given time. The diagram implies that the *marginal* group of machines earns no quasi-rent — not even something for depreciation — but that the intra-marginal machines earn anything from a handsome return on their cost down to a sum barely enough to make it worth while to use them until they have to be discarded. When the demand curve in the diagram shifts upwards, more spindles and looms are started up; when it shifts downwards, more are shut down.

In deciding whether to keep a certain group of spindles and looms in operation, a mill treasurer might talk as follows about a contract currently being advertised for bids:

"According to my cost-accounting records, my over-all cost of producing this particular kind of cloth is so-and-so with cotton at present prices. To break even on this contract I must bid not less than such-and-such a figure. But times are bad, hence if I do not take this business I may get nothing else to keep my machines going, and then I shall lose so-and-so many dollars a day merely for taxes, interest, and depreciation. Is it not better, therefore, to accept the business at a small loss than to shut down at a greater loss? Yes, indeed! Consequently the problem resolves itself into guessing what is the best price I can try for and still not lose the business to one of my competitors who also wants

---

piece and the extra wear-and-tear of plant. This is the special cost which a manufacturer has in view, when his works are not fully employed, and he is calculating the lowest price at which it will be worth his while to accept an order, irrespectively of any effect that his action may have in spoiling the market for future orders, and trade being slack at the time."

Arbitrary write-downs of plant and machinery as a result of receiverships and reorganizations do not reduce *prime* cost, because interest and depreciation do not enter into prime cost as defined above.

For any given state of business activity, the higher the price, the less the sales, as shown by the shape of the demand curve; but if activity improves, the demand curve shifts to the right, and causes both sales and prices to rise.

to minimize his own losses. Such being the case, it is up to me to guess what my competitor's cost is, and what sort of machinery he has available for use on this contract. If I think the competition is going to be severe, I will name a figure that will reduce my losses hardly at all, because it will at least keep my organization together, but if I think that few of my competitors have machinery as good as mine not already engaged on other contracts, I will shave my over-all costs only a little.

"If times were good, of course, I would try to get a price well above my over-all costs, and would seek the biggest profit I could get without losing the business to some one else."

3.   OBSOLESCENCE

If a new and very efficient piece of equipment is built, a place for it in the supply curve in Diagram 13 must be made by crowding all higher-cost equipment to the right, causing a permanent change in the shape of the supply curve. In the iron and steel industry, for instance, as one new furnace after another is built, each usually more efficient than its predecessors, it comes to pass eventually that all of the old furnaces become crowded so far to the right in the diagram as to lie beyond the demand curve and become extra-marginal. This process of moving the supply curve to the right causes the price to fall step by step,[5] with the result that gradually the quasi-rent earned by any given furnace becomes less and less until it vanishes altogether. This gradual decline in quasi-rent from year to year is foreseen, of course, by the entrepreneurs, and allowed for from the very beginning. They calculate as best they can on a falling annuity of quasi-rents, and regulate their original investment accordingly, realizing that from these dimin-

---

[5] Except as prevented by monopolistic control of prices.

ishing quasi-rents they must accumulate a depreciation or obsolescence fund sufficient to repay the principal sunk in the investment, and must also get Interest and Business Profits on their venture.

The steady shift of the supply curve to the right, as a

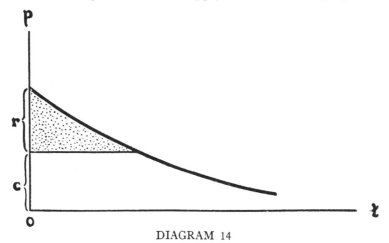

DIAGRAM 14

THE DECLINE IN QUASI-RENT CAUSED BY INVENTION

result of the invention and construction of more and more efficient machines, causes the price, as determined by the intersection of the demand and supply curves, to fall with the passage of time in somewhat the manner shown by the time chart in Diagram 14.

In this chart, time in years is measured on the horizontal axis, and price on the vertical axis. If c is the prime cost for any given machine, p the selling price, and r the quasi-rent, then

$$p - c = r$$

As p falls with the passage of time t, r declines until it reaches zero, after which time the machine from which it is derived ceases to be used any longer. The shaded area represents the annuity of quasi-rents earned by the machine during its entire lifetime. In equilibrium the present worth of this annuity should equal the cost of the machine.[6]

As the quasi-rent from an existing machine comes in year by year, part of this income, if dividends are to continue indefinitely, must be set aside and reinvested in a new and better machine whose quasi-rent shall replace that of the old machine when the old machine has become obsolete because it cannot produce cheaply enough. In the case of a large business, reinvestment in new machines will begin little by little before the old machines are wholly obsolete, and in due course the company will come to own a series of machines of all grades of newness, each earning a different quasi-rent according to its age and efficiency. If it is the aim of the management to draw off a constant sum yearly with which to pay a steady dividend, and if, as usually happens, the initial quasi-rents earned by new machines tend to be less than were the initial quasi-rents from the old, then the management must plan to increase the total number of its machines as time goes on. That such a decline in initial quasi-rents is likely, the upward concavity of the price curve $p = f(t)$ in Diagram 14 would imply.

Just what rate of reinvestment is necessary to yield uniform dividends is an unsolved theoretical problem in the economics of investment, but we shall try to throw some light on it in an empirical way when we come to the study of United States Steel in a later chapter.[7]

The prevailing notion that industries must become less profitable as their rate of growth declines will not bear critical examination. If the slackening of growth is a thing foreseen, and puts in its apearance slowly enough for all

[6] Cf. Marshall, *Principles*, footnote on page 424.
[7] Chapter XXII, §§ 3 and 13.

to understand and plan upon, then profits should hold up nevertheless, for entrepreneurs, in adding new capacity, will always try to estimate the useful life of their investment, and will take into account not only the savings offered by improved designs but also the length of time before these new designs will themselves be outmoded. If demand is expanding but slowly, then entrepreneurs can feel that still better machines will not be installed as soon by competitors as if the market were growing by leaps and bounds.

This problem of reinvestment against competitive obsolescence does not arise in the case of outright monopolies like the utilities, however, because the law permits the utilities to adjust their rates in relation to the demand in such a way as to secure a "fair return on a fair value." Legally the railroads are accorded the same privilege, but in practice they have not been able to devise a rate schedule that will produce the allowed return, because it would be more than the traffic could bear. Their task has been made harder by the loss of three fourths of their passenger traffic to the automobile, and by the fact that in hiring labor they have had to deal with trade unions whose monopolistic strength is equal to that of the railroads themselves.

The utility and rail issues between them probably represent more capital goods than all the industrial issues put together; hence in this book we are justified in devoting as much space as we do to formulas that apply mainly to legal monopolies.

4.   CUT-THROAT COMPETITION

A great many people believe that corporate earning power can be retained only by self-restraint in competitive price cutting; they see nothing in the organization of production itself to insure *automatically* some measure of profit no matter how free the competition. In this view they are wrong, however; for nearly every company tends to earn a quasi-rent on its intra-marginal equipment. The better the equipment, the more the rent. Likewise, the better the times, the more the rent. For inefficient plants, of course, operation capable of returning a new dollar for an old are impossible whenever general business gets dull, but during such times these plants close down. Their closing is the *automatic* thing that reduces supply and permits the better plants still to earn some quasi-rent. So long as business men seek day-by-day profit, and do not try to drive each other out of busines permanently even at the cost of dissipating their own quick assets, some measure of profit should accrue at all times to industry.

It should be clear from the context that the word "profit" is used loosely above to signify earnings before taxes, interest, and depreciation. The possibility that all quasi-rent may go to the tax-gatherer is not considered here, but is reserved for discussion later, in the chapter on taxes. Likewise the fate of the public utilities, or of other monopolies which cannot close down when prime costs are not covered, is not under discussion here.

5.   THE EFFECT OF HIGHER WAGES ON EARNINGS

Offhand it might seem that a rise in wages within any particular industry would surely make the industry less profitable to its owners; but careful analysis shows that such need not *always* be the case. In fact, for industries which cater to a very inelastic demand, and in which wages are the major element of costs, the reverse is often true; and a rise in wages, if it takes place uniformly throughout the entire industry, often produces an *increase* in profits. Especially is this true for the more efficient producers if their efficiency is due to the use of labor-saving machinery, because for these fortunate intra-marginal producers a rise in wages increases their competitive advantage. Since they use less labor per unit of output than their competitors, higher wages increase their competitive advantage. Although their own costs go up somewhat, their competitors' costs go up still more. While these intra-marginal producers do not normally enjoy an increase in their *volume* of business as a consequence of their improved competitive position — for a low-cost producer can usually get all the business he can handle in either good times or bad — nevertheless these favored producers should enjoy a sharp rise in the *price* of their product, because their marginal competitors will be forced to add the increase in wages to the selling price of their wares.

Even if most of the firms in the industry have both low- and high-cost equipment, a rise in wages may still prove advantageous to all of them, because the best equipment owned by each will become more profitable when selling prices are forced up enough to cover the added cost of operating marginal equipment.[8] In the end, therefore, a general wage increase throughout a single industry may benefit owners as well as workers. But such an outcome, be it remembered, will occur only if six necessary conditions are fulfilled, namely:

1. The demand must be inelastic.
2. Wages must be so much more important than raw

[8] When wages in the steel industry were increased in March 1937, some $2.00 a ton *on the average*, prices were raised about $4.00 a ton. Many people criticized this action, saying that the rise in prices was too much; but this criticism shows a failure to understand the difference between *average* and *marginal* costs. While it may be true that the rise in prices was *somewhat* excessive, nevertheless it is certainly not true that the rise should economically have been held down to the lower figure mentioned above.

For a statement of a view contrary to that expressed here, see President Roosevelt's denunciation of the rise in price of copper, steel, etc., reported in the *New York Times* for April 3, 1937, pp. 1 and 6.

materials in determining total costs that a change in wages will produce an important change in the relative costs of marginal and intra-marginal equipment.

3. The wage increase must fall on all companies in the industry and none must escape the added burden.

4. Other industries in the economic system must not nullify the gains for this particular industry by making increases in wages and selling prices on their own account, thus causing an all-round reduction in the purchasing power of money.

5. Selling prices must be determined by competition and not by monopoly or monopolistic competition,[9] because in the latter case the burden of the wage increase *may* fall on profits instead of selling prices.

6. Selling prices must be raised enough to cover the full increase in costs on the highest-cost equipment employed.

6. THE EFFECT OF SHORTER HOURS ON EARNINGS

Shorter hours, since they usually go hand in hand with higher wages per hour, have to that extent the same effect on the earnings of capital as an outright increase in wage rates. And if overtime, in addition, commands a specially high wage rate of its own, the cost of the marginal unit of output will be raised all the more, with the result that prices will be raised also, their rise usually being enough to offset nearly the entire increase in the cost of producing the last unit of output. Such a rise in prices, unless it substantially reduces the volume of sales because the demand is too elastic, will increase the profit on intra-marginal output a great deal, and may benefit the owners of the enterprise even more than the workers — all at the expense of the consumers, of course.

Even if shorter standard hours are not accompanied by

[9] Cf. Chamberlin, *Monopolistic Competition.*

overtime work, the owners may still benefit from the change if the demand is inelastic enough to keep the plants running nearly as many hours per year as formerly. Plant utilization at nearly the original rate may be achieved either by running more shifts per day in many departments or by operating more days per week during the period of usual seasonal dullness.

7. LABOR MONOPOLIES

It goes without saying that no one manufacturer could possibly benefit from granting higher wages or shorter hours if his competitors did not do likewise. And ordinarily his competitors will not do so unless forced to. Hence, ordinarily, wages in any particular industry do not rise faster than wages throughout industry in general. On special occasions, however, as in the spring of 1937, this may not be so; for if certain labor unions, such as those under the leadership of John L. Lewis and the C. I. O.,[10] win the closed shop, or otherwise succeed in monopolizing the supply of labor in a number of industries such as coal, autos, and steel, these labor unions can assure employers that *all* plants within each given industry will be forced to grant the same wage and hour concessions. Under these circumstances, each employer can feel sure of being able to pass his higher costs on to consumers, and so each can safely accede to the desires of Labor, knowing full well that the demand from consumers is so inelastic that output will not be seriously curtailed. And at the higher wage levels the low-cost producers can henceforth make even more money than before. Thus the workers always, and the owners sometimes,[11] might stand

[10] The C. I. O. unions usually embrace industries, the A. F. of L., crafts.

[11] Henry Ford even goes so far as to charge collusion between Capital and Labor to defraud consumers, but this is most unlikely. For Ford's views, see the *New York Times*, May 15, 1937, p. 1, col. 5, paragraph 11.

to gain from a labor monopoly, while the helpless public would have to pay the price.

The only protection for the public from exploitation in this way is the outlawing of labor monopolies with the same thoroughness that all other artificial [12] monopolies deserve. Not all labor unions are labor monopolies, of course, because not all unions successfully embrace their *entire* industry; but any union that does so control an entire industry must certainly be disbanded or restrained [13] if the public is not to suffer exploitation.

If the C. I. O. should grow until it included a really important fraction of the country's workers, and if it should force large increases in hourly wages, the result would be a serious increase in the price of many articles, and of the cost of living as a whole. The name "wage inflation" might well be given to the process whereby labor monopolies thus forced up wages and the general price level. Inflation of this sort could not be stopped merely by balancing the federal budget.

A rise in wages within a particular industry not accompanied by a general rise in wages throughout all industry can be achieved only by a labor monopoly within the given industry. Trade unions acquire such a monopoly by executing a closed-shop agreement with employers, and professional men by making their bar examinations, actuarial examinations, and the like, extremely difficult. For industry as a whole, however, no artificial raising of wages is possible at present, because there exists today no nationwide monopoly of labor. Any gains won by union labor now are at the expense of non-union labor, for high wage rates

---

[12] By an artificial monopoly is meant a monopoly like the old Standard Oil trust, in contrast to a natural monopoly like Consolidated Edison of New York, which latter cannot wisely be disbanded and must therefore be regulated.

[13] An example of such restraint is the unwritten law which nowadays prevents the Railroad Brotherhoods from calling a nationwide strike.

in one craft reduce employment opportunities there and force the excess labor into other occupations, thus lowering wage rates elsewhere. For industry as a whole, the return to Labor, and also the return to Capital, are determined by the general economic laws of Distribution. To upset the ratio in which Labor and Capital now share the national dividend, some federal legislation restricting the supply of labor on a great scale, as by a thirty-hour week, would be necessary. Certainly such a law would, on balance, hurt Labor at once by reducing the national dividend to be shared in, and hurt it still more in the end by reducing the opportunities for investing current savings at a profit.

Not by the struggle of social classes, but by the supply and demand for labor, is the general rate of wages determined. Wages depend mainly on the marginal productivity of labor. Contrast the views of President Roosevelt, who says, "If labor is to be a commodity in the United States, in the final analysis it means that we shall become a nation of boarding houses instead of a nation of homes." [14] Economists believe that competition between employers is fully able to keep the level of wages from collapsing, and that such competition, rather than minimum-wage laws or labor unions, is what really sustains wages today. Labor, in fact, is now, and always has been, a "commodity" in President Roosevelt's sense, ever since the passing of serfdom.

Since wages as such already absorb three fourths of the national income,[15] and since wage-earners through their ownership of savings accounts and insurance policies also receive a part of the remaining fourth of the national income, little more could be gained for Labor by encroaching

[14] Speech at Dallas, Texas, June 12, 1936, reported in the *New York Times*, June 13, p. 1, col. 1.
[15] Paul H. Douglas, *The Theory of Wages* (New York: Macmillan, 1934), chap. V.

further on the share of Capital. Even if Capital surrendered all its income, Labor would receive only 10 per cent or 15 per cent more.[16] Not industrial warfare, therefore, but increased marginal productivity of labor, bringing in its wake a larger national income for all to share in, is the real key to "the more abundant life" for the masses and the "underprivileged." The way to increase the marginal productivity of labor is to use more capital and better methods of production. Verily the saver and the inventor are Labor's best friends.

8.   COLLECTIVE BARGAINING

Organized labor is eagerly pressing for the universal adoption of collective bargaining and the closed shop. Those who now enjoy these advantages are fervently crusading for their adoption by the rest of the laboring population. How little they seem to understand on which side their own bread is really buttered!

A single union, protected by a closed-shop agreement, can exact an outrageous monopoly price from the public, but an all-inclusive group of unions would have almost no one else to exploit. In this country, to be sure, collective bargaining in industry would leave the farmers outside the monopolistic group, but in this country Labor is seeking an alliance with Agriculture in the guise of a Farmer-Labor Party. Such an alliance leaves no consumers to exploit but the owners of savings, the widows and orphans who must depend on life insurance policies, the hospitals and charitable foundations, the universities, churches, and research laboratories, and whatever income the few rich may have left after paying their taxes. Not a very promising or

---

[16] Statistics on the share of Labor in the national dividend are given in the issue for July 1936 of the *Letter* on economic conditions, published by the National City Bank of New York. The remuneration for those who are self-employed as well as those who work for wages is here included in Labor's share.

desirable field for exploitation, is it? How much shrewder it would be for the present trade unions to let well enough alone, and not seek to organize any new unions! Perhaps the realization of this fact lies behind the feud between the old American Federation of Labor and the new Committee for Industrial Organization.[17]

[17] Cf. J. R. Walsh, "A Labor Movement for the United States" in *Explorations in Economics* (New York: McGraw-Hill Book Company, Inc., 1936), pp. 292–305, esp. p. 304.

CHAPTER XVII

TAXES AND SOCIALISM

I.   TAXES AND VALUE RECEIVED

Taxes have a far-reaching effect on the value of securities, because taxes today are heavy and the tax structure is such that its burden falls mainly on the earnings of property.

But let us first ask whether these heavy taxes may not be a *quid pro quo*.[1] What does the taxpayer get for his money? Not just what he wants and no more than he wants, as in the case of goods and services bought in the competitive markets, for the taxpayer when he pays his taxes deals with a monopolist of a peculiar sort, a monopolist who forces him not only to pay a monopoly *price*, but also to buy a certain *quantity* no matter whether he needs it or not. Thus every householder, for instance, is forced to pay taxes for the support of the public schools whether he has children or not. And every corporation must likewise pay local taxes at full rates even though it never makes use of the schools. Although a corporation benefits from having its workers educated in the public schools, so do the workers themselves. There is no more real logic in expecting a corporation to educate its workers than in expecting

---

[1] Cf. President Roosevelt's Message to Congress on June 19, 1935, in which he speaks of "the widely accepted principle that taxes should be levied in proportion to ability to pay and in proportion to benefits received," and then goes on to say that "income [is] the measure of benefits. . . ." See the *New York Times*, June 20, 1935, p. 2, col. 2.

See also Alfred Marshall, "National Taxation after the War," in *After-War Problems*, ed. by W. H. Dawson (Macmillan, 1917), esp. pp. 317–324, and F. W. Taussig, *Principles of Economics* (Macmillan, 1929), chap. 68.

it to feed and clothe them. If a corporation operates in a mill town where no other industry helps to support the community, it makes little difference, to be sure, whether the corporation pays taxes for the schools directly, or pays higher wages to permit the workers to support their own schools; but if the same corporation operates in a large community alongside other industries, it may pay more or less than its fair share of taxes, depending on whether it uses much capital or little. Clearly the services offered by municipalities and paid for by taxes, while often indispensable, are nevertheless not in the same class with ordinary supplies and raw materials consumed by a corporation and paid for as prime costs of production.

In the same way, federal taxes are no *quid pro quo*. Until recently the principal use of federal revenues, directly or indirectly, has been to make war. The largest expenses of the federal government have been for the army, the navy, bonuses to the veterans, and interest on Liberty Loans. It can hardly be said that the World War was a profitable investment of the federal taxpayers' money in the sense that every taxpayer benefited in proportion to his particular contribution. In the future, another non-productive expense of the Treasury threatens to be benefits to farmers, financed by income taxes. Capital cannot feel that in paying income taxes for such purposes it is buying a service that adds to the profits of business and the marginal increment of which just barely pays for itself.

In saying that government services are not an ordinary factor of production, bought and paid for as ordinary goods and services are, we are not denying, of course, that government does many useful things that private business could not do so well or so cheaply, and many other things that private business could not do at all. Neither are we saying that taxes should be reduced. We are only saying that taxes are no *quid pro quo*.

2.   THE INCIDENCE OF PROPERTY AND INCOME TAXES

The direct taxes on the quasi-rents of capital goods are of two sorts: fixed taxes in the form of levies on assessed values, and participating taxes in the form of levies on corporate incomes. The fixed taxes are usually collected by municipalities and are called property taxes, while the participating taxes are collected by the states or the national government and are called income taxes. A new kind of fixed tax, called the capital-stock tax, has also been introduced recently and is collected by the federal government.

Property taxes on structures already erected cannot be shifted, because their amount is invariant whether operations are full or curtailed. The incidence of these taxes is on the property owner alone.[2] The incidence of income taxes on established enterprises is also on the proprietor. As no saving in income tax can be achieved without hurting net income itself, management has no choice but to shoulder the whole burden of the income tax. Both property and income taxes come out of quasi-rents — the source from which interest and dividends also are paid. As a result, any increase in property or income taxes on existing capital goods means an equal decrease in common dividends.

3.   THE EFFECT ON DIVIDENDS OF HIGHER TAXES

An increase in the property-tax rate of $10 a thousand, for instance, say from $15 to $25 a thousand, such as has

---

[2] Or, more exactly, on the owner of the structure at the time the tax was enacted. The effect of growing demand is discussed in § 6 below.

occurred during the past generation, is as burdensome, in a typical case, as the grant of a first mortgage equal to 25 per cent of a corporation's assets — a fact which the following calculations concerning a hypothetical company show:

Total assets $100,000,000

		INCOME ACCOUNT	
		At Start	*At End*
Earnings before taxes, @ 8%		$8,000,000	$8,000,000
Property taxes,	@ $15/M	−1,500,000 @ $25/M	−2,500,000
Balance for interest		$6,500,000	$5,500,000
Hypothetical bond issue	$25,000,000		
Hypothetical interest rate	@ 4%		
Hypothetical interest charge		−1,000,000	
Balance for stockholders		$5,500,000 =	$5,500,000

The rise in fixed taxes is thus seen to be equivalent to mortgaging the company in favor of the local government to the extent of 25 per cent of the corporation's assets.

Likewise, an increase in the income-tax rate from 1 to 15 per cent, such as has occurred during the same period, is equivalent, in the case of a typical company again, to declaring a stock dividend of 80 per cent in favor of the federal government. If the company in question is the one just described, and has, for instance, an equal amount of preferred and common stock outstanding, then the effect on common dividends will be as follows:

INCOME ACCOUNT (cont.)

		At Start		At End
Balance for stockholders after increased local taxes		$5,500,000		$5,500,000
Income taxes	@ 1%	−55,000	@ 15%	−825,000
Net income		$5,445,000		$4,675,000
Required for reinvestment,[3] @ 2% of plant		−2,000,000		−2,000,000
Balance for dividends		$3,445,000		$2,675,000
Preferred dividends		−1,717,500		−1,717,500
Common dividends		$1,727,500		$ 957,500

If, for instance, the number of shares in the first place was 957,500, then the cash dividend per share would be $1.80 $1.00

To find the stock dividend which would reduce the original cash dividend as much as the higher income tax has done, note that an increase in the number of shares to 1,727,500 would give a cash dividend per share of $1.00

Hence the equivalent stock dividend would be

1,727,500 shares − 957,500 shares = 770,000 shares, or 80.4%

The actual burden of the increased income tax is even worse than the equivalent of an 80-per-cent stock dividend as computed above; for the hypothetical stock given to the government would rank above the rest of the common stock, and even above the preferred stock in dividend priority, because the government stock would pay dividends even if the earnings covered only interest requirements and left nothing for preferred and common dividends.

The foregoing burdensome effect of higher taxes applies only to old investments, of course, and not to new ones, for

[3] See Chapter VI, § 3, for a discussion of the priority in practice of reinvestment requirements over dividends.

entrepreneurs in making new investments will take cognizance of the new tax rate, and will refrain from building new plant unless the quasi-rents obtainable promise to be enough larger than formerly to cover the new and higher level of taxes. Since the rise in taxes referred to has taken place gradually rather than suddenly, and has occurred during a period of great industrial growth, business has been able to shift much of the burden of the new taxes to the general public, who have been forced to pay the new taxes either in the form of lower interest rates, or lower money wages, or higher costs of living.

4. INDUSTRIALS, UTILITIES, AND RAILS

Industrials during the period from 1900 to 1930 were greatly affected by rising taxes, but utilities were not, because in law the latter were entitled to a "fair return on a fair value," with the words "fair return" meaning the return to security holders *after all taxes*. In theory, therefore, utility stockholders could be indifferent to the tax burden, because they could always recoup their taxes from their customers by charging higher rates. In practice, moreover, it was possible, at least until the depression, to make the public shoulder the tax burden, because costs in the industry fell so fast and demand increased so rapidly that the higher taxes could be shifted to the consumer by the simple device of lowering rates somewhat less rapidly than otherwise would have been done. But during the depression many special taxes were piled onto the utilities, who were considered "depression proof" and hence unworthy of sympathy; and with demand shrinking the companies soon found themselves unable to shift the incidence of the new taxes in accordance with their legal rights, for higher energy rates were politically impossible to obtain.

Like the industrials and the utilities, the rails also were

subjected to rising taxation during the last generation. Although the rails are just as much entitled to a "fair return on a fair value" as the electric utilities, they cannot enforce their rights in practice. Their rates are set already at about the right level to bring in the maximum gross revenues. Were the railroads to raise their rates, they would lose business to waterways and trucks and induce the building of branch factories throughout the country to save freight. Yet it is not high taxes but high wages that is the real hindrance to a fair return for the rails. Railroad labor unions hold a monopoly over a service which the railroads must buy; with their great political power in Congress, these unions can extort higher wages whenever railroad earnings rise enough to cover them. In effect then, the employees, not the nominal shareholders, are the real common stockholders of the railroads.

So long as one government authority rules on wages and another on rates, neither can control the *difference* between income and outgo, which difference is the source of interest and dividends. Not until the United States Supreme Court rules — which it may never do — that some given wage increase is unconstitutional because confiscatory,[4] will railroad stockholders be receiving the protection of the courts to which they are entitled. Individual roads, of course, may give satisfactory returns to investors, but only because these roads are intra-marginal producers and able, therefore, to operate at a profit on rate levels and wage scales that keep part of the industry on the verge of bankruptcy.

But since the labor unions are trying to ride two horses at once and are seeking to raise wages and increase em-

---

[4] Quite possibly the Supreme Court may hold to the fiction that freedom of contract exists in the negotiations between rail labor and its employers, and hence any contract they make is valid regardless of its effect on earnings.

ployment both at the same time they can accomplish neither objective in full, and are unable, therefore, utterly to strangle the railroad industry. If they were to push wages too high, they would make too much mileage unprofitable and force too many men out of work. In the last analysis, neither the cost of living nor social justice sets the level of rail wages, but rather the curtailment of service which the public will tolerate on the one hand, and the loss of jobs which the union members can endure on the other. Should the unions push wages so high as to bankrupt most of the railroads and force government ownership, railroad workers would then find themselves in the same class with postal clerks, with their power to strike gone forever — a loss which they dread above all else. Boundless though the monopoly power of the rail unions might seem to be, therefore, extortion cannot in fact be practiced to an unlimited extent, and so the securities of the intra-marginal railroads do not in truth deserve the scorn with which all railroad securities are so often viewed today.[5]

5.   HIGH TAXES AND THEIR EFFECT ON SAVING

The taxation of quasi-rent does not cease with the distribution thereof. Not only do property holders pay federal, state, and local taxes from earnings at the source, but also they pay federal and state income taxes on these same earnings when received as interest and dividends. Those families who are best able to save because their personal incomes are largest pay exorbitant surtaxes, and then must surrender a good share of their principal recurrently for estate and inheritance taxes. Our present system of

---

[5] Concerning the outlook for the rails, see *Transportation Development in the United States* (New York: Academy of Political Science, Columbia University, 1937), including addresses by Joseph B. Eastman, William J. Cunningham, Thomas W. Lamont, Winthrop M. Daniels, and others.

taxing capital hinders the formation of capital in two ways: by cutting profits it reduces the will to invest, and by "soaking the rich" it reduces the power to save. The effect on

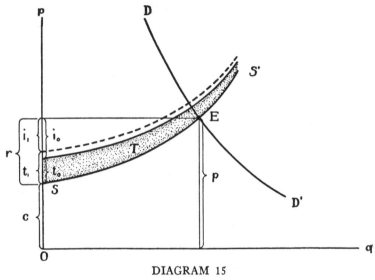

DIAGRAM 15

INCIDENCE OF PROPERTY AND INCOME TAXES

the rate of interest is important, as will be shown in a later chapter.[6]

6.   HIGH TAXES AND THEIR EFFECT ON INVESTMENT

An increase in taxes will delay the erection of new plant. Additions and betterments which are thought to be profitable at the old tax rates will be considered unwarranted at the new rates, and entrepreneurs will wait until a further growth of demand or improvement in technique takes place to increase the prospective quasi-rent [7] obtain-

[6] Cf. Chapter XX, § 15.
[7] Ordinarily the term "quasi-rent" is applied only to the return on *old* investments of capital, but Marshall himself, in a case like that above, speaks of "the

able on new investments in the industry. Diagram 15 shows this effect of taxes in the case of a single industry.

In this diagram DD' is the demand curve, and SS' the supply curve. In the present state of the art, the prospective quasi-rent obtainable on a new unit of plant is shown by the distance r at the left-hand edge of the demand and supply diagram. If t is the tax per unit of capacity, then

$$r - t = i$$

is the net return on the investment-per-unit-of-capacity, I. As pointed out in Chapter XVI, § 3, the investment should not exceed the present worth of the declining annuity of net earnings expected from it.

The shaded area T is the total tax levied on the industry. If the assessed value for the purposes of the property tax conforms to the cost less depreciation of the various plants, and if abatements are secured when for one reason or another individual plants become unprofitable and fall in market value (as proved by their going through receivership, for instance), then the rate of the property tax will turn out to be roughly proportional to the quasi-rent r earned on any given productive unit in the industry. Likewise the income tax will be roughly proportional to the quasi-rent of each plant. With both property and income taxes being proportional to quasi-rent, it follows that the total tax levied on the industry will take the form of a cutlass blade as shown in the diagram. The equilibrium of supply and demand will occur where the *lower* edge of the blade crosses the demand curve at the point of equilibrium E. The point of the cutlass is shown as broken off because property owners usually raze their extra-marginal equip-

confident expectation of coming quasi-rents [that] is a necessary condition for the investment of capital in machinery, and for the incurring of supplementary costs generally." Cf. his *Principles*, p. 424, footnote.

ment when it becomes too high-cost to compete even in boom times, for such a destruction of plant saves property taxes.

An increase in property and income taxes will not reduce output, as a sales tax would, but will discourage the erection of new plant by reducing the net earnings on new investment from i_o to i_1 in the diagram. Entrepreneurs will then wait until demand increases and raises the price p, or until technological improvements lower the prime cost c, enough to offset the higher taxes t_1 and make i as large as before. If neither of these developments takes place, entrepreneurs must wait for the accumulation of savings to lower the interest rate to a point where the reduced income i_1 is considered high enough to warrant the new investment I. During the interval while entrepreneurs are waiting for these changes in demand, technique, or interest rates, existing properties find themselves protected by the higher tax from competition with new properties.

7. GOVERNMENT DEFICITS

With very good reason do business men dislike a deficit in the budget of their city, state, or national government. Such a deficit means increased taxes on quasi-rents, a fall in dividends, a discouragement to new investment, and stagnation in the capital-goods industries. Technological advances which could otherwise be exploited become insufficiently profitable now to assure the payment of *both* taxes and interest. Hence entrepreneurs refuse to borrow, and emissions of new securities fall off. Men wait for still greater technological advances on the one hand, and for a decline in interest rates on the other hand. The fall in interest rates is impeded, however, by the reduction in savings caused by the higher levies on large personal incomes and inheritances.

Even though the deficit in question is only a threat of higher taxes to come, rather than the reality of such taxes now, the mere prospect of higher taxes is sufficient to discourage investment in capital goods. And even if the business community thought the deficit would result in inflation rather than in higher taxes, nevertheless the same stagnation would result, for then savers would not lend except at prohibitive rates of interest. Consequently, if the government has a large deficit, the only thing that will restore business confidence, reopen the market for new issues, and set the heavy industries humming, is such a reduction in government expenses as to balance the budget at a moderate level of taxation.

Taxes are no negligible item in business calculations. Some 30 or 40 per cent of distributable quasi-rent goes out in taxes in normal times. As we shall see later in the case of the United States Steel Corporation, the tax burden of that corporation is now 35 per cent of distributable quasi-rent at a normal rate of operations. Table I shows how the taxes of this particular company have risen in the last generation.

In the case of urban real estate owned by large corporations, the tax burden today is equally high. For example, take the case of land and buildings yielding a monthly rental of $10,000 (after expenses and repairs), and worth $900,000, thus:

Total quasi-rent	$120,000
Less depreciation, @ 4% of present depreciated value	− 36,000
Distributable quasi-rent	$ 84,000
Less property taxes, @ $25.66/$M$, for instance	− 23,100
Less capital stock tax, @ $1.00/$M$	− 900
Income	$ 60,000
Less income tax, @ 15%	− 9,000
Net income	$ 51,000

TABLE 1

Quasi-Rents Distributed for Taxes by the U. S. Steel Corporation

(in thousands of dollars)

Year	Taxes on Iron Ore Mines	Other Property Taxes	Total State & Local Taxes	Federal Income Tax	Federal Capital Stock Tax	Total Taxes	Income Tax Rate
1901	. . . . . .	. . . . . .	. . . . . .	. . . . . .	. . . . . .	not available	nil
1902	. . . . . .	. . . . . .	. . . . . .	. . . . . .	. . . . . .	2,391	nil
1903	. . . . . .	. . . . . .	. . . . . .	. . . . . .	. . . . . .	2,973	nil
1904	. . . . . .	. . . . . .	. . . . . .	. . . . . .	. . . . . .	3,053	nil
1905	. . . . . .	. . . . . .	. . . . . .	. . . . . .	. . . . . .	3,646	nil
1906	. . . . . .	. . . . . .	. . . . . .	. . . . . .	. . . . . .	4,356	nil
1907	. . . . . .	. . . . . .	. . . . . .	. . . . . .	. . . . . .	5,384	nil
1908	. . . . . .	. . . . . .	. . . . . .	. . . . . .	. . . . . .	5,361	nil
1909	. . . . . .	. . . . . .	. . . . . .	. . . . . .	. . . . . .	8,704	1 %[a]
1910	. . . . . .	. . . . . .	. . . . . .	. . . . . .	. . . . . .	9,161	1 %[a]
1911	. . . . . .	. . . . . .	. . . . . .	. . . . . .	. . . . . .	9,622[b]	1 %[a]
1912	. . . . . .	. . . . . .	. . . . . .	. . . . . .	. . . . . .	9,840[b]	1 %[a]
1913	. . . . . .	. . . . . .	. . . . . .	. . . . . .	. . . . . .	13,226	1 %[c]
1914	. . . . . .	. . . . . .	. . . . . .	. . . . . .	. . . . . .	12,646	1 %
1915	. . . . . .	. . . . . .	. . . . . .	. . . . . .	. . . . . .	13,640	1 %
1916	. . . . . .	. . . . . .	18,800	. . . . . .	. . . . . .	26,600	2 %
1917	. . . . . .	. . . . . .	23,367	+ 233,465[d]	. . . . . .	= 252,265	4 %[d]
1918	. . . . . .	. . . . . .	29,594	+ 274,278[d]	. . . . . .	= 297,645	12 %[d]
1919	. . . . . .	. . . . . .	38,724	+ 52,000[d]	. . . . . .	= 81,594	10 %[d]
1920	. . . . . .	. . . . . .		+ 37,500[d]	. . . . . .	= 76,224	10 %[d]

TABLE 1 (Continued)

Year	Taxes on Iron Ore Mines	Other Property Taxes	Total State & Local Taxes	Federal Income Tax	Federal Capital Stock Tax	Total Taxes	Income Tax Rate
1921	......	......	......	......	......	37,684	10 %[d]
1922	......	......	......	......	......	35,798	12½%
1923	......	......	......	......	......	55,083	12½%
1924	......	......	31,513	+13,764	......	= 45,277	12½%
1925	......	......	35,299	+15,624	......	= 50,923	13 %
1926	......	......	35,313	+17,086	......	= 52,400	13½%
1927	......	......	34,817	+11,474	......	= 46,291	13½%
1928	......	......	36,016	+14,960	......	= 50,976	12 %
1929	......	......	37,739	+17,233	......	= 54,972	11 %
1930	......	......	36,047	+12,005	......	= 48,052	12 %
1931	14,216	+19,858→	34,074	+174	......	= 34,248	12 %
1932	12,682	+18,951→	31,633	+173	+499	= 32,305	13¾%[e]
1933	12,736	+17,600→	30,336	+375	+999	= 31,710	13¾%[e]
1934	13,859	+17,399→	31,259	+2,889	+1,633	= 35,780	13¾%[e]
1935	13,624	+18,612→	32,236	+4,405[b]	+1,736	= 38,377	13¾%[e]
1936	15,187	+20,210→	35,397	+11,608[b,h]	+1,809	= 48,814[g]	15 %[d,f,i]

[a] Excise tax on income.
[b] Includes Federal excise tax.
[c] For period from Mar. 1 to Dec. 31.
[d] Excess profits tax also levied.
[e] Consolidated returns taxable at 14¼%.

[f] Tax on undivided earnings also levied.
[g] Exclusive of Social Security Taxes of $4,082,000.
[h] Includes Undistributed Profits Tax.
[i] Excess profits tax also payable if earnings are high.

In this case total taxes are $33,000 = $23,100 + $900 + $9000; and 33,000/84,000, or 39 per cent, of the distributable quasi-rent goes for taxes. A government deficit so large as to force an increase in taxes of one half would reduce the net income on this property from $51,000 to $34,500, or from 5.7 to 3.8 per cent. No wonder that rising taxes stifle the heavy industries and create unemployment!

8.   GROSS AND NET INTEREST RATES

When taxes intervene, there results a situation in which there is no such thing as *the* interest rate, for taxes serve to drive a wedge between the marginal productivity of savings in the hands of the borrower and the rental value of savings in the hands of the lender. Thus, for example, it might happen that the *borrower* could make a marginal increment of savings produce a gross return of 6 per cent, whereas under the same circumstances the *lender* would be able to get a net return of only 4 per cent; such would be the case if property taxes and corporate and personal income taxes absorbed the other 2 per cent; under these circumstances the gross interest rate would be 6 per cent, the net 4 per cent.

Yet neither 6 per cent nor 4 per cent would be the *market* rate, because some of the taxes would be paid by the borrower and some by the lender. Thus if property taxes and corporate income taxes absorbed one fourth of the earnings of new capital, these taxes would use up $1\frac{1}{2}$ per cent of the 6 per cent gross return, and the market rate of interest, therefore, would be $4\frac{1}{2}$ per cent; and if personal income taxes absorbed one ninth of the saver's income,[8] these latter taxes would use up $\frac{1}{2}$ per cent of the $4\frac{1}{2}$ per cent market

[8] Or, more exactly, if the last increment of the saver's income was in the bracket where the normal tax plus the surtax is at the rate of one ninth, or 11 per cent.

rate, and would leave a net return of 4 per cent. The 6 per cent gross return would then be the marginal productivity of savings and the 4 per cent net return would be the reward for abstinence that economists talk about in discussing the forces that determine the rate of interest. But there would be no *equality* between marginal productivity and reward for abstinence, nor any approximation to such equality; for the rate of tax on the use of savings is far too high to be treated as a mere error of approximation. Indeed, taxes on the earnings of capital nowadays are so heavy that changes in tax rates themselves are fully able to offset changes in the demand or supply of savings, and fully able to put the market rate up or down in opposition to the other forces which usually are mentioned as of prime importance in determining the interest rate. In particular, if the New Deal and all it stands for in the way of heavy taxation of capital for the benefit of the poor is to give us a much higher level of taxes, we should expect the gross return from capital to rise and the net return to decline, while the volume of saving and investing decreased, merely because of the tax rate and wholly without regard to the direct effect of the New Deal on the ability of corporations and wealthy individuals to save.

What the effect of a wider spread between the gross and the net return would be on the *market* rate of interest would depend on the slopes of the demand and supply curves for savings and on the kind of taxes that were increased. If both corporate and personal taxes were increased in the same proportion, and if both were equally heavy in the first place, an increase in the total tax rate would tend to raise the market rate when the demand curve was steeper than the supply curve, and lower it when the reverse was true. Unfortunately very little is known about the true slopes of the demand and supply curves for savings, but we do know that more of the total tax on the earnings of capital is paid by the borrower than by the lender. Hence we may say that *if* the two curves had the same steepness,[9] and if both kinds of taxes were increased in the same degree, the effect of the increase in taxes would be to decrease the market rate of interest. The left-hand figure in Diagram 16 illustrates [10] this reasoning. In these diagrams DD' is the demand curve, and SS' the supply curve. The full lines represent the gross and net interest rates under the old tax rate, the dotted lines under the new; thus g is the old and g' the new gross rate, n the old and n' the new net rate. The burden of the tax is shown resting three fourths on the borrower and one fourth on the lender each time, with the result that m is the old and m' the new market rate. Geometrically it follows from the equal steepness of the two curves that an increase in the gap between g and n will lower m. But the drop in m to m' will be only half as great as the drop in n to n'.

Numerically the diagram might be interpreted as follows: At the old tax rate the gross return was 6 per cent, the net return 4 per cent, and the market rate $4\frac{1}{2}$ per cent. At the new tax rate, if taxes are doubled, the gross return will need to be 7 per cent, the net return will be 3 per cent, and the market rate 4 per cent. Thus the market rate will decline $\frac{1}{2}$ per cent, while the actual rates that borrower and lender respectively must consider before making their bargain will each move 1 per cent in the direction of discouraging the borrowing and saving of money. In other words, the *market* rate of interest in its decline will not fully reflect the cut in the reward for abstinence; neither

[9] One curve being positive and the other negative in its slope, however.

[10] Although the effect of a nation-wide system of taxes on all quasi-rents is in reality a problem of *general* and not *partial* equilibrium, it is hoped that, by care in definition, the diagrams used herewith can nevertheless be made of assistance in presenting the argument. Cf. footnote 12, below.

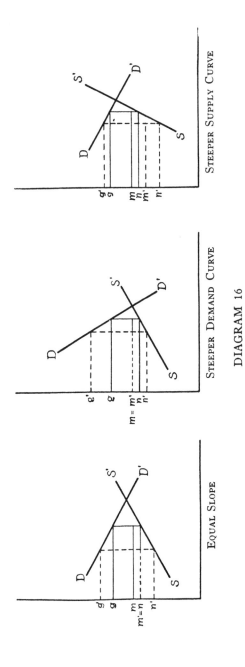

DIAGRAM 16

THE EFFECT OF TAXES ON THE MARKET RATE OF INTEREST

will it give a correct impression of the higher gross return now required by borrowers to justify the erection of new equipment. The decline in the market rate will make it appear to uncritical observers that plant expansion has somehow been stimulated, whereas the truth of the matter is that high taxes are strangling the growth of industry.

As said before, if we knew that the demand and supply curves had the same steepness, then we could infer the effect of higher taxes on the market rate of interest, and we could make a true interpretation of any fall in this rate, but since we do not know the slopes of these curves, we cannot predict the market effect of higher taxes. Whichever way the *market* rate moves, however, we can be sure that the *gross* return required by borrowers will be increased by a rise in taxes, and that any fall in the market rate that may be due merely to an increase in the tax rate is no cause for optimism on the expansion of industry.

If the relative slopes of the demand and supply curves should be such that an increase in taxation drove the market rate down, corporations with bond issues already outstanding would take advantage of the opportunity to bring their interest costs down too, and would call their present issues and replace them with new issues bearing a lower coupon rate. Heavy refunding operations, in other words, would be encouraged by the higher taxes, while flotations involving new capital would be distinctly discouraged. The disparity today between the amounts of refunding and new-money issues being offered for sale may perhaps be partly explained, therefore, by the recent rise in the tax burden.

9. PAY-ROLL TAXES

Unlike property and income taxes, with which we have been concerned so far, pay-roll taxes — such as those employed under the Social Security Act — are not paid out

of quasi-rents, for the incidence of pay-roll taxes is altogether different from that of property and income taxes.

The incidence [11] of a nation-wide tax on wages is as

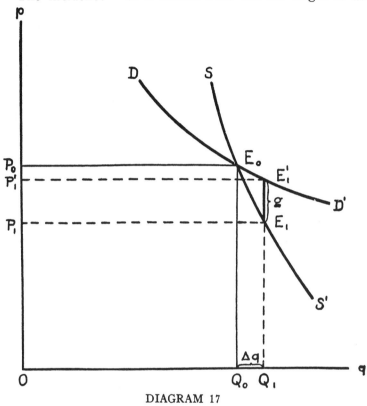

DIAGRAM 17

THE INCIDENCE OF A TAX ON WAGES

shown in Diagram 17.[12] The curve DD' is the demand
curve, and represents the demand price p for various quantities q of labor hired, the price being expressed in terms of

[11] Cf. Paul H. Douglas, *Social Security in the United States* (New York
and London: Whittlesey House, McGraw-Hill Book Company, Inc., 1936),
pp. 62–68.

[12] Although the theory of wages is a question of *general* and not *partial*
equilibrium, it is hoped that, by care in definition, a diagram reminiscent of the

units of wage-goods paid per man-hour of labor employed. The demand curve is drawn with an elasticity *greater* than one on the assumption that the more the labor employed, the more the national dividend and the more the collective share of wage-earners in this dividend; for entrepreneurs can afford to offer an increment in total wages for each increment in the product of labor.

The curve SS' is the supply curve and represents the supply price for various quantities of labor; the curve shows how many man-hours of labor q would be forthcoming for any given wage p. The supply curve is drawn with a negative slope [13] on the assumption that a fall in wages would cause the laboring population to work somewhat longer hours and send more of their women and children into the factories in an effort to maintain the family's standard of living; but the elasticity of supply is shown as being less than one on the assumption that the effort to compensate for the decline in wage rates by harder work would stop short of completely offsetting the loss in real income.

It will be noticed that this diagram is drawn contrary to all ordinary demand and supply diagrams in that the supply curve falls below the demand curve to the right of the point of intersection. How can our diagram, therefore, possibly yield a stable equilibrium between demand and supply? To answer this question, consider what would happen if the quantity of labor offered for hire should chance to be in excess of the equilibrium quantity OQ_o by the small amount Δq. In this case laborers would be willing to work for less than the equilibrium price OP_o and would accept a price OP_1. To entrepreneurs such a price would

---

Marshallian demand and supply curves can be made of use in clarifying the argument.

[13] Frank H. Knight, *Risk, Uncertainty, and Profit* (Boston and New York: Houghton Mifflin Company, 1921), pp. 117–118.

afford a gain, g, represented by the distance between the demand and supply curves. The existence of this gain would cause entrepreneurs to compete with each other for the available supply of labor, and as higher and higher wages were offered to attract workers from other employers, the supply of labor itself would decrease, until at last equilibrium would be reached at the intersection of the demand and supply curves. Likewise, if the supply of labor should chance to be too small for equilibrium, with workmen demanding too short hours and too high wages, entrepreneurs could not use even this small supply of labor at a profit, and would proceed to lower wages under the threat of discharging those who would not accept the pay cuts; and then workmen, in order to retain their standard of living, would consent to longer hours until equilibrium was restored.[14]

The difference between the diagram as drawn above and applied to labor and a similar diagram so drawn and applied to a commodity like cotton lies in the fact that a laborer, if paid more than his supply price, tends to *decrease* his output, whereas a farmer when overpaid tends to *increase* his output. The upshot of the foregoing argument, therefore, is that Diagram 17, however strange it may seem at first sight, correctly depicts the attainment of equilibrium in the labor market.[15]

If now the diagram is extended to show the incidence of

[14] For statistical evidence concerning the actual slope of the short-run supply curve for labor, see Douglas, *Theory of Wages*, chaps. XI and XII, and esp. p. 314. Concerning the slope of the demand curve, see Douglas. p. 152.

Douglas presents the foregoing argument on pp. 498–499.

[15] W. L. Sargent, in his *Recent Political Economy* (London, 1867), p. 76, argues in favor of a supply curve for savings with a negative slope like that of the supply curve for labor shown above. Equilibrium in such an event would be attained for savings in the same way as for employment, because buyers and sellers would act in the same way in each case if the price happened to be too high or too low.

a tax on wages, it will be seen that such a tax reduces wages by more than the amount of the tax. Let the line segment g now represent the amount of the tax per man-hour. Then OP_1 will represent the new wage received by the laborers, and OP_1' the new cost of labor to the employers; the difference P_1P_1' will be the tax. The total wages received by the laboring population as a whole will be represented by the new rectangle $OQ_1E_1P_1$, which will be smaller in area than the old rectangle $OQ_oE_oP_o$, because the supply curve SS' has an elasticity less than unity. If the proceeds of the tax, represented by the area $P_1E_1E_1'P_1'$ are returned to Labor, however, in the form of old-age or unemployment benefits, the total share of workers in the national dividend will be $OQ_1E_1'P_1'$, which will be larger in area than the original share $OQ_oE_oP_o$, because the demand curve DD' has an elasticity greater than unity. The national income itself will also be increased by the tax on wages, because the extra hours of labor induced by the tax on wages will result in a larger product from society's outfit of men and machines. And the share of Capital in the national dividend will likewise be increased, for the very assumption of an elastic demand curve for labor implies also that Capital should find it worth while to pay larger sums for greater quantities of labor. Hence a tax on wages, if spent for the benefit of the public and not wasted in war or useless monuments of peace, increases the income of nearly everyone. Were it not for the disutility entailed in the extra work that is forced upon people, it could be said that the general welfare, as well as the national dividend, was also increased by the tax.

The foregoing argument rests on the implicit assumption that workers consider the tax a genuine deduction from their wages, and not a mere postponement of wages whereby they receive in their old age whatever they do not get in their youth. Postponed wages, rather than lost wages, are what the tax amounts to in fact, but it is most unlikely that the workers will so consider it. For if they did, it would mean they were quite willing to have their wages postponed by law, and would have done so of their own accord otherwise. Yet it is a known fact that workers do not of their own free will save such a large fraction of their wages as 9 per cent when employed.[16] Hence we must assume that they do not like to save so much and would consider the forced saving of this amount a hardship which would have to be made good by extra hours of work.

10. DISGUISED CAPITAL LEVIES

In addition to income and property taxes and pay-roll taxes, already discussed, there are two other kinds of taxes which affect the investment value of securities directly or indirectly. These taxes are the estate tax and the capital-gains tax.

While a light estate tax, such as could easily be amortized out of income by the rich from generation to generation, might induce enough extra saving by the rich to absorb itself, a heavy estate tax, such as could not possibly be amortized, is likely to encourage the rich to squander their estates in haste before the tax-gatherer can lay hands on them. But if an estate is not squandered, and if it is assessed for confiscatory taxes, its holdings of securities will be put up for forced sale and will have to be bought by someone. The money to buy the securities may come either from private savings or from bank borrowings; if from savings, the tax will reduce the flow of new capital into private industry, and if from borrowings, the tax will inflate the deposits of the banking system. Which is the more likely to happen? If only the very rich are over-

---

[16] The total pay-roll tax will be 9 per cent eventually, with 6 per cent going for old age benefits and 3 per cent for unemployment benefits.

taxed, probably the merely well-to-do will be able to save enough to absorb the recurrent capital levies on the big estates, but if the well-to-dō also are over-taxed, then no one is left who is able to buy with his savings the securities being sold; for the poor as a class ordinarily save but little in spite of their great numbers, and the ultimate recipients of the proceeds of the tax — namely, the veterans, the farmers, and those on relief, or those who sell to them — cannot be expected to do enough extra saving to finance the tax. Hence the securities undergoing sale will have to be bought with borrowed money, the funds therefor being raised by the hypothecation of other securities; and the result will be an increase in collateral loans, with the proceeds of the loans going to the government. Estate taxes under these extreme circumstances will then be paid with borrowed money, and the process will be inflationary. The outcome is what always happens when taxes exceed taxable income; such taxes are financed by inflation, and much of their weight falls ultimately on those who suffer from the rising cost of living that inflation produces. Only in the special case where the excessive tax is used to pay off government obligations held by the banks can such a tax be kept from becoming inflationary.

From the government's own point of view, it is living on its capital when it uses the proceeds of confiscatory estate taxes to pay its current expenses. President Roosevelt, when he proposed the last increase in estate taxes in 1935, urged that the proceeds be used exclusively for paying off the government debt;[17] he urged, in other words, that the government, when it reduced its income-producing assets by taxation, should likewise reduce its income-bearing liabilities by redemption. It remains to be seen, however,

[17] *New York Times*, June 20, 1935, p. 2, cols. 3 and 4, "Text of Roosevelt's Message on New Taxes," Part I, last paragraph.

whether any such principles of sound finance will be adhered to for long. Unless they are, the tax will merely dissipate the nation's largest present holdings of securities and its largest sources of future savings without any permanent offsetting gains to the taxpayers as a whole. To the extent, moreover, that future savings are thus impaired, the rate of interest in the years to come will tend to be raised.

Taxes on capital gains, like estate and inheritance taxes, are in reality a capital levy, for capital gains are not true income, but only the bartered hope of future *increases* in income. If John Doe buys United States Steel at $30 and sells it at $70, no income of $40 arises from the national point of view. All that happens is a transaction recognizing the change that has already occurred in marginal *opinion* concerning future dividends. Such transactions based on waves of optimism are not additions to the national income, and no tax levied on the results of this optimism in the stock market can be paid out of anything but the previously existing national income. Therefore any such tax is only a capital levy. To be sure, if John Doe does not sell his United States Steel after it goes to 70, he may eventually get a corresponding increase in dividends on which he will have to pay income taxes, but if he does sell his stock at once and reinvest the proceeds in bonds, he will have to pay a capital levy merely for the privilege of swapping securities; and in addition he will be obliged to pay an income tax on the interest from the new bonds when it is received. Even though John Doe, on his part, pays his lawful tax on his capital gains, Richard Roe, to whom he sells his Steel, will also have to pay a further tax on his dividends received. Thus both buyer and seller will pay a tax on the same increase in dividends, and the government will collect *two* taxes on the same future income (if indeed it should materialize). The first tax, however, will be paid out of capital,[18] and only the second will be a true income tax.[19] Therefore it is correct to say that taxes on capital gains are a kind of capital levy collected in boom years, and provocative of inflation like any other capital levy when excessive.

11.   TAXES ON UNDIVIDED PROFITS

Noteworthy among the fiscal innovations of the New Deal is a tax on undivided profits.[20] The most serious drawback to such a tax is that these *so-called* profits usually do not exist at all. Amazing though it may seem, the undistributed earnings of the average corporation are not really earnings from the investor's point of view, but only obsolescence reserves wrongly credited to surplus. As will be brought out in great detail in the chapter on United States Steel, the reinvested earnings of the average corporation in practice prove barely able to keep the company

[18] By "capital" is here meant "capital claims," not "capital goods"; taxes do not consume present bricks and mortar as such, but only revise the distribution of the earnings from these bricks and mortar.

[19] The taxation of capital gains bears certain analogies to the taxation of income saved and invested, discussed by Marshall, in *After-War Problems*, p. 323, footnote. Marshall points out that income saved and not consumed is taxed once as income, and then in effect taxed again at the same rate when it yields a return after being invested. The taxation of savings, like the taxation of capital gains, is thus a form of double taxation.

[20] The following table shows the rate of tax payable on undistributed net income. (See the *New York Times*, June 21, 1936, p. 30, col. 1, Section 14 D.)

Bracket	Rate of Tax
0%– 10%	7%
10%– 20%	12%
20%– 40%	17%
40%– 60%	22%
60%–100%	27%

Thus if a company distributed four fifths of its earnings in dividends, and retained one fifth, it would have to pay a tax of 7 per cent on one tenth of its earnings, and of 12 per cent on another tenth, or an average tax of 9½ per cent on the two tenths of its earnings which were retained for reinvestment in the business.

abreast of the times, and serve merely to maintain the *status quo* of dividend-paying power.[21] Only such companies as reinvest an unusually large amount succeed in raising their dividend-paying power in the end. Hence a punitive tax on reinvested earnings, like that recently enacted, would, if successful, make all stocks slowly lose their present dividend-paying power. But because all competitors would be subject to the same tax, the process would be retarded, to be sure, for obsolescence would be slower then than now for A, if B likewise were restrained from making improvements.

To reduce corporate saving and reinvestment is the avowed aim of the tax.[22] But such saving and reinvestment is the established method for reducing costs and improving product; therefore why not call the new tax "the tax on progress"?

Many corporations have sought to avoid the tax by revising their dividend and assessment policies. Instead of paying out 80 per cent, let us say, of their earnings once and for all, these corporations have paid out 100 per cent for the moment and have then assessed their stockholders to get 20 per cent back again. The assessment was not called by that bitter name, of course, for another word for the same thing is in common use; to wit, the word "right," applying to the practice of selling new stock to present stockholders for less than the market price. This practice, as already explained in Chapter V, § 5, is tantamount to a stock dividend plus an assessment. As a way of effecting a contribution by stockholders to offset in part the distribution to them of too much of the company's earnings, it is

[21] See also Chapter VI, § 3.

[22] Cf. the views of Secretary Wallace of the Department of Agriculture, set forth in a series of lectures on the business cycle at the University of North Carolina, and reported in the *New York Herald Tribune*, April 29, 1937, p. 6, cols. 2 and 3.

altogether successful, and it is one answer, therefore, to a tax on undivided profits and reinvested earnings.[23] For convenience, the contributions can be made less often than the distributions, the rights being offered but once in two or three years, let us say, while the dividends can still be paid quarterly as now.[24]

While the use of rights is one answer to the undistributed profits tax, it is not the perfect answer, because the flow of the dividend money from a corporation to its stockholders and back again is subject to the personal income tax, both state and federal. The marginal increment of this money, in the case of a stockholder with an income of $13,000, and a surtax net income of just over $10,000, for example, would bear a normal tax of 4 per cent, a surtax of 7 per cent, and a state tax (in Massachusetts, for instance) of 6.6 per cent, or a total tax of 17.6 per cent. Thus every dollar set aside for reinvestment by the corporation would be reduced to $100¢ — $17.6¢ = $82.4¢ before it could be put back into plant and equipment. For wealthy stockholders, who would be subject to even higher taxes, the loss would be still more. If the bookkeeping for the new stock issue is included, it may be said that the cost of using rights ranges all the way from 8 or 9 per cent for the small stockholder up to 86 per cent for the multimil-

---

[23] Notable among the companies resorting to this method of tax avoidance is Sears, Roebuck & Co., which offered rights to its stockholders in December 1936. See the *New York Times*, October 27, 1936, p. 37, col. 1.

[24] President Roosevelt himself seems to have in mind some such result as here outlined, to judge by the newspaper reports of his press conference on the proposed measure. The account in the *New York Times*, March 4, 1936, p. 2, col. 6, reads as follows: "He suggested . . . that the officers divide the profits among the shareholders, and at the same time send the minority stockholders an offer to reinvest their dividends in the purchase of new stock to provide capital for plant expansion."

Unfortunately such "offers" are commands, not invitations, for the stockholder cannot decline without financial loss. His only option is to pay up or sell out.

lionaire; indeed on the average the cost of using rights
may well approach the figure of 27 per cent set by the law
as the maximum penalty on the reinvestment of earnings.
Hence for a corporation that is not retaining all its earnings and is not subject to the maximum rate of tax, it is
better to pay the undistributed profits tax in the first
place than to attempt to avoid it by the use of rights.

The effect of the undistributed profits tax is to make
reinvested earnings no longer much the cheapest source
of new capital, because now reinvested earnings have to
pay nearly the same tax as all other savings derived from
corporate income. In the past, when a stockholder's income emerged in the cash account of a corporation, as explained in Chapter V, § 7, the money could be reinvested
in the same business without paying a tax, and only such
savings as were drawn out and invested elsewhere were
subject to tax. But now the taxes laid on stockholders'
savings are roughly the same wherever the money is invested. Now every dollar of corporate income has to pay
a tax of 7 to 27 per cent before it can be put into plant and
machinery. If a new building in the past required $100,000
of corporate saving, and if the tax should be in the 17 per
cent bracket, for instance, the building would now require
$120,500; thus the effect of the tax in this case would be
to raise the cost of the capital goods financed by corporate
saving 20½ per cent. The burden could not be avoided by
the use of borrowing instead of reinvestment to finance
the capital outlay, because bonds issued for such a purpose ordinarily would be unsuitable for institutional investors, and would have to be sold to the stockholding
class in society, who could only buy them with the proceeds of dividends less taxes. Hence, no matter how the
capital outlay was financed, it would still have to pay a
high tax. In the past, saving, or rather corporate saving,

was tax-free, while consumption (paid out of personal incomes) was heavily taxed; now both are taxed. The ultimate result will be to discourage savings as compared with consumption, and to raise the rate of interest. The reduction in corporate saving will hurt the heavy industries the worst, and these, unfortunately, are the very ones that have suffered most from unemployment.

A curious misconception is current to the effect that corporations are carried through depressions by their surpluses. Obviously their *surpluses* have nothing to do with the matter; instead, it is their *cash* which they use for wages, materials, taxes, interest, and dividends in time of need, or at any other time, for that matter. If the surpluses are all invested in bricks and mortar, they are of no use for meeting operating expenses; only to the extent that a surplus has been kept in current assets can it be drawn upon for current expenses.

Another misconception is current, to the effect that the new tax, by causing the distribution of a higher percentage of earnings on dividend account, will increase the velocity of money [25] and thus promote prosperity. The same misconception is responsible for the assertion that the increase in dividends during a boom will make the boom worse, while the decrease during a slump will make the slump worse. Fallacies all! Earnings not paid out to stockholders in any year are spent on plant instead, and thus reach consumers all the same. Only if the undistributed earnings are retained as idle cash — a rare event with corporations already strong financially — does the retention of such earnings shrink consumer purchasing power. In a boom, if a corporation should pay higher dividends because of the

[25] The *New York Times* account (*loc. cit.*) reads as follows:

" 'Is one of the purposes of the program to increase the velocity of money?' a correspondent asked.

"The president replied in the affirmative."

tax, the act would not add more fuel to the fire, for the extra payment would subtract just that much from what otherwise would have been spent on plant. If it be assumed that the reinvested earnings would have gone into marketable securities instead of plant, the answer is still the same, because investment in marketable securities is merely the loaning of money to others, who in turn spend the money on plant. Even though the corporation itself bought none but seasoned securities, those who received the cash would have to buy, at the last link of the chain, new issues the proceeds of which would be devoted to plant outlays by the borrowing corporation. When all is said and done, then, it makes no difference in a boom whether earnings are paid out or reinvested; in either case they make an equal contribution to business activity.

Likewise, under the old policy of underpaying dividends in prosperity and overpaying in depression, formerly followed for the sake of uniformity in dividend rates in the long run, no help comes from the payment of unearned dividends. Funds so dispersed during a depression must be drawn from the year's provision for depreciation, and thus diverted from reinvestment in plant. If payments exceed the year's depreciation charge, so that the balance must be taken from current assets, then the buyers of such assets must finance their purchases out of savings, thus reducing consumer purchasing power among savers by exactly the amount it is increased among dividend receivers. Should the buyers of the current assets being liquidated resort to bank borrowing, the consumers' incomes would be augmented, to be sure, by the amount of the bank borrowing, and the process of paying unearned dividends would then become inflationary, and as such would be helpful in overcoming a depression quite as any other inflationary process would be. The payment of unearned dividends would benefit the stockholders themselves no more, however, than if they went to the bank and borrowed the amount of the unearned dividend themselves, using the stock as collateral; for the payment of unearned dividends makes a stock worth less. When one considers the depressing effect on the prices of raw materials and bonds, moreover, when a corporation liquidates its inventories and marketable securities for the payment of unearned dividends, it would seem that such a payment could only be deflationary in the end. Evidently the old practice of overpaying dividends in depression must be adjudged more harmful than the new policy of keeping dividends in line with earnings. Hence, whichever way one looks at it, and whether one considers booms or depressions, one cannot say that the new tax need make the business cycle worse. Surely it is not correct to argue that the new tax is a tax on stability — though it certainly is a tax on progress.

It is a mistake to say that the greater variability of dividends that would result from changing the rate of dividend from year to year as earnings changed would make stock prices go up and down more. To begin with, stocks could hardly be more volatile than they are now! General Motors, for instance, fell from $91\frac{1}{4}$ to $7\frac{5}{8}$ in the depression, a decline of 92 per cent; could it have done much worse if the dividend had been passed altogether? In the second place, if no pretense is made of equalizing dividends from year to year, people will make their own allowance for variability, and will be less likely to be misled by the peculiarities of any particular company's dividend policy.

The direct yield of the undistributed profits tax to the Treasury may not be large, but the real help to federal revenues will come from the newly levied normal tax on all dividends, and from the higher surtaxes paid by big stockholders. The new tax, therefore, amounts to a device for lowering the present exemptions in the personal income tax so as to assess the man of moderate means more heavily. It also amounts to a device for raising the surtax net income of large stockholders. Unless the courts can be persuaded to order a liberalization of the Treasury's rules on depreciation and income, so as to bring these rules into line with the economic facts of obsolescence — a revision that would be far in advance of current practice among even professional accountants themselves — there will be no defense for the large stockholders against the tax, and one more force will have been set at work to hasten the dissipation of the capital of wealthy men.[26]

The decrease in the volume of saving that will result from "soaking the rich" may be great, for according to the Brookings Institution, two thirds of all the savings in the country are made by families with incomes over $10,000, although these families constitute only 2.3 per cent of all families.[27]

If the rich were to pay their taxes by decreasing their expenses and reducing their standard of living to a less luxurious level, it might be said that high taxes were beneficial to the national economy insofar as these taxes reduced the cost of supporting a (supposedly) parasitic class in society. But if the rich refuse to economize, and if they pay their high taxes out of their savable surpluses, then no such benefit results; on the contrary, the poor of the next generation are injured by the failure of our own generation to add as much as it could to the capital equipment of the country. And even if the rich were to reduce their standard of living in order to pay their taxes, the lessened cost of supporting

[26] Cf. Anderson, "Eating the Seed Corn," in which the tax on undivided profits is discussed in particular.

[27] Cf. Harold G. Moulton, Maurice Leven, and Clark Warburton, *America's Capacity to Consume* (Washington, D. C.: The Brookings Institution, 1934), pp. 93–94.

the upper classes might not be all clear gain for the rest of the nation, for in the past many of the luxuries bought by the rich have turned out to be of ultimate benefit to the poor; thus the rich and well-to-do, by freely purchasing such new devices as automobiles, radios, and oil furnaces at high prices when first introduced, have helped to finance the development of these inventions in their infancy and made possible their perfection and sale to the poor in great numbers at low prices in the end.

Not what the rich get, but what they spend, not Henry Ford's income, but his scale of living, is the measure of the social injustice resulting from his great fortune. Judging by any such standard as this, it can only be said that the United States under capitalism has enjoyed the benefits of free enterprise at a very cheap price in terms of the rewards paid to successful entrepreneurs.

12.   HIGH SURTAXES AND TAX-EXEMPT SECURITIES

If a man who has demonstrated his investment skill by his success in building up his own income to $50,000 a year should be offered the choice of (1) a tax-free New York State bond yielding 2.80 per cent to maturity, or (2) a subscription to new common stock where the money would earn 10 per cent less various taxes, he would probably choose the tax-free bond, for reasons to be given presently, although the tax-free application of his capital might be the less useful one from the standpoint of the welfare and prosperity of the country as a whole. The reason why the high return of 10 per cent offered by private industry might not appeal to this skillful investor is shown by the following calculation, where it is assumed that earnings average 10 per cent, being 15 per cent in good years and nothing in bad years:

Principal invested in new stock	$10,000
Rate of return in two out of three years	×15%
Gross return after depreciation and before taxes	$1,500
Property taxes, @ 2½% of principal	−250
Capital stock tax, @ $1/M	−10
Balance	$1,240
Corporate income tax, @ 15%	−186
	$1,054
Reinvestment requirement, @ 20%	−211
Tax on reinvested earnings *	−20
Balance for dividends, subject to personal income tax	$ 823
State income tax, @ 8% (as in New York) ..	−66
Balance subject to Federal tax	$ 757
Normal tax on dividends, @ 4%	−30
Surtax on dividends, @ 31%	−235
Dividends received in two out of three years	$ 492
Average yearly dividend	$ 328
Yield on taxable investment	3.28%
Price of tax-free New York 3½'s of 1970	115
Number of years to maturity	33 yrs.
Yield on tax-free investment	2.80%
Differential in favor of taxable stock	0.48%

* The excess profits tax of 5 per cent on all income over 12½ per cent of the value of the company's capital stock is not included in the tax deductions, because it is assumed that the 15 per cent return from the new assets would be diluted by a lower return from the company's old assets. Likewise the New York state franchise tax is not included, for it is assumed that the money is being invested outside of the state.

Our hypothetical investor probably would not consider the foregoing differential of ½ per cent in favor of the common stock sufficient to cover the greater risk and lower marketability of the suggested investment therein. Certainly he would not consider the differential sufficient if he were asked to put his money into a new enterprise like a moving picture theater or an apartment house for which the marketability would be notably poor. The foregoing calculation shows, therefore, that our present tax structure makes it almost impossible for large numbers of meritorious new ventures to secure equity money. For where can the rising entrepreneur possibly obtain venture money if all income-receivers above $50,000 are driven away by taxation, and if few below that level have much income they can risk in non-marketable, long-term speculations?

In the years 1926 to 1931, after the war-time surtaxes had been reduced to a maximum of only 20 per cent, capital expansion and technological progress suffered from no such prohibitive burden of taxation as this. Perhaps it is no mere coincidence that our last great period of prosperity in the heavy industries burst upon us immediately after a decade of exorbitant surtaxes came to an end in 1926.

The New Deal has finally succeeded in closing the last loopholes in the tax law. By putting a tax on reinvested earnings and subjecting capital gains to the regular surtax instead of the flat rate of $12\frac{1}{2}$ per cent that applied in the 1920's, the Treasury has at last made it impossible to avoid a good part of one's taxes on a risky venture by letting earnings accumulate and taking one's profit only at the end of many years when one sells out. At the very time when the country, because of heavy unemployment, is most in need of new industries, a well-nigh prohibitive tax has been put on the launching of new ventures. While some innovations can still be started by inducing big corporations to exploit them, nevertheless by and large the financing of innovations has been made much more difficult, and so the rise in the standard of living and the national income will surely be slower than it might have been under more enlightened tax policies.

Taxes on junior money do not merely prevent the raising of junior money; they also prevent the raising of senior money, for the one is of no use without the other. If the public utilities, for instance, cannot sell stock year by year, then they cannot sell bonds for long either, because the safety of the senior money depends on the presence of an adequate margin of junior money to carry the risks of the enterprise. The same is true of the railroads, and of many building projects. It is only the exceptional corporation that is so large and so free from senior obligations today that it can safely finance its expansion for years to come with bond money supplied by insurance companies and small investors. Hence the present discouragement of equity financing means the discouragement of all financing. No wonder that recent bond issues have been so largely confined to refunding!

Mistaken are those who say that interest rates are too low to permit of a long depression now. *Gross* interest rates, as seen by borrowers, are not low, but high, and have been made even higher by the tax on undistributed profits and the surtax on capital gains. Unless these taxes are repealed, or tax-exempt securities are abolished, business may be very slow to recover, and stocks may sink to prices so cheap that the rich no longer will want to switch out of them.

13. THE REDISTRIBUTION OF WEALTH

Since government services, as pointed out in § 1, are not an ordinary factor of production like land, labor, capital, and management, and are not paid for in the same way, taxes are not a cost of production, but rather a *device for redistributing the national dividend*. The effect of taxes on quasi-rents is to redistribute in part the shares going to Land, Labor, Capital, and Management as Rent, Wages, Interest, and Profits. If taxes are heavy, then the picture of distribution as drawn by classical economists will need to be redrawn substantially, and we shall have to say that competition distributes, but taxes redistribute, the national dividend. In a democracy taxes are used mainly to make Capitalism socialistic. Probably this is desirable, but we shall not digress to debate the question here. Suffice it to say that with some 40 per cent of all quasi-rent apparently going into taxes at the source,[28] and another 10 per cent into taxes when received or spent by property owners, the nation has already gone 50 per cent socialistic, if the extent of public participation in the earnings of capital be taken as the measure of socialism.

The abolition of private property, not the leveling of wages, seems to be the essence of socialism in practice. In the U. S. S. R. although wage rates vary between individuals, and interest is paid to savers, the State nevertheless enjoys the ownership of mines, factories, ships, canals, and so forth. In this country the State owns the schools and parks, highways and sewers, most of the canals and waterways, and will eventually own the railroads and perhaps even the electric-light plants and the oil fields, if recent trends continue. Thus it is clear that even with us the State already owns a good share of society's outfit of capital goods. To go entirely socialistic, the State would need only to take over completely the ownership of the factories, stores, apartment houses, farms, and mines from which it already draws off half the income as taxes.

We of today whose immediate past has been capitalistic think that capitalism is normal and socialism abnormal, but if we look back over history and see the long periods during which feudalism and other non-capitalistic systems have prevailed, we must realize that the capitalism we have known may well prove to be only a passing phase in economic history.

[28] See § 7.

When income and inheritance taxes are used to raise money to pay doles, the function of taxation to *redistribute* the national income is very clear; but when property taxes are used to support public schools, a new service, namely popular education, is added to the national dividend, and the redistribution of income then takes place not in cash but in kind, with the result that the function of taxation to redistribute income is obscured in the process. If education were sold at cost by municipalities at so much a child-year, just as water is sold by them at so much a thousand cubic feet, then the process would be capitalistic and no redistribution of income would be involved, but now the arrangement is socialistic — and wisely so. But being socialistic, it tends to reduce the national dividend as a whole in a capitalistic society, for the cost of a tax is always more than its yield. Since a tax tends to raise prices, it is a burden not only in itself but also as a check on consumption. In general, taxes are worth while if the gains from the redistribution of the national dividend more than offset the losses from the reduction thereof, but not otherwise.

In passing it should be pointed out that the redistribution of income and the redistribution of wealth amount to the same thing in the end. Since the wealth of the rich consists largely of factories and machines which the owners can neither eat nor wear, but only draw an income from, it matters not whether the wealth itself once and for all, or the income therefrom year after year, is seized by the tax-gatherer.

Not only does half the *income* of capital fail to reach the nominal owners of capital, but also a large share of the *management* of capital escapes their control in practice. It is a commonplace that large corporations like United States Steel and American Telephone are not governed by the stockholders but rather by a clique of officers and directors who feel nearly as much responsibility toward workers, customers, and the public, as toward the stockholders. Here again is a condition that is a far cry from the pure capitalism discussed in economic textbooks. Especially is this true when management thinks, as is somewhat the fashion nowadays, that wages should be governed by the level of profits rather than by the marginal productivity of labor, as shown by the prevailing wage elsewhere.

The taxing of Capital to educate Labor, or to defend it from bandits, invaders, or disease, is a purely socialistic undertaking to which we have long been accustomed, and which is approved by everyone. But the degree to which it is being done has been increasing steadily. Statistics on the United States Steel Corporation show that its tax rate has risen from 1.7 per cent of its quasi-rent in 1902 to a probable 35 per cent of normal quasi-rent today.[29] Sometime the point will be reached where saving and investment will be so severely handicapped that modern nations cannot increase taxes on Capital any further. Then they must either go over to Socialism entirely, or call a halt on further measures to "share the wealth." It would seem that our present system could hardly carry any great increase in the present burden of doles, AAA benefits, soldiers' bonuses, and naval armaments if the new taxes are to be levied on Capital alone.

As taxes on quasi-rents drive a wedge between saving and investment, such taxes result, if overdone, in stopping the expansion and modernization of plant altogether. However desirable it may be to "share the wealth," excessive taxation to accomplish this purpose ends in destroying the

[29] For statistics on industry in general, see W. L. Crum, "Corporate Tax Payments," in *Explorations in Economics*, pp. 487–497, esp. Table 2, which shows the share of the government to have been 33% of earnings after depreciation and before interest and taxes in the pre-New-Deal years of 1922–1933.

wealth itself. Even if savers, in spite of low interest rates, were willing to refrain from consuming their own capital, nevertheless the physical plant itself could not be maintained intact unless enough quasi-rent was left after taxes to provide for depreciation. If such a condition of over-taxation should arise, one striking symptom of it would be chronic, non-cyclical business depression,[30] with the greatest unemployment in the heavy industries. Another symptom would be very low interest rates, with large issues of bonds for refunding purposes at the onset of the period, but a complete absence of issues of new capital to be devoted to plant and equipment.

[30] Cf. Fritz Machlup, "The Consumption of Capital in Austria," in *The Review of Economic Statistics*, January 1935. This article concludes with the following words: "Austria was successful in pushing through policies which are popular all over the world. Austria has impressive records in five lines: she increased public expenditures, she increased wages, she increased social benefits, she increased bank credits, she increased consumption. After all these achievements she was on the verge of ruin."

CHAPTER XVIII

WHERE IS THE INTEREST RATE DETERMINED?

I. THE SUPPLY AND DEMAND FOR SAVINGS

At first thought it might seem that the rate of interest was determined in *all* of the capital markets acting together, and that wherever securities representing the ownership of capital goods were sold, some contribution to the determination of the rate of interest would be made. That such a view is wrong, and that only a small part of the dealings in stocks and bonds are relevant to the setting of the interest rate, we shall now go on to show.

From the description of capital goods and the quasi-rents they fetch which has been given in Chapter XVI, it is evident that capital as a whole does not come into the market daily for hire and rehire, and does not suffer a change in its earnings as interest rates move up and down; for the accumulated savings of the past no longer exist in liquid form, having long since been committed to bricks and mortar and embodied in tangible capital goods, which now receive, not interest, but quasi-rent. If these capital goods are mortgaged, their owners, to be sure, must pay *contractual* interest out of their quasi-rents, retaining the balance as profits for themselves if the balance be positive, or supplementing the balance out of their own pockets if the balance be negative. But this payment of contractual interest is not flexible, and does not vary with the true rate of interest that is currently being determined elsewhere.

Not past savings, but only present savings, can freely be converted into whatever kind of new capital goods now seems most profitable; only present savings are now lying unused and unspoken for; and only present savings can now fetch the high price, or must now accept the low price, that results from the present state of demand.[1] Hence it is current savings, and not capital in general, that enter the equilibrium of supply and demand wherein the rate of interest is each day determined. Hence also it is *new* securities, not old securities, whose price gives rise to the rate of interest day by day, for current savings are borrowed, and new capital goods are financed, by the sale of *new* issues, not by the resale of old issues. Therefore the rate of interest is determined in the market for new issues only,[2] and whatever rate emerges there will merely be transferred to old issues as well.

2.   THE CONTRAST BETWEEN SECURITY AND COMMODITY MARKETS

Stocks and bonds are not like wheat, cotton, and other commodities, which are continually being used up, and continually being replaced, and the carryover of which serves only to smooth out the fluctuations in quantities demanded and supplied; for stocks and bonds are not consumed, but once produced remain in the "carryover" forever after. Consequently the accumulation of stocks and bonds from the past vastly exceeds the emission of new issues in the present. As for the securities already in the carryover, their price is set by marginal opinion concerning their future payments, and no factor but the rate of interest to be used in discounting these future payments is directly affected by the flow of new securities. The supply of

[1] The question of hoarded savings, that is, uninvested past savings, need not detain us here, since we are discussing not the *monetary*, but only the *real*, rate of interest in this chapter.

[2] Cf. Marshall, *Principles*, p. 533: "The phrase 'the general rate of interest' applies in strictness only to the anticipated net earnings from new investments of free capital. . . ."

these new securities arises from the need of borrowers for current savings, while the demand arises from the accumulation of savings by lenders. The current savings themselves, to be sure, are like wheat and cotton in that they consist of finished goods and services that are continually being produced, exchanged, and consumed, according to a process which converts the unused real income of savers into new capital goods; but the new securities, on the other hand, which represent the ownership of the new capital goods, are unlike commodities, because once issued they remain forever in the market.[3]

3.   THE SUPPLY OF NEW ISSUES

In the market where new issues are sold and where the rate of interest is determined, free and unhampered bargaining between borrower and lender and competitive bidding and offering in the conversion of current savings into new capital goods take place only with respect to certain kinds of new securities, not all kinds. Genuine bargaining and genuine formation of capital occur only in the case of new issues of *bonds*, not in the case of *stocks*, surprising though this one-sidedness may seem. The reasons for this one-sidedness in the capital markets as they are organized today will become clear if we compare the market for stocks with that for bonds.

If it were customary today, as once it was, to promote a great enterprise by organizing a new company, selling its shares, and spending the proceeds for the construction of plant and equipment, new issues of stock, like new issues of bonds, would really convert savings into capital goods, and would really help to set the interest rate.[4] In the old days,

---

[3] Except as they may be eliminated by retirement through sinking funds and the like, an operation involving the reinvestment of surplus earnings discussed in § 3 below.

[4] Keynes seems to have such an unreal process as this in mind when he says,

companies to trade overseas, or to establish plantations, dig canals, and build railroads, were actually floated with sales of stock by their promoters, but today such a procedure is largely obsolete. Only an occasional small mine or new invention is ever financed in this way now, and such ventures are never listed on the New York Stock Exchange in their infancy and never absorb a significant part of the nation's savings. Hence the sale of *shares* by new enterprises today cannot be considered an important factor in determining the rate of interest.

Whenever the sale of shares does occur today in sufficient volume to affect the demand and supply of savings, the sale does not take place under such conditions as would represent the requisite combination of free bargaining between buyer and seller and genuine conversion of savings into capital goods, for nowadays it almost always happens that if the one condition is fulfilled, the other is not. Thus, if the new issue is freely priced, it almost always represents the ownership of some old and well-established enterprise which is being sold out by its original owners or their heirs for the purpose of diversifying the family holdings; such shares are not really *new* shares at all, even though they may be newly listed on the stock exchange, and the sale of these shares does not result in the creation of *new* capital goods, but only in the exchange of existing securities between various investors and the interchange of ownership of existing capital goods. The family sellers almost never use the proceeds of their sale to buy bricks and mortar and embark on a new venture; instead they almost always buy existing securities, and thus absorb, directly or indirectly, the very stocks and bonds which others have liquidated to

"The measure of success attained by Wall Street, regarded as an institution of which the proper social purpose is to direct new investment into the most profitable channels in terms of future yield, cannot be claimed as one of the outstanding triumphs of *laissez-faire* capitalism" (*General Theory*, p. 159).

buy the family's shares. Only in the special case where the founders of an enterprise sell out at a profit does the sale of their stock absorb the savings of the community, and even then the absorption is only as much as the excess of the offering price over the book value of the new shares. In the case of these privately held issues, the saving that in the beginning created the assets behind them took place outside the stock market when the proprietors invested their personal savings in the enterprise or let it grow up out of earnings.

Almost the only time when the sale of new shares ever represents the genuine conversion of savings into new capital goods is when a going concern offers rights to its own stockholders; but when this happens, the price of the new shares is always set well below their current market value, and so there occurs no bargaining between borrower and lender, no haggling over price between supplier and demander of savings. Thus when one condition for the determination of the rate of interest in the stock market is fulfilled, the other is not. The occasion seems never to arise nowadays when the sale of new issues of stock can fairly be viewed as a process wherein the rate of interest is independently determined. As will be shown, the stock market in this respect is vastly different from the bond market.

Whatever effect on the rate of interest the sale of stock on rights has is slight and wholly indirect, and wholly expressed in the bond market. If rights are offered, or if, in more candid terms, stockholders are assessed for new money,[5] savings which might otherwise have been available for the purchase of bonds, and capital goods which might otherwise have been built with the proceeds of bonds, are perforce built with the proceeds of stocks. Thus the supply

[5] For a discussion of the true nature of rights, see Chapter V, § 5.

and demand for *borrowed* capital are both reduced, but reduced equally; and this reduction makes little difference, therefore, in the final rate of interest.

Equity capital is usually obtained by a process that is wholly independent of the pricing mechanism of the stock market. If the capital comes from corporate saving, this saving goes on without reference to the particular price or course of prices for the company's shares in the open market; managers approve the enlargement or modernization of plant not because their company's stock is selling high or low, but because they believe such a step will increase future earnings. Can anyone imagine that Mr. Ford, whose company has been built up to an enormous size out of earnings, made it a practice to consult the ticker for the price of his stock before deciding to build a new assembly plant, power house, or glass factory? Of course not. His stock is unlisted and its market value does not interest him. Yet if the pricing mechanism of the stock market were really relevant to the formation of capital, and if stock prices really reflected the cost of procuring savings in the same way that bond prices reflect this cost,[6] Mr. Ford or any other industrialist would be obliged to take these stock prices into account. Untenable, therefore, would seem to be the theory, advanced by some writers,[7] that high prices for shares promote, and low prices retard, the formation of new capital.

With bonds the case is quite different, and with bonds

[6] Contrast the views of Keynes, who says of the 1929 bull market that "very high prices of common shares, relatively to their dividend yields, offered Joint-Stock enterprises an exceptionally cheap method of financing themselves" (*Treatise*, II, 195). After all, dividends payable on stock issued for "rights" are not a *cost* like contractual interest on bonds; instead dividends are a division of *profits*.

[7] Contrast the views of Keynes expressed in his *General Theory*, p. 151. The observed concurrence of high stock prices and heavy outlays merely reflects the response of both prices and building to a common influence, namely, good prospects for future earnings.

the market price is a deciding factor in the formation of new capital; for bonds, unlike stocks freely priced, are really used to finance great construction projects; and when so used, new bonds, unlike most new stocks, are sold to savers at a price as high as can be obtained, not at a price below the market. With new issues of bonds genuine bargaining between borrower and lender occurs, and every new issue is priced on its merits. The price, therefore, is significant, and actually represents the cost of new capital. Hence, it is in the bond market, not in the stock market, that the long-term rate of interest is determined. The bond market, not the stock market, is where savings compete for an outlet, and where enterprises compete — really compete — for financial support. In this market, unlike the stock market, no specious rights are issued, no dividends are withheld, nothing is done without the consent of the investor. The rate of interest that thus emerges in this competitive market is reached in coöperation with the mortgage market and the market for short-term loans,[8] to be sure, but thereafter the rate of interest that results from the activities of all three markets,[9] whatever it may be, is merely carried over without further change into the stock market, and applied to the appraisal of common stocks there.

4.   INTEREST RATES AND NEW INVESTMENT

The interest rate that emerges in the bond market in the manner just described is of great importance in determining the amount of new investment in capital goods, as we shall now go on to show.

Although quasi-rent is the source from which interest and dividends are paid, it is also the source from which

[8] For a discussion of the connection between long- and short-term interest rates, see Chapter V, § 4, Chapter X, Chapter XIX, § 10, and Chapter XX, § 3.
[9] The effect of marginal opinion on bond prices and interest rates is described in Chapter III, § 2.

several other outlays of equal or greater amount must likewise be paid. A complete list of the costs which must be covered by the annuity of quasi-rents earned by a piece of equipment during its life is given in order of priority below:

1. Property taxes
2. Maintenance, in part [10]
3. Repayment of the principal [11]
4. Interest on the principal
5. Income taxes
6. Business profits, if possible

From the above list it will readily be seen that for some kinds of capital goods interest in itself is only a small item in the total of overhead costs, whereas for others it is a major item. Thus in the case of a motor truck, whose life is short, interest is unimportant, whereas in the case of a tunnel, whose life is well-nigh perpetual, interest is the major item. Hence a decline in the rate of interest would do little directly to induce the manufacture of motor trucks, but it might do much to induce the drilling of tunnels.

Whether a decline in the rate of interest by itself would provide a large new outlet for savings depends, not on the possibility of increasing our equipment of motor trucks,

[10] While those maintenance outlays that are caused by the wear and tear of actual operations are properly chargeable to prime costs, since they can be avoided by letting the machinery stand idle, those that are caused by weather and age are chargeable to overhead, since they go on whether the plant is used or unused. Along with these latter costs must also be included the cost of supervising such unavoidable maintenance.

[11] Charges for depreciation, depletion, and obsolescence are here taken care of by the requirement that the principal shall be repaid out of earnings. Fire insurance premiums are not listed here as a separate expense; instead they are treated like installments on the principal, because they provide the fund out of which obsolete structures are so often replaced. In fact, it is all too often true that the only provision for obsolescence or depreciation which property owners make is the payment of fire insurance premiums, and the only replacements they make are with fire insurance collections.

steam shovels, farm implements, etc., but rather on the possibility of increasing our equipment of tunnels, dams, breakwaters, etc. If property taxes on new permanent structures of the latter kind were only light enough, then interest would be almost the sole cost to be covered by their quasi-rents, with the result that a decline in the rate of interest would justify an enormous outlay on many improvements heretofore considered too costly. Railroad curves could be straightened, grades could be reduced by fills and tunnels, roadbeds could be ballasted, bridges could be built, and many other things could be done to shorten distances and save coal, labor, and time in the hauling of freight and passengers. Ship canals, locks, drydocks, and the like could be built to facilitate water-borne commerce. Motor highways could be straightened and regraded; hydroelectric dams, power plants, and transmission lines could be erected; rapid-transit subways could be sunk; dikes and levees could be thrown up; swamps and marshes could be drained; soil erosion could be combated; sewage systems could be installed; and reservoirs, irrigation works, and waterworks could be built. All this new construction, moreover, could be made with costlier but more durable materials, with wood giving way to brick and steel, and flimsy sheds to solid and enduring structures.[12] Perhaps even dwelling houses could be built so well as to need very few repairs each year thereafter; in this event, a low rate of interest would promote the absorption of much capital in house building.[13] Any investment, in short, which promised a saving in prime costs, and which was very durable

[12] In the light of the above list, it would hardly seem that Keynes was right in maintaining that the opportunities for investing new savings are "strictly limited." See his *General Theory*, p. 375. Surely no building contractor or real-estate salesman, coming in daily contact with countless would-be buyers who can hardly find money enough for a small down payment on a new house, would ever agree with Keynes's view that people nowadays tend to save so fast that they can find no profitable outlet for their savings.

[13] Compare the remarks of Marshall, who says, "The demand for durable

and very cheap to maintain, would pay for itself, and would be well warranted, provided that property taxes as well as interest rates were low enough.

It would be necessary, of course, for the credit of the borrower to be sound and free from impairment by other commitments; thus it would do no good to have the cost of a railway tunnel well justified by the savings it would produce if the railroad that wished to borrow found its credit already impaired by high wages and low traffic. There can be little doubt but what low interest rates in the 1930's would have caused much larger capital outlays of the sort just described if only the credit of the railroads and other potential borrowers had been better and the property taxes to which the new improvements would have been subject had been lower.

For certain kinds of capital outlays to be encouraged by a low rate of interest it is also necessary for the business outlook to be good, and for demand to be active. Obviously, there is scant inducement to build a new hydroelectric plant, for instance, if demand is so slack that present plants are not used to capacity. While a low rate of interest helps to throw the balance of advantage from a steam plant using little capital to a hydroelectric plant using much capital — provided that demand warrants the construction of any new plants at all — nevertheless, if demand is slack, a low rate of interest may pass entirely unheeded.

And finally, for a low rate of interest to encourage capital outlays in general, it is necessary for building costs to show a horizontal or rising trend. For if building costs are headed downward, it may be judged cheaper to build later and pay a higher rate of interest on a smaller sum of money invested.

New inventions increase the opportunities for investing

stone houses in place of wood houses which give nearly equal accommodation for the time indicates that a country is growing in wealth, and that capital is to be had at a lower rate of interest" (*Principles*, p. 581).

savings profitably, and help, in a time like the present when technological progress is so rapid, to support the rate of interest; but to this statement, repeated by so many writers on economics, one qualification needs to be added, as follows: the *prospect* of a new invention has the opposite effect from the *presence* of the same invention, for the prospect induces people to postpone capital outlays until the new invention has been perfected and can be embodied in the proposed capital good. Thus the prospect of continued improvements in the steam locomotive makes railroad managers unwilling to let out too many replacement orders now, and also makes them unwilling to embark on electrification projects as a substitute for steam traction. Likewise the prospect of continued improvements in building construction and the means of transportation makes the obsolescence of houses and neighborhoods so high as to prevent great emphasis on durability in the design of dwellings. Can it be possible that at the present time, therefore, the rapidity of technological progress is so very high that it is depressing the rate of interest temporarily for the reason that expected obsolescence has increased in many lines of investment? Such an effect, to be sure, is indeed possible in specific cases, but it is doubtful if these cases are numerous enough to account for much of the dearth of new borrowing today.

5. NOTE ON KEYNES'S THEORY OF INTEREST

For purposes of exposition it may help to contrast the views set forth above with the new theory of interest recently advanced by Keynes in his *General Theory of Employment, Interest and Money*.

It is hard to agree with his premises when he writes:[14]

[14] See esp. p. 167. Quoted by permission of the publishers, Harcourt, Brace and Company.

. . . the rate of interest cannot be a return to saving or waiting as such. . . . The rate of interest is the reward for parting with liquidity . . . [it] is a measure of the unwillingness of those who possess money to part with their liquid control over it.[15] The rate of interest is not the "price" which brings into equilibrium the demand for resources to invest with the readiness to abstain from present consumption. It is the "price" which equilibrates the desire to hold wealth in the form of cash with the available quantity of cash. . . .

When he writes thus, he implies (1) that cash is liquid while securities are not; (2) that cash is safe to hold while securities are not; (3) that people will accumulate savings without the inducement of interest, whereas they would be loath to part with these savings once accumulated except on payment of interest.

These premises do not seem to be correct, for the following reasons:

1. The marketability of many securities, such as government bonds, is so great that they are practically as liquid as cash.

2. The very best securities, such as government bonds, are just as safe as cash to hold, because they are sure to be paid off in cash at maturity,[16] and customarily sell at a price at which the market believes the chance of intermediate depreciation to be exactly balanced by the chance of intermediate appreciation.[17] Hence only those investors who disagree with the market by being distinctly bearish on the intermediate outlook will prefer cash to bonds. All other investors will consider the interest received to be net income and no mere insurance premium to compensate them for the possibility of partial loss of their principal in case they should have to sell before maturity.

3. It seems distinctly incorrect to claim that the entire

---

[15] Cf. Chapter III, § 2.
[16] Cf. Chapter XIX, § 1.   [17] Cf. Chapter V, § 8.

amount of current savings would be laid up just the same even if no one were to receive any reward for saving. While it is true that some people would save in the absence of any interest whatsoever, it is doubtful if all present savers would do so. In other words, when Keynes writes, "If a man hoards his savings in cash, he earns no interest, *though he saves just as much as before,*" [18] he slurs the point; for the average man probably will not save as much as before if he must hoard his savings in cash and cannot lend them at interest. The true explanation for his hoarding in the beginning is simply his hope of getting a higher rate of interest in the end when he finally does see fit to buy securities.

Merely because we do not agree with Keynes's theory *in toto*, however, it does not follow that we must reject his theory completely. So much of it as is valid may be salvaged and incorporated into the classical theory by making use of the notion of a frequency curve covering the distribution of market opinion along the lines suggested in Chapter III, § 2.

[18] *Loc. cit.* Italics mine.

PART IV

THE OUTLOOK FOR INTEREST RATES AND THE PRICE LEVEL

CHAPTER XIX

POLITICS, INFLATION, AND GOVERNMENT BONDS

The present section of this book (Part IV) looks both forwards and back: forwards, in the sense that, by appraising the worth of Government Bonds, it is the first of the Case Studies; and back, in the sense that, by completing the groundwork for the rest of the studies, it is the last of the Theory.

Viewed as a Case Study, on the one hand, this section undertakes to find the present worth of future coupons and principal for Government Bonds by asking first, "What will be the purchasing power of these coupons and principal?" (Chapter XIX), and second, "What rate of interest should be used in discounting this purchasing power of coupons and principal?" (Chapter XX). Like the other Case Studies, and unlike the earlier sections of this book, the present one on Government Bonds is set forth with the reservation that its conclusions are "subject to change without notice" if any unforeseen events occur, as they surely will, from time to time.

Viewed as groundwork, on the other hand, this section seeks to answer the two most important general questions confronting the investor today; namely, "What is going to happen to the price level?" and "What is going to happen to interest rates?" An answer to these questions is needed before any attempt can be made to appraise specific securities in the pages to follow. Viewed as groundwork again, this section, more than any other part of the book, seeks to discover the economic consequences of the New Deal so far as the investor is concerned.

I.   INTEREST RATES AND THE PRICE LEVEL

While there are no riskless investments in existence in the broadest sense of the word, nevertheless there is a class of investments, namely, government bonds, which are often called riskless.[1] Government bonds are riskless in the sense that they will certainly be paid off in legal tender, for the government itself controls the printing press and can always provide money of some sort to meet its obligations. In this sense its credit does not depend on its taxing power, as does that of a city or state, but only on its power to create fiat money.[2]

Whether this money will be of the usual value or not is another question. If lenders expect a decline in the purchasing power of money, they ought to demand compensation in the form of a higher interest rate in terms of money, as Fisher pointed out so clearly in his "Appreciation and Interest."[3] Thus the money rate of interest should move with the general price level, even though the real rate of interest remains constant.

[1] A comprehensive manual on government bonds, entitled *United States Government Securities*, is published by C. J. Devine & Co., Inc.

[2] The repurchase of one's own obligations is also a riskless investment. Such an investment was made by the U. S. Steel Corporation in 1930 (see Chapter XXII) when it paid off a large part of its funded debt. Repayment of debt reduces interest charges and adds to net income. The increase in net income is subject to the corporation income tax, however, and so the return on this kind of riskless investment is impaired to that extent. Hence it did not pay the Steel Corporation to call its bonds down to the very last dollar. Because the last hundred million of bonds could never cause the Corporation embarrassment in bad times, there was no use in putting the stockholders' money into such an investment with money rates what they were at that time.

[3] Irving Fisher, "Appreciation and Interest," *Publications of the American Economic Association*, Third Series, vol. XI, No. 4 (August 1896), pp. 331–442. See also his *Theory of Interest* (New York: Macmillan, 1930), chap. II, "Money Interest and Real Interest," and chap. XIX, "The Relation of Interest to Money and Prices"; also his *Rate of Interest* (New York: Macmillan, 1907), Appendix to chap. V, § 1, "History of Theory of Appreciation and Interest." See also Marshall, *Money, Credit, & Commerce*, p. 74, and *Principles*, p. 594.

The most striking confirmation of this theory in recent years is the behavior of French government bonds during the post-war inflation in that country, as shown by Chart II.[4] When the general price level was rising fastest, these bonds made their extreme low, because it was just at this point that investors were most pessimistic; but as soon as the speed of inflation decreased, investors took heart again, and bonds began to recover. With each decrease in the speed of inflation thereafter, investors set a lower and lower limit on the shrinkage still to be expected in the purchasing power of future payments. The result was that the low for the bond curve was coincident with the steepest part of the cost-of-living curve.

A similar confirmation of the theory is to be seen in what Keynes[5] calls the "Gibson Paradox." For nearly a hundred and fifty years, high prices for commodities have gone with low prices for consols, and vice versa, as shown by Chart III.[6] At first this seems out of harmony with the French experience to the extent of one fourth of a cycle, but the answer is not far to seek. In the English experience the rise and fall of general prices were very slow, and seemed to observers of the time as a trend without end. Consequently investors would continue to forecast rising prices even when the peak of the rise had been reached, and falling prices even at the low. In fact, nothing made them so sure of the future trend as the long duration of the past trend. Con-

[4] Data from *Bulletin du Bureau de la Statistique Générale* (Paris: Imprimerie Nationale, 1932), p. 124, and monthly supplements. See also James Harvey Rogers, *The Process of Inflation in France* (New York: Columbia University Press, 1929), pp. 257–262 and Chart XLIX.

[5] For Keynes's own explanation of the Gibson Paradox, see his *Treatise*, II, 203–208.

[6] The bond yields are those of British consols, and the commodity prices are a combination of the Silberling, Sauerbeck and Statist index numbers. Chart reprinted from *Trends in Interest Rates*, by Edwin Walter Kemmerer (New York: Manhattan Foundation, Inc., 1936), with the permission of the author.

CHART II

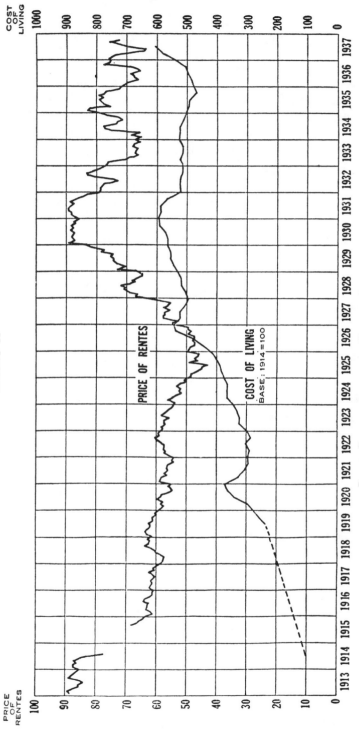

RENTE PRICES DURING THE FRENCH INFLATION

sequently, borrowers and lenders were most completely
wrong in their forecasts just at the turning points. Exactly
when commodity prices were ready to turn down, everyone
was most sure of a rise; and so all contracted their loans

CHART III

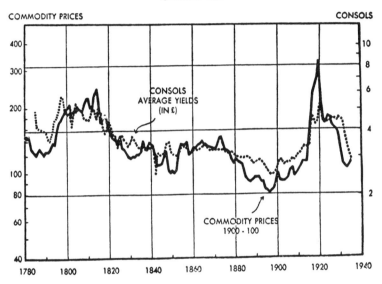

BRITISH BOND YIELDS AND COMMODITY PRICES

at the highest rate of interest. The converse was true at
the bottom of the cycle.

In the United States, a notable instance of falling prices
and low interest rates is to be found in the period of the
1890's. Prices had been declining since 1864, and were
just ready to turn upward under the influence of the gold
discoveries in the Rand and the cyanide method for treat-
ing gold ores; but leading investors were oblivious to these
new things, and based their forecasts solely on the extrapolated trend of the past generation. They did not reason

explicitly, of course, on the rational connection between price trends and interest rates, but did so implicitly when they said experience showed that low yields were nevertheless satisfactory to the investor in the end. Contemporary opinion on the subject has been preserved for us in a collection of letters [7] written in 1899 by bankers and trustees in answer to a request for advice by the Equitable Life Assurance Society. That the advice given was unanimously wrong is not surprising, because prevailing opinion never shows the future course of prices but only explains the present position thereof. It was precisely the bullishness of expert opinion which accounted for bond quotations' being as high as they were then, and no further rise ought to have been expected without an increase in bullishness.

During the recent depression likewise, the spectacular decline in interest rates was related in part to the expected course of commodity prices. If money is gaining in purchasing power, borrowers and lenders both should allow for this in their dealings; and if the fall of commodity prices is expected to be fastest in the immediate future, short-term loans should carry the lowest interest rates, and a fall that is swift enough should even send the rate to zero. Likewise, if inflation instead of deflation is under way, short-term interest rates again should respond more than long-term rates, because both borrowers and lenders will expect prices to rise fastest in the early years of a loan. In theory interest rates should act in this way always, and in practice they do very often, as shown by Leonard P. Ayres in his booklet entitled *Inflation*.[8] Our own formulas, given in Chapter V, § 4, entitled "Compound Interest at a Changing Rate," and in Chapter VIII, § 2, entitled "Bonds with

[7] Reprinted in Rose, *A Scientific Approach to Investment Management*, Appendix II. [8] Published by the Cleveland Trust Company, 1936, p. 27.

Inflation or Deflation Impending," show how the coupon rate on a long-term bond can rise only a little and still offset a sharp but short inflation, whereas the coupon rate on a short-term bond must rise a lot in order to offset, in a few years, the same amount of inflation.

In any actual case where inflation or deflation is clearly foreseen, if long- and short-term interest rates do not behave as here described, it is because some offsetting force is at work (as described in § 10, below), or because people do not act in a rational manner. Lack of rationality is, of course, a difficulty met with on occasion in other branches of economics as well, such as the theory of wages and the theory of monopoly; but we do not on that account discard these other theories, nor should we in this case discard our theory of long- and short-term interest rates for fear that people may sometimes fail to see.and act on prospective changes in the price level. This is especially so because we are engaged in measuring investment value, not in forecasting market price, in deciding what one *should* pay, not what one *must* pay, for a given security.

Lack of rationality, moreover, though it often appears in slight degree, seldom asserts itself in an overwhelming degree in economic behavior; and to say that investors would buy bonds at a price inconsistent with their convictions regarding the future purchasing power of money would be to say that men are fools — something that economic science is not in the habit of doing. Therefore, if we wish to know what people in general expect regarding the future course of prices, we have only to look at quotations for government bonds. Government bonds, being riskless, are the barometer of *expected* inflation or deflation. As to whether the prevailing expectation is right or wrong, we are not concerned just yet. All we seek is a measure of the expectation itself.

The foreign exchange rate does not measure the same thing as bond prices do, and the common belief that it is the most sensitive and reliable index of future inflation is a mistake. When steady, it merely measures the degree of inflation already attained and has no forecasting significance. When changing, it merely indicates the best speculative guess, if a country is temporarily off the gold standard, as to the figure at which resumption of gold payments will eventually be attempted. Thus, in the case of the United States in 1933–34, the declining foreign exchange quotation was no measure at all of internal inflation, and showed only what shrewd traders thought would be the eventual degree of *devaluation* (as contrasted with inflation).

In certain exceptional circumstances, to be sure, the rôle of government bonds and foreign exchange is reversed, but this case need be mentioned only to prevent its being used as an argument against the theory expounded above. It is illustrated by the fall in United States government bonds in the autumn of 1931 and again in the spring of 1932, when this country was experiencing two serious runs on its gold reserves. Each time the exchange rate stayed close to par, because gold payments kept it there for the time being. Government bonds, however, fell, because they were promises to pay gold in the *future*, and their ultimate value in gold was open to doubt, since the run might become serious enough to render their payment in full impossible when the time came. Short-term bonds fell less than long-term bonds, since they stood a better chance of maturing before it was too late to get gold payments.[9] In this connection it is worth noting that long-term government bonds fell lower during the outward gold flows of

[9] Intermediate-term bonds, on their part, while they might not mature in time to be paid in gold, nevertheless stood a better chance of maturing in time to be paid in less seriously depreciated paper money.

1931 and 1932 than during the bank panic of 1933; evidently the fear of our going off the gold standard was more of a factor in 1931 and 1932 in determining their market price than was any necessitous selling by certain banks in need of cash in 1933. In these exceptional circumstances, therefore, bonds, rather than the exchange rate, were forecasting the eventual time and degree of devaluation. In ordinary circumstances, however, government bonds are the weathervane that forecasts the *expected* trend of commodity prices, particularly the cost of living. To judge by present prices — namely, those of June 1937 — the bond market is supremely confident that inflation will not occur.

Let no one say that the rise in bonds from 1932 to 1936, taking place at a time when commodity prices were likewise rising, disproves the logical connection between bond prices and the expected purchasing power of money. Nothing of the sort; for it is precisely in accordance with theory that bond prices should rise as commodity prices approach the end of their recovery, and that bond prices should be back to normal when the rise in the cost of living is thought to have come to a stop. Therefore it is still correct to say that the bond market itself is supremely confident of no inflation ahead. In this expectation it may be wrong, but such at least is the correct interpretation of its present level of prices.

It is incorrect to argue, as some writers do,[10] that bond prices cannot discount a well-foreseen rise in commodity prices, because a *well-foreseen* rise is inherently impossible for the very good reason that speculators would send commodity prices up at once if a rise was thought sure to come eventually. Nothing of the sort; for most commodities are perishable, and cannot be bought up in advance and stored for several years in hopes of higher prices. Neither

[10] Cf. Keynes, *General Theory*, p. 142.

can the cost of living be raised by speculative anticipation, because a rise in the cost of living must await an increase in the money income of consumers as compared with the quantity of goods offered for sale to them.

2.   THE DEGREE OF DEPRECIATION THAT INFLATION WOULD WARRANT

Many promises have been made by the Roosevelt Administration to raise the general price level.[11] If people really thought the government could do so, and if investors knew by experience what this always means in terms of shrunken purchasing power, then government bonds would surely sell a great deal lower than they currently do. Just how much lower they ought to sell we can determine exactly, once the necessary assumptions regarding the future course of commodity prices have been made. For the sake of example, let us consider the following three possibilities: Either

(1) The index of the cost of living will rise to the 1926 level during the next four years, or

(2) The index of the cost of living will rise to the 1926 level during the next twenty years, or

---

[11] Cf. President Roosevelt's radio speech on October 22, 1933 reprinted on page 1 of the *New York Times* the next day, in which he announced his gold-buying program and made the following statements:

"If we cannot raise farm prices one way we will do it another. Do it we will. . . .

"Finally, I repeat what I have said on many occasions, that ever since last March the definite policy of the government has been to restore commodity price-levels. . . .

"The object has been to make possible the payment of public and private debts more nearly at the price-level at which they were incurred.

"It is the government's policy to restore the price-level first. . . ."

See also the *New York Times* for July 6, 1933, p. 1, where he is reported seeking a return to the price level of 1924–25.

Likewise see the *New York Times* for October 11, 1934, p. 1, col. 1, where he is again reported determined to raise prices.

The 1926 level of prices has often been mentioned as President Roosevelt's objective.

(3) The index of the cost of living will rise enough during the next twenty years to offset the devaluation of the dollar to 59.08 per cent of its old parity.

These three possibilities will affect long- and short-term bonds differently. The longer a bond has to run, the more its price must change to alter its yield and reflect movements in the general price level; therefore we shall choose for our calculations the longest issue now outstanding, the Treasury $2\frac{3}{4}$'s of 1956–59. For simplicity we shall assume that these bonds will be called [12] in 1956, with the result that they will have about twenty years more to run. To find the proper value for these bonds in each of the three possible cases mentioned above, we shall use formula (33).[13] In order that the application of the formula may be quite clear, all the knowns used in the formula, as well as all the original data, will be included in Table 2.[14]

For illustration, data as of November 16, 1936 are used in the calculations. An interest rate of 2.60 per cent (the same as the then-prevailing yield to maturity) is employed, and this rate is assumed to remain steady throughout the period in question. In speaking of a 2.60 per cent rate, the real rate in goods is meant, not the rate in paper money or gold. A riskless rate is also meant. Whether the riskless rate that actually will be collected during the next twenty years will prove to be 2.60 per cent is not the question. All that is needed is a fair statement of what people expect.

For simplicity the computations are made with interest compounded annually instead of semi-annually, even

[12] Actually the bonds will probably be allowed to run to maturity, for the reasons given in the next chapter (Chapter XX, § 6), but the foregoing simplification of the assumptions makes little difference in the answer.

[13] See Chapter VIII, § 2.

[14] The index of the cost of living used in the computation is the index number of the National Industrial Conference Board; it is published monthly in the *Survey of Current Business* by the United States Department of Commerce and has a base of 1923 = 100.

though the coupons are in fact payable semi-annually; but this simplification introduces no substantial error into the answer.

TABLE 2

The Effect of Expected Inflation on the Fair Value of Treasury $2\frac{3}{4}$'s of 1956–59

Formula (33):

$$V_o = pC_o \left\{ w \left(\frac{1 - w^n}{1 - w} \right) + \frac{u^n}{i} \left[v^n - v^{n'} \left(1 - \frac{i}{p} \right) \right] \right\}$$

	Case 1	Case 2	Case 3
	Data		
Coupon Rate:	$p = 2\frac{3}{4}\%$	$p = 2\frac{3}{4}\%$	$p = 2\frac{3}{4}\%$
Principal:	$C_o = \$100$	$C_o = \$100$	$C_o = \$100$
Pure Interest Rate:	$i = 2.60\%$	$i = 2.60\%$	$i = 2.60\%$
$v = \dfrac{1}{1+i}$	$v = 0.9747$	$v = 0.9747$	$v = 0.9747$
Life of Bond:	$n' = 20$ yrs.	$n' = 20$ yrs.	$n' = 20$ yrs.
Price Index at Start:	$H_o = 85.7$	$H_o = 85.7$	$H_o = 85.7$
Duration of Price Rise:	$n = 4$ yrs.	$n = 20$ yrs.	$n = 20$ yrs.
Price Index at End:	$H_n = 103.8$	$H_n = 103.8$	$H_n = \dfrac{85.7}{.5908}$
			$= 145.1$
	Variables of Computation		
	$v^n = 0.9024$	$v^n = 0.5985$	$v^n = 0.5985$
	$v^{n'} = 0.5985$	$v^{n'} = 0.5985$	$v^{n'} = 0.5985$
$u^n = \dfrac{H_o}{H_n}$	$u^n = 0.8256$	$u^n = 0.8256$	$u^n = 0.5908$
	$u = 0.9532$	$u = 0.9905$	$u = 0.9740$
$w = uv$	$w = 0.9291$	$w = 0.9654$	$w = 0.9494$
$w^n = u^n v^n$	$w^n = 0.7450$	$w^n = 0.4941$	$w^n = 0.3536$

$v^{n'} \left(1 - \dfrac{i}{p} \right) = v^{n'} \left(1 - \dfrac{.0260}{.0275} \right) = (.5985)(0.05455) = 0.0326$, in all three cases

	Answers		
	$V_o = 85\frac{1}{8}$	$V_o = 88\frac{1}{4}$	$V_o = 68\frac{3}{4}$

Table 2 shows that price-raising to the 1926 level in four years would have made these $2\frac{3}{4}$'s worth $85\frac{1}{8}$, or in twenty years $88\frac{1}{4}$; while if devaluation should achieve its implied purpose in twenty years, the bonds would be worth only $68\frac{3}{4}$, instead of $102\frac{9}{32}$, the prevailing price in November 1936. In every case the bonds would have been worth par [15] at the end of the four- or twenty-year periods, of course, and should have risen slowly as inflation progressed and approached its end. In theory the bonds ought to hit their low in the very beginning, but in practice this would not happen, because investors would neither believe in nor understand inflation until it had been with them for some time and had made substantial progress. By then the inflation would already be partly over, and so at that time a decline to the extreme lows just computed would not be warranted.

The fact that bond quotations are today well above par does not prove that inflation will never come, but only that it is not expected and allowed for already.

3. CAN GOVERNMENT BOND PRICES BE PEGGED?

Some of those who think inflation a serious possibility still insist that long-term government bonds will not fall, even after inflation begins, because they believe in the power of the Treasury to rig the market and peg the price.[16] They maintain that the Treasury, with its "Stabilization Fund" of $2,000,000,000 and its control of the open-market operations of the Federal Reserve System, can put the price where it pleases and keep it there. Such being the case, they say, why should anyone fear a decline and wish to sell?

[15] Or, more precisely, $101\frac{30}{32}$ (the amortized value at 2.60 per cent) in the case of inflation ending in four years.

[16] Cf. J. Franklin Ebersole's address before the Massachusetts Coöperative Bank League, reprinted in the *Proceedings* of their 46th Annual Convention (Boston, 1934), pp. 116–121.

Banks and insurance companies, to be sure, who care nothing about the cost of living [17] because their liabilities are expressed in paper money only, will not be driven to sell for the reasons that actuate private investors. Since most of the government bonds are owned by these financial institutions, who feel they are obliged to buy them for income, and since the amount of long-term debt in the hands of individuals, colleges, hospitals, and charitable endowments is small, there might seem, superficially, to be nothing to worry about. Such is not the fact, however, because inflation would cause private investors to shift from bonds into stocks, or into real estate and commodities. Inflation would make individuals want to sell bonds of every kind, including non-government issues. When these latter issues became cheaper than government issues, the financial institutions would sell government bonds, which they had been counted upon to retain, in order to replace them with corporate bonds; and nothing but the exhaustion of the supply of corporate bonds held by private investors could bring this process to a stop. Thus governments would be driven down with the rest of the list, unless the Treasury and the Federal Reserve System stood ready to absorb the entire supply, and end with the ownership of all such bonds outstanding. But why should the government, which really wants to distribute bonds, accumulate them instead, just to hold the price, when this would still leave it unable to sell any new issues?

Even if the Federal Reserve Board should revise its rules so as to permit member banks to borrow on long-term Treasury issues at par regardless of how low the market fell — even then, to repeat, the price might not stay up, because most banks might refuse to go into debt in order to speculate in governments.

---

[17] Except as it may affect their own operating expenses in a severe inflation.

Perhaps there is another explanation of the strength in governments, however, an explanation that involves the use of a different kind of support by the national authorities. Perhaps the market thinks that in an emergency the commercial banks would not be allowed to switch out of governments into corporate issues, and that a financial dictatorship in Washington would allot the outstanding and new issues by a system of quotas, subjecting all financial institutions to a regimen of forced feeding. That a dictatorship over banking lurks in the background, and could be used to support government bond prices in time of need, is true; and Marriner S. Eccles, Governor of the Federal Reserve Board, has bluntly said as much.[18] Things would not need to come to such a pass, however, before the federal authorities could get their way, because the banks could be forced to submit in the beginning to anything they knew was inevitable in the end. Some may argue, then, that this fact explains current high bond prices in the face of impending inflation (if indeed inflation does impend).

The trouble with this argument is that it proves too little. It may explain the price of government bonds, but not of all bonds. Perhaps the federal authorities stand ready to ration their own bonds, but certainly they contemplate no such support for all bonds, including state, municipal, and corporate issues. Yet in 1936 the best of these issues likewise sold at record highs. Why?

4.   WILL INFLATION REALLY COME?

Unless inflation is really a serious possibility, there need be no mystery, of course, to present quotations. Most in-

---

[18] In his testimony before the House Banking and Currency Committee, he said: "It would be unfortunate for the bankers if the government, by reason of a deficit, couldn't get their coöperation, because under the circumstances the government would take over the banking system" (*New York Times*, March 10, 1935, p. 31).

vestors now feel that politicians are helpless in dealing with the general price level, and nothing that the law-makers can do, short of starting a panic, will suffice to change the purchasing power of money. What good has been done by the open-market operations of the Federal Reserve Banks? say these disillusioned investors. What has devaluation accomplished,[19] except in the case of a few things like wheat and cotton? What good has the purchase of silver done? What good would it do to issue greenbacks, for new paper money would only be redundant, and would only drive out old paper money such as Federal Reserve notes? To these arguments there is much force. Verily, the politician who promises to lift the price level and free the people from their bondage of debt will soon find he has attempted the impossible.

Even though rising prices cannot be had merely by passing a law, nevertheless inflation could develop of its own accord in due time. Such spontaneous inflation should make bonds go down as much as deliberate inflation would. A spontaneous rise in general prices need not be rapid. Even if it took twenty or thirty years to run its course, it should still send bonds down, as shown by the calculations in Cases 2 and 3 above. Whether it *would* send bonds down, and how soon and how far they would fall, would depend on how quick the public was to understand what was happening. Although the investment value of bonds would be reduced the instant inflation became likely, their market price would fall only when the marginal investor became convinced that he stood to lose a part of the future purchasing power of his money. Our problem here, however, is not to forecast market prices, but to estimate investment value. Hence it behooves us to inquire with care into the question of what is likely to happen to the cost of living in

---

[19] The price rises of 1936 seem to have been due not to devaluation, but to drought, fear of war abroad, and hope of prosperity at home.

the generation ahead as a result of the devaluation of the franc in 1928 (and again in 1936), of the dollar in 1934, and of the pound, as seems probable, in due time.[20]

5. GOLD SUPPLIES AND THE PRICE LEVEL

To begin with, we must decide whether the 1913 price level, or the 1922–1930 price level, represented the true equilibrium level at the former gold values for the various currencies. As far as France was concerned at the start of the depression, nothing had happened to *force* the subsequent price decline of 1931–1933, because internal prices in France had risen from 1913 to 1928 somewhat less than the franc itself had been devalued in 1928. As far as England and the United States were concerned, however, a dangerous situation existed, because internal prices had risen some 50 per cent from 1913 to 1928 without any offsetting devaluation. Yet it is true that the United States, though it had not devalued, had done something else which, in the eyes of some economists, might have been expected to produce the same effect on prices as devaluation. This country had adopted the Federal Reserve System in 1913, and had made changes in it later, which had entailed a great reduction in the reserve ratio for the bank deposits of the country. Kemmerer has figured that this reduction was more than enough to permit the rise of 50 per cent in prices that took place between 1913 and 1928.[21] But is it true that the price level in any country depends on its own gold reserves alone? Can any country let its own prices rise faster than prices elsewhere, regardless of its gold reserve to start with, and still stay on the gold standard with-

[20] The likelihood of inflation and the prospects of a return to gold are discussed in the *Proceedings* of the Academy of Political Science, May 1936. See also the report of the University of Minnesota Conference on *The Prospects for Inflation.*

[21] See his speech delivered before the American Statistical Association, October 27, 1931 (mimeographed).

out a change of parity? If there had been no war in Europe
in 1914–1918, and if our own prices had risen after the
Federal Reserve System began operations, would not gold
have flowed out of this country, and kept on flowing until
it was all gone? As soon as we had tried to stop the flow,
would not the price rise have ended? Moreover, would not
international commodities, like wheat and cotton, copper
and oil, have remained at the same prices both here and
abroad? Therefore, would not a mere 8 or 10 per cent rise
in our prices, let us say, instead of the full 50 per cent implied by the change in our banking laws, have been all
that could properly have been expected? While the acquisition of some of our gold by European nations would
have permitted their prices to rise too, ending even with
ours, surely the world-wide rise would never have been to
the post-war level. Hence it cannot be claimed that the
introduction of the Federal Reserve System, with its lowered gold requirements, was equivalent in this country to
the devaluation of the franc and other currencies abroad.

Neither did the withdrawal of gold from circulation in
England, France, and elsewhere during the War add enough
to bank reserves abroad to support the higher price level of
the post-war decade. Furthermore, the transition of India
from a silver to a gold standard in 1928 was an offsetting
influence tending to increase the amount of gold needed
to support the world price level.

All things considered, then, the 1913 level of commodity
prices seems more likely to have been the equilibrium level
at the old parities than the 1926 level.[22]

Had the *gold exchange* standard used in the 1920's succeeded, the 1926 level could have been held with less diffi-

[22] Cf. George F. Warren and Frank A. Pearson, *Prices* (New York: J. Wiley
& Sons, Inc.; London: Chapman & Hall, Ltd., 1933), p. 367, who wrote as
follows in 1932: "If all the former gold-using countries return to the gold basis
and if the United States continues to maintain its present monetary standard,

culty, but now this measure is discredited. Likewise, if London had continued to be the sole great money market, and if New York and Paris had not arisen as rivals, a smaller gold reserve would have sufficed for settling international balances, because these balances could have been cleared through London without movement of funds into or out of that center. Moreover, if investors nowadays were not so fearful of monetary malpractice, and if speculators in foreign exchange were not so given to transferring huge sums from one money market to another, the present excess gold reserves would not be needed, and commodity prices the world over would not be held down by the necessity of maintaining them. As it is, though, reserves greatly in excess of the legal minimum are necessary in practice, because no country has an internal price structure so flexible as to bob up and down with every wave of gold flow, letting the country stay on the gold standard in spite of huge surges of capital. Since the effect on prices of keeping these excess reserves is the same as of increasing the reserve ratio itself, is it any wonder that general prices in terms of the old parities could not be sustained at the 1926 level, or even at the 1913 level, once the flight of capital from place to place got under way with full force during the depression? The recent increase in new gold being mined would seem inadequate to offset these capital movements, and even the redistribution of the excess gold reserves of the United States might not be enough to overcome this difficulty if all nations tried to return to the gold standard.

---

it is to be expected that commodity prices will average below pre-war for the next ten years."

Dr. Benjamin M. Ánderson, Jr., of the Chase National Bank, seems to take a different view, however, and seems to believe that the price level of the 1920's was the equilibrium level for the gold supply of the world at that time. His views on the future of commodity prices are quoted in the *New York Times*, January 7, 1937, p. 38, col. 1.

Should all the important countries in the world go completely off the gold standard, with the result that any movement of capital from one money market to another could not avoid pushing the exchange rate up against this selfsame capital movement, then these great flights of capital from place to place would be ended for good and all. And even though a single country like the United States remained on the gold standard,[23] the result would still be the same, for capital could not go out of this country into England, for instance, without putting the pound up, or come back into this country without putting the pound down, and moving the pound enough in either case to throttle down in short order an otherwise well-nigh unlimited flow. For such an automatic check to work England would have to be really off gold, of course; the check would not work if some exchange equalization fund were operating with nearly unlimited resources to keep the exchange rate fixed. But since the British Equalization Fund, as a matter of fact, is not used for the purpose of rate-fixing, but is used only for smoothing out minor fluctuations and discouraging manipulation, capital movements, as far as London goes, tend to be self-limiting.[24]

So long as any country is off the gold standard, then, its internal price level can go its own way without let or hindrance from abroad, but as soon as the country returns to the gold standard, its own price level becomes tied at once to the price levels of all other countries on the gold standard. Until September 1936 there remained in the world two important gold-standard countries, France and the United States. The price level of each was tied to that

[23] As far as *international* payments are concerned, the United States is on the gold standard, at least partially, though as far as *internal* redemption of its currency is concerned, it is not.

[24] At the present moment an exception to this statement must be made, because the recent Tri-Partite Agreement seems to be forcing the British into a form of exchange pegging for the time being.

of the other in two ways: directly, through the action of international commodities, which are kept at the same price in all countries by arbitrage; and indirectly through the action of gold flows,[25] which reduce central bank reserves and deflate member bank deposits before inflation can proceed very far in any country where prices begin to rise.[26]

So long as France stayed on the gold standard and we ourselves continued our use of gold for settling international balances, there was no danger of an extreme inflation in this country, with a rise here of 50, 100, or 500 per cent in all prices. Instead, what was happening here during 1934–35 as a result of our own devaluation was a readjustment between various prices within this country, such as would have brought export commodities back to their pre-depression relation to domestic commodities, with the result that our price index would have returned to the level of the 1920's. Such a readjustment, in fact, was already well under way before France went off gold in September 1936, and this readjustment had partly undone the maladjustments of 1930–1932. It will be remembered that during the early years of the depression, when the 1926 price level was in the process of breaking down, export commodities like wheat and cotton had fallen sharply in this country and domestic commodities and the cost of living had followed slowly but surely. Had there been no devaluation by us in 1933–34, a new internal equilibrium would

[25] The extent of the internal price rise that would be needed to produce an outflow of gold from the United States would depend in large measure on the degree to which the dollar is undervalued now. If the pound, which is the most important foreign currency for us, is now selling too high at $5.00, and should be selling around $4.20, let us say, for equilibrium, then the dollar would appear to be undervalued by roughly 15 per cent at present.

[26] For a more elaborate description of the operation of the gold standard see R. G. Hawtrey, *The Art of Central Banking* (London: Longmans, Green and Co., 1932), chap. IV, and Keynes, *Treatise*, chaps. XXI, XXXIV, XXV, and XXXVIII.

probably have been reached eventually for all prices at the low level already reached by export prices, which latter were down to pre-war figures in 1932. This earlier process of adjustment by deflation was abruptly ended in 1933, however, by our temporary abandonment of the gold standard, and by our subsequent devaluation of the dollar in 1934 to 59.08 per cent of its old parity. Such a devaluation in itself was enough to permit the rise of an export commodity like wheat from a price of 59.08 to one of 100, an increase of 69.3 per cent, or more than the increase in the general price level between 1913 and 1926, when prices rose from 69.8 to 100.[27] Evidently our devaluation in 1934 was more than enough to offset the change that had taken place in our own price level in the 1920's as a result of the War. Hence it also allowed some leeway for riding the ebb and flow of gold movements so common nowadays. Therefore, if the 1913 price level was for this country the normal level before devaluation, on the basis of the world's gold stock in 1933, then the 1926 level was probably the normal after devaluation, on the basis of the same gold stock. The tendency was strong, moreover, after our devaluation, for all prices to rebound at once to the higher level, and for the disequilibrium among prices to be rectified by the return of all prices to the relative values prevailing in the 1920's, since many prices had been sticky during the depression, and some had declined hardly at all from the 1926 level.

6.   THE INVESTOR'S COST OF LIVING

Why do government bonds, and other high-grade bonds as well, stay up, if reflation in general prices to the 1926 level is well under way and if the resulting fall in the pur-

---

[27] According to the index of the United States Bureau of Labor Statistics, included in Table VII of Appendix II.

chasing power of money is not yet completed? Why do not bonds decline, if the cost of living is going to continue to rise until it reaches the 1926 level; that is, if prices are going to rise from 85.7 to 103.8, let us say, as measured by the index of the National Industrial Conference Board for October 1936 as against the year 1926? For this paradox two explanations are possible: one, that market prices and investment value do not coincide, that is, that the rank and file of investors do not foresee the impending price rise and do not allow for it in their forecasts; the other, that the index itself is in error, that is, that the index does not measure the cost of living for the investing class in society. Since the index is heavily weighted with food prices, and since it takes but little account of the inflexible items in the budgets of the well-to-do, may not the second explanation be the true one, for may not it be a fact that the index overstates the rise in the cost of living to be expected by the well-to-do as a result of our devaluation in 1934, just as it overstated the fall in the cost of living previously enjoyed by these same people as a result of the depression? If the well-to-do are to see their cost of living rise only 4 or 5 per cent, let us say, instead of by the amount implied by the index, during the period ahead when wholesale commodities themselves are returning to the 1926 level, then the change in the purchasing power of money for investors will not be great enough, or certain enough, to warrant any aversion on their part to fixed-income-bearing securities. If the latter explanation is correct, we can say that what the bond market is really forecasting is a horizontal secular trend of certain prices — namely, investors' prices — with a probable rise in other prices — namely, wholesale prices — and with the end of disorder among most prices, but without inflation in the price level as a whole.

Let us now turn from the question of index numbers to

the consideration of several recent events of great importance in the monetary world, and see if any of these events
has set in motion forces that will of necessity upset this
reassuring forecast of the bond market and produce a rise
in the investor's cost of living. To begin with, let us consider the recent monetary moves made by France.

7. SIMPLE DEVALUATION BY FRANCE

If, on the one hand, France in September 1936 had entirely suspended the purchase and sale of gold by her central bank, as England did in September 1931, our own
price level would have been cast adrift completely, for then
France would have been completely off the gold standard,
and the United States would have been wholly without a
rock to anchor to. If, on the other hand, France had simply
devalued her currency and resumed gold payments at a
new and lower figure, as Belgium did in March 1935, our
own price level would still have been tied to gold, albeit
at a new parity. Mere devaluation by France, with gold
payments resumed at a lower rate for the franc, would
only have protected this country the more from inflation
here. Devaluation in France, by promoting a rise in prices
there, would have tended to draw gold from the United
States, and would have caused, had it not been for our
excess holdings of gold, a fall in prices here.[28] So long as
France remained on the gold standard, then, no matter
at how low a figure, she would have helped to protect us
from inflation, provided we too stayed on gold. She would
not have prevented us, however, from enjoying a reflation
to the 1926 level, because the gold supply of the world
was ample to support the 1926 level.

[28] In this connection it might be pointed out that a further drop in the
franc from the level of 4.65¢ at which it held till March 1937 would have a
tendency to depress international commodities and undermine the American
price level.

What France actually did was neither simple abandonment of the gold standard nor simple devaluation within the gold standard. Neither England's course nor Belgium's was hers. Instead she followed a mid-way course, choosing devaluation within limits so broad as to represent virtual abandonment of gold. Devaluing her currency between 25 and 34 per cent, as she did, and giving the franc a new gold content varying between 49 and 43 milligrams,[29] compared with its former gold content of 65½ milligrams, she placed the new gold points so far apart that the exchange rate became practically independent of the gold content of the monetary unit and settled at a figure that was really determined by the balance of trade, as with England, rather than by the redeemability of the unit, as with Belgium. Apparently the new gold points were chosen in such a way as to make sure that they would fall astride of the "natural" value of the franc, the word "natural" being used to mean the value around which the franc would float if allowed to drift freely in the foreign exchange markets in the absence of panicky capital movements.

Let us talk for the moment as if there were no Tri-Partite Agreement now in existence and see what in theory would be the resulting state of the foreign exchanges. With England and France both off gold, the fixed gold value of the American dollar would be of no consequence. The gold content of the dollar could be raised from $35 an ounce to $36 or $37, let us say, or lowered by the same amount, without affecting exchange rates (except insofar as speculators might try to use the news to fool the public). If our price of gold were raised greatly, of course, say to $50 an ounce, such a move would make it profitable for Frenchmen to buy gold in France at the value of 43 milligrams per franc, ship the gold to New York, convert it into paper

[29] Nine-tenths fine.

dollars, repurchase paper francs, and repeat the operation, thus driving up the price of the franc in dollars and affecting the exchange rate, just as would have happened in the past in response to a cut in the gold content of the dollar. But if the United States should make any such wide change in the price of gold as this, or even if the President should only lower the gold content of the dollar from 59.08 per cent of its old value to 50.00 per cent thereof, as permitted by law, it is extremely likely that the French would also drop their own gold point below 43 milligrams per franc, with the result that no gold exports from France would occur, and no effect on exchange rates would be produced by the President's action. Under these circumstances, therefore, it would seem that the President was powerless to alter the exchange rate from its normal level by any change in the official price of gold,[30] and that the foreign exchanges, now that France is off gold, would continue to float freely at levels determined only by the currents of international trade.

With all currencies afloat, no price levels would be tied together, and any country could enjoy a domestic inflation without its being promptly halted by an outflow of gold to other nations. Therefore, now that France has abandoned the gold standard, our own adhesion to it will be of no help in preventing us from having an inflation here, except as the Tri-Partite Agreement, to be discussed in the next section, may act as a substitute for certain features of the ordinary gold standard.

8.   THE TRI-PARTITE AGREEMENT

To what extent does the Tri-Partite Agreement on exchange rates, announced September 26, 1936, serve to

[30] Excepting, of course, a *lowering* in the American price of gold so great as to cause an outflow of gold to France and a welcome restocking of her bank

replace the gold standard in preventing inflation in this country?

To begin with, the agreement may be terminated by any of the signatories on twenty-four hours' notice, with the result that if an incipient inflation here should cause a rise in domestic prices and an increase in imports and a decrease in exports of international commodities, together with an outflow of gold such as would threaten bank reserves, stiffen interest rates, and force the contraction of loans and deposits, the agreement could, and doubtless would, be promptly denounced; and would prove, therefore, no check on domestic inflation.

Only so long as we continue to sell gold at the present price does the Tri-Partite Agreement protect us against inflation. But so long as we do, if our price level should begin to rise, with the result that imports grew and exports shrank and our demand for foreign currencies to pay for our excess of imports increased, then the dollar would tend to drop in the foreign exchange market, and the pound and the franc would tend to rise; and then if England and France did not wish to see their currencies rise against the dollar, they could buy paper dollars in the foreign exchange market, selling paper pounds and francs to American importers, and they could later convert their paper dollars into gold, bring the gold home, and reimburse their stabilization funds at their central banks by converting the gold back into the same number of paper pounds and francs as they had to start with. The foregoing process would cause an outflow of gold from the United States in response to inflation here in just the same way as would occur under the gold standard. Therefore, so long as — but only so

---

reserves and her war chest, with an attendant *rise* of the dollar against foreign currencies. Such a move by the President would be most unpopular, however, especially among the farmers, and is really out of the question.

long as — the President does not raise the price of gold, and does not place an embargo on exports of it, the Tri-Partite Agreement helps to protect us from inflation.

It is assumed, of course, that England and France will gladly do all they can to keep their own exchange rates down, and that they will gladly buy gold from us whenever necessary, and will do so in spite of the fact that this means exchanging the fertility of their fields and the sweat of their brows for a miserable heap of cold and sterile metal that is of no use to anyone. For now that it has become government policy to forbid the private ownership of gold, gold is no longer of use even for hoarding. Since gold derives its value essentially from the fact that it is the best store of wealth during a period of war, revolution, anarchy, pillage, and conflagration, because it is very scarce and is bright and shiny and can be buried in secret places without fear of spoilage, how is it possible for gold to remain of value if hoarders are denied the right to keep it? Either the anti-hoarding law will come to be thought unenforceable by everyone, or else the central banks will eventually find themselves sitting on a heap of worthless bullion, of no value for anything, not even for settling international balances.

But aside from the question of the short-sightedness of destroying the demand for the very stuff of our bank reserves, a mistake that was made several years ago, it nevertheless remains true that the Tri-Partite Agreement could conceivably be made to operate as an automatic check on inflation [31] in this country so long as the President was will-

---

[31] At the very least, the Tri-Partite Agreement must mean that this country will abstain from the one device for manipulating exchange rates that remains open to any country when everyone is off gold; namely, the device of printing paper money without limit and using the new money to buy foreign currencies. Ordinarily a national stabilization fund could not afford to risk buying anything but gold abroad, but if the printing presses at home are subject to no restrictions, purchases of foreign currencies can be *forced* to show a paper

ing to let it do so. Even if the French franc should undergo a further decline, or the English pound should weaken, the Tri-Partite Agreement would still help to protect the United States from inflation because it would still commit us to *sell* gold on demand.

9. VOLUNTARY CHECKS ON INFLATION

Although new powers for controlling credit and preventing inflation, such as the power to raise reserve requirements,[32] were given to the Federal Reserve Board by the

---

profit to the fund if this buying is continued long enough. The Tri-Partite Agreement by implication rules out such methods of currency warfare.

The Tri-Partite Agreement was at first called the Gentlemen's Agreement by most of the newspapers reporting it.

[32] In an "off-the-record" speech to bankers in Boston, later quoted in the *Boston Evening Transcript*, December 17, 1936, p. 1, and in the *New York Times*, December 19, 1936, p. 27, col. 2, Chairman Eccles of the Federal Reserve Board spoke of other new methods of credit control that might be needed, such as taxes on foreign investments in this country for the purpose of restricting further capital imports, and such as the use of tax revenues to retire the national debt and extinguish bank deposits. The first method, if successful, would only prevent the harm which *future* gold imports might do, and the second, like so many others, presupposes a balanced budget, and is useless in stopping any inflation that might get started with the budget still unbalanced.

The newspaper accounts contain no mention of any reference by Eccles to debt refunding as a means of credit control (cf. § 12 below), although refunding the government short-term debt and transferring it from the banks to their depositors is a far more powerful way of reducing bank deposits than Eccles' own process of paying off the debt with tax receipts. It is worth noting, however, that the last period of debt retirement in this country coincided with the last great stock-market boom.

Other things being equal, of course, debt retirement by the government out of taxes, like debt retirement by individuals out of earnings, causes deflation, or, more exactly, business stagnation, because debt retirement causes the purchasing power paid out to consumers in wages, rent, interest, and dividends to be less than the aggregate sales value set on the consumers' goods by their makers. Cf. Chapter XX, § 20, footnote 43.

Prior to 1935, the only important methods of credit control at the disposal of the Federal Reserve Banks consisted of raising the rediscount rate and selling acceptances or government securities in the open market.

The United States Treasury itself has recently acquired certain new powers for controlling credit, the most important of which is the power to shift huge sums of money from the member banks to the Federal Reserve Banks. Every dollar of government deposits so shifted subtracted about 90 cents from the

Banking Act of 1935, these powers probably will not be used with sufficient vigor, at least in the next few years, to stop an inflation, because the United States Treasury is likely to veto their use. The Treasury is apparently committed to low interest rates as long as the national debt is so largely composed of short-term issues, whose maturities must continually be provided for. Never will government finance be safe until the threat of temporary embarrassment (as the euphemism goes) is removed once and for all by the refunding of the floating debt into long-term bonds. This refunding can be performed successfully if general prosperity returns soon enough, bringing with it higher governmental revenues from taxes and lower governmental outlays for relief. If the budget is thus balanced before the debt becomes too large, and if the country, at the time when refunding is attempted, is on the gold standard externally, so that an automatic check on inflation exists, then long-term bonds can probably be sold in quantities great enough to pay off all the short-term notes and bills. But until this refunding operation has been com-

excess reserves of the banking system under the reserve requirements in force until August 1936; and under those now in force (June 1937) every dollar so shifted subtracts about 80 cents from excess reserves.

The power of the United States Stabilization Fund to buy gold anywhere, if used to buy gold from the Federal Reserve Banks in exchange for government deposits at these Banks, would not tighten money directly, for it would not reduce excess reserves; but it might tighten it indirectly, for it should reduce the reserve ratio of the Federal Reserve Banks and force them to sell bonds and acceptances and reduce rediscounts.

The power of the Federal Reserve Board to raise margin requirements on brokers' loans would be of some use in controlling credit if brokers' loans were bigger, but with security loans as small as they are now, no important reduction is possible. The power to control brokers' loans is important, not because inflation can occur in stocks, nor because the stock market absorbs credit, for neither of these things is true (cf. Chapter IV, §§ 2 and 3, and Chapter III, § 4, but because any power to prevent the making of bank loans, no matter on what security, whether on stocks, bonds, commodities, or real estate, is tantamount to the power to prevent demand deposits themselves from rising, and it is rising demand deposits that open the way to inflation.

pleted, the Treasury cannot easily acquiesce in any measures tending to tighten credit and raise short-term interest
rates. Should a credit inflation get started, therefore, before the short-term debt has been refunded, it would be
likely to run a long way before Washington brought itself
to take the right steps to stop it. Such an inflation could
bring a large and rapid rise in the general price level, even
to 200 or 300 per cent of the present figure, and could
cause a severe drop in bond prices, should it be found that
the Treasury was stubbornly unwilling to sell its short-
term bills at a heavy discount.

10.   EXPLANATION OF LOW SHORT-TERM INTEREST RATES

The persistence of very low short-term interest rates
even now, long after the ending of deflation, seems inconsistent with any expectation of price stability in the years
just ahead. According to our theory connecting interest
rates and the purchasing power of money, should not low
short-term interest rates now mean a forecast of declining
commodity prices in the near future? If everything else
were equal, this would be true, but so many special circumstances complicate the short-term money market today
that the explanation of the low rates prevailing now had
best be made from another angle, and reconciled afterwards with our previous theories.

Short-term interest rates are low today because member
bank reserves are far in excess of the legal minimum, as
everyone knows; and these excess reserves are the deliberate creation of the Treasury, which wants to depress
interest rates in order to cheapen the cost of its own borrowings. The manipulations of the Treasury working
through the Federal Reserve Banks are entirely effective,
however, only for short-term rates. By filling the member
banks with excess reserves, the Treasury can make the

banks *wish* to buy both short- and long-term loans, but it cannot make them *dare* to buy both kinds of loans at any price no matter how high. The banks will dare to buy the *short*-term loans, to be sure, even at a fractional rate of interest, because these loans are riskless by reason of their early maturity. The *long*-term loans, on the contrary, the banks dare buy only at a price that allows for the probability that interest rates will rise as time goes on, because the banks must always reckon on the likelihood that one day the excess reserves will be "mopped up" by order of the government itself, if a balanced budget and a funding of its short-term obligations should result from a normal business recovery and make the present excess reserves unnecessary as well as unsafe.[33] Because the banks must reckon on this probable change in Treasury policy, they cannot forecast the indefinite continuance of excess reserves and low short-term interest rates, and cannot apply a uniform rate, therefore, in discounting all the future coupons and the principal of long-term issues. Instead they must apply compound interest at a changing rate [34] in estimating the fair value of long-term bonds, and consequently the manipulations of the Treasury, however much they may depress short-term rates, are powerless to depress long-term rates to anywhere near the same degree, or even to reduce these rates much below their natural level.

From this reasoning it follows that a collapse in long-term bond prices is entirely within the range of possibility even with present or still greater excess reserves. A fortunate corollary of this conclusion is that bankers are so afraid to buy long-terms, and yet so unable to find enough short-terms, that the excess reserves are turning out to be less of a menace to the price level than might otherwise

[33] Cf. § 12 in the present chapter.
[34] See Chapter V, § 4, and Chapter XX, § 10.

have been expected. A further corollary is that manipulation of the short-term rate by the Federal Reserve Banks is of little use in controlling business activity, because business men do not care how much or how little they pay for interest expense so long as they know that the abnormal rate is only temporary.

If the marginal productivity of capital for short-term purposes were higher than the market rate of interest on such loans, borrowers would flock to the banks for credit, and demand deposits would increase by leaps and bounds. But such phenomena are not in evidence. Low money rates in themselves have produced little or no increase in commercial loans. Why? The answer is that the opportunities for investing additional sums profitably for *short* periods are very small. Existing technical knowledge reveals many opportunities for the *permanent* or *semi-permanent* investment of new capital, but few for the temporary investment thereof. While it is true that permanent structures might be built with short-term loans subject to constant renewal, business men know that such loans would have to be renewed later at higher rates, with the result that the average rate in the end would be the same as if the money had in the beginning been borrowed on long-term once and for all.[35] Hence it remains true that the need for purely temporary accommodation is indeed so small that the demand proves to be very inelastic.

To say, as some bankers do, that lack of demand for commercial loans explains present low interest rates is to fail to tell the whole story, for even if commercial loans were in demand, interest rates would still be no higher than now so long as excess reserves remained as large as they are now. Of course, if commercial loans were actually in great demand, excess reserves would tend to decrease,

[35] Cf. Chapter X, § 2.

for the making of loans would increase deposits and required reserves as well, thus reducing excess reserves and raising interest rates. But just so long as excess reserves do remain as high as at present, whether from lack of demand for commercial loans or from other causes, money rates will tend to remain easy.

There being adequate reasons to explain low short-term rates regardless of the short-term outlook for the purchasing power of money, we may say, therefore, that low *short*-term rates do not imply a fall in commodity prices in the immediate future (or at any other time, for that matter). Instead, low short-term rates reflect a low *real* [36] rate of interest over the next few months or years, while higher long-term rates reflect a higher *real* rate of interest over longer periods.

II.   BUSINESS RECOVERY AND THE FEDERAL BUDGET

It is a common assumption these days that a cyclical recovery in business will come soon enough to balance the federal budget automatically. Even though our recovery to date has been largely in consumers' goods, it is assumed that this recovery will spread into producers' goods as well. The recent large orders for rolling stock for the railroads, and for generating equipment for the utilities, is encouraging; but the continued dearth of new issues of securities for purposes other than refunding is discouraging, because it suggests that high taxes are making it unprofitable in most industries to invest new capital,[37] and that the only effect of low interest rates is to induce the refunding of

[36] *Real* is here used in the technical economic sense implying measurement in terms of goods and services rather than in terms of paper money of indeterminate worth.

[37] In the case of the utilities, who are normally large borrowers, other things than taxes also inhibit borrowing. Among these things are the anti-holding-company law and the competition of the Tennessee Valley Authority.

those debts with which corporations are saddled already. While it is true that many companies find it best to complete their refunding before trying to borrow new money, since the refunding improves their show of earning power, still it is by no means certain that a great increase of corporate borrowing is about to take place and carry our national economy into a period of full-blown, well-rounded prosperity such as attended the large security flotations of the 1920's.

There is a further question as to whether full recovery is possible without more of an expansion in foreign trade than can be achieved in the near future. An increase in foreign trade probably does not need to wait upon a general return to the gold standard,[38] but it may have to wait and even wait in vain for a return of faith in peace, the lack of which faith is now making so many nations seek self-sufficiency for military reasons. Yet the shrinkage in foreign trade is less of an impediment to full recovery in the United States, which does only 6 or 7 per cent of its business abroad,[39] than would be a failure of corporations in general to issue new securities wherewith to borrow current savings for plant expansion.

Should complete recovery fail to come, and come early enough and strongly enough, and should heavy outlays for relief and light yields from income taxes continue to create deficits, then investors would grow more and more discouraged over the mounting government debt and the growing bank deposits, and at last they might lose hope entirely, finally despairing of the government's ever ceasing

[38] Frank D. Graham in an article entitled "The Place of Gold in the Monetary Standards of the Future," printed in the *Proceedings* of the Academy of Political Science, May 1936, argues that a return to gold is not even desirable, let alone necessary.

[39] S. E. Harris, *Exchange Depreciation* (Cambridge: Harvard University Press, 1936), p. 242.

to add to its debt. Now continual increases in debt, if the borrowing exceeds the saving within the nation, mean continual increases in bank deposits. No matter whether the borrower be public or private, government or corporation, institution or individual, national borrowing in excess of national saving means that commercial banks must finance the excess by buying the bonds or notes and making a credit to deposits against them. Usually when either a government [40] or a private concern borrows, the proceeds go in the end to labor and are spent for the means of subsistence. Even if public works are built, and materials are bought as well as wages paid, the money finds its way in the end into the hands of workmen who spend it on their families. If these workmen are not engaged in making consumers' goods, the national dividend, in terms of consumers' goods, is not increased, and in this case prices must rise. While the money incomes of these workmen become bigger, their real incomes stay the same; therefore only the price of what they buy goes up. In other words, inflation, not prosperity, results. The process is described in detail by Keynes,[41] who speaks of investment exceeding saving.

If inflation begins to occur in a minor degree only, to be sure, in a society in which there is much unemployment because wage rates have been held too high by union rule or stubborn custom, inflation then proves a tonic, able to put the patient to work again. But if inflexible prices are not to blame, and if inflation goes on and on without increasing real incomes, then governmental expenses likewise rise, but taxes usually lag. In that event, prices get out of all control, and disaster follows. Such a disaster can

[40] The principal exception is when the government borrows for such agencies as the RFC, which buys doubtful assets from banks and insurance companies, who take good government bonds in exchange. See "Commodity Prices and Public Expenditures" by S. E. Harris in the *Review of Economic Statistics*, February 15, 1935.

[41] Keynes, *Treatise*, I, 141. In his later *General Theory*, p. 83, however, he repudiates this discrepancy between saving and investment.

come, however, only if governmental borrowing (1) exceeds national saving, and (2) fails to stimulate business when prices have risen a little, and also (3) fails to produce a sufficient rise in tax receipts.

At present none, let alone all, of these conditions seems to be fulfilled. Federal borrowing does not seem to be exceeding national saving; rising prices are not failing to stimulate business; higher prices are not failing to increase tax receipts. Hence the near-term prospects of federal spending by itself are not those of an uncontrollable inflation, and a much larger annual deficit would be needed to produce inflation automatically.

12.   GOVERNMENT BORROWING AS A CAUSE OF INFLATION

While it is true that bank deposits have increased during the last four years by almost the same amount as the rise in the national debt, and while it is likewise true that the increase in deposits can be ascribed almost wholly to the purchase of government securities by the banks, it does not follow from this increase in deposits that a corresponding increase in the price level is to be expected in due course,[42] for the very fact that deposits have already increased so much without forcing prices up indicates that much "hoarding" of deposits has been going on.[43] Some of the increase in deposits has been devoted to financing an increase in the volume of business, to be sure, and some to financing a cyclical rise in prices, but the remainder has undoubtedly been hoarded. This "hoarding" of deposits might better be described as the accumulation of funds on deposit by savers.[44] Ordinarily these savers would have invested their savings in new bond issues, and the borrowers who issued

[42] Cf. Ayres, *Inflation*, p. 24, where the opposite interpretation of the facts is presented.

[43] Cf. Harris, *Exchange Depreciation*, p. 190, footnote.

[44] The life insurance companies, for instance, in the spring of 1937 were holding many hundreds of millions of dollars uninvested in this way.

the bonds would have come into possession of the deposits owned by the savers and would then have proceeded to hire labor and buy materials, with the result that the deposits would have been put back into circulation. During the last few years, however, many savers have been afraid to buy long-term bonds because of the risk of inflation, and have been unwilling to buy short-term notes because of the inadequacy of the yield; consequently they have let their savings pile up in the form of idle deposits. If the fear of inflation had been absent, and if bond yields had been higher, these savings of individuals and corporations would have been available for the purchase of government bonds, and the government deficit could have been financed to a greater extent with savings rather than with newly-created bank credit. Under these circumstances the deficit would have caused less growth of deposits on the one hand and less "hoarding" of deposits on the other.

Yet so long as the hoarded deposits remain uninvested in other new issues, they remain available for investment in government issues whenever the fear of inflation departs and the government is willing to offer an adequate rate of interest to savers.

If business recovery, high taxes, and government economy should bring the federal budget into balance in due course, the fear of inflation might largely subside.[45] Then it would be wise indeed for the government to act promptly to prevent later trouble for itself and inflation for the country. Trouble for itself in an emergency would be possible if the recurrently maturing short-term debt was not converted into long-term bonds, and inflation for the country would be likely if the accumulated uninvested deposits

[45] As pointed out in Chapter III, § 2, it is only the extra-marginal investors, and not all investors, who now fear inflation seriously; and it is only these bearish investors who are hoarding their savings in cash because they think bonds too high.

were not prevented from being loaned to industry. At the first opportunity, therefore, the government, a large part of whose recent borrowings have been on short term from the commercial banks, should fund its floating debt by issuing long-term bonds, and should sell these bonds to private lenders, and use the proceeds to pay off the banks. Even though the government might be obliged to pay 2 or even 3 per cent more in interest on its debt so converted, it would still be sound finance to do so, for it is better to borrow at 3 or $3\frac{1}{2}$ per cent for forty or fifty years than to borrow at $\frac{1}{2}$ per cent for a few years and later be obliged to pay $4\frac{1}{2}$ or 5 per cent or even more after inflation has sent interest rates up; and it is certainly wise not to be always at the mercy of the money market for renewing some big short-term note issue every few months. So obvious is the wisdom of funding the floating debt that we can almost take it for granted that any administration, whether Democratic or Republican, will try to do so at the first opportunity.

But the floating debt cannot be funded on a great scale without taking it out of the banks and placing it with private lenders; for the banks, though willing to hold short-term paper, do not want long-term bonds. The banks, with their heavy liabilities on deposit account, cannot run the risk of temporary depreciation that goes with any long-term bond; but private individuals, on the other hand, who have no such demand liabilities, can afford to overlook fluctuations in market prices so long as the interest and principal of their bonds are paid as expected. Of necessity, therefore, funding the debt involves transferring the debt from the banks to their depositors, who are the general public.

When a borrower transfers a debt from a bank to its depositors, the effect on bank deposits is the same as if the bank itself had sold some of its bonds to its own depositors, which in turn is the same as if a depositor had paid off a loan of his own. All three acts involve the cancellation of loans or investments against deposits, of assets against liabilities. Thus the funding of the government debt, and the consequent transfer of the debt to private lenders, would inevitably reduce demand deposits by exactly the amount of the debt so funded and so transferred.

Since demand deposits are "means of payment," and are a form of money so far as their effect on the price level is concerned, their partial annihilation by debt-funding would be deflationary if it were not for the fact that the deposits that would disappear would be the very ones which have been "hoarded" and whose velocity of circulation has been zero and which have not served to raise the price level to date because they have been kept out of use awaiting investment by their owners.

If everything turns out for the best, so that the federal budget is balanced, then the funding of the floating debt at some future date will offset the accumulation of the deficit up to that date (at least to the extent that the deficit has been paid for with short-term borrowings from the banks), and the recent increase in demand deposits will disappear, and consequently the final effect of the government deficit on the price level will turn out to be nil. In other words, since everything *may* work out in this way, it cannot be said that the deficit has irrevocably set forces to work that *must* produce a substantial degree of inflation.

Summarizing our conclusions so far, we see that, while much has been done since April 1933 to *permit* prices to rise, nothing yet mentioned will *compel* them to rise. Up to the present these permissive measures have failed to lure the country into inflation. But may they not soon frighten it into inflation? That is the question next to engage our attention.

13.   LOSS OF CONFIDENCE AS A CAUSE OF INFLATION

Now that various permissive measures have cleared the way for a large increase in the quantity of active money, real inflation could develop at any time merely from a loss of confidence.[46] Even though further government borrowing, with its attendant increase in bank deposits, should remain too small to make trouble in itself, if the business and financial community became convinced that trouble in the end was sure, they would proceed to discount the future at once.

During 1935 and 1936 the conservative attitude of the Supreme Court remained a bulwark to confidence. From the invalidation of the NRA in June 1935 until President Roosevelt's attack on the Court in February 1937, business felt sure of its constitutional rights, and industrial activity grew apace. Thus the Supreme Court in the 1930's, like foreign loans in the 1920's, served to hold a rickety structure together. In the one case the businessman's distrust of the New Deal and in the other the inflated level of prices[47] were a constant menace to the continuation of prosperity, but in each case a particular factor served to hold off the collapse. Not long after the foreign lending ceased in the 1920's came the crash of 1929. Let us hope the analogy holds no further today, for if confidence in business recovery in general should disappear, confidence in the dollar in particular might soon vanish too.

One of the first things [48] that would happen if confidence in the dollar should falter would be that financiers would

[46] Cf. the unsigned article entitled "Inflation is What?" in *Fortune*, December 1933.

[47] Cf. § 5, above.

[48] The very first thing that would happen might be a profit-taking stampede in the stock market (cf. Chapter III, § 6), where the fall in prices would cause people to begin making a pessimistic reappraisal of the outlook.

try to get their money out of the country. They would sell their bonds and send the cash abroad in the form of gold so long as the Treasury would permit gold exports. The gold exports would not be made by the financiers themselves, of course, but would be handled by foreign stabilization funds under the terms of the Tri-Partite Agreement; nothing but the provocation of the gold exports would be the direct work of the financiers. Soon an embargo on gold would be laid down, however, and then the financiers would sell paper dollars for francs and pounds, quickly driving the exchange rate down to a level where it would be too costly to export any more capital in this way. Next they would turn to commodities like wheat, cotton, copper, etc., and would buy these at home and sell them abroad, thus getting their wealth out of the country by the process of denuding the nation of its raw materials. During all this process, government and other bonds would fall in price, partly because of the liquidation by capitalists but mostly because of a mere revision of opinion by buyers and sellers alike, led by the speculators. The great drop in bonds would end all new financing, but as such financing to date has been largely for refunding instead of for plant expansion, the ending of bond flotations would not of itself produce much of a decline in business activity.

Only after the financiers had caused a very severe drop in the exchange rate and in the price of bonds, and a spectacular rise in export prices, would the business community begin to make its own response to the prospect of inflation; for business men have to reckon with future taxes as well as with future prices. Even though business men expected building costs to rise, they would not try to anticipate this rise by investing in new plant unless they felt that the rise in future prices would more than offset the rise in future taxes. But loss of confidence in the ability of the government ever to balance its budget, such as was assumed above in explaining the action of the financiers, implies just such an unwillingness or inability of the government to lay ade- quate taxes, and just such a resort to bank borrowing as would increase the quantity of money and the height of the price level rapidly. Under such circumstances it is smart business to borrow and build. The borrowing would have to be done on short-term, of course, since the bond market would be closed to everyone, including the government it- self. Everyone would be selling short-term paper to the banks, who, because of their vast excess reserves, would be eager buyers. The money thus borrowed would be spent for labor and materials, and wages and commodity prices would rise. Unemployment would cease, sales would be large, and inventory profits high; prosperity, in short, would be here.

But the majority of voters would be bitterly dissatisfied, for the majority would be hard hit by the high cost of living. While at first they would find the reduction in unemploy- ment a relief, in the end they would find their wage scales too inflexible to keep up with rising prices. Throughout the length and breadth of the land the cry would go up to stop this inflation. Stop it, stop it, at any cost, even if everyone, including the poorest worker, should have to pay an income tax. Then such a tax would be levied, and then all unnecessary expenses, like "benefits" to the farmers and "bonuses" for the veterans, would be cut out, and then the budget would be balanced at the new and higher price level. The financiers would bring home their gold, the bond market would rise, the business men would fund their floating debt with long-term bond issues, and all borrowers would be permanently richer, all creditors permanently poorer.

Because such a large part of the nation's investment in

capital goods is ordinarily made each year by the railroads and utilities, however, both of whom in an inflation would suffer so much from rising costs as to lose their credit standing at once and become unable to borrow, it is hard to get an inflation started. In our economy the required speculative borrowing and building must be done by small business men, farmers, and home owners, rather than by the railroads and the electric light companies; and consequently the circle of those who look for rising prices must include many more persons than the select group who run the great corporations; it must reach out and include millions of persons of smaller means and less education. For the very reason that in this larger group a longer time is needed for a new idea to take hold and for a new fashion in belief to spread, inflation, which is partly a phenomenon of social psychology, would be slow to get started. Were the rails and the utilities able to borrow like anyone else in the face of inflation, the delay would not be so great.

At present the fear of inflation is absent, to judge by the prices now ruling in the bond market. Business men now expect a normal cyclical recovery in trade that will balance the government budget automatically. But if they should ever lose their faith in recovery, then inflation could be expected to begin in due course. As pointed out above, the first warnings of such an inflation would be a collapse in bond prices and an embargo on gold exports.

If government bond prices should drop, an interval of time would elapse before all commodity prices rose, because time would be needed for fear to spread and for borrowing and spending to take up the slack in employment. First would come the panic in the bond market and the embargo on gold, then the lull, and finally the steady rise in the cost of living. During this lull, this gestation period, it would still be possible for the federal government to make a counter-attack and recapture its lost credit standing by reducing expenditures and raising taxes. Perhaps, therefore, a panic in the bond market would suffice to chasten Congress; if not, perhaps the panic would suffice to unseat the "ins" at the next election, thus producing a reversal of policies and removing the fear of inflation before the price rise had gone far.

Although the first warning of inflation, if it should get started, would be given by weakness in government bond prices, few would doubt the government's ability to pay its interest. Not the burden of the debt to the taxpayer, but the effect of the borrowing on money and prices, would be the real cause for concern. Likewise, not the effect up till now, but the effect in the future, would be the determining consideration; for speculation would anticipate inflation from public borrowing and bring it about by private borrowing long before the inflation developed mechanically to a serious degree from the mere excess of expenses over taxes. Carried along by such private borrowing, inflation might well run its course entirely without the issuance of any new paper money by the government to pay its debts.

Not yet has the nation been frightened into inflation in this way by any of the New Deal policies, alarming though some of them have seemed at the time. The repudiation of the gold clause in government bonds,[49] the Warren gold-buying plan, and the deliberate creation of huge federal deficits, each in turn gave a great shock to confidence, but

---

[49] Default on the gold clause in government bonds was indeed unavoidable, but it is too bad that default was made to look like repudiation — so much like repudiation, in fact, that the Supreme Court should find itself obliged to condemn the measure unanimously. If more time had been available for consideration of the problem, it is possible that the government could have devised a plan for the *pro rata* discharge of its obligations, with all creditors being treated alike, as in any other bankruptcy, and all creditors being offered the choice of either (1) their fractional share of the gold in the Treasury, or (2) the extension of their loans on a paper-money basis.

still no inflation has resulted. Apparently the nation can no more be frightened into inflation than it can be lured into it. But can it not be *forced* into inflation? Measures to do this latter thing are at hand, for any scheme that increases the cash income of the consumers without increasing the volume of goods offered for sale tends to force prices up. Among such schemes are farm relief, unemployment relief, and collective bargaining. Let us now turn, therefore, to a consideration of the inflationary prospects of the various New Deal measures for "increasing purchasing power" under a "managed recovery."

14.   FARM RELIEF AND INFLATION

An insidious threat of inflation lurks in the New Deal program of farm relief, regardless of whether relief takes the form of "benefits" under the old Agricultural Adjustment Act, or of "rentals" under the new Soil Conservation Act, because either of these measures, if allowed to stand, would establish the principle that it is a proper function of the federal government to redistribute the national dividend on a great scale between the various groups of voters.[50] The government credit can stand its ordinary expenses for military, naval, and other purposes; it can stand a heavy burden of relief for a while; but it cannot stand gifts to every Tom, Dick, and Harry whose vote is needed to win the next election, because to such gifts there is no limit. The AAA, which started out as a lofty program to (1) give cash benefits to farmers, (2) curtail output, and

[50] "It is hereby declared to be the policy of this act also to secure . . . reestablishment, at as rapid a rate as the Secretary of Agriculture determines to be practicable and in the general public interest, of the ratio between the purchasing power of the net income per person on farms and that of the income per person not on farms that prevailed during the five-year period August 1909–July 1914, inclusive, as determined from the statistics available in the United States Department of Agriculture, and the maintenance of such ratio" (*New York Times*, February 28, 1936, "Text of AAA Substitute Measure as Adopted," p. 16, col. 3, Sec. 7 (A), esp. item 5).

(3) pay its own way with processing taxes, threatens to degenerate into a political scheme to do the first thing only, namely to give cash to farmers in order to hold the farm vote. When the new Soil Conservation Act was drawn up, the Ways and Means Committee of the House dropped from the Act even the temporary substitute for processing taxes, on the ground that income-tax receipts were turning out to be higher than expected for the first quarter of 1936. Likewise, the curtailment feature of the Act threatens to become inoperative, because under the Supreme Court decision on the AAA farmers are likely to find a way to evade their obligations to reduce output as required by the "soil conservation" program.[51]

It is true that the farmers, like many other people, have inadequate incomes and that many of them are in great distress. In fact, what with the partial loss of our export market for farm products, and what with the rapid mechanization of agriculture, the farmer's troubles have become a chronic drain on general prosperity. For the good of the nation as a whole, however, the permanent solution would not seem to be to give a special subsidy to the agricultural class, but to raise instead the standard of living of their customers, so that the masses in the cities could afford a better diet. A better diet takes more land and labor for its production and thus would make the farmers' land and labor worth more.

A further way to facilitate the exchange of products be-

---

[51] That the act is really designed to raise prices rather than to conserve fertility is revealed by the following item, for instance, from the *New York Times* article of March 23, 1936, entitled "AAA Plan Brings Protests by Wire," pages 1 and 7, which reads in part as follows:

"Because many crops are classed as 'soil-depleting' under certain conditions in one section of the country and as 'soil conserving' in others, one official said the matter of classification may be decided largely on a State or local basis.

"Heavy responsibility will be placed on county and State committees for determining whether a farmer has used some crop for 'conserving' or 'depleting' land."

tween farm and factory is to lower the cost of factory goods. Then the farmer will buy more from the city man, and thus let the city man buy more from him. The ordinary principles of international trade between nations apply equally well to trade between groups of producers within the same country. If the aim is to "restore the balance between industry and agriculture," it does not therefore follow from the principles of international trade that the only way to do so is to raise agricultural prices; it would work even better to lower industrial prices or to increase industrial demand for farm products.

The old AAA was not the success from the farmers' own point of view that it is commonly supposed to have been. Devaluation, drought, and urban prosperity, much more than crop curtailment, account for the observed rise in farm prices. Had there been no processing tax on farm products, farm prices would have risen even more than they did. In hogs, for instance, for which the demand curve is much flatter than the supply curve, the tax put prices down by nearly the full amount of the tax,[52] with the result that what the corn-hog farmer gained in benefit payments he lost in lower prices. In cotton, the tax lowered the export price, with the result that the loss on export sales offset the tax collected for the farmers on domestic sales. Curtailment of acreage at home caused expansion abroad, and reduced the world crop so little as to fail to compensate the cotton farmers for their smaller volume of cotton to sell. In wheat, where the crop was greatly reduced by the drought, acreage curtailment was so slight that it would have had almost no effect on world prices if normal weather had given average crops and kept the country on an export basis, because a 10 or 15 per cent cut in the United States

[52] See Geoffrey Shepard, "The Incidence of the Cost of the AAA Corn-Hog Program," in the *Journal of Farm Economics* for July 1934.

crop would have amounted to almost nothing in the world markets. In wheat, however, most of which is used at home, the processing tax can be levied on most of the crop, and for this part of the crop, therefore, a domestic price, tax-on, much above the world price, can be obtained; hence in the particular case of wheat it may be said that the AAA could have succeeded. But only in wheat could the AAA have been made to work, because only in wheat were there to be found the conditions necessary for success, to wit: (1) inelastic demand — wherein wheat differs from pork, for which there are many substitutes; (2) domestic sales far in excess of export sales — wherein wheat differs from cotton.[53] Wheat, however, contributes much less to farm income than corn and hogs, or cotton. Success with the minor, failure with the major crops, this was the lot of the AAA. How long would it have taken the farmers to find this out if the Supreme Court had not intervened?

Even if the Republicans had won the 1936 election, huge cash payments to farmers would still have remained as a threat to the budget.[54] In fact, the domestic allotment plan advocated by Landon might well have cost more than the AAA. It remains to be seen, moreover, whether the new national policy of taxing one group to make gifts to another will stop at the present limit of a half-billion yearly to farmers alone. Why draw the line at a mere half-billion?

[53] A comparison of how the cotton farmers actually did fare with how they would have fared without the AAA requires certain new theoretical apparatus not yet to be found in the literature of economics. The solution requires a set of simultaneous equations for all the demand and supply curves, both foreign and domestic, that are involved; allowance for the abnormal carryover must also be made. I have attacked the first part of the problem in an unpublished study entitled "Economics of the Processing Tax," and the second part in an article entitled "Speculation and the Carryover," published in the *Quarterly Journal of Economics*, for May 1936. See also Joseph S. Davis, "The AAA as a Force in Recovery," *Journal of Farm Economics*, February 1935.

[54] See the unsigned article entitled "The Taxpayer Takes up Farming" in *Fortune*, March 1936.

the farmers will say. Why exclude the coal miners, or the railroad workers, or the veterans? other groups will say. Indeed it looks at times as though nothing but a crisis in government credit, with a big drop in government bonds, would rid the nation of the "benefit-bonus" mania. Perhaps even a credit crisis would not suffice, and a real inflation will be needed.

When and if the great political issue becomes farm relief versus stopping inflation, the break-down of the old Republican and Democratic parties is possible, with the emergence thereafter of an Agrarian versus an Industrial party. If the fight is fierce enough, it is even possible that first the Supreme Court and then the Senate will go down in the struggle, leaving this country in the end with the House of Representatives supreme. A more likely development, however, would seem to be a third party movement in which the farmers and radicals would quit the old Republican and Democratic parties and form a new Progressive party of their own, leaving the conservative Easterners in control of the Republican party, and the conservative Southerners of the Democratic. Certainly, the present control of each party is anomalous, the Republican party now being led by Westerners who cannot carry their own states, and the Democratic party by Left-Wingers who defy the conservative wishes of the South whence their party draws its main strength.

Let the reader be his own political prophet, and decide for himself what are the chances for such a measure of governmental economy in the near future as will bring expenses within the nation's taxpaying power. Let him not overestimate this power, however, by making comparisons with England or France, because the American taxpayer may well prove less docile than his brothers across the sea. Then if the reader is an optimist, he will hold the long-term bonds of the government, if a pessimist, the short-term notes, no matter how low their yield.

15. WAGE RATES, UNEMPLOYMENT, AND THE BURDEN OF RELIEF

Like farm relief, unemployment relief, however humane its motive, is a measure whose inflationary possibilities must not be overlooked by the intelligent investor. The first question that presents itself is this: Will the burden of relief always remain so high that the federal budget can never be balanced? If so, inflation is inevitable. It behooves us, therefore, to inquire into the causes of unemployment, and to find out if it must always be so heavy.

Although humanitarians may deny that labor is a commodity, it nevertheless remains true that its price is determined by the equilibrium of demand and supply, just as the price of a commodity is determined.[55] So long as free competition persists, the rate of wages will tend to settle eventually at a point where there is only frictional unemployment and where the worker is paid a wage equal to his marginal productivity. If competition is interfered with, however, whether by the NRA, the WPA, minimum-wage laws, or the closed shop, so that the rate of wages is set too high, unemployment will result, people will be thrown on relief, and a burden will fall on taxpayers that may prove so heavy as to cause deficits and ultimately inflation itself.

What are the causes of unemployment, therefore, and are they largely temporary or permanent? An answer to these questions will throw much light on the investment value of long-term government bonds.

The temporary causes of unemployment at the present stage of recovery are to be found partly in the inactivity of the building trades, with the consequent lessening of rail-

[55] Cf. Chapter XVI, § 7, and Chapter XVII, § 9.

road traffic, freight-car buying, steel making, etc. Inactivity in building results, in turn, from high taxes on real estate [56] and from the unwillingness of home-buyers to borrow money when their confidence in their future earning power is weak. The wages of building mechanics also are rather high, but actual wages (as contrasted with official union wages) are now lower than during the last building boom, at least in the case of artisans working independently as sub-contractors; hence high wages cannot be blamed as an insurmountable cause of inactivity in building. The other causes, like high taxes and lack of confidence, do not seem serious enough to prevent forever an increase in building, especially since good roads and the automobile are constantly tempting urban dwellers to move further out into the suburbs and build new houses for themselves in the country. Lower rates of interest on home mortgages are also tempting people to build. It is to be hoped that inactivity in construction, therefore, may correctly be listed as a temporary and perhaps a fast-disappearing cause of general unemployment.[57]

Government interference with wage rates, however, seems to be a more persistent cause of unemployment. Although the NRA as such is now dead and buried, many of its rules live on. The shorter working week, for instance, makes it necessary to pay higher hourly wages, which means that fewer men can qualify as worth the higher rate. Those who cannot qualify must stay on the dole. The WPA, by subsidizing the unemployed, prevents them from competing for available jobs and from driving the prevail-

---

[56] For non-residential building the capital-gains tax is also a serious deterrent to building in some cases, because it prevents owners from trading freely in real estate. Controller Tremaine of the State of New York is a vigorous advocate of the abolition of this tax. See the *New York Times*, April 26, 1937, p. 27, col. 1.

[57] Cf. George F. Warren and Frank A. Pearson, "The Building Cycle," *Fortune*, August 1937, p. 85.

ing wage down to a point where they would become worth their hire. The strongly pro-labor, pro-union attitude of the Roosevelt administration, by making employers feel they cannot get a fair deal if government mediation becomes necessary during a strike, likewise tends to force wages up by lowering the resistance of corporations to wage demands. Thus high wages, as in the automobile industry, restrict the demand for labor, and produce higher prices and smaller sales of finished goods.

While high wages cause the displacement of labor by machines, they also increase the demand for labor to make machines, with the result that the net effect on unemployment during the period of "tooling up" may be the reverse from the effect after the new machines are installed; but the boom in the machine-tool industry is in any event less important than the NRA, the WPA, and the labor unions in its effect on general employment.

A further cause of unemployment is the lack of skill that handicaps most of the unemployed.[58] These unfortunate men cannot find a job, not because there are no jobs at all to be had, but because they cannot qualify as expert machinists, steel workers, or what not; and the reason they cannot qualify is sometimes that their own friends, as union members, have favored a union policy of not training enough apprentices, and sometimes that the manufacturers themselves have neglected, especially during the depression, their social obligation to train an adequate body of skilled labor. The problem of providing young men with skill enough to find good jobs and be worth good wages, and of retraining those who become technologically unemployed, is one of the most important in the whole question of unemployment, and must be settled before useful work can be found for all the millions now out of work.

[58] See the survey on unemployment in *Fortune*, October 1937, p. 99.

The foregoing more persistent causes of unemployment would not seem to be serious enough, however, to keep a rich and gifted nation like the United States in a permanent state of depression, nor to produce such a heavy burden of relief as to ruin the value of its money. Consequently it does not seem reasonable to say that inflation in this country is inevitable because the necessary outlays for relief make it impossible to balance the budget.

16.   THE THIRTY-HOUR WEEK

If Labor should succeed in forcing industry to accept the thirty-hour week [59] together with a rise in hourly wages sufficient to keep weekly earnings as high as before, costs of production would rise throughout industry. Manufacturers would have to take on many new workers to offset the shorter week for their present workers. Since these workers would have to be drawn from those now unemployed, they would be less efficient, on the average, than those who have already been able to find jobs when employers are free to pick and choose. Hence, on the average, the hourly output of workers would fall. But at the same time hourly wages would rise by the amount required to maintain weekly earnings as high as before. Therefore unit costs would rise a great deal. If a forty-hour week was replaced by a thirty-hour week, hourly wages would rise to $^{40}\!/_{30}$, or 133 per cent, of the present rate; but marginal unit costs of production would rise even more, say to 140 or 145 per cent of present costs, because of the fall in the skill and industriousness of the average employee.

With a rise in marginal unit costs of 40 per cent or more, manufacturers would seek to increase their selling prices to

[59] As demanded in a resolution passed by the American Federation of Labor at its 1936 Convention in Tampa. See the *New York Times*, November 28, 1936, p. 1.

the same extent. Competition between producers would not prevent such a rise in prices, for all producers would be confronted with the same increase in marginal unit costs. If prices rose 40 per cent, while the weekly earnings of the workers now employed stayed as at present (and if workers bought nothing but manufactured articles), these workers would suffer a fall in their real incomes to $100/140$, or 71 per cent, of the present level. To the extent that the present workers buy things other than manufactured articles, they would not have to pay higher prices for consumers' goods, to be sure, and to this extent their loss from the thirty-hour week would be reduced; but the net effect of the thirty-hour week on the cost of living would still be very bad. Hence workers would demand a rise in money wages, which in turn would produce higher selling prices and still further provoke inflation. For the worker who is fortunate enough to have a job now, the proposed change to a thirty-hour week would certainly be no blessing. Since most of the laboring population and the members of trade unions are already employed, is it not strange for them to advocate a measure tending so much to their own disadvantage?

The real beneficiaries of the scheme would be those who would be taken out of the ranks of the unemployed and put to work at good wages. The community as a whole would suffer, however, because a motley crew working thirty hours a week could not produce as much as a picked crew working forty hours a week. Capitalists might gain at the expense of the masses, moreover, because "sharing the work" would put the burden of relief of the unemployed on the wage-earners themselves, whereas now it rests on those who pay the income tax.

As an ultimate ideal, of course, the thirty-hour week is desirable. People would certainly get more joy out of life if they had more time for recreation, for outdoor games, companionship, reading, and travel. Labor is undoubtedly right in seeking leisure as well as material things in its drive for the more abundant life. If the technical productivity of our economic system can be made great enough in the course of time, and if enough new workers can be drawn from the ranks of the unemployed or drained off the farms, then the thirty-hour week might be made to succeed a generation or so from now; but if not, or if the measure is introduced too soon and too suddenly, it will help to produce inflation, and then inflation will cause a political turnover, with the result that in the end the unsound measure will have to be abandoned, after which the inflation will be halted at some new and higher price level.

It is a debatable question as to whether an increase in leisure can be hastened by legislative means. Some people think that long hours and low wages depress the efficiency of workers to the point where their work is really worth but little, whereas short hours and high wages increase efficiency to a point where a short week's work becomes really worth as much as a long week's work. If this is so, legislative intervention is certainly to be desired. Probably it is so sometimes, but not always, and for some kinds of work, but not for all. It would seem much more likely that legislation shortening the hours and raising the wages of miners, for instance, would increase their efficiency and value than that similar legislation would so affect machine operatives doing light and easy work already. It is really a problem, not for the economist, but for the physiologist, psychologist, and efficiency engineer, who have only begun to explore the possibilities of great advances in human efficiency. The truly scientific way to proceed would be first to experiment systematically in a laboratory with shorter hours, and then to pass legislation if it should be proved beyond doubt that the proposed schedule would not lead to a shrinkage in the national dividend. If shorter hours can really be proved to be more economic, moreover, employers can be expected to grant them voluntarily in many cases, and no legislation may be needed to effect the change.

But if it is not a problem of efficiency, but a problem of giving people the particular mixture of leisure and goods which they like best, even at the cost of some sacrifice in their standard of living in terms of material things, then, if the force of custom is too strong, legislation will be needed. Again it will be found that some people like to work hard and live well, others prefer leisure and a frugal diet. The ideal solution would be steady work for the industrious, irregular work for the leisurely. If human happiness is our goal, let every man live according to his own tastes.

Such freedom for all, however, is not what the proponents of the thirty-hour week seem to have in mind. Apparently they are thinking instead of creating an artificial shortage of labor in order to force wages artificially high. If their scheme, rather than leading to higher efficiency, should result merely in a rise in money wages, as is more likely, it would tend strongly to produce inflation and depress the price of government bonds. Fortunately this scheme is not likely to be enacted as law.

17. PAY-ROLL TAXES FOR SOCIAL SECURITY

A reckless and stupid blunder was made by the Republicans in the closing weeks of the 1936 campaign when they criticized the pay-roll taxes used by the Democrats to finance the old age and unemployment benefits of the Social Security Act. Now the cat is out of the bag, and before long every workman will suspect, and with good reason, that the entire burden of the plan, whether the tax is paid by employer or employee, falls on him alone, and that the capitalist feels none of the incidence of the tax.[60]

When the workman discovers this fact, there are three things which he may possibly say:

(1) "The plan, by forcing me to save 6 per cent of my earnings for my old age, is good for me. I need to have someone in Washington tell me how to spend, and *how not to spend*, my own money."

(2) "I've no use for the scheme; it isn't worth the cost. I'll take my chances on holding my job till I die, or else I'll live on my children, as my father and grandfather did before me. Old age insurance is something no poor man can afford, because he needs his money for the doctor and the dentist, the education of his children, and recreation enough for himself to make life worth living."

(3) "Let's make the rich man pay for this thing. Tax very heavily all those with incomes over $4,000, for instance, and distribute the proceeds to the poor as old age and unemployment benefits. After all, don't Republicans and Democrats alike admit that every man has a *right* to security? It is up to the government to find a way to provide it."

The reader can decide from his own knowledge of human nature which of these answers the working man is most likely to make, and which the politicians will consider it the best politics to espouse. If the last answer is the most likely one, and if the beneficiaries of Social Security presently succeed in getting something for nothing, are they not likely to go on and demand still higher benefits, claiming that the present pension scale is altogether inadequate?

If the pay-roll tax for Social Security is abolished, government revenues to the extent of four billion dollars a year

[60] Cf. Chapter XVII, § 9.

eventually will be lost, but government expenses of the same amount will remain. And if the scale of benefits is later raised, the disparity may reach six or seven billion dollars. Does anyone think this sum can be raised by taxes on the higher incomes?

Extremely menacing to the bond market, therefore, was the recent criticism of pay-roll taxes, and any reconsideration of Social Security by Congress seems only too likely to put the fat into the fire.

The sad truth is that social security, or anything else intended to provide a substantially higher standard of living for the masses of the people, is not to be obtained by giving Labor a larger share in the national income, because the masses already collect 85 or 90 per cent of the national income. The only way to improve the welfare of Labor is to increase its efficiency, either by giving it new lands to till, as the great explorers from Christopher Columbus to George Rogers Clark did, or by putting better tools into its hands, as the great inventors from James Watt to Thomas Edison did. Redistribution of the national income, or socialism in other words, will not make the average man better off. Nor will it make him happier, unless he likes the camaraderie of "equality for all" better than he likes the hope of rising in the world on his own merits.

That Social Security benefits and taxes will actually be increased to an intolerable degree is not really to be expected, however, for experience seems to show that some measure of common sense will always be shown by the American people no matter how much at the mercy of a grasping minority they seem to be for a time.

18. PRICE RIGIDITIES

If *all* prices were free to move with the same ease as the price of cotton, wheat, apples, or potatoes, for instance, the introduction of new taxes would not affect the general price level, because taxes would be shifted forwards and backwards with ease, and land, labor, capital, and management would each absorb its theoretical share of the burden of any tax without a change in the price level and the quantity of money in circulation. But if some prices are rigid, such as wages, for instance, and if a pay-roll tax, like the one for Social Security, cannot be shifted back to labor directly by means of wage cuts, then it must be shifted there indirectly by means of higher prices [61] and a reduced purchasing power for labor's wages. Today such an indirect shifting is possible because the banking system is not loaned up, whereas some years ago this indirect shifting might not have been possible. With trade unions strong, and with the New Deal hostile to wage cuts, a tax on pay rolls may be expected, therefore, to be followed by a rise in selling prices, with the tax apparently being shifted forward to the "consumer," but with the tax actually being shifted backwards to the worker, since the worker himself is really the principal consumer in this country. In other words, the real effect of the tax will be to raise the cost of living for the worker.

To this rise in the cost of living the worker may be expected to respond with demands for higher money wages. These in turn will probably be granted widely under the New Deal, and passed on to consumers, and a vicious spiral of rising prices may get under way. Possibly the Social Security Act may prove to be one of the long-dreaded sparks that will help to light the fires of inflation.[62] Certain

[61] Cf. the 1935 Annual Report of the J. I. Case Co., p. 6, which says, "These [higher taxes] cannot be offset by economies in operations and higher selling prices are inevitable."

[62] For a discussion of the particular circumstances under which the Social Security Act could produce, not immediate inflation, but ultimate deflation, see Chapter XX, § 20, footnote 43.

it is that nothing in the present banking position in the shape of deposits outstanding, money rates, or excess reserves seems likely to hinder the development of an inflation so begun.

Far more menacing than the Social Security Act, however, is the C. I. O. movement, for the burden of the Social Security taxes is small indeed compared with the weight of the C. I. O. exactions in the form of higher wages and lower output per man. The C. I. O. movement, aiming at labor monopolies in various industries, threatens to raise costs and selling prices for a wide variety of goods and services, with the result that the cost of living will go up, still higher wages will be demanded, and a disease best described as "wage inflation" will attack our economic life. Inflation of this sort seems inevitable unless the C. I. O. movement is checked, because the ordinary devices for stopping inflation, like balancing the budget, would be of no avail against inflation of this sort. At present our best hope seems to be a defeat of the C. I. O. movement itself by a public opinion aroused against its principal weapons, such as the sit-down strike and the mobbing of non-strikers. But if all hopes fail, the C. I. O. seems all too likely to provoke enough inflation to cause severe embarrassment to the rails and utilities, with a resulting cessation in capital outlays by them, and a corresponding recession in the heavy industries, followed by a fresh depression throughout business generally, with wage inflation and unemployment getting continually worse. In fact, in June 1937, the stock market had already begun to take cognizance of this ugly possibility, and the subsequent rally in July and August was caused partly by the C. I. O.'s loss of the steel strike.[63]

[63] The other cause of the rally, of course, was the defeat in the Senate of President Roosevelt's plan to pack the Supreme Court with six new judges.

19.   THE PROBABLE SEVERITY OF INFLATION

Should inflation get started in this country, it need not be all-consuming, for in this country inflation would not be under forced draft as it was in Germany or France. In Germany it was useless to try to balance the budget with higher taxes, because the more the tax receipts, the more the Allies would demand in reparations. In France [64] it was considered unpatriotic to question the Army's ability to force the collection of reparations whereby Germany would pay the cost of rebuilding the devastated regions. Therefore the French franc was tied to the German mark, and inflation among the vanquished caused inflation among the victors. In this country, however, no external circumstances are at work to fan the fires of inflation. Neither do we find ourselves engaged in a great war like the Revolutionary War, the War of 1812, the Civil War, or the World War, which alone have been responsible for all the great inflations this country has ever had in the past. Today, by contrast, our price rise is not under forced draft,[65] and with us, therefore, a fire would show nothing but bad management, for with us a fire could easily be put out as soon as enough people got burnt and became angry about it. Hence the worst that is to be feared today is a rise in the cost of living so high as to cause a majority of Senators and Representatives to be thrown out and new men to be elected in their places. A rise of 50 or 60 per cent in

[64] For an illuminating account of the domestic political background of the French inflation, see Eleanor L. Dulles, *The French Franc, 1914–1928* (New York: Macmillan, 1929).

[65] Major L. L. B. Angas seems to hold that a forced draft is not necessary, and that the fires of inflation will fan themselves. Is it not true, however, that our own price level is tied to the world-wide price level, especially for speculative commodities like wheat and cotton, sugar and copper, and that no wild inflation can get under way in this country so long as the Tri-Partite Agreement holds, and England and France are free to support our exchange by buying gold from the United States Treasury at the present price? For a statement of Angas's views, see his debate with Stephen M. Foster in *Barron's*, January 25, 1937, p. 3.

prices [66] should certainly be enough to produce such a political turnover.

If the New Deal is really unsound, it is very likely to produce inflation in the end, and thus cause its own downfall. A philosopher, in fact, would say that, where universal suffrage prevails, inflation is the ultimate sanction against bad government.

20. CONSIDERATIONS OF PROBABILITY

To declare categorically, in this uncertain world, that inflation will or will not come, and that bonds should or should not decline, would be foolish indeed, for no one knows with certainty what will happen; the most that any wise man can say is that one event seems more likely to happen than another, that the *probabilities* for the future are such and such in his estimation. A careful estimate of the *probabilities* is all that the investor has to go on; beyond that he has to take his chances with uncertainty, just as does the field marshal in going into battle, or the young man in choosing a career. The majority of life's decisions, in fact, have to be made on the basis of estimated probabilities, and the investor in doing likewise is only facing reality, regardless of whether or not the logicians argue that the theory of probability is not strictly applicable to forecasting future economic developments. Whatever the logical difficulties still to be resolved in the practical application of the theory of probability, experience shows that it pays to think and act in terms of this theory, and that in the long run most people succeed better if they consider all the possibilities and allow for the chance of mishap as well as for the likelihood of things as usual. The theory of probability requires that we should give weight to *all* the possibilities, that we should average the likely with the unlikely,

[66] Concerning the difficulties of stopping a boom even after the budget is balanced, see "The Mechanism and Possibilities of Inflation," by J. Franklin Ebersole, in the *Review of Economic Statistics*, February 15, 1935.

that we should choose, to use the technical term, the *mean* and not the *mode* of the probability curve.

In this particular case, what is the mean [67] of the probability curve for the investment value of government bonds? Surely the mean is not the figure that allows *no* weight for the possibility of inflation. And even if the most likely event is no inflation at all, nevertheless some weight must be given to the chance that the unexpected will happen, and some allowance must be made for the risk that the cost of living will rise as much as assumed in Cases 1, 2, and 3 of § 2 above. If any weight at all is given to these (presumedly) less likely possibilities, the mean estimate of the investment value of the 2¾'s of 1956–59 cannot possibly be as high as the recent market price [68] of 102 ⁹⁄₃₂.

To be more exact, we should say that the mean cannot possibly be as high as this if the bonds are to yield the rate of 2.60 per cent assumed in the calculations. Only if the real interest rate were lower than 2.60 per cent, only if it were substantially lower, in fact, could it be said that the market was allowing for *all* the possibilities, unlikely as well as likely, and only then would the recent yield include a premium for the risk of inflation. How low the real interest rate would need to be to leave room at recent prices for serious inflation is shown by the following rough calculation:

If without inflation the real interest rate were zero, the 20-year 2¾'s would have a present worth of

$$(100) + (20) (2\tfrac{3}{4}) = 155$$

But if the price level should be about to rise at once to a figure of 155, and if the real interest rate remained at zero, these bonds would have a present worth of only

$$\frac{100}{155} \text{ of } 155 = 100$$

Conversely, a zero interest rate would be necessary to leave room for a sudden rise to 155 by the price level in the near future.

[67] Cf. Chapter V, § 8.   [68] As of November 16, 1936.

While a gradual rise in the price level to the figure just assumed would not impair the value of the bonds quite so much as a sudden rise, nevertheless it is clear that an extremely low interest rate would be required to provide for a rise in the price level to the degree assumed, which level is even then slightly less than would correspond to the recent reduction in the gold content of the dollar. Inasmuch as the bond market is assuming today, without much doubt, a real rate of interest very close to 2.60 per cent, it is obvious that the market is giving extremely little weight to the possibility of substantial inflation.

21. SUMMARY

The inflationary measures and events of recent years discussed in the foregoing pages may be classified into three groups:

First, those measures which, by removing old restraints and allowing a wild boom in business, merely *permit* inflation; among these measures are devaluation by the United States and France, and insistence on low interest rates by the Treasury. Offsetting these measures are the feeble Tri-Partite Agreement and the recent raising of reserve requirements to an extent insufficient wholly to eliminate the excess reserves. Measures of this first kind seem to have been without effect, so far as producing real inflation to date is concerned.

Second, those measures which, by impairing confidence and by inciting a flight from the dollar, rashly *provoke* inflation; among these measures are the repudiation of the gold clause in government bonds, the Warren gold-buying plan, and the deliberate creation of federal deficits. Measures of this second kind seem likewise to have been without effect in producing inflation to date.

Third, those measures which, by increasing money incomes and by forcing the cost of living up, actually *compel* inflation; among these measures are government borrowing on bank credit and spending for farm relief, for unemployment assistance, and for public works; government taxation of pay rolls when wages are rigid; and government encouragement of demands for higher wages. Measures of this third kind are already beginning to drive the price level up, and no one knows when it will stop.

If inflation should come at all, it may come either as a climax to a boom, or as a sequel to a panic after prosperity is over. Inflation of the first sort seems unlikely, because extreme activity in business would permit the government to balance its budget, refund its short-term bonds, transfer its debt from the banks to the public, and consent to the elimination of excess reserves. Inflation of the second sort, however, is more likely, because the present recovery in business may burn itself out without bringing the budget into balance, and may leave the government face to face with a natural recession in business at a time when its debt is still piling up. Such a recession, coming at the end of a long bull market in stocks, might touch off a panic in the stock market and cause a flight from the dollar, an embargo on gold exports, and a rise in foreign exchange rates. Aggravated by high and inflexible wage-rates, the recession might bring a great increase in unemployment, and the economic machine might stall because of a maladjustment of prices. The decline in tax receipts and the increase in borrowing would then cast grave doubt on the ultimate purchasing power of the dollar. Although money incomes would be partially sustained by government outlays for relief, real incomes would shrink, because high taxes and lack of confidence would cause business men to curtail output. The cost of living would stubbornly climb, and no one would know at first where the rise would end. Under these circumstances, a collapse in bond prices would be unavoidable.

CHAPTER XX

THE FUTURE OF INTEREST RATES

1.   WHAT DOES THE MARKET ITSELF EXPECT?

In the preceding chapter we have seen what present
quotations for government bonds imply concerning the
future price level; in the present chapter we shall see what
they imply concerning future interest rates. With the implications of the bond market concerning inflation we
could not wholly agree; perhaps with its implications concerning interest rates we cannot agree either. But be this
as it may, our first task in the present chapter is to find out
exactly what the market itself expects, and afterwards we
can go on to form our own conclusions.

Since we have already discussed in the preceding chapter
the question of inflation, and have shown there that present
bond prices are predicated on no inflation ahead, let us
assume in the present chapter, for the sake of argument,
that bond prices depend on interest rates alone, and that
the market need make no allowance for any forthcoming
change in the purchasing power of money, because none is
expected. Should this assumption be false and should inflation become probable, nominal interest rates would be
affected, of course, for bonds would drop, as explained in
the preceding chapter, and bond yields would rise. Interest rates in terms of paper money would thus respond to the
outlook for the purchasing power of money, but interest
rates in terms of goods and services, *real* interest rates, in
other words, could remain substantially unchanged. In this
chapter it is *real* interest rates that we wish to discuss, and
therefore in this chapter we shall make such an assumption
concerning inflation or deflation as will do most to simplify
and clarify the argument. Moreover, inasmuch as the bond

market itself expects no inflation, we ourselves shall not be guilty of introducing any implausibility if we too assume no inflation.

2. THE DIFFERENTIAL ON TAX-EXEMPT ISSUES

If bond prices are to depend on real interest rates alone, they must be independent of corporate earnings; hence for our purposes only the highest grade bonds, the so-called "riskless" issues, can be considered.

Likewise, if bond prices are to depend on interest rates alone, they must be independent of taxes. State and municipal bonds are the only wholly tax-free issues in existence,[1] for Federal bonds are subject to the surtax on incomes. But this does not mean that "Aaa" municipals show the pure interest rate, for these issues, which are bought mostly by heavily taxed millionaires, sell in a fenced-off market of their own, where they are exempt from competition with the main body of securities. Treasury bonds, in contrast to municipal bonds, compete with all other issues, because Treasury bonds, like other bonds, are taxable if held by individuals, and individuals are the marginal holders of these bonds, as we shall show in due course. Hence Treasury bonds correctly reflect the pure interest rate for the market as a whole. Proper allowance, however, must be made for the fact that Treasury bonds, although not so completely tax-exempt as to be suitable for tax avoidance by very rich investors, are still tax-exempt enough to command a somewhat better price than corporate bonds. Just how much difference in yield should emerge is the next question for us to answer.

Let us begin by considering all the riskless bonds on the market, exclusive of wholly tax-exempt municipals and

[1] With the exception of United States Treasury Notes, Bills, and Certificates of Indebtedness, which are too short in term for our purposes.

Treasury Notes and Bills. This group of riskless bonds will be composed of Treasury bonds, on the one hand, and (well-nigh) riskless corporate issues, on the other hand, with the Treasury issues exceeding the corporate issues in amount. The supply of these issues at any one time may be taken as fixed, since it consists of the total inventory of these bonds in existence, which inventory is subject to but very slow increase as new issues are brought out. Thus the relative price of Treasury and corporate issues, like the relative price of gold and silver or diamonds and emeralds, is determined mainly by the quantities already in existence and the demand for each, and only to a slight degree by the new increments currently being produced.

The demand for these riskless issues will come from several sources. To begin with, the banks and insurance companies will wish to hold some given quantity of riskless bonds, determined largely by the amount of their total assets; next, private individuals will desire a certain quantity of riskless bonds; and lastly, charitable institutions, universities, foundations, etc., will wish to hold such bonds. Each source of demand will have its own degree of preference for Treasury over corporate issues, depending on the relative tax advantages of the one or the other type of bond. For banks and insurance companies, Treasury bonds, which are tax-exempt save for the Federal Excess Profits Tax, will be preferable to corporate bonds [2] to the extent of the 15 per cent tax [3] on the income of these banks and insurance companies.[4] For private individuals, Treas-

[2] Corporate bonds are partly tax-exempt for *life* insurance companies, for if these bonds are held as reserves against policies (i.e., are not held as investment for capital funds) their income is exempt to the extent of $3\frac{3}{4}$ per cent (or 4 per cent in certain cases). See the Instructions issued with the Life Insurance Company Income Tax Form by the Treasury Department.

[3] In states where state as well as federal income taxes are levied, the differential would be even higher than this.

[4] Other corporations (such as manufacturing companies) also enjoy the same

ury bonds, which are exempt from the normal income tax of 4 per cent, but subject to the surtax, are preferable to corporate bonds to the extent of only 4 per cent difference in return.[3] For charitable institutions, which pay no taxes at all, Treasury bonds would not be preferable to corporate bonds in the slightest, and so charitable institutions would not buy Treasury bonds at all if their prices were above those of corporate bonds. As a result of their several tax rates, therefore, each group of buyers will be willing to pay different prices for Treasury bonds as compared with corporate bonds.

If a given riskless corporate bond with twenty-five years to run bore a 3 per cent coupon and sold at par, the banks with their income-tax rate of 15 per cent would be willing to accept from a Treasury bond instead a yield of 85 per cent of 3.00 per cent, or 2.55 per cent, while private individuals with their normal tax rate of 4 per cent would demand 96 per cent of 3.00 per cent, or 2.88 per cent, and charitable institutions with their lack of tax differential would demand 100 per cent of 3.00 per cent. If the banks and insurance companies alone could absorb all the Treasury bonds, they would establish a difference in yield of 15 per cent, but if private individuals must be called in to absorb the marginal increment of these bonds, a difference in yield of 4 per cent will result; while if charitable institutions are the marginal holders, no difference in yield at all will result.

In point of fact, the actual difference in yield, as nearly as can be told, is neither 15 per cent, nor 4 per cent, nor 0 per cent, but 9 per cent, for Treasury $2\frac{7}{8}$'s of 1955–60,

---

tax differential on Treasury bonds that banks and insurance companies do, but such corporations ordinarily would not hold *long*-term Treasury issues, since short-term issues are a better substitute for cash in the bank and do not have the appearance of being a permanent investment of undistributed stockholders' funds retained for purposes of tax evasion.

with twenty-four years to run sell at $100^{11}\!/_{32}$ to yield 2.86 per cent, while a typical well-nigh riskless corporate bond like the Standard Oil (New Jersey) 3's of 1960 sells [5] at $97\frac{7}{8}$ to yield [6] 3.13 per cent.

The reason why the difference in yield is 9 per cent instead of 4 per cent, as it should be if individuals are the marginal holders, is probably because the Standard Oil bonds are not considered so completely riskless as Treasury bonds, with the result that the 5 per cent discrepancy between the theoretical parities for the yields is in reality a premium for risk. Thus in the case of the Standard Oil bonds the tax-exempt riskless yield would be 2.86 per cent, the same as for Treasury bonds, while the taxable riskless yields would be 2.97 per cent and the actual yield 3.13 per cent after allowance for both taxes and risk.[7]

If the banks and insurance companies decided to increase their holdings of riskless long-term bonds, they would buy more Treasury issues, because these issues now give them a better yield than corporate issues do, and if the time was ever reached when these institutions absorbed the entire supply, the price of Treasury bonds might jump to where these bonds would yield a full 15 per cent less than riskless corporate bonds. The purchase of government bonds by the Social Security Fund might also have a similar effect on prices.[8]

As soon as private investors were excluded from the government bond market, Treasury issues could rise without

[5] As of June 15, 1937.
[6] The ratio of the two yields is 2.86%/3.13% = 91%. Hence Treasury bonds yield 91 per cent as much as (well-nigh) riskless corporates; in other words, their yield is 9 per cent less.
[7] In states where state as well as federal income taxes are levied, the differential would be greater than 4 per cent, and this fact may in part explain the actual differential.
[8] Compare the remarks of Allan M. Pope, President of the First Boston Corporation, quoted in the *Annalist*, May 29, 1936, p. 787.

making interest rates in general fall. If banks and insurance companies became the sole holders of governments — a condition which does not now prevail — the price of governments would no longer represent the pure interest rate at all, for the price would then be indeterminate within limits, and might vary between one which gave governments a yield 4 per cent less than corporates to one which gave them a yield 15 per cent less. Between these two limits the price could move up or down according to the whim of the various banks trading among themselves. Thus the Treasury $2\frac{7}{8}$'s of 1955–60, if the taxable riskless rate were really as high as the yield of 3.13 per cent displayed by the Standard Oil 3's, might sell anywhere between $97\frac{30}{32}$, at which they would yield 3.00 per cent, and $103\frac{21}{32}$, at which they would yield 2.66 per cent. But outside of these limits, if the yield went above 3.00 per cent private investors would buy Treasury bonds away from the banks and dispose of corporate issues, while if the yields went below 2.66 per cent the banks would sell governments and buy corporates. Between these limits, however, so long as riskless corporates continued to yield 3.13 per cent, governments would be free to fluctuate in a meaningless way.

Even though riskless corporates may be fewer in number than Treasury bonds, they can still be the true index of the pure interest rate, because, unlike governments, they are firmly tied, through a suitable premium for risk, to the great bulk of more risky corporate bonds, and to preferred stocks, mortgages, etc., in the market for new issues wherein the interest rate is determined.[9]

As already said, if the banks and insurance companies held all the long-term governments, the price of these bonds would be partly indeterminate, but since no such exclusion

[9] Cf. Chapter XVIII.

of private investors actually exists,[10] no such latitude for prices results. Therefore it is permissible for us to use Treasury bonds, if we wish, to measure the pure interest rate, provided, of course, that for other reasons also these issues seem to be the best for the purpose.

3. FUTURE SHORT-TERM INTEREST RATES

The assertion that short-term interest rates are normally lower than long-term rates for the reason that short-term loans are safer from depreciation than long-term loans is incorrect, because (1) short-term rates often are not lower than long-term rates, and (2) the *net* risk on long-term loans is zero, for the hope of temporary appreciation is balanced against the fear of temporary depreciation. If short-term interest rates are low, the possibility that they may continue low is one good reason for hoping that long-term bonds will go up, instead of fearing that they may go down. Hence it is not correct to say that long-term interest rates include a premium for a special risk that is not present in short-term rates.

A bond market in which high-grade bonds of different maturities are bought and sold is like a commodity market in which future contracts in wheat or cotton are bought and sold. Such a bond market quotes futures on interest rates [11] instead of futures on commodity prices. Thus the comparative prices of two bonds, one maturing in 1954 and the other in 1959, for instance, imply a particular rate of

---

[10] *The American Banker* for December 1936 states that, on June 30, 1936, banks and insurance companies together held 66.8 per cent of the government bonds outstanding at that time; hence we know that the remaining 33.2 per cent of the federal debt must have been held by individuals, corporations, charities, etc.

[11] Cf. Keynes, *General Theory*, p. 168. "If the rates of interest ruling at all future times could be foreseen with certainty, all future rates of interest could be inferred from the *present* rates of interest for debts of different maturities, which would be adjusted to the knowledge of the future rates."

interest for the period from 1954 to 1959. If bonds maturing in 1954 sell high, while those maturing in 1959 sell low,
even though both carry the same coupon and both have the
same security, these prices will imply a high rate of interest for the intervening period, and borrowers will wish to
borrow up to the nearer date only, while lenders will prefer
to lend through to the later date. Some method of calculation is needed by each party to help it decide whether
to favor the longer or the shorter period in its borrowing
or lending. The calculations of each party should compare
the rate implicit in bond prices for the period 1954 to 1959
with the short-term rate that seems likely to prevail when
these years come. For the borrower has the choice of issuing bonds of the 1954 maturity, and then of seeking temporary accommodation from 1954 to 1959, or of issuing
bonds of the 1959 maturity once and for all.[12] Likewise
the lender has the choice of buying bonds running to 1954
only, and then of putting his money out on short-term later,
or of tying up his funds until 1959 once and for all. What
each will do depends on what each expects interest rates
to be during the five-year period in question.

An interesting practical aspect of this problem appears
in federal financing, where the question presents itself as
follows: Was it good business for the Treasury in September 1936 to offer a yield of 2.67 instead of 2.61 per cent
in order to make its 2¾'s mature in 1959 instead of 1954?
What rate was the Treasury implicitly committing itself to
pay for the use of the money during the extra five years?
Was this rate more or less than would probably have been
required on short-term in these years when the time came?

Although no exact method for computing this future
rate is yet in common use, we shall find that the intuition
of the market has arrived at prices for the two maturities

[12] Cf. Chapter X, § 2.

that imply a reasonable interest rate for the intervening period, this rate being $3\frac{1}{8}$ per cent, as we shall see.

4.   TREASURY BONDS GIVE THE BEST DATA

The ideal instrument for measuring the future short-term interest rates expected by the money market would be a large, well-seasoned issue of riskless or nearly riskless serial bonds, with maturities every six months until fifty or sixty years from now. No such issue is in existence, how-ever, and so we must choose the best thing actually avail-able. For this purpose a riskless corporate issue like Chesapeake and Ohio equipment trust 3's of 1937–50, rated "Aaa," might be used, except that they do not include maturities that are distant enough to give us all the in-formation we need, and no thoroughly reliable list of prices for all the various maturities is available day by day. State of Massachusetts $2\frac{1}{4}$'s of 1937–66 might also be used, except for the fact that municipals, being wholly tax-ex-empt, sell in a fenced-off market, and therefore do not cor-rectly reflect the actual pure interest rate. United States Treasury bonds, with irregular maturities extending from 1940 to 1959, remain as a possible issue of quasi-serial riskless bonds. While these bonds do not have a uniform coupon rate, the formulas can still be made to handle them, and a study of their yields shows that the diversity of cou-pon rates does not in itself produce any diversity of yields, the yields all being determined only by the number of years to maturity.[13] These issues have the great advantage of being very active in the market, with the result that each day's prices may be taken to represent the carefully con-sidered and currently revised opinion of a large group of

[13] With the exception of the two or three issues which happen to be selling well below par; these discount bonds, however, will be omitted from the calcula-tions.

experts. While the fact that all the issues but one are callable before maturity might at first sight seem to introduce an element of uncertainty into the calculations by making the exact date of payment debatable, a careful comparison of yields will show, in a way to be explained soon, whether the market expects the bonds to be paid at maturity or to be called beforehand. In spite of their lack of exactly annual maturities, therefore, Treasury bonds would seem to be the best means available for inferring the future short-term interest rates implicit in the present structure of bond prices.

While these implications are what we are seeking to discover at present, they do not necessarily coincide, of course, with our own expectations, the deduction of which is being deferred to later portions of this chapter.

5.   "RIGHTS" PERTAINING TO TREASURY NOTES

With Treasury issues, unfortunately, it is not possible to begin with the very shortest maturities, because the notes due within a few months carry a negative yield. This negative yield results from the Treasury's habit of making its new bond issues sell above par when offered, and of giving preferential treatment to note holders when these new issues are allotted; thus holders of maturing notes are allotted new bonds for the full value of their holdings, while cash subscribers to new bonds must accept only their *pro rata* share. It is as though invisible "rights" were attached to the notes, and it is the value of these rights which carries the notes up to a figure where their yield is apparently negative. If one could get a quotation on the notes "ex-rights," however, he would see that the notes really do afford a positive yield, as we shall now show.

It is only reasonable to suppose that Treasury notes "ex-rights" would afford the same yield as Treasury bills of the same maturity, which carry no preferential subscription privileges for new bonds. In August 1936, for instance, when Treasury bills sold at a discount to yield 0.15 per cent for the shortest maturities, namely two months and less, the same yield would seem to have been fair for Treasury notes of this maturity. Such a yield would have implied a fair value on August 11 for the $1\frac{1}{2}$ per cent notes due September 15 of $100\frac{4}{32}$ as contrasted with the actual market price of $100\frac{26}{32}$. Evidently the conversion privilege attached to the notes was considered at that time to be worth $\frac{22}{32}$ of a point; in other words, it was thought at that time that the next issue of long-term bonds offered by the Treasury would sell at $100\frac{22}{32}$. Three weeks later, when the offer was actually made, it turned out to be so attractive that the notes rose to $101\frac{9}{32}$ bid, and when the new bonds came on the market on September 15, they sold between $101\frac{9}{32}$ and $101\frac{5}{32}$ during the first day of trading. Back in August, however, dealers did not foresee such an attractive offer, and so at that time they appraised the "rights" attaching to the notes at the lower value of $\frac{22}{32}$ mentioned first.

If the "rights" attaching to the notes of September 15, 1936, were worth $\frac{22}{32}$, the rights attaching to other notes were probably worth no more, and possibly worth less, but how much less it is hard to say except in the particular case of the 3's due April 15, 1937. These latter, by comparison with Treasury bills of the same maturity, should have been selling to yield 0.30 per cent, and their fair value, therefore, would seem to have been $101\frac{26}{32}$ as compared with the actual market price of $102\frac{9}{32}$; evidently the conversion privilege attached to these notes was appraised at $\frac{15}{32}$, compared with $\frac{22}{32}$ for the September 1936 issue.

Apparently the more distant the conversion privilege, the less it was thought to be worth. A privilege seven months distant in this case was appraised $\frac{7}{32}$ of a point lower, for $\frac{22}{32} - \frac{15}{32} = \frac{7}{32}$. Possibly a privilege that might be exercisable twenty-two months hence would be valued at zero by the market, and probably one exercisable three or four years hence would be valued thus. If so, it would be fair to state that such an issue as the $3\frac{3}{8}$ per cent Treasury bonds of June 1940, not due until nearly four years from August 1936, contained no element of conversion value in its then price of $108\frac{7}{32}$. Likewise all later issues would contain no element of "rights" in their then prevailing prices, and no adjustment would need to be made to these prices in using them to infer the future interest rates implicit in the present structure of government bond prices.

6.   PROBABLE REDEMPTION DATES

To ascertain just when the market expects each Treasury issue to be redeemed, the procedure is to make two separate arrays of these issues, as shown in the first two columns below, one array according to call date, and the other according to maturity date, with the yield to the one or the other redemption date set beside each issue in each array. From these two arrays a third array may then be constructed by choosing one issue after another according to its expected redemption date. The third array will include, therefore, a mixture of call dates and maturity dates. Each issue will be listed as payable at the one or the other date according to the best indications available, and the yields will be consistent with each other and with the chosen term of each bond. It will be noted that neither of these first two arrays gives consistently rising yields, whereas the third array does. For the particular day chosen, June 15, 1937, the construction of the third array happened to

be relatively simple, because for this day it was only necessary to take the first ten bonds from column one, and the
other nine from colmun two. The three arrays are shown
in Table 3.

The nineteen choices of redemption dates mentioned
above give the third array of yields in Table 3. These
yields, it will be noted, show a consistent increase from
year to year in a way that the yields in neither of the first
two arrays do, and this very consistency may be taken as
proof that the third array displays the real expectations of
the bond market. The only inconsistencies in the third
array are the slight ones pertaining to the 4¼'s of 1947–52,
the 2½'s of 1949–53, and the 2¾'s of 1956–59, the first of
which seems to be explained by the special tax features [14]
of the issue and the second and third by the discount from
par at which the bonds are selling.[15] Because of these inconsistencies these three issues will be omitted from our
calculations henceforth.

7.   COMPUTATION BY THE APPROXIMATE METHODS

Three methods of computing implied future short-term
interest rates are available to us, of which two are approximate and one exact. But the exact method is so intricate
that it is better to use the approximate methods first in
order to find out roughly what the right answer is, and to
have figures at hand that will serve as a partial check on
the more elaborate calculations to follow.

What do the government issues in Table 3 show regarding the expectations of the bond market as to future

[14] The 4¼'s of 1947–52 are the only Treasury issue which may be offered at
par for the payment of estate taxes even if the market price should happen to be
below par.

[15] Discount bonds habitually sell on a lower yield basis than premium bonds
because many small trustees dislike the bother of writing off the premium on
premium bonds year by year.

TABLE 3

United States Treasury Bonds

June 15, 1937

	Arranged in Order of Call Dates			Arranged in Order of Maturity Dates					
	Issue	Price	Yield to Call Date	Issue	Price	Yield to Maturity Date	Issue	Yield to Redemption Date	
1940	3 3/8's of June 40–43	105 12/32	1.53[c]	...	....	...	3 3/8's of June 40–43	1.53[c]	1940
....	...	....	...	...	....	...	...	...	
1941	3 3/8's of Mar. 41–43	106 10/32	1.62[c]	...	....	...	3 3/8's of Mar. 41–43	1.62[c]	1941
....	3 1/4's of Aug. 41	106 1/32	1.73[n]	3 1/4's of Aug. 41	106 1/32	1.73[n]	3 1/4's of Aug. 41	1.73[n]	
1942	...	....	...	...	....	...	...	...	1942
....	...	....	...	...	....	...	...	...	
1943	3 3/8's of June 43–47	106 19/32	2.20[c]	3 3/8's of Mar. 41–43	106 10/32	2.20[c]	3 3/8's of June 43–47	2.20[c]	1943
....	3 1/4's of Oct. 43–45	106 6/32	2.20[c]	3 3/8's of June 40–43	105 12/32	2.41[c]	3 1/4's of Oct. 43–47	2.20[c]	
1944	3 1/4's of Apr. 44–46	106 2/32	2.29[c]	...	....	...	3 1/4's of Apr. 44–46	2.29[c]	1944
....	4's of Dec. 44–54	111 10/32	2.35[c]	...	....	...	4's of Dec. 44–54	2.35[c]	
1945	2 3/4's of Dec. 45–47	102 18/32	2.42[c]	...	....	...	2 3/4's of Dec. 45–47	2.42[c]	1945
....	3 3/4's of Mar. 46–56	109 19/32	2.52[c]	3 1/4's of Oct. 43–45	106 6/32	2.42[c]	3 3/4's of Mar. 46–56	2.52[c]	
1946	3's of June 46–48	103 29/32	2.51[m]	3 1/4's of Apr. 44–46	106 2/32	2.48[c]	...	...	1946
....	3 1/8's of June 46–49	104 19/32	2.55[m]	...	....	...	...	...	
1947	...	....	...	3 3/8's of June 43–47	106 19/32	2.62[c]	...	...	1947
....	4 1/4's of Oct. 47–52	115 24/32	2.51[c]	2 3/4's of Dec. 45–47	102 18/32	2.47[c]	4 1/4's of Oct. 47–52	2.51[c]	
1948	2 3/4's of Mar. 48–51	100 14/32	2.70[m]	3's of June 46–48	103 29/32	2.59[m]	3's of June 46–48	2.59[m]	1948
....	...	....	...	...	....	...	...	...	
1949	3 1/8's of Dec. 49–52	104 14/32	2.71[m]	3 1/8's of June 46–49	104 19/32	2.68[m]	3 1/8's of June 46–49	2.68[m]	1949
....	2 1/2's of Dec. 49–53	97 19/32	2.73[m]	...	....	...	...	...	

TABLE 3 (Continued)

	Arranged in Order of Call Dates			Arranged in Order of Maturity Dates					
	Issue	Price	Yield to Call Date	Issue	Price	Yield to Maturity Date	Issue	Yield to Redemption Date	
1950	....	....	...	....	....	...	....	...	1950
....	....	....	...	....	....	...	....	...	
1951	2¾'s of June 51–54	99 19/32	2.79[m]	2¾'s of Mar. 48–51	100 14/32	2.71[m]	2¾'s of Mar. 48–51	2.71[m]	1951
....	3's of Sept. 51–55	102 14/32	2.79[m]	....	....	...	....	...	
1952	....	....	...	4¼'s of Oct. 47–52	115 24/32	2.96[c]	....	...	1952
....	....	....	...	3⅛'s of Dec. 49–52	104 14/32	2.77[m]	3⅛'s of Dec. 49–52	2.77[m]	
1953	....	....	...	....	....	...	....	...	1953
....	....	....	...	2½'s of Dec. 49–53	97 19/32	2.68[m]	2½'s of Dec. 49–53	2.68[m]	
1954	....	....	...	2¾'s of June 51–54	99 19/32	2.78[m]	2¾'s of June 51–54	2.78[m]	1954
....	....	....	...	4's of Dec. 44–54	111 10/32	3.15[c]	....	...	
1955	2⅞'s of Mar. 55–60	100 11/32	2.85[m]	....	....	...	....	...	1955
....	....	....	...	3's of Sept. 51–55	102 14/32	2.83[m]	3's of Sept. 51–55	2.83[m]	
1956	....	....	...	3¾'s of Mar. 46–56	109 19/32	3.07[c]	....	...	1956
....	2¾'s of Sept. 56–59	99 11/32	2.80[m]	....	....	...	....	...	
1957	....	....	...	....	....	...	....	...	1957
....	....	....	...	....	....	...	....	...	
1958	....	....	...	....	....	...	....	...	1958
....	....	....	...	....	....	...	....	...	
1959	....	....	...	....	....	...	....	...	1959
....	....	....	...	2¾'s of Sept. 56–59	99 11/32	2.79[m]	2¾'s of Sept. 56–59	2.79[m]	
1960	....	....	...	2⅞'s of Mar. 55–60	100 11/32	2.86[m]	2⅞'s of Mar. 55–60	2.86[m]	1960

[c] Evidently to be redeemed on call date.
[m] Evidently to be redeemed on maturity date.
[n] Non-callable.

interest rates? Let us apply the simplest method of calculation first, and use the formula

(37f) $(n' - n)i = n'i_{n'} - ni_n$

where

n = number of years to redemption of shorter
        bond

n' = number of years to redemption of longer
        bond

i_n = yield to redemption of shorter bond

$i_{n'}$ = yield to redemption of longer bond

i = interest rate during intervening years from
        n to n'.

The essence of this method of approximation is revealed
by the following example:

Just as we can say that

3% = average rate

if   2% = rate in first year

and   4% = rate in second year

so also we can say, by turning the computation around, that

4% = rate in second year

if   2% = rate in first year

and   3% = average rate.

Thus we are able to solve for the unknown second-year rate of 4 per
cent when the known first-year and average rates of 2 and 3 per cent
are given.

The foregoing method is applied by the use of formula
(37f) in Table 4, and a similar computation applied to a
group of short-term Treasury notes is given in Table 5.

TABLE 4

Approximate Future Short-Term Interest Rates as Shown by Treasury Bonds

June 15, 1937

Expected Date of Redemption	Term	Yield	$n'i_{n'} - ni_n = (n'-n)i$			Interval $(n'-n)$	Computed Rate i	Issue	Period Covered
June 15, 1940	(3)	(1.53)	4.5900	– 0.0000 =	4.5900	3	1.53%	3⅜'s of June 40–43	June 15, 1937 to June 15, 1940
Mar. 15, 1941	(3¾)	(1.62)	6.0750	– 4.5900 =	1.4850	¾	1.98%	3⅜'s of Mar. 41–43	June 15, 1940 to Mar. 15, 1941
Aug. 1, 1941	(4⅛)	(1.73)	7.1363	– 6.0750 =	1.0613	⅜	2.83%	3¼'s of Aug. 41	Mar. 15, 1941 to Aug. 1, 1941
June 15, 1943	(6)	(2.20)	13.2000	– 7.1363 =	6.0637	1⅞	3.23%	3⅜'s of June 43–47	Aug. 1, 1941 to June 15, 1943
Oct. 15, 1943	(6⅓)	(2.20)	13.9333	– 13.2000 =	.7333	⅓	2.20%	3¼'s of Oct. 43–45	June 15, 1943 to Oct. 15, 1943
Apr. 15, 1944	(6⅚)	(2.29)	15.6483	– 13.9333 =	1.7150	½	3.43%	3¼'s of Apr. 44–46	Oct. 15, 1943 to Apr. 15, 1944
Dec. 15, 1944	(7½)	(2.35)	17.6250	– 15.6483 =	1.9767	⅔	2.07%	4's of Dec. 44–54	Apr. 15, 1944 to Dec. 15, 1944
Dec. 15, 1945	(8½)	(2.42)	20.5700	– 17.6250 =	2.9450	1	2.95%	2¾'s of Dec. 45–47	Dec. 15, 1944 to Dec. 15, 1945
Mar. 15, 1946	(8¾)	(2.52)	22.0500	– 20.5700 =	1.4800	¼	5.92%	3¾'s of Mar. 46–56	Dec. 15, 1945 to Mar. 15, 1946
June 15, 1948	(11)	(2.59)	28.4900	– 22.0500 =	6.4400	2¼	2.86%	3's of June 46–48	Mar. 15, 1946 to June 15, 1948
June 15, 1949	(12)	(2.68)	32.1600	– 28.4900 =	3.6700	1	3.67%	3⅛'s of June 46–49	June 15, 1948 to June 15, 1949
Mar. 15, 1951	(13¾)	(2.71)	37.2625	– 32.1600 =	5.1025	1¾	2.02%	2¾'s of Mar. 48–51	June 15, 1949 to Mar. 15, 1951
Dec. 15, 1952	(15½)	(2.77)	42.9350	– 37.2625 =	5.6725	1¾	3.24%	3⅛'s of Dec. 49–52	Mar. 15, 1951 to Dec. 15, 1952
June 15, 1954	(17)	(2.78)	47.2600	– 42.9350 =	4.3250	1½	2.88%	2¾'s of June 51–54	Dec. 15, 1952 to June 15, 1954
Sept. 15, 1955	(18¼)	(2.83)	51.6475	– 47.2600 =	4.3875	1¼	3.51%	3's of Sept. 51–55	June 15, 1954 to Sept. 15, 1955
Mar. 15, 1960	(22¾)	(2.86)	65.0650	– 51.6475 =	13.4175	4½	2.98%	2⅞'s of Mar. 55–60	Sept. 15, 1955 to Mar. 15, 1960
					65.0650	22¾			

TABLE 5

Approximate Future Short-Term Interest Rates as Shown by Treasury Notes

June 15, 1937

Issue	Term	Yield	$n'i_{n'}$	$-$ ni_n	$= (n'-n)i$	Interval $n'-n$	Computed Rate i	Period Covered
3¼'s of Sept. 1937		negative						
2⅝'s of Feb. 1938*	(⅝)	(0.42)	0.2625	− 0.0000	= 0.2625	⅝	*0.42%*	June 15, 1937 to Feb. 1, 1938
3's of Mar. 1938	(¾)	(0.39)	0.2925	− 0.2625	= 0.0300	⅛	*0.24%*	Feb. 1, 1938 to Mar. 15, 1938
2⅞'s of June 1938	(1)	(0.51)	0.5100	− 0.2925	= 0.2175	¼	*0.87%*	Mar. 15, 1938 to June 15, 1938
2½'s of Sept. 1938	(1¼)	(0.63)	0.7875	− 0.5100	= 0.2775	¼	*1.11%*	June 15, 1938 to Sept. 15, 1938
1½'s of Mar. 1939	(1¾)	(1.14)	1.9950	− 0.7875	= 1.2075	½	*2.42%*	Sept. 15, 1938 to Mar. 15, 1939
2⅛'s of June 1939	(2)	(1.20)	2.4000	− 1.9950	= 0.4050	¼	*1.62%*	Mar. 15, 1939 to June 15, 1939
1⅜'s of Sept. 1939	(2¼)	(1.29)	2.9025	− 2.4000	= 0.5025	¼	*2.01%*	June 15, 1939 to Sept. 15, 1939
1⅜'s of Dec. 1939	(2½)	(1.31)	3.2750	− 2.9025	= 0.3725	¼	*1.49%*	Sept. 15, 1939 to Dec. 15, 1939
1⅝'s of Mar. 1940	(2¾)	(1.40)	3.8500	− 3.2750	= 0.5750	¼	*2.30%*	Dec. 15, 1939 to Mar. 15, 1940
1½'s of June 1940	(3)	(1.43)	4.2900	− 3.8500	= 0.4400	¼	*1.76%*	Mar. 15, 1940 to June 15, 1940
1½'s of Dec. 1940	(3½)	(1.51)	5.2850	− 4.2900	= 0.9950	½	*1.99%*	June 15, 1940 to Dec. 15, 1940
1½'s of Mar. 1941	(3¾)	(1.54)	5.7750	− 5.2850	= 0.4900	¼	*1.96%*	Dec. 15, 1940 to Mar. 15, 1941
1⅜'s of June 1941	(4)	(1.55)	6.2000	− 5.7750	= 0.4250	¼	*1.70%*	Mar. 15, 1941 to June 15, 1941
1¼'s of Dec. 1941	(4½)	(1.53)	6.8850	− 6.2000	= 0.6850	½	*1.37%*	June 15, 1941 to Dec. 15, 1941
1¾'s of Mar. 1942	(4¾)	(1.70)	8.0750	− 6.8850	= 1.1900	¼	*4.76%*	Dec. 15, 1941 to Mar. 15, 1942
					8.0750	4¾		

* Due February 1, 1938; all other notes due on the 15th of the month.

TABLE 6

Approximate Future Short-Term Interest Rates as Shown by Five Selected Treasury Bonds, Using Simple Interest Method

Expected Date of Redemption	Term	Yield	$n'i_{n'} - ni_n = (n' - n)i$	Interval $(n' - n)$	Computed Rate i	Issue	Period Covered
June 15, 1940	(3)	(1.53)	4.590 − 0.000 = 4.590	3	1.53%	3⅜'s of June 40–43	1937–40
June 15, 1943	(6)	(2.20)	13.200 − 4.590 = 8.610	3	2.87%	3⅜'s of June 43–47	1940–43
June 15, 1948	(11)	(2.59)	28.490 − 13.200 = 15.290	5	3.06%	3's of June 46–48	1943–48
June 15, 1954	(17)	(2.78)	47.260 − 28.490 = 18.770	6	3.13%	2¾'s of June 51–54	1948–54
Mar. 15, 1960	(22¾)	(2.86)	65.065 − 47.260 = 17.805	5¾	3.10%	2⅞'s of Mar. 55–60	1954–60
			65.065	22¾			

TABLE 7

Compound Interest Method for Finding Five Future Short-Term Interest Rates as of June 15, 1937

Expected Date of Redemption	Yield to Redemption i_n	$(1 + i_n)$	$\log (1 + i_n)$	Number of Years to Redemption n	$n \log (1 + i_n)$	Log of Quotient	Interval $n' - n$	$\log (1 + i)$	$(1 + i)$	Rate for Period	Period Covered
June 15, 1940	1.53%	1.0153	0.00659	3	0.01977		3	.....	.....	1.53%	1937–40
June 15, 1943	2.20%	1.0220	0.00945	6	0.05670	0.03693	3	0.01231	1.0288	2.88%	1940–43
June 15, 1948	2.59%	1.0259	0.01111	11	0.12221	0.06551	5	0.01310	1.0306	3.06%	1943–48
June 15, 1954	2.78%	1.0278	0.01191	17	0.20247	0.08026	6	0.01338	1.0313	3.13%	1948–54
Mar. 15, 1960	2.86%	1.0286	0.01225	22¾	0.27869	0.07622	5¾	0.01326	1.0310	3.10%	1954–60

A graph of these yields is shown in Chart IV. In this chart the main outlines only are of significance, for the individual peaks and valleys probably represent nothing but day-to-day irregularities in market price. A study of this chart suggests that the many separate short periods may be grouped into a few longer ones in a way that will remove the sharp and meaningless fluctuations without obscuring the real course of events. Such a grouping would reduce the number of periods to five; the computations for this grouping are given in Table 6. We can now proceed to use the second and more accurate method of approximation for determining implicit short-term interest rates. The formula is

$$(37\text{d}) \qquad (1 + i)^{n'-n} = \frac{(1 + i_{n'})^{n'}}{(1 + i_n)^n}$$

and the calculations are given in Table 7.

8. COMPUTATION BY THE EXACT METHOD

With these two approximate calculations as a guide, we can now proceed to compute the required short-term rates by the exact method,[16] whose formulas are as follows:

$$(29\text{d}) \qquad V_1 = \pi_1 a_{\overline{n}|i_1} + Cv_1{}^n = M_1$$

$$(1\text{p}) \qquad V_2 = \pi_2 a_{n\overline{1}|i_1} + Cv_2{}^{n'} = \frac{M_2 - \pi_2 a_{\overline{n}|i_1}}{v_1{}^n}$$

$$(1\text{p}) \qquad V_3 = \pi_3 a_{n\overline{n}|i_1} + Cv_3{}^{n''} = \frac{M_3 - \pi_3 \left(a_{\overline{n}|i_1} + v_1{}^n a_{n\overline{1}|i_2} \right)}{v_1{}^n v_2{}^{n'}}$$
$$\text{etc.}$$

$$(29\text{e}) \qquad 2i_1 = f(V_1,\ 2\pi_1,\ \tfrac{1}{2}n)$$
$$\text{etc.}$$

---

[16] Cf. Chapter X, § 4.

CHART IV

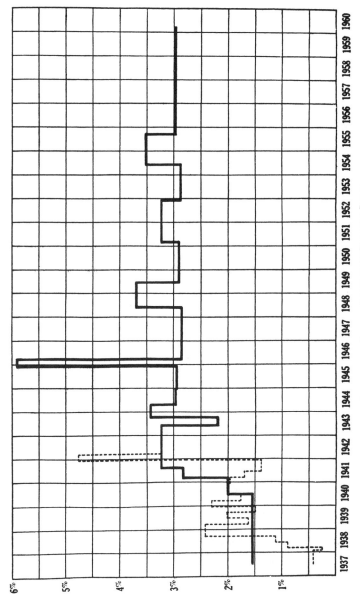

APPROXIMATE FUTURE SHORT-TERM INTEREST RATES

Notes: ------   Bonds: ——————

For simplicity of notation, V_1, V_2, V_3 and n, n', n'' may be redefined as follows:

V_1 = value of shortest bond

V_2 = value of next shortest bond

V_3 = value of third shortest bond

n = number of interest periods to maturity of shortest bond

n' = number of additional interest periods to maturity of next shortest bond

n'' = number of additional interest periods to maturity of third shortest bond, etc.

The calculations are given in Table 8.

In these computations the values of $a_{\overline{n}|}$ and v^n are obtained from Glover's Tables [17] by interpolation. For v^n it is best to interpolate the logarithms rather than the natural numbers. In Table 9 on page 357 is set forth a comparison of the expected future interest rates given by the exact method and the rates given by the approximate methods. It will be noted that the exact method gives higher rates in distant years than the approximate methods, because these latter neglect the coupons paid and use only the principal in their calculation.

The forecast of rising short-term interest rates set forth in Table 9 is bullish on the stocks of such banks as have refrained from holding high-grade long-term bonds, and, by the same token, it is bearish on the stocks of fire and life insurance companies, most of whom are heavily committed to bonds of the very kind that will depreciate most in the years to come. As a hedge against such depreciation, the insurance companies should increase their holdings of bank

[17] Glover, *Tables of Applied Mathematics*.

TABLE 8

EXACT METHOD FOR FINDING FIVE FUTURE SHORT-TERM INTEREST RATES AS OF JUNE 15, 1937

Issue	$3\frac{3}{8}$'s of 40–43	$3\frac{3}{8}$'s of 43–47	3's of 46–48	$2\frac{3}{4}$'s of 51–54	$2\frac{7}{8}$'s of 55–60
Assumed Date of Payment	June 15, 1940	June 15, 1943	June 15, 1948	June 15, 1954	Mar. 15, 1960
Price in thirty-seconds	$105\frac{12}{32}$	$106\frac{19}{32}$	$103\frac{29}{32}$	$99\frac{19}{32}$	$100\frac{11}{32}$
Price in decimals $M =$	105.3750	106.5938	103.9063	99.5938	100.3438
Number of Half-Years in Period $n =$	$3 \times 2 = 6$	$3 \times 2 = 6$	$5 \times 2 = 10$	$6 \times 2 = 12$	$6 \times 2 = 12$ [a]
Semi-Annual Interest Rate for Previous Period $i =$	none	.767%	1.464%	1.571%	1.609%
Present Worth of Annuity at Former Rates $a_{\overline{6}\vert i_1} =$	nil	5.842	5.842	5.842	5.842
Present Worth of Annuity at Former Rates $v_1^6 a_{\overline{6}\vert i_2} =$	....	....	5.448	5.448	5.448
Present Worth of Annuity at Former Rates $v_1^6 v_2^6 a_{\overline{10}\vert i_3} =$	....	....	....	8.043	8.043
Present Worth of Annuity at Former Rates $v_1^6 v_2^6 v_3^{10} a_{\overline{12}\vert i_4} =$	....	....	....	....	8.116
Sum $(a_{\overline{6}\vert i_1} + \cdots + v_1^6 v_2^6 v_3^{10} a_{\overline{12}\vert i_4}) =$	nil	5.842	11.290	19.333	27.449
Coupon Rate for Half-Year $=$	1.6875	1.6875	1.5000	1.3750	1.4375
Product of Sum and Coupon Rate $\pi(a_{\overline{6}\vert i_1} + \cdots + v_1^6 v_2^6 v_3^{10} a_{\overline{12}\vert i_4}) =$	nil	9.8584	16.9350	26.5829	39.4579
Price $M =$	105.3750	106.5938	103.9063	99.5938	100.3438
Price less Product = Difference $M - \pi(a_{\overline{6}\vert i_1} + \cdots + v_1^6 v_2^6 v_3^{10} a_{\overline{12}\vert i_4}) =$	105.38	96.74	86.97	73.01	60.89
First Discount Factor $v_1^6 =$	....	.9552	.9552	.9552	.9552
Second Discount Factor $v_2^6 =$	....	....	.9165	.9165	.9165
Third Discount Factor $v_3^{10} =$	....	....	....	.8557	.8557
Fourth Discount Factor $v_4^{12} =$	....	....	....	....	.8257
Product $(v_1^6 v_2^6 v_3^{10} v_4^{12}) =$	1.00000	.9552	.8754	.7491	.6185
Value of Bond at Start of this Period = Quotient $V =$	105.38	101.28	99.35	97.46	98.45
Length of this Period $\frac{1}{2}n =$	3 yrs.	3 yrs.	5 yrs.	6 yrs.	6 yrs.
Coupon Rate for Full Year $2p =$	$3\frac{3}{8}$%	$3\frac{3}{8}$%	3%	$2\frac{3}{4}$%	$2\frac{7}{8}$%
Annual Interest Rate for this Period = Answer $j_{(2)} = 2i =$	*1.533%*	*2.928%*	*3.141%*	*3.219%*	*3.161%*
Semi-Annual Interest Rate for this Period $i =$	.767%	1.464%	1.571%	1.609%	1.581%
Period Covered	1937–40	1940–43	1943–48	1948–54	1954–60

[a] For simplicity in calculation, this particular bond is treated as though it matured in June instead of March, or in 6 instead of in $5\frac{3}{4}$ years after the preceding bond.

stocks, provided they can find banks with portfolios sufficiently free from long-term bonds.

9.   IMPLIED YIELD TO PERPETUITY

When short- and long-term Treasury bonds show the yields to maturity derived in the foregoing calculations, what yield to perpetuity should a perpetual Treasury bond display, assuming that the interest rate found to apply for the terminal years 1954–1960 is to continue in force beyond the year 1960 without change forevermore?

TABLE 9

COMPARISON OF RESULTS BY THE THREE METHODS

Period Covered		Interval	Approximate Methods		Exact Method
			Simple	Compound	
June 1937 to June	1940 ..	3 years	1.53%	1.53%	1.533%
June 1940 to June	1943 ..	3 years	2.87%	2.88%	2.928%
June 1943 to June	1948 ..	5 years	3.06%	3.06%	3.141%
June 1948 to June	1954 ..	6 years	3.13%	3.13%	3.219%
June 1954 to March 1960 ...		5¾ years	3.10%	3.10%	3.161%

The formula for answering this question has been worked out in Chapter X, § 3, and is as follows in this particular case:

$$(\text{1j}) \qquad \frac{1}{\bar{\imath}} = a_{\overline{6}|i_1} + v_1{}^6 a_{\overline{6}|i_2} + v_1{}^6 v_2{}^6 a_{\overline{10}|i_3}$$

$$+ v_1{}^6 v_2{}^6 v_3{}^{10} a_{\overline{12}|i_4} + \frac{v_1{}^6 v_2{}^6 v_3{}^{10} v_4{}^{12}}{i_5}$$

Here $\bar{\imath}$ is the desired yield to perpetuity, and v_1, v_2, etc., are the discount factors for the near-by periods 1, 2, etc., while $a_{\overline{6}|i_1}$, $a_{\overline{6}|i_2}$, etc., are the corresponding annuity factors.

The value of $\bar{\imath}$ may easily be computed with the aid of figures contained in Table 8 thus:

$$\frac{1}{\bar{\imath}} = 27.449 + \frac{0.6185}{1.581\%}$$

$$= 27.449 + 39.121$$

$$= 66.57$$

$$\bar{\imath} = \frac{1}{66.57} = 1.502\%$$

$$2\bar{\imath} = 3.004\%$$

Q. E. F.

The foregoing calculation shows that the Treasury, if it wished, could sell a 3 per cent perpetual bond, or "consol," almost at par; for such a bond ought to command a price [18] of $99^{28}/_{32}$ to be in line with the other issues already outstanding.

The "yield to perpetuity" might well be called *the* long-term interest rate, for any other long-term rate is a vague notion indeed, because it depends on the particular length of time to which it applies. If we call the yield to perpetuity, calculated as shown above, *the* long-term interest rate, then we may compare this rate of 3 per cent for a government issue with the corresponding rate of $4\frac{1}{2}$ per cent offered by such very high grade non-callable preferred stocks as American Can preferred,[19] and we may point out that the differential between the two rates, covering taxes and risk, is $1\frac{1}{2}$ per cent rather than $1\frac{5}{8}$ or $1\frac{3}{4}$ per cent as might appear from a casual glance at the yields to maturity for government bonds published in the newspapers.

[18] $\dfrac{(3.000\%)}{(3.004\%)} (100) = 99.87 = 99^{28}/_{32}.$

[19] Closed at $156\frac{3}{4}$ on June 15, 1937.

10.   IMPLIED FUTURE MARKET PRICES

The expected future interest rates calculated in Section 8 by the exact method imply a corresponding expected behavior of market prices during the life of the bonds. If the $2\frac{7}{8}$'s of 1955–60, for instance, are to yield the computed rates during the five sub-periods, their market prices must move as calculated in Table 10, where the course of prices is given in the next to the last column, and should be read in reverse order, going from bottom to top of the column. Incidentally, this table serves as a useful check on the calculation performed in Section 8 above.

In bold letters, where all who run may read, the bond market is now proclaiming that long-term bonds are going to fall, and that in particular the course of prices for the $2\frac{7}{8}$'s mentioned above will be as follows:

June 15, 1937	100.34
June 15, 1940	96.26
June 15, 1943	96.09
June 15, 1948	96.86
June 15, 1954	98.44
June 15, 1960	100.00

(For simplicity in calculation the maturity date is assumed to be in June instead of March, and the term twenty-three years instead of twenty-two and three quarters.)

If this forecast of future bond prices, implicit in the structure of present bond prices, proves to be correct, temporary losses will result for those who amortize their bonds at a *constant* interest rate. In the present money market, a *constant* rate is wrong, and can only lead to wrong results. The right rate to use is a *changing* rate, such as will amortize long-term bonds very heavily at first, and may even reduce their book value below par for a while. If such a

TABLE 10

IMPLIED COURSE OF THE MARKET VALUE OF TREASURY 2⅞'s OF 1955-60

Period	Term $\frac{1}{2}n$	Short-Term Yield Annual $2i$	Semi-Annual i	Annuity Factor $a_{\overline{n}\rvert}$	Present Worth of Coupons $\pi = 1.4375$ $\pi a_{\overline{n}\rvert}$	Discount Factor v^n	Future Price M_n	Present Worth of Future Price $M_n v^n$	Present Worth of Entire Bond $(a_{\overline{n}\rvert} + M_n v^n)$	Date
1954-60 ...	6 yrs.	3.161%	1.581%	10.854	15.60	.8284	100.00	82.84	100.00	June 15, 1960[a]
1948-54 ...	6 yrs.	3.219%	1.609%	10.835	15.58	.8257	98.44	81.28	98.44	June 15, 1954
1943-48 ...	5 yrs.	3.141%	1.571%	9.188	13.21	.8557	96.86	82.88	96.86	June 15, 1948
1940-43 ...	3 yrs.	2.928%	1.464%	5.704	8.20	.9165	96.09	88.06	96.09	June 15, 1943
1937-40 ...	3 yrs.	1.533%	.767%	5.842	8.40	.9552	96.26	91.94	100.34	June 15, 1940
										June 15, 1937

[a] For simplicity in calculation, the maturity date is assumed to be in June instead of March, and the term 23 years instead of 22¾.

TABLE 11

APPROXIMATE FUTURE SHORT-TERM INTEREST RATES AS SHOWN BY TREASURY BONDS

Expected Date of Redemption	Term	Yield	$n'i_{n'} - ni_n = (n' - n)i$	$(n' - n)$	Computed Rate i	Issue	Period Covered
			As of July 14, 1936				
June 15, 1940	(3 11/12)	(1.17)	4.5825 − 0.0000 = 4.5825	3 11/12	1.17%	3⅜'s of June 40-43	July 14, 1936 to June 15, 1940
June 15, 1943	(6 11/12)	(2.04)	14.1100 − 4.5825 = 9.5275	3	3.18%	3⅜'s of June 43-47	June 15, 1940 to June 15, 1943
June 15, 1948	(11 11/12)	(2.47)	29.4342 − 14.1100 = 15.3242	5	3.06%	3's of June 46-48	June 15, 1943 to June 15, 1948
June 15, 1954	(17 11/12)	(2.65)	47.4792 − 29.4342 = 18.0450	6	3.01%	2¾'s of June 51-54	June 15, 1948 to June 15, 1954
Mar. 15, 1960	(23⅔)	(2.73)	64.6100 − 47.4792 = 17.1308	5¾	2.98%	2⅞'s of Mar. 55-60	June 15, 1954 to Mar. 15, 1960
				23⅔			
			As of Feb. 27, 1937				
June 15, 1940	(3 7/24)	(1.24)	4.0817 − 0.0000 = 4.0817	3 7/24	1.24%	3⅜'s of June 40-43	Feb. 27, 1937 to June 15, 1940
June 15, 1943	(6 7/24)	(1.86)	11.7025 − 4.0817 = 7.6208	3	2.54%	3⅜'s of June 43-47	June 15, 1940 to June 15, 1943
Mar. 15, 1948	(11 1/24)	(2.32)	25.6167 − 11.7025 = 13.9142	4¾	2.93%	2¾'s of Mar. 48-51	June 15, 1943 to Mar. 15, 1948
Mar. 15, 1955	(18 1/24)	(2.53)	45.6454 − 25.6167 = 20.0287	7	2.86%	2⅞'s of Mar. 55-60	Mar. 15, 1948 to Mar. 15, 1955
				18 1/24			
			As of Apr. 30, 1937				
June 15, 1940	(3⅛)	(1.58)	4.9375 − 0.0000 = 4.9375	3⅛	1.58%	3⅜'s of June 40-43	Apr. 30, 1937 to June 15, 1940
June 15, 1943	(6⅛)	(2.41)	14.7613 − 4.9375 = 9.8238	3	3.27%	3⅜'s of June 43-47	June 15, 1940 to June 15, 1943
Mar. 15, 1948	(10⅞)	(2.75)	29.9063 − 14.7613 = 15.1450	4¾	3.19%	2¾'s of Mar. 48-51	June 15, 1943 to Mar. 15, 1948
Sept. 15, 1955	(18⅜)	(2.84)	52.1850 − 29.9063 = 22.2787	7½	2.97%	3's of Sept. 51-55	Mar. 15, 1948 to Sept. 15, 1955
Mar. 15, 1960	(22⅞)	(2.85)	65.1938 − 52.1850 = 13.0088	4½	2.89%	2⅞'s of Mar. 55-60	Sept. 15, 1955 to Mar. 15, 1960
				22⅞			

rate is used, no embarrassing depreciation should be suffered.

For clarity it must be pointed out that a decline in bonds such as that portrayed in the table above is not what we shall mean hereafter by a bear market in bonds, because the decline shown above is an *expected* decline, and is entirely consistent with *present* interest rates. Only a decline greater than that shown in the table, and more than is now expected, would constitute a bear market in bonds according to our definition, and only such a decline would indicate a change in the long-term interest rate of the sort that will be forecast in later sections of this chapter.

11. CHANGING EXPECTATIONS CONCERNING FUTURE INTEREST RATES

During the last twelve months the market has changed its mind to some extent concerning the future of interest rates. This change of expectations is computed in Table 11,

TABLE 12

RECENT CHANGES IN EXPECTED FUTURE INTEREST RATES [a]

Period Covered [b]	As of July 14, 1936	As of Feb. 27, 1937	As of Apr. 30, 1937	As of June 15, 1937
1937–40	1.17%	1.24%	1.58%	1.53%
1940–43	3.18%	2.54%	3.27%	2.87%
1943–48	3.06%	2.93%[c]	3.19%[c]	3.06%
1948–54	3.01%	2.86%[d]	2.97%[e]	3.18%
1954–60	2.98%	. . .	2.89%[f]	3.10%

[a] The data for this table are derived in Table 12 below.

[b] From June 15 of the first year to June 15 of the second, except in 1960, when March 15 is the closing date.

[c] June 15, 1943 to Mar. 15, 1948.

[d] Mar. 15, 1948 to Mar. 15, 1955.

[e] Mar. 15, 1955 to Sept. 15, 1955.

[f] Sept. 15, 1955 to Mar. 15, 1960.

where the simple-interest method of approximation is applied to government-bond yields on various significant dates. Table 12 summarizes the findings of Table 11.

The dates used in Tables 11 and 12 are important for the following reasons:

July 14, 1937, because it was the last day before the announcement of the first increase in member bank reserve requirements;[20] likewise it was the day when near-by short-term interest rates, as reflected in the yields on Treasury bills, made their all-time low.

February 27, 1937, because it was the approximate day when the longest-term Treasury bonds made their all-time high; this was four weeks after the second increase in reserve requirements was announced.

April 30, 1937, because it was the day before the second half of the second increase in reserve requirements [21] went into effect, and the approximate date when short-term rates made their high in response to the measures being taken to tighten the money market at this time.

June 15, 1937, because it was the date of the quarterly Treasury financing. No distortion of prices, however, such as often occurs on these occasions, took place this time.

Table 12 shows that near-by interest rates were but slightly affected by the 1936 increase in reserve requirements, because this first increase left excess reserves still very large.[22] The 1937 increase, however, was much more effective,[23] because for many individual banks it eliminated excess reserves altogether.

The table [24] also shows that the Federal Reserve Board's action did not greatly affect the market's appraisal of the

[20] The first increase amounted to 50 per cent, and took effect August 15.

[21] The second increase amounted to 33⅓ per cent and raised required reserves to *twice* the level prevailing before August 15, 1936. This increase was announced January 31; one half took effect March 1, and one half May 1.

[22] Excess reserves were reduced from about 3 billion to about 1.9 billion by the first increase.

[23] Excess reserves were reduced to about half a billion by the second increase.

[24] A similar comparison of expected future interest rates, computed this time

distant future. Instead the effect was mainly confined to the six years immediately ahead, during which time very easy money had been expected to prevail for the sake of facilitating Treasury borrowing and refunding. As the market moderated its expectations concerning these six years, the price of short- and medium-term bonds fell substantially. Long-term bonds, however, fell only enough to allow for a change in their true yield during a *portion* of their life — namely, the first few years thereof — leaving their true yield thereafter largely unaffected. Thus the substantial decline in all bonds in the spring of 1937 was caused by Federal Reserve action affecting the near future rather than by loss of confidence concerning the distant future.

12.   THE FUTURE NORMAL INTEREST RATE

It should be noted that Chart IV, showing expected interest rates, and Table 9, both show rising rates in the first few years only, with steady rates thereafter. Starting with

by the exact method, is given below:

COMPARISON OF EXPECTED FUTURE INTEREST RATES

	As of Sept. 22, 1936
Sept. 22, 1936 to June 15, 1940	1.095%
June 15, 1940 to June 15, 1943	2.879%
June 15, 1943 to Dec. 15, 1944	3.340%
Dec. 15, 1944 to Dec. 15, 1947	2.845%
Dec. 15, 1947 to June 15, 1954	3.333%
June 15, 1954 to Sept. 15, 1959	3.254%
	As of June 15, 1937
June 15, 1937 to June 15, 1940	1.533%
June 15, 1940 to June 15, 1943	2.928%
June 15, 1943 to June 15, 1948	3.141%
June 15, 1948 to June 15, 1954	3.219%
June 15, 1954 to Mar. 15, 1960	3.161%

Since September 22, 1936, when part of the foregoing calculations were made, interest rates have actually risen, just as the relative prices of Treasury bills forecast they would at that time.

1.53 per cent in the first three years, the rate rises to 3.14 per cent six years hence, and then continues at about that figure all the way to 1960. Why should interest rates be expected to rise no more than this when once they recover from their present extreme lows? Is such an expectation reasonable, or is the market grossly mistaken in its forecast, and should the thoughtful investor take care not to be misled by current prices? What interest rate, in fact, should the investor use in his calculations for the period after 1943? In other words, what is a reasonable normal to count on once the government's deficit financing and refunding is out of the way?

For the immediate future, the table of expected future interest rates shown above forecasts a continuation of very easy money. As pointed out in the previous chapter, the interest rate for the immediate future is an artificial figure subject to the will of the Treasury Department. Not the supply and demand for savings to be used in the creation of capital goods but the amount of excess reserves in the banking system determines the interest rate on short-term loans contracted today. Likewise the excess reserves three years hence, or the lack thereof, together with the rediscount rate then prevailing, will determine the *short-term* rate then, and the same ten and twenty years from now. The *long-term* rate now, however, is not determined by excess reserves *now*, but by the expectations concerning excess reserves and short-term rates over a *long period* of time. These expectations are greatly modified, however, by the realization that the long-term interest rate so produced must conform to the equilibrium of the supply and demand for savings, and that any effort by the banking authorities to keep the short-term rate permanently too low, and thus to depress the long-term rate from its natural position, will defeat itself in the end, because if the long-term rate is too low, too many new bonds will be sold, bank deposits will rise, and inflation will take place continuously.[25] Since unending inflation is bad politics, people know that permanent maintenance of large excess reserves and low short-term rates is out of the question. Therefore the market must expect the abolition of excess reserves and the raising of the rediscount rate in due course.

To be precise, the market evidently expects the excess reserves to be done away with soon enough to let short-term rates rise to normal in six years, with the result that rates will advance from the present level [26] of $4/10$ per cent to about 2 per cent by 1940, and will continue rising to $3\frac{1}{8}$ per cent by 1943.

Such a rise could not occur, of course, without the consent of the Treasury, and such consent is hardly to be expected so long as the Treasury has new loans to float.[27] Therefore a rate of $3\frac{1}{8}$ per cent in 1943 means that by then the Treasury is expected to be out of the market, to be through with its manipulation of excess reserves, to have washed its hands of the whole business. Clearly this sit-

[25] Cf. Ludwig von Mises, *Theorie des Geldes und der Umlaufsmittel*, 1st ed. (Munich and Leipzig: Dunker and Humblot, 1912), bk. III, chap. V, § 4, esp. pp. 430–433. See also the English translation (1935) of the second edition (1924), published by Harcourt, Brace and Company under the title *The Theory of Money and Credit*, pp. 362–364. While Von Mises argues that the banks, by the liberal emission of credit, cannot depress interest rates permanently, and will only bring on a crisis if they try to do so, he does not go on to say, as we do, that the long-term rate is the result of the successive short-term rates that the banks see fit to set. In other words, while Von Mises distinguishes between the actual or money rate (*Geldzins*) and the equilibrium or natural rate (*natürliche Kapitalzins*), as we do, he does not distinguish between the short- and the long-term rate, nor show how these latter are related mathematically. Von Mises insists that the *Geldzins* should be made to equal the *Kapitalzins*, whereas the present book maintains that the chain of short-term rates (and thus the long-term rate) should be made to equal the *Kapitalzins*, if inflation or deflation is to be avoided.

[26] As of June 1937, for Treasury notes maturing in March 1938.

[27] Major Angas argues to the contrary, holding that such a violent boom will develop soon that the Federal Reserve Board will be *forced* to tighten money. See footnote 65 in Chapter XIX, § 19.

uation cannot arise until the federal budget is balanced, and until the federal short-term debt has been funded as well. For as long as the federal debt is rising, or even so long as any near-by maturities are outstanding to plague the Secretary of the Treasury, he will abhor high interest rates, and will insist on easy money, so that he can "point with pride to the high credit of the United States." [28] But once the budget is balanced, and once the short-term notes are all replaced by long-term bonds with maturities in the distant future, the Secretary of the Treasury can begin to concern himself with "the manifest danger inherent in the potentially inflationary easy money rates," and can "take a leading part in removing this hazard to the welfare of the great masses of our people."

Whichever party is in power in Washington, the problem is the same. To balance the budget, fund the short-term debt, and "mop up" the excess reserves, so as to raise interest rates before inflation can occur — that is the task for any party that hopes to be returned to power.

Evidently the market expects this task to be completed by 1943 or a year or two sooner. In the nature of things, the date could hardly be any later if inflation is to be avoided, and, as pointed out in the preceding chapter, the bond market is supremely confident that inflation will not occur.

If interest rates are to be back to normal by 1943, the Federal Reserve Board must have completely removed the excess reserves by that time, and in the preceding two or three years fifteen or twenty billions of short-term issues must have been refunded. For this program to be carried through on such a great scale, it would be necessary to have the full confidence of private investors, since the banks

---

[28] In theory a rise in present short-term rates ought to depress long-term bonds but little, and so in theory the Treasury could ignore a rise in near-by short-term rates. But in practice such complacency is not likely to be exhibited.

themselves could not wisely consent to exchanging all their short-terms for long-terms. But even if the banks should consent, they would demand a balanced budget as assurance of freedom from intermediate shrinkage in market value, and the private investor would likewise demand it as assurance of freedom from permanent shrinkage in purchasing power. Therefore the course of interest rates forecast by present prices must imply a genuinely balanced budget, or even a small surplus by 1940 or thereabouts.[29]

Are these expectations concerning the dates when the budget will be balanced, the debt refunded, and the excess reserves completely eliminated, reasonable? These are questions which have already been touched upon in the preceding chapter, dealing with inflation. But the reader must remember that unless these expectations are reasonable, long-term bonds are too high; for no other expectations are consistent with the present structure of bond prices.

But even if these expectations concerning the period from 1937 to 1943 are reasonable, there still remains the question of whether the expectations concerning the years from 1944 to 1960 are also reasonable. Should these latter expectations be unreasonable, and should the interest rate properly to be expected for these more distant years be higher than $3\frac{1}{8}$ per cent, it would follow that bond prices today ought to be lower. In the 1920's, a rate of $3\frac{1}{8}$ per cent would have been considered unreasonably low to expect for the future. In the years 1922 through 1929, the average yield to maturity for Liberty bonds and Treasury bonds was nearly 4 per cent. We must not let the present period of artificial ease blind us, therefore, to the possibility

---

[29] President Roosevelt himself, in his message to Congress on January 8, 1937, forecast a balanced budget eighteen months earlier than this, namely, in the year to end June 30, 1938. See the *New York Times*, January 9, 1937, pp. 1 and 6.

TABLE 13

COMPUTATION OF FAIR VALUE OF 2⅞'S OF 1955–60 AT AN INTEREST RATE OF 3¾% FROM 1943 TO 1960

Period	Term	Short-Term Yield Annual $2i$	Semi-Annual i	Annuity Factor $a_{\overline{n}|}$	Present Worth of Coupons $\pi=1.4375$ $\pi a_{\overline{n}|}$	Discount Factor v^n	Future Market Price M_n	Present Worth of Future Price $M_n v^n$	Present Worth of Entire Bond $(\pi a_{\overline{n}|} + M_n v^n)$	Date
1943–60	16¾ yrs.	3.750%							100.00	Mar. 15, 1960
1940–43	3 yrs.	2.928%	1.464%	5.704	8.20	.9165	89.19	81.74	89.19 [a]	June 15, 1943
1937–40	3 yrs.	1.533%	.767%	5.842	8.40	.9552	89.94	85.91	89.94	June 15, 1940
	22¾ yrs.								94.31	June 15, 1937

[a] The process of computation is begun by deriving this figure directly from the bond tables; then this same figure is inserted in the M_n column, and thereafter the computation proceeds as shown in the table.

that real interest rates will return to the level prevailing in the last period of prosperity.

13. THE SENSITIVENESS OF PRICES TO CHANGES IN THE FUTURE INTEREST RATE

Before proceeding to discuss the forces that will tend to raise or lower the long-term interest rate in the future, let us pause to see how much difference it would make to use whatever new rate we may decide upon. In other words, let us stop to compute the magnitude of the change in bond values that a change in the interest rate would produce. The computations for a rate of $3\frac{3}{4}$ per cent from 1944 to 1959 are shown in Table 13 for the $2\frac{7}{8}$'s of 1955–60.

Similar computations using other possible rates for these years give the series of present values as functions of future normal interest rates shown in Table 14.

TABLE 14

FAIR VALUE OF TREASURY $2\frac{7}{8}$'S OF 1955–60 AT VARIOUS FUTURE NORMAL INTEREST RATES

Interest Rate for 1943–60	Fair Value Today	Actual Price Today
$4\frac{1}{4}\%$	$89^{15}\!/_{32}$	. . .
$4\ \%$	$91^{27}\!/_{32}$	. . .
$3\frac{3}{4}\%$	$94^{10}\!/_{32}$	. . .
$3\frac{1}{2}\%$	$96^{28}\!/_{32}$	. . .
$3\frac{1}{4}\%$	$99^{18}\!/_{32}$	$100^{11}\!/_{32}$
$3\ \%$	$102^{11}\!/_{32}$	. . .
$2\frac{3}{4}\%$	$105^{8}\!/_{32}$	. . .

Evidently the present value of these bonds is not extremely sensitive to the future normal interest rate applying to the years 1943–1960, and an error in choosing the right rate for this period would be less serious than a mistake on the question of inflation. One reason for this lack of sensitiveness is that we are likely to make only a small error in our choice of the interest rate, whereas we might make a large error in our guess concerning the future purchasing power of money. Another reason is that the particular bonds chosen for illustration do not have a very long term; had we selected some bond of really distant maturity, like the Atchison general 4's of 1995, a change in the interest rate for the years after 1943 would have been more important. If the Treasury $2\frac{7}{8}$'s were to mature in 1995 instead of 1960, an interest rate of $3\frac{3}{4}$ per cent instead of that of $3\frac{1}{8}$ per cent assumed by the market would reduce their value about 14 points [30] instead of only 6. For a perpetual bond or a preferred stock the reduction in value would be even more.

14. WHAT DETERMINES THE LONG-TERM INTEREST RATE?

So much for the bond market's guess concerning future interest rates, now for our own.

With the market's forecast, or implication, of rising short-term interest rates during the next five or ten years we should not quarrel, but with its forecast of a normal rate of only $3\frac{1}{8}$ per cent when refunding is over we cannot entirely agree, for reasons to be discussed in the remainder of this chapter. Let us proceed, therefore, to examine in detail the forces that are at work today to change the interest rate to be expected after this depression from what it was before the depression.

The rate of interest depends on the supply and demand for new savings;[31] in the absence of a change in these two factors the rate should be the same in the future as in the past. To forecast the rate of interest we must ask, therefore, whether anything is happening today to change the

[30] The exact value would be $86^{13}\!/_{32}$ as compared with the present price of $100^{11}\!/_{32}$. The calculation may be made in the manner shown in Table 13 above.

[31] Not on the supply and demand for capital as a whole; see Chapter XVIII. The effect of the quantity of money on the rate of interest, stressed so much by Keynes in his *General Theory*, is discussed in Chapter III, § 2.

rate of accumulation, on the one hand, or the opportunities for investment, on the other, from what prevailed before the depression of 1931–1935.

15. TAXES AND THE SUPPLY OF SAVINGS

As for the rate of accumulation, several influences have recently been set at work to reduce the volume of saving from what it was in the 1920's. Because taxes are high, business profits are less. Taxes, moreover, are being levied in just such a way as to cut into the nation's savings the most. Corporate saving is being penalized by the new tax on reinvested earnings, and the incomes of the rich, who are best able to save, are now being taxed with extreme severity,[32] while their estates also are being confiscated in part by taxation when they die.[33] It is now impossible for very rich families to keep their fortunes intact beyond a single generation. Not even by leaving their incomes as undistributed profits in the corporations in which they are stockholders can they escape confiscatory taxation; the new revenue laws taxing reinvested earnings have given the *coup de grâce* to that procedure. No longer can the nation hope to be enriched by future Fords, Mellons, Carnegies, or Du Ponts. Henceforth it must rely on the little fellows, millions of them, to provide the funds for industrial expansion.

Taxes, moreover, are by no means the only new drag on saving. Low interest rates themselves in many cases reduce the power to save. Thus the reduction in the interest rate on the federal, state, and municipal debts in the United States, and the government debt in Great Britain, has reduced the income of many wealthy people and im-

[32] Such a man as Hearst, for instance, now pays more than 80 per cent of his income to the government in taxes. See the *New York Times*, October 23, 1935, p. 1, col. 3.

[33] Cf. Chapter XVII, § 12.

paired their power to save. In Germany and Italy the regulation of business has gone so far that these countries will henceforth be unable to make their former contribution to the world's supply of savings, and in France inflation threatens to occur again and impoverish the *rentier* class, and greatly reduce its power to save.

In the United States, where the well-to-do have a good part of their capital invested in railroad and public-utility securities, investment losses threaten to be very heavy ultimately. If most of the railroads should go through bankruptcy, their common stocks and some of their junior bonds would be wiped out. The incomes of many well-to-do families would be reduced and their power to save would be permanently impaired. If the reduction in interest charges were to accrue to the benefit of the common stockholders, to be sure, then what the wealthy lost on interest account they would recover on dividend account, and no net reduction in their power to save would result; but no such transfer from bondholder to stockholder will occur, for the very fact of bankruptcy means that distributions to security holders in general are too heavy, and that whatever is saved on interest account by reorganization must be diverted to wages and materials. Thus reorganization of the railroads would produce a permanent redistribution of the national income in favor of the poorer classes, and would reduce, to that extent, the volume of savings. While the public utilities have not yet reached such a serious condition as the railroads, government competition and heavy taxation together with rising expenses and inflexible rates point down the road to eventual reorganization, with resulting losses by security holders and reduced savings by the families who have hitherto been the main source of new capital.

Although a number of able economists have expressed

a fear of chronic "oversaving" in the future, the foregoing considerations make it seem that their case was still to be proved.

16.   INVENTIONS AND THE DEMAND FOR SAVINGS

Offsetting the decline in the supply of savings, mentioned above, is the possibility that the demand for savings, also to be considered, may decline likewise, for it may turn out that the opportunities for investment in the next generation will be less than in the past.

The period 1900–1930 saw the exploitation of two inventions which created an enormous demand for new capital. These inventions were the steam turbine, making possible the electric power industry, and the gasoline engine, making possible the automobile. The steam turbine, on the one hand, by producing five or ten times as much energy with the same amount of coal as did the old reciprocating engine,[34] caused the building of electric power plants, transmission lines, and conveyor-belt factories, and by reducing the cost of power, prompted the manufacture of countless things that had been too costly to sell before. The gasoline engine, on the other hand, by offering to every man a new device for saving time, labor, and money,[35] led to a great investment in automobiles, automobile factories, steel plants, oil wells, refineries, filling stations, highways, bridges, and new residential districts. Between them, the

---

[34] Cf. Abbott P. Usher, *A History of Mechanical Inventions* (New York: McGraw-Hill Book Company, Inc., 1929), p. 363: "The Edison station at Chicago [with reciprocating engines] used in 1900, 6.90 pounds of coal per kilowatt hour. . . . In 1924 turbines at the Duquesne Light Company's Colfax station at Pittsburgh consumed 1.29 pounds per kilowatt hour."

The Weymouth Station of the Boston Edison Company in 1930 used only 0.9 pound per kilowatt hour, and the mercury turbine, now being introduced, promises to cut coal consumption to 0.6 pound per kilowatt hour.

[35] The old term "pleasure vehical" originally applied to the automobile shows how little the true significance of this new invention was understood in the beginning.

steam turbine and the gasoline engine far more than filled the gap that was beginning to appear in the demand for new capital as the world completed its railway net about 1900. But what will arise in the next generation to take the place of these two inventions in the capital market? At present nothing important seems to be in sight. Perhaps nothing is needed, however, for perhaps these two inventions have not yet been fully exploited, and their demands for new savings have not yet been fully satisfied. Even though the possibilities of the turbine seem to have been largely realized [36] (as discussed in Chapter XXV), those of the gasoline engine have not. In causing the relocation of residential districts, at least, the motor car has made only a beginning in its demand for new capital. Moreover, should something occur to take the building of houses out of the handicraft stage and put it into the factory stage,[37] with the result that vastly better dwellings could be built for the same price, a great building boom could develop and could create an enormous demand for savings in the coming generation. If there is any truth whatsoever in the theory that inventions appear spontaneously when the time for them is ripe, then the factory-made house should become a commonplace in the not too distant future.

Whether or not this particular invention is made, it is hazardous in the extreme, as the history of the last 150 years shows, to forecast now, with science in its present stage of development, a hiatus in the flow of new inventions seeking fresh savings for their exploitation. Surely the safest forecast is to say that in that race between inven-

---

[36] According to Schumpeter's theory of the business cycle, this might account in part for the 1931–1935 business depression, and a new period of prosperity would have to wait for a new invention to exploit.

[37] Roger W. Babson has suggested that the manufacturers of automobile trailers may be the ones to solve the problem of the pre-fabricated house.

tion and accumulation, where the rate of interest is determined, invention will run as fast as ever.

At the present moment, moreover, the building of armaments is becoming so important as to perform the office of a new invention in eating up the savings of many nations and reducing the flow of new capital into private projects.[38] With armies so much bigger now than fifty years ago, and with their mechanical equipment in the form of guns, tanks, aeroplanes, forts, and battleships so expensive, preparation for war can alter employment, living costs, and interest rates as greatly as the railroad, the turbo-generator, and the automobile did in their time.

Too much weight should not be given to the fact that the population of the United States is growing more slowly than formerly, for the change between the decade of the twenties and the generation ahead — the two periods we wish to compare — is small. Moreover, the low birth rate of the last few years is deceptive; it reflects the postponement of marriages during the depression, and is likely to be followed by a recovery. It indicates, not a decline in potential fertility, but a voluntary effort to raise the standard of living; not the end, but the beginning of a great expansion in consumption, requiring huge new capital outlays for its achievement. The low birth rate, in other words, only shows how great is the ultimate need for more savings in this country. Nor is our own country the only one seeking to raise its standard of living; the tropics in particular need great amounts of new capital if they are ever to attain a higher level of civilization.

The "oversaving" which is said to be chronic today is an illusion. If the railroads could recover their credit

[38] The world outlay on arms in 1936 was three times as large as in 1913 and amounted to 11 per cent of all industrial production, according to the Institut für Konjunkturforschung, quoted in the *New York Times*, January 6, 1937, col. 1.

standing, if the utilities could be freed from government competition, and if the government would stop creating uncertainty, a vigorous demand for investment funds would soon appear. If junior money could be relieved of excessive taxation, a way could soon be found to put senior money to work. If insurance companies, savings banks, and wealthy individuals were confident that money would remain easy, and that bond and stock prices would hold up, they would stop hoarding their income, and would invest it at once, in order to secure a return from it without further delay. In short, it is the inability of borrowers to borrow, and unwillingness of lenders to lend, that gives the market an appearance of supersaturation at present; and it is bad news and bearishness, rather than oversaving, that stops the circulation of money saved and produces deflation and depression as a result.

17. THE ELASTICITY OF THE DEMAND FOR SAVINGS

All the successful inventions and improvements in technique of the last generation and all the further innovations which could be perfected with a little thought can be grouped into two classes, those which would pay and those which would not pay at high interest rates — high and low interest rates here being taken to mean rates above or below the average rate of the last generation. Since business men are always looking for profitable ideas to exploit but are quite careful to reject unprofitable ones, it follows that most of the innovations in the first class but few of those in the second have already been applied. Those technically successful innovations which have not yet been applied await only a lower rate of interest. Consequently, if one were to draw up a demand curve for new capital covering a period of a few years only in the future, he would find this curve rather steep for interest rates above, and nearly

flat for interest rates below, those prevailing in the past.
The elasticity of the curve, in other words, would increase
substantially as one passed from high to low interest rates.
The steep part of the curve would apply to the few very
good inventions of the years just ahead, and the flat part
to the many less good inventions of the years gone by and
of the years ahead as well.

From this peculiarity of the demand curve for savings it
follows that a sudden and permanent fall in the real interest
rate substantially below the average figure for the past
generation is impossible, for savings could not possibly
increase enough in any single year,[39] or even in four or five
years, to exhaust at once the entire accumulation of long-
neglected opportunities for investing at low interest rates.[40]
Therefore, if the market rate of interest for long-term loans
is found to have fallen abnormally low for the moment,
as at present, some special explanation must be sought.
Among the explanations frequently heard nowadays are
three which deserve special consideration, and to which the
next three sections will be devoted.

[39] Contrast the view expressed by Marriner S. Eccles in an article in *Fortune*
for April 1937, entitled "Controlling Booms and Depressions," wherein he speaks
of "oversaving" as a menace to prosperity, and goes on to say (p. 182), "By
providing that the expenses of the government be financed largely out of taxes
on the higher and intermediate income groups we diminish the total savings of
the community and hence the total amount seeking investment and threatening
to remain idle, thus obstructing the monetary flow." Evidently Eccles and Keynes
see eye-to-eye.

Is it not true, however, that "oversaving," that is, saving in excess of investment in capital goods, occurs only because savers are temporarily bearish on
the security markets, and refuse to buy new issues at high prices? If so, the
natural remedy is either a fall in security prices or an increase in confidence
among investors. Surely savers would not refuse to lend their cash for an interest return unless they thought security prices were *temporarily* higher than they
could be expected to remain. Clearly such a situation does not require a *permanent* system of taxation for its correction.

[40] For a discussion of the other overhead costs besides interest which also
affect new investment, see Chapter XVIII, § 4.

18. FOREIGN LENDING

For some time to come, it is said, capital may find itself cooped up within the lending countries, and afraid to venture forth from England, France, and the United States into Asia, Africa, and Latin America. Without a return to the political and monetary stability of the days before the War, it is argued, interest rates will tend to be depressed to some degree in the lending countries. It must be admitted that these assertions would seem to be correct so far as they go; nevertheless they cannot gainsay the argument of the preceding section concerning the great elasticity of the demand for savings at low rates of interest, with the resulting tendency for interest rates to hold up.

It is further maintained by some writers that the United States must expect a permanently lower level of interest rates at home because during the War this country changed from a debtor to a creditor nation. It remains to be seen, however, if we are really a creditor nation; for if our credits turn out to be bad because we cannot collect our war debts and our post-war loans to Germany and Latin America, then we may find ourselves a debtor nation again after all. In fact, only to the extent that we have actually repatriated our own securities held abroad can we feel sure that we have moved permanently in the direction of becoming a creditor nation.

Furthermore, it is extremely doubtful whether the debtor-creditor relationship between Europe and America has much to do with pure interest rates in the United States; for a great many stocks and bonds have come to be "international securities" in recent years, are held by investors in many different countries, and are bought and sold on the stock exchanges of New York, London, Paris, Amsterdam, and other financial centers. In every one of these markets, the same security commands the same price at the same time — or at least as nearly so as the arbitragers can contrive. Hence in the pricing of these securities the same interest rate prevails everywhere. Throughout the entire world, all riskless loans tend to bear the same rate of interest, and whatever divergence in rates appears is due to differences in risk. Thus if British consols go up or down, United States government bonds should do the same. Whatever difference in yield exists between the two should reflect either the difference in income-tax rates, or the difference in maturity dates, or the difference in the prospects for domestic inflation. In fact, it should be possible to compare British consols and Treasury bonds exactly, and compute in this way the relative prospects for inflation in the two countries. The analysis would show whether war in Europe or the New Deal in America was deemed the greater menace to the future purchasing power of money in the two countries. A similar comparison with French *rentes* would prove that the policies of *Le Front Populaire* were considered far more alarming, than anything either of the two Anglo-Saxon countries had to face.

The fact that British consols made their high in January 1935 at 94⅜, while United States Treasury long-terms made theirs in February 1937, does not mean that interest rates made their peak in London two years before they did in this country, for we know on theoretical grounds that interest rates in both centers are *always* the same. Instead, the downturn in England in 1935 merely reflected the prospects for higher personal income taxes there as the necessity for rearmament against Germany and Italy became obvious during the course of the year.

19.   WAR AND THE DESTRUCTION OF CAPITAL

While it is probable that the destruction of capital goods during the World War, and the failure to make the usual replacements, additions, and betterments during these years, created an abnormal demand for savings in the 1920's and tended to raise the interest rate somewhat above the level that would otherwise have prevailed then, yet it must be remembered that the war years were a period of extreme activity during which many industries increased their plant investment enormously, with the result that the capital equipment of the world did not receive as great a setback as might be thought. Whatever shortages were created by the war were more in houses than in machines. In fact, it is a question whether the great depression of the 1930's has not created a larger deficit in capital goods than the World War did. If so, interest rates need be no lower in the next decade than in the past decade.

Moreover, it is unfortunately by no means certain that the world will be spared from great wars in the next generation; in fact, the danger of war is now so serious that it must perforce be reckoned among the possible causes of higher interest rates in the future.

20.   THE SOCIAL SECURITY ACT

The Social Security Act,[41] with its plan for the accumulation of old-age pension funds invested in government bonds to the extent of fifty billion dollars or so, is sometimes pointed to as a source of savings likely to push interest rates down in the future. If we assume that the scheme will be carried out as planned, and that reserves against future liabilities will actually be set up and invested in bonds, and

[41] Cf. the article by Paul H. Douglas, entitled "The United States Social Security Act" in the *Economic Journal* for March 1936; see also the book *Social Security in the United States* by the same author.

that the fund will not be used to finance government deficits but will be put into industrial plant and equipment, directly or indirectly, and that it will not be drawn on in an emergency to support the unemployment insurance scheme that is a part of the same Social Security Act — in short, if we concede no chance at all of miscarriage, then and only then do we need to make any allowance for the effects of the extra saving on the future rate of interest.

In order for the pay-roll tax to affect the interest rate, it is necessary that the proceeds of the tax should be loaned out in competition with those private savings which are ordinarily relied upon to finance industrial expansion. Such competitive investing of Social Security revenues could occur directly or indirectly — directly, if the government used its tax receipts to build electric power systems like the T. V. A., for instance, and indirectly, if (1) the government used its tax receipts to buy in its own bonds, *and if* (2) the sellers then reinvested the proceeds in new issues of corporate bonds. Obviously the indirect method is likely to be more important than the direct.

If the Social Security Fund purchased long-term government bonds as fast as its own resources piled up, and if the sellers of governments immediately reloaned their money and bought new issues regardless of their high prices, then the result would be that the forced savings of the workmen would find their way into private industry in the end, and the addition of these extra savings to the usual stream of savings would tend to depress the interest rate. Nevertheless, for the reason that the demand for savings below the average rate of the last generation is probably very great, as pointed out in § 16 above, the decline in interest rates that would result is probably not very large.[42] Furthermore, the existing supply of *long*-term government

---

[42] For possible effects on the price of government bonds as contrasted with other bonds, see Section 2 above.

bonds is too small to provide investments for the Social Security Fund for long, and when this supply is exhausted, the effects of such investing would cease, and the Fund would have to turn elsewhere for outlets for its premium income.

If, however, the Social Security Fund did not go into the market for the long-term bonds that are outstanding already, but bought only such long-term bonds as might be issued henceforth, the effect on the rate of interest would depend on the particular circumstances under which the new bonds came into existence. If these new bonds were created year by year as part of a Treasury refunding operation, and if the proceeds of the bonds were used to pay off currently maturing *short*-term issues, the effect on long-term interest rates would probably be small, because most of the government's short-term debt is held by the commercial banks, which would merely credit investments and debit deposits when they found they could not renew their short-term loans to the government. As the deposits of the banks declined, excess reserves would grow, to be sure, but the banks themselves probably would not go into the long-term bond market and buy new corporate issues, for the banks would not want to replace their expiring short-term issues with new long-term bonds bearing low coupons and subject to serious depreciation before maturity; consequently bond prices and long-term interest rates would not be affected by such Treasury refunding conducted through the Social Security Fund. The price level, however, would be affected, because with each circuit flow of money from producer to consumer and back again, a slice of purchasing power would be withheld as pay-roll taxes, and the buying power of the public would each time be reduced slightly below the sales value [43] set on con-

---

[43] For the reason that the cash received by consumers as wages, dividends, interest, and rentals, and available for the purchase of consumers' goods, would

sumers' goods by their producers; hence, other things remaining equal, the effect of such a financial policy would be to cause business stagnation. Unless bank borrowing elsewhere by private business was heavy enough to offset this forced saving by public authority and make investment equal saving for the nation as a whole, the tax would prove deflationary in the end.[44] The effect of the tax would thus be felt on the price level rather than on the interest rate.

If, on the other hand, the revenues of the Social Security Act were not used for debt retirement, but devoted to building capital goods of the sort which do not compete with private industry — whether these goods were productive assets like roads and schools or non-productive assets like battleships and forts — no such impairment of consumer purchasing power would result from the operations of the Fund, and no business stagnation would tend to develop. Moreover, since neither roads and schools nor battleships and forts would bring forth a stream of consumers' goods to be offered for sale, neither of them would have the same ultimate effect on the price level for consumers' goods that ordinary capital goods like railroads and factories built with private savings have, and no tendency for general prices to fall would be observed when government saving and investing of this sort was completed. And here also the Act would prove to be without effect upon the rate of interest.

If the revenues of the Social Security Act were not spent for capital goods at all, but were merely used to pay doles

---

always be less than the cash outlays already incurred by producers in bringing these goods to market; the discrepancy being the amount of cash paid by the producers to the government as pay-roll taxes, but not passed on to consumers as income of any sort wherewith to purchase the aforementioned goods.

[44] For a discussion of the particular circumstances in which the tax might have *inflationary*, rather than deflationary, effects in the beginning, see Chapter XIX, § 18.

to the unemployed or bonuses to the employed, the scheme would become a mere device for levying an income tax on one workman and giving the proceeds to another; under these circumstances also, no effect on the rate of interest would be felt.

Finally, if the plan were changed to a "pay-as-you-go" scheme, with the result that the accumulation of reserves invested in government bonds was abandoned, as recommended by many experts,[45] obviously the Social Security Act would then cease to be a possible factor in interest rates. Although the Republican attack [46] on the reserve principle during the 1936 campaign has naturally aroused stubbornness in the Democrats, it is fairly likely that in due course the original sponsors of the Act will make whatever changes seem sensible — unless, of course, the Treasury should seek to use the Social Security Fund to finance its own deficit, a step that we hope will never be resorted to. While old-age pensions, or personal savings to provide for life's declining years, are greatly to be desired from the humanitarian point of view, it would be a cruel deception to tax the wages of the workingman and then cause part of the impounded proceeds to be lost by inflation. Yet in providing the means for government extravagance the Social Security Act seems to be promoting just such an inflation.

To conclude, if we could be sure that the reserve feature of the Social Security Act would be retained in the face of

[45] See *An Appraisal of the Federal Social Security Act*, by Winthrop W. Aldrich, chairman of the Chase National Bank, published in July, 1936.

See also the report to the Twentieth Century Fund quoted by Landon and reprinted in the *New York Times*, October 1, 1936, p. 18; this report was financed by the Filene Foundation, organized by Edward A. Filene, a supporter of Roosevelt.

[46] See Landon's speech at Milwaukee reprinted in the *New York Times*, September 27, 1936, p. 31.

Likewise in the article by Reinhard A. Hohaus in the *Transactions* of the Actuarial Society of America for October, 1936, entitled "Reserves for National Old Age Pensions."

all the expert advice to the contrary, and if we could be sure that the Fund would first invest in existing long-term governments and then in newly issued ones, which latter would be used to refund the Treasury's floating debt, then we could say that the first effect of the Social Security taxes would be to lower the long-term interest rate slightly for a while, and the second effect would be to depress business activity somewhat as the refunding proceeded; but since we are not sure that the Fund and the Treasury will act in this way, we cannot say with certainty what effect the Social Security Act will have on the interest rate or the business cycle.

21.   THE PROBABLE FUTURE INTEREST RATE

When all is said and done, then, and taxation, invention, rearmament, foreign lending, war, and Social Security have all been considered, it would seem that real interest rates would soon begin to rise from their present extremely low level, and that they would eventually reach the level of the 1920's again. It would appear that the reduction in the supply of savings as a result of world-wide over-taxation, and the increase in the demand for savings as a result of general rearmament, would offset whatever slackening may occur in the peacetime demand for savings as the result of fewer new inventions. Indeed, were it not for the fact that higher taxes increase the spread between gross and net interest rates, and tend to depress the market rate (which lies between the other two [47]), the market rate might be expected to go even higher than in the 1920's.

The forecast, heard so often recently, of even lower long-term interest rates in the future, is based almost exclusively on *monetary* considerations and follows from the belief that excess bank reserves will force commercial banks still

[47] Cf. Chapter XVII, § 8.

further into the bond market. A discussion of this purely monetary argument is to be found in the preceding chapter, where it is maintained that excess reserves, while they may reduce *short*-term interest rates and may even depress *nominal* long-term rates for a while and produce inflation in the end, cannot alter the *real* rate of interest permanently, for this rate includes an allowance for changes in the purchasing power of money.

To show more clearly the general level of real interest rates to be expected in the next generation, a comparison of the expected future rates with typical rates at present and in the past generation is given in Table 15. It need hardly be said that the rates given would vary with the stage of the business cycle, the credit of the borrower, the section of the country, and the size of the loan. Table 15

TABLE 15
INTEREST RATES, PAST, PRESENT, AND FUTURE

	Past	Present	Future
Government bonds, long-term	4 %	2⅛%	4 %
Good stocks, horizontal trend	5¾%	4¾%	5¾%
Commercial paper, prime names	5 %	1 %	5 %
Home mortgages, Eastern cities	6 %	5 %	6 %

shows a decline in interest rates from the past to the present, and a recovery in the future.

In the Current Case Studies of Book II, the rate of interest that will be used for discounting future dividends is 5¼ per cent, a figure midway between the figures of 4¾ per cent and 5¾ per cent shown in Table 15. This midway figure is chosen in order to allow for the fact that it will take time for the rate to reach its normal of 5¾ per cent, with the result that the yield to perpetuity beginning now, when short-term rates are very low, will work out to less than 5¾ per cent.[48]

[48] Cf. Chapter XX, § 9.

If the rate of interest for good stocks is going to rise from the present estimated normal of $4\frac{3}{4}$ per cent to a future normal of $5\frac{3}{4}$ per cent as forecast above, a corresponding fall in the price of stocks should be expected, unless opinion changes regarding the dividends to be received from them in the future. But since the rise in interest rates with returning prosperity is likely to coincide with a rise in earnings also, the effect of the rise in interest is likely to be obscured, except in the case of the very best non-callable preferred stocks. Thus American Can common, for instance, whose earnings would increase, would not be obviously depressed by the rise in interest rates, but American Can preferred, whose dividend would remain unchanged, would visibly decline. Now selling at $156\frac{3}{4}$ to yield $4\frac{1}{2}$ per cent [49] on its $7 dividend, this preferred stock might suffer a decline of nearly 20 per cent, to 127, as a result of the rise in yields on securities of this sort to $5\frac{1}{2}$ per cent.

22. THE EXCESSIVE PRICE OF BONDS

It would seem that the market, with its forecast of a riskless future interest rate of $3\frac{1}{2}$ per cent (computed in Section 8), was naming a figure that was distinctly low, and that $3\frac{3}{4}$ or 4 per cent would be more reasonable. We are forced, then, to the conclusion that bonds are altogether too high. And they are too high not merely because present prices allow no premium for insurance against the risk of inflation, as pointed out in the last chapter, but also because present long-term yields, as pointed out in this chapter, are too small, even assuming no inflation to come, and should be larger to correspond with what seems to be

---

[49] This yield of $4\frac{1}{2}\%$ applies to a preferred stock; the yield of $4\frac{3}{4}\%$ mentioned in Table 15 applies to a common stock not preceded by senior securities.

a reasonable expectation for the real rate of interest in the future.

The prudent investor in Treasury $2\frac{7}{8}$'s of 1955–60, for instance, ought to demand a concession of 10 or 12 points from present prices to cover the *probability* of higher interest rates and the *possibility* of inflation. Yet if so great a decline as this should occur within the next year or so, it would almost certainly not be the result of a mere increase in wisdom by investors generally; instead it would undoubtedly be a symptom of trouble ahead and of deterioration in the outlook. Therefore it may be asserted that no prices now prevailing or likely to prevail soon could make high-grade long-term bonds desirable investments for the average private individual, nor really safe investments for those financial institutions which would be embarrassed by temporary depreciation [50] in market prices.

[50] Depreciation in excess of that implied by the current array of long- and short-term prices, and mentioned in Section 10 above, is here referred to.

BOOK II: CASE STUDIES IN INVESTMENT VALUE

FOREWORD TO THE CASE STUDIES

To show how the theory and formulas of Book I may be applied is the aim of the Case Studies in Book II, and to illustrate as many principles as possible has been the motive in selecting the particular stocks for study. The Case Studies are arranged in the order of simplicity of formulas used, with the result that all the Current Studies happen to come first, and all the Post Mortems second. It is hoped that the reader, as he goes from the simple cases to the complex, will become more and more convinced of the indispensability of suitable formulas of evaluation in any serious attempt to estimate investment value.

PART I

CURRENT STUDIES

CHAPTER XXI

GENERAL MOTORS

I. THE MEANING OF INVESTMENT VALUE

Because it lends itself to appraisal by the simplest methods, the common stock of the General Motors Corporation has been chosen as the first case to illustrate our Theory of Investment Value. Assuming, for reasons to be given later, that the secular trend of the company's earnings will be horizontal,[1] we can estimate the worth of its stock by the simple formula

$$(8a) \qquad\qquad V = \frac{\pi}{i}$$

which states that the investment value V of such a stock is to be found by capitalizing its normal dividend π at the going rate of interest i for long-term issues moderately free from risk.

During the bull market [2] of 1932–1936, General Motors rose [3] from $7\frac{5}{8}$ to 77, but it has since declined, and on June 15, 1937 it sold at 50. If the stock was really worth 50, the investor who bought it at the price could hope to receive a fair return on his money over the years to come, but if the stock was still too high on June 15, the buyer then could only plan to be a speculator pure and simple, intend-

---

[1] For a discussion of the tendency of industries to grow rapidly at first, and then ever more slowly, according to a Gomperz curve, see Chapter VII, § 2, and Chapter XI, and also Simon S. Kuznets, *Secular Movements in Production and Prices* (Boston and New York: Houghton Mifflin Company, 1930). The growth of the motor industry in particular is treated in Ralph C. Epstein, *The Automobile Industry* (Chicago & New York: A. W. Shaw Company, 1928).

[2] The high for the 1921–1929 bull market was $91\frac{3}{4}$.

[3] A notable speculation in General Motors stock by President Alfred P. Sloan is discussed in Chapter III, § 7, footnote 25.

ing to profit only by finding another buyer who was a "bigger sucker" than himself. The pure investor, however, would buy only for a dividend return, and only on the basis of intrinsic value carefully estimated; and he therefore would not need to concern himself with forecasting the course of the market, for if General Motors was really worth 50, he would get a fair return from dividends during the years to come even if the stock went down the day after he bought it and never touched the purchase price again, not even once during the next hundred years.

It follows, therefore, that the future market action of this stock will in no sense confirm or refute the appraisal we shall make of it, for investment value is one thing, and the market price another — today, tomorrow, or many years hence. To try to test the Theory of Investment Value by the performance of the market would be to rest our argument on the false premise that the market, while wrong now, will be right later and will stay right.

It is the common practice nowadays to reckon that a stock is worth, let us say, ten, or twelve, or fifteen times its earnings. The earnings of General Motors in 1935 being $3.69 a share, its value then, according to the old rule-of-thumb which settled on the figure ten as the proper multiplier, should have been 37. In 1936, however, the company earned $5.35 a share, in which case the stock should have been worth 54 that year. But if the stock was worth 54 in 1936, how could it have been worth only 37 in 1935, with one-year interest rates at a fraction of 1 per cent in the meantime?

To answer this question, a common practice is to take the *average* earnings of recent years. If care is used to include a whole number of business cycles, and if the secular trend of earnings is horizontal, this practice will give good results, provided the right multiplier for earnings per share is used. As to what is the right multiplier, however, there is no agreement among authorities. Investment Analysis until now has been unable to settle this point;[4] and yet it is highly important to do so with certainty. Let us see if the theoretical analysis of Book I cannot be invoked to resolve the difficulty.

According to this analysis, a stock is worth the present value of its future dividends, with future dividends dependent on future earnings. Thus, if 5 per cent is a fair return from an investment, a stock should sell at twenty times its normal future dividend. Every dollar of dividends thus means twenty dollars of investment value. But what earnings are needed to produce a dollar of dividends? That is the question. If two dollars of earnings are needed to support one dollar of dividends, then a stock is worth only ten times earnings, but if $1.25 of earnings, for instance, is all that is needed, then a stock is worth sixteen times earnings. True value thus depends on the distribution rate for earnings, which rate is itself determined by the reinvestment needs of the business.

2. THE NORMAL DIVIDEND FOR THE STOCK

To find out what the distribution rate of General Motors has been in the past, we need its record of earnings and dividends, as given in Table 16. This table shows that during the eleven years from 1926 through 1936 average earnings per share were $3.52 and average dividends $2.71, with the result that the distribution rate, when preferred dividends are included, has been 78.2 per cent, as shown in Table 17. Although this distribution rate is somewhat higher than the rate of 72.62 per cent given in the last Annual Report[5] for the entire period from 1909 through

---

[4] Cf. the article entitled, "Is Earning Power a Safe Guide?" by "The Trader" in *Barron's*, September 20, 1937.   [5] *Annual Report* for 1936, p. 55, col. 6.

1936, the discrepancy is to be accounted for by the fact that dividends were relatively low from 1909 to 1925, because of the large reinvestment requirements of the business at that time. During those years the secular trend of the company's sales was so sharply upward that very large

TABLE 16

THE GROWTH OF GENERAL MOTORS

Year	Earnings per Share[a]	Dividends Declared on Common[a]	General Motors' Sales throughout the World[b]	Production of All Companies in the U. S. and Canada[b]	General Motors' Share of Total[c]
1921	$-1.16	$0.53⅓	214,799	1,682,365	12.8%
1922	1.24	0.26⅔	456,763	2,646,229	17.3%
1923	1.68	0.64	798,555	4,180,450	19.1%
1924	1.15	0.64⅔	587,341	3,737,786	15.7%
1925	2.80	1.60	835,902	4,427,800	18.9%
1926	4.11	2.50	1,234,850	4,505,661	27.4%
1927	5.20	3.10	1,562,748	3,580,380	43.6%
1928	6.14	3.80	1,810,806	4,601,141	39.4%
1929	5.49	3.60	1,899,267	5,621,715	33.8%
1930	3.25	3.00	1,174,115	3,510,178	33.4%
1931	2.01	3.00	1,074,709	2,472,359	43.5%
1932	-0.21	1.25	562,970	1,431,494	39.3%
1933	1.72	1.25	869,035	1,985,909	43.8%
1934	1.99	1.50	1,240,447	2,869,963	43.2%
1935	3.69	2.25	1,715,688	4,119,811	41.6%
1936	5.35[d]	4.50	2,037,690	4,616,857	44.1%

[a] Adjusted to present capitalization. The number of common shares was reduced in 1924 in the ratio of 1 new for 4 old shares, increased on September 11, 1926 in the ratio of 1½ new for 1 old, increased again in September 1927 from 1½ old to 3 new, and increased once more on January 7, 1929 from 3 old to 7½ new; all of which may be summarized thus:

$$4 \rightarrow 1 \rightarrow 1\tfrac{1}{2} \rightarrow 3 \rightarrow 7\tfrac{1}{2}$$

On June 30, 1926, the outstanding minority interest in the Fisher Body Corporation was acquired by an exchange of shares, resulting in a still further increase in capitalization.

[b] Number of cars and trucks. The General Motors' sales from Annual Reports, year by year. The production of all companies from Annual Report for 1932, p. 13, and for 1936, p. 12.

[c] Ratio of the two preceding columns.

[d] After the tax of 5¢ a share on undistributed earnings.

sums were needed for reinvestment to increase capacity, whereas in recent years growth has almost ceased, and reinvestment on so large a scale has not been necessary.

TABLE 17

DISTRIBUTION RATE OF GENERAL MOTORS [a]

All Eleven Years 1926–1936	First Four Years 1926–1929	Last Seven Years 1929–1936
$\beta = \$0.22$	$\beta = \$0.22$	$\beta = \$0.22$
$\pi = 2.70$	$\pi = 3.25$	$\pi = 2.39$
$\beta + \pi = \$2.92$	$\beta + \pi = \$3.37$	$\beta + \pi = \$2.61$
$\beta = \$0.22$	$\beta = \$0.22$	$\beta = \$0.22$
$\gamma = 3.52$	$\gamma = 5.24$	$\gamma = 2.54$
$\beta + \gamma = \$3.74$	$\beta + \gamma = \$5.46$	$\beta + \gamma = \$2.76$
$q = \dfrac{\beta + \pi}{\beta + \gamma} = \dfrac{\$2.92}{\$3.74}$	$q = \dfrac{\beta + \pi}{\beta + \gamma} = \dfrac{\$3.37}{\$5.46}$	$q = \dfrac{\beta + \pi}{\beta + \gamma} = \dfrac{\$2.61}{\$2.76}$
$q = 78.1\%$	$q = 61.7\%$	$q = 94.6\%$

[a] The distribution rate for the capitalization as a whole, including preferred stock as well as common, may be found by means of formula

(83a)
$$q = \frac{\beta + \pi}{\beta + \gamma}$$

where
β = preferred dividends per share of common stock
π = common dividends per share of common stock
γ = earnings per share of common stock
q = distribution rate (after depreciation and taxes)

In the earlier years of its history, General Motors grew faster than the automobile industry as a whole, and as time went on sold a larger and larger percentage of the total output, as shown by the last column in Table 16. In 1927, a spectacular increase in General Motors' share occurred when Ford suspended the production of his Model T in order to re-tool for his new Model A. But since 1929, the Ford and the Plymouth have been able to give the Chevrolet much stronger competition, and earnings have never again reached the 1928 peak of $6.14 a share. Although prior to 1928 the secular trend of earnings was upward, since then the trend seems to have been horizontal. Even if some future years should see the unit sales of the industry at a new high in excess of the 1929 figure, the price of cars will doubtless be so much lower than in 1929 that dollar sales and dollar profits will not exceed the peaks of the last boom. Hence it seems fair to forecast a trend for the company's earnings and dividends that is merely horizontal.

The eleven-year average earnings of $3.52 per share, derived from Table 16, contain the results of four good, four bad, and three fair years as regards industrial activity in general; probably these eleven years constitute a fair sample of the ups and downs of general business and give a fair picture of the average earning power of General Motors. Perhaps, however, the future reinvestment requirements of the business are slightly overstated by the record of the past eleven years, because this period included the years 1926 to 1929, in which capacity was being increased enough to raise the output from 1,234,850 units to 1,899,267 units. If so, the average distribution of 78.1 per cent computed in Table 17 for the past eleven years is too low. As a matter of fact, the rate in the seven years following the completion of the expansion program in 1929 was 94.6 per cent, as compared with only 61.7 per cent in the first four years, when the expansion program was still under way. It would seem altogether reasonable, therefore, to choose a future distribution rate that was somewhat higher than the average rate for the past eleven years, and a future rate [6] of 83⅓ per cent would seem to be more nearly right.

A future normal distribution rate of 83⅓ per cent, if applied to future normal earnings of $3.52 (the same as the average for the past eleven years), would give a future normal dividend of $2.90, as computed in Table 18.

[6] The actual distribution rate in 1936, the first year in which the Undistributed Profits Tax was in effect, was 84 per cent. Evidently the new tax did not produce any noteworthy change in General Motors' established dividend policy.

TABLE 18

FUTURE NORMAL DIVIDEND OF GENERAL MOTORS

(83c) $\pi = q(\beta + \gamma) - \beta$

where

$\beta = \$0.22$, the preferred dividend $\left.\right\rangle$ per share

$\gamma = \underline{\ \ 3.52}$, the earnings on common $\left.\right\rangle$ of

$\beta + \gamma = \overline{\$3.74}$, the earnings on investment $\left.\right\rangle$ common

$q = \ \ \ \ 83\frac{1}{3}\%$, the distribution rate

$q(\beta + \gamma) = \overline{\$3.12}$ the total distribution $\left.\right\rangle$ per share

$-\beta = -.22$ the preferred dividend $\left.\right\rangle$ of

$\pi = \overline{\$2.90}$ the common dividend $\left.\right\rangle$ common

3.   COMPETITION IN THE MOTOR INDUSTRY

During the last ten years most of the small automobile companies have gradually been losing their earning power, as Table 19 shows. Only General Motors and Chrysler now remain in the list of those able to pay large dividends. The past decade has seen receivership for Willys-Overland, Studebaker, Hupp,[7] and several smaller companies, and the loss of most of their earning power by Hudson, Nash, Packard, and many other companies that once were highly profitable.

Apparently the cause of these troubles, in addition to the depression, has been the improvement in the smaller and less expensive cars in comparison with the larger and more costly ones. The light cars have become so good that the public has not thought it worth while to pay the extra cost of heavy cars, and, in consequence, the sales of heavy cars have declined greatly and the earnings of their makers have vanished in the process. Even among the small cars, moreover, only the Chevrolet and the Plymouth have remained really profitable, and others, like the Terraplane made by Hudson and the small cars made by Nash and

[7] While Hupp was not actually in receivership in June 1937, its operations had been almost at a standstill for some time.

TABLE 19
The Trend of Earnings of Various Motor Companies
(in thousands of dollars)

	General Motors	Chrysler	Ford	Hudson	Nash	Packard	Willys-Overland	Studebaker	Hupp
1921 ...	-38,681	-3,251	......	916	2,226	-3,487	-13,999	10,410	890
1922 ...	54,474	832	......	7,243	7,613	2,116	2,780	18,086	3,764
1923 ...	72,009	2,678	82,263	8,004ᵃ	9,280	7,082	13,034	18,342	2,636
1924 ...	51,623	4,116	100,435	8,073ᵃ	9,280	4,805ᵈ	2,087	13,774	1,614
1925 ...	116,016	17,126	79,890	21,379ᵃ	16,256	12,191ᵈ	11,423	16,620	3,797
1926 ...	186,231	15,449	75,271	5,373ᵇ	23,346	15,843ᵈ	1,820	13,042	3,505
1927 ...	235,105	19,485	-42,787	14,431	22,671	11,743ᵈ	6,342	11,938	2,719
1928 ...	276,468	30,992	-72,221	13,457	20,820	21,885ᵈ	5,905	13,947	8,790
1929 ...	248,282	21,902	81,798	11,595	18,014	25,183ᵈ	-5,196	11,346	3,469
1930 ...	151,009	234	44,461	325	7,601	9,034	-9,074	1,000	-923
1931 ...	96,877	2,112	-53,586	-1,991	4,808	-2,909	-14,021	448	-4,249
1932 ...	165	-11,254	-74,862	-5,429	1,030	-6,824	-6,628	-8,355	-4,515
1933 ...	83,214	12,129	-3,924	-4,410	-1,189	107	in	-4,876	-1,778
1934 ...	94,769	9,535	6,860	-3,239	-1,625	-7,291	receiver-	-1,462	-4,398
1935 ...	167,227	34,976	3,566	585	-610	3,316	ship	-1,976	-2,607
1936	238,482	62,111	26,427	3,306	1,061ᶜ	7,053	nil	2,188	-1,079

ᵃ 13 months ending Dec. 31.
ᵇ 12 months ending Nov. 30.
ᶜ Includes wholly owned subsidiary, Seaman Body Corporation, from July 16, 1936.
ᵈ Years ending Aug. 31.

Studebaker, have not sold in sufficient volume to be good money-makers.

It is interesting to conjecture as to why competition between the Chevrolet and the Plymouth has not eliminated all profits even on these cars, and the following explanation [8] is put forward as a suggestion:

The Chevrolet and the Plymouth are also in competition with the Ford, which likewise sells in great volume. The Ford Motor Company, however, unlike General Motors

[8] It should be emphasized that this explanation is only a surmise, and in the nature of things can be no more than this, for the reason that the published financial statements of the Ford Motor Company are too scanty to serve as a complete proof for any theory. The only financial statements currently available on Ford are the annual balance sheets filed with the Massachusetts Commissioner of Corporations. Since no income accounts accompany these balance sheets, no record of dividends paid is available, and we can only surmise that these dividends were small because the Ford family did not seem to have any reason for taking their profits out of the company. If no dividends at all were paid, earnings would have been as shown in Table 20. The earnings represent net income after heavy charge-offs, without doubt; whether they represent net income after extraordinarily and arbitrarily heavy charge-offs, no one knows. For whatever light it may throw on this problem, the following comparison of changes in Surplus and in Net Current Assets year by year is given:

Year Ending	Change in Net Quick Assets	Change in Profit and Loss Surplus
Feb. 28, 1922[a]	$ 54,743,000[a]	$ 57,601,000[a]
Feb. 28, 1923	96,708,000	119,299,000
Dec. 31, 1923	−18,293,000	82,263,000
Dec. 31, 1924	44,368,000	100,435,000
Dec. 31, 1925	69,024,000	79,890,000
Dec. 31, 1926	43,387,000	75,271,000
Dec. 31, 1927	−111,281,000	−42,787,000
Dec. 31, 1928	−88,796,000	−72,221,000
Dec. 31, 1929	97,964,000	81,798,000
Dec. 31, 1930	57,301,000	44,461,000
Dec. 31, 1931	−51,522,000	−53,586,000
Dec. 31, 1932	−66,549,000	−74,862,000
Dec. 31, 1933	21,519,000	−3,924,000
Dec. 31, 1934	22,260,000	3,759,000
Dec. 31, 1935	−241,000	2,701,000
Dec. 31, 1936	17,861,000	19,689,000

[a] Ten months, ending February 28, 1922.

and Chrysler, has not been profitable recently, but has only broken even, as Table 20 shows. Perhaps Ford's failure to make money in recent years has been due to his inability to operate as nearly at capacity as General Motors and Chrysler. To some extent his low earnings may also have been due to the fact that his eight-cylinder motor is more expensive to build than a six, yet does not fetch so high a price. Be that as it may, Ford, in setting his price each year for his new models, has had to figure on getting his re‑tooling expense back on a relatively low rate of operations. The price he has had to name, therefore, has been one that permitted General Motors and Chrysler, with their higher rate of operations in relation to capacity, to make a good profit. This profit has been due, of course, to the willingness of General Motors and Chrysler to follow Ford's lead in pricing; had they tried to undersell him and had they tried to drive him out of business, they would have made no money themselves. Moreover, they would have had a long, hard fight on their hands, because the Ford Motor Company is enormously rich, its net current assets on December 31, 1936 being $393,000,000 as against $340,000,000 for General Motors and $65,000,000 for Chrysler. Even though General Motors and Chrysler have known how to make cars that the public liked better than the Ford (if willingness to pay more than the cost of an article is a fair test of popularity), they have been wise in not trying to push their advantage too far. While they have competed with price cuts and improvements in quality until they have driven all their rivals but Ford nearly out of business, beyond that point they have not pressed the fight. Instead they have let Ford remain as the marginal producer. That Ford, for the present at least, is really a marginal producer, would seem to be indicated by Table 20, which shows that his profit per car is very low. The various

TABLE 20

COMPARISON OF LEADING MOTOR COMPANIES

	Earnings before Interest[a]			Number of Cars and Trucks Sold			Profit per Car		
	General Motors	Chrysler[b]	Ford[c]	General Motors	Chrysler[b]	Ford[d]	General Motors	Chrysler[b]	Ford
1921	$ −38,681,000	$ −3,251,000	....	214,799	12,000	1,013,958	$ −180	...	...
1922	54,474,000	832,000	....	456,763	53,000	1,351,333	120	...	...
1923	72,009,000	3,036,000	$ 82,263,000	798,555	67,000	2,090,959	90	...	$39
1924	51,623,000	5,047,000	100,435,000	587,341	82,000	1,993,419	88	...	50
1925	116,016,000	17,410,000	79,890,000	835,902	137,668	1,990,995	139	$127	40
1926	186,231,000	15,701,000	75,271,000	1,234,850	170,392	1,655,125	151	92	44
1927	235,105,000	19,674,000	− 42,787,000	1,562,748	192,083	454,601	150	102	− 94
1928	276,468,000	32,615,000	− 72,221,000	1,810,806	360,399	818,859	153	91	− 88
1929	248,282,000	25,420,000	81,798,000	1,899,267	450,543	1,951,092	131	56	42
1930	151,099,000	3,334,000	44,461,000	1,174,115	269,899	1,485,602	129	12	30
1931	96,877,000	5,255,000	− 53,586,000	1,074,709	272,118	762,058	90	2	− 70
1932	165,000	− 8,462,000	− 74,862,000	562,970	222,512	420,531	0	− 4	− 178
1933	83,214,000	16,216,000	− 3,924,000	869,035	451,734	437,408	96	36	9
1934	94,769,000	12,369,000	6,860,000	1,240,447	597,759	858,534	76	21	8
1935	167,227,000	37,382,000	3,566,000	1,715,688	843,599	1,335,865	97	44	3
1936	238,482,000	62,201,000	26,427,000	2,037,690	1,066,299	1,194,800	117	58	22

[a] To the nearest $1,000.

[b] Includes Dodge Bros. from July 31, 1928.

[c] As computed from balance sheets submitted to the Massachusetts Commissioner of Corporations.

[d] Production, not sales.

small companies which still hang on, producing at a loss, are what may be called "extra-marginal" producers. The earnings of General Motors and Chrysler today, therefore, would seem to be in the nature of an economic rent such as the user of good land gets in competition with the user of poor land; but in their case the rent arises from better management rather than from better natural resources; hence this rent might be given the technical name of "business profits" by some economic theorists.

4. THE INTEREST RATE TO USE

In the extremely easy money market of June 1937, a fair interest rate to use for capitalizing General Motors' normal dividend of $2.90, computed in Table 18, would seem to be 4¾ per cent.[9] Such a rate would be high, of course, in comparison with the "yield to perpetuity" of 3 per cent currently applicable to government bonds,[10] which carry with them a risk of loss by inflation [11] such as does not beset a common stock like General Motors. Industrial enterprises, however, have the habit of going to seed eventually, with only the best being able to survive for two or three generations. Such an old-time standby as Amoskeag, for instance, founded in 1831 and enormously profitable as recently as 1919, is now in liquidation. In view of this risk, therefore, an interest rate of 4¾ per cent would seem to be none too high.

Yet the future of General Motors is not excessively uncertain, for the company has recently taken on products

[9] See the discussion of present and future interest rates in Chapter XX, § 21.
[10] Cf. Chapter X, § 3, and Chapter XX, § 9.
[11] For a discussion of the likelihood of inflation, see Chapter XIX. Incidentally, inflation tomorrow should not make General Motors sell higher today. The formula used above for a company with horizontal earnings would still apply, for the increase in the dollar amount of future dividends because of inflation would be just offset by the decrease in the purchasing power of these dividends. Cf. Chapter IV.

other than automobiles, from which it can expect rising earnings in the future. These products include electric refrigerators, radios, oil burners, domestic lighting units, and Diesel-electric locomotives. For a time the Corporation was also interested in aviation, and it plans to renew its activities in that field when the legal status of the industry permits. Although the earnings from these side lines are now small in comparison with the earnings from automobiles, the time may come when they will be large. The competitive outlook for the company's automobile business, moreover, is satisfactory. If the Ford Motor Company should be turned over to the public because Henry Ford's heirs could not pay the estate taxes in any other way, this company would probably seek to earn a better profit than has recently been its practice under its founder, and then the stockholders of General Motors and Chrysler would benefit accordingly. Suffice it to say that whereas the General Motors Corporation, unlike companies in certain other lines of business, must make its way on its efficiency alone, without benefit of favored location or ownership of superior natural resources,[12] it can still count on a satisfactory competitive situation to lend security to its earning power. Hence a very high rate of interest does not need to be used in capitalizing its normal dividend.[13]

While the sit-down strikes against General Motors and Chrysler in the winter and spring of 1937 resulted in substantial wage increases and a serious fall in the efficiency of labor, at least for a time, nevertheless it is probable that the higher costs will not rest permanently on the stockholders, but will be shifted to the public in the form of higher prices, without causing any serious decrease in sales

[12] Contrast the position of the U. S. Steel Corporation, for instance, whose ore reserves and railroad holdings are discussed in Chapter XXIII, § 7 and § 8.
[13] Cf. the section entitled "Uncertainty and the Premium for Risk," Chapter V, § 8.

in the long run. Should things work out thus, the 1937 labor troubles of the industry would not require us to revise our estimate of future normal dividends, nor impel us to use a higher rate of interest in discounting these dividends. Only in comparison with other current interest rates, however, would the rate of 4¾ per cent chosen above be fair; for such a low rate takes no account of the economic forces at work to raise all interest rates to a higher level in due course. As pointed out in Chapter XX, the return on the best listed common stocks should eventually rise to 5¾ per cent; hence a rate of 5¼ per cent today would represent a fair average for present and future combined.

5. THE INVESTMENT VALUE OF THE STOCK

If the normal dividend of $2.90, computed in Table 18, was capitalized in June 1937 at the going rate of 4¾ per cent mentioned in the preceding section, the investment value as thus determined would be 61,[14] while if the normal dividend was capitalized at the proper rate of 5¼ per cent, thus making allowance for a coming rise in general interest rates, the investment value would be 55¼.

In November 1936, when general interest rates as shown by the prices of long-term government bonds were even lower than in June, the going rate on common stocks was 4½ per cent, and at that time the proper relative value of General Motors was 64½. Evidently the bull market high of 77, made at the time of the Automobile Show in November 1936, while generous, could not be called grossly extravagant as bull markets go.

---

[14] It goes without saying that any price estimated in the text is to be treated only as a rough approximation. This approximate character of prices could have been implied by the use of a range of prices, such as 57–65 in this particular case. This practice has not been followed, however, lest the reader find it too hard to check the arithmetic in the argument.

CHAPTER XXII

UNITED STATES STEEL

I. INTRODUCTION

The investment value of United States Steel, like that of any other stock, is the present worth of all its future dividends. Even though no dividends have been paid recently,[1] there is good reason to expect them to be resumed later, at an average rate which it is our problem to estimate. Whoever buys this stock now for less than its investment value will have two chances to profit — either by a rise in price, or by the receipt of a large income on his outlay. At present no good way of making a reasonable estimate of the investment value of the stock seems to be in general use, and most people would be hard put to it to make even a guess. Since its market price has varied between $261\frac{3}{4}$ and $21\frac{1}{4}$ during the last eight years, the range for guess-work is very wide, even if one thinks that the fair value must certainly lie within the range covered by the market — something not necessarily true.

It should be clearly understood that the estimate of investment value which we shall reach by the method to follow is not a precise figure, but only a first approximation to the truth. As such it is much better than nothing at all, however, for investors will find it a real help to them in deciding whether to buy or sell the stock now.

Since the purpose of this study is to offer a method, rather than to hand down a finding, no attempt will be made to prove beyond question the correctness of every assumption introduced; hence the reader should feel free

---

[1] Prior to October 1, 1937.

to revise any assumption to suit his own judgment. While using the same method we shall use, he can then reach the appraisal that seems fairest to him personally. As time alone can show what is really the true investment value of this or any other stock, no one can do more now, in advance of the event, than to make his own estimate to the best of his ability. Such estimates, even though they are not exactly right, are by no means worthless on that account, but are a helpful guide to action, just as are the uncertain estimates of the merchant concerning demand, or of the engineer concerning costs, or of the employer concerning the ability of a prospective employee.

Dividends, it was shown in Chapter XVI, are paid out of the quasi-rent earned on the capital goods owned by a corporation. Because the United States Steel Corporation is not a public utility, the price of its product is not regulated by any public authority, and its quasi-rents are neither limited nor protected by law. No rule of a "fair return on a fair value" connects earnings and assets, as in the case of the utility stocks discussed in later chapters, and so United States Steel must be appraised by a method entirely different from those which we shall use for American Telephone, Consolidated Gas, and American and Foreign Power.

United States Steel has been chosen to illustrate the methods applicable to certain industrials, because its accounts go back so far and are available to the public in such detail. The company is typical of those enterprises which make a wide variety of products, continually adding new ones and dropping old ones, with the result that their earnings do not undergo a long-term rise and fall like that of concerns which exploit only a single product during their lifetime.

But it is only by continually improving its methods so as to reduce costs that the Steel Corporation can retain its earning power throughout the years in the face of the forces of obsolescence. Although a public utility company can ignore obsolescence for a time, since it holds the monopoly of the market for a given area, the Steel Corporation, which enjoys no such monopoly, must always make the maintenance of its competitive strength a first object of its policy. No dividends can safely be paid to stockholders until provision has been made for new investment to maintain earning power. Just what proportion of earnings must be reinvested, and what can be paid out, we shall seek to learn by a study of the Corporation's accounts.

It makes no difference in the end whether the funds for reinvestment come from "depreciation" or from "surplus earnings," for it is the asset and not the corresponding liability that possesses earning power. After all, no one really knows where to draw the line between the Reserve for Depreciation and the Surplus; it is all a matter of opinion, on which even the experts will disagree. In order not to entangle our conclusions in such an argument, therefore, we shall avoid the difficulty by using earnings before depreciation in our calculations. Any other course would only beg the question in some of the problems to be considered hereafter.

To estimate the value of the Steel Corporation's stock, we must first estimate its normal quasi-rent, or earnings before depreciation and taxes. Next we must estimate the reinvestment requirements of the business. Then we shall find that whatever distributable balance is left over after paying property taxes, bond interest, income taxes, and preferred dividends can go to the common stockholders, and will determine the investment value of their stock.

2. THE TREND OF THE COMPANY'S EARNINGS

Apparently rising, but really horizontal, has been the trend of the Steel Corporation's earning power during the last thirty-five years, for the apparent trend has been distorted by the change in the purchasing power of money that has taken place since the formation of the company in 1901, which change has served to inflate the earnings of post-war years. Chart V shows a rising trend for actual earnings, a horizontal trend for deflated earnings.[2] Since the curve of deflated earnings begins in prosperity and ends in depression, it might appear to have a downward rather than a horizontal trend, but, in computing the slope of the trend, care should be taken not to make the mistake of using a fractional instead of a whole number of business cycles.

Two details of the chart are of interest: first, the huge profits on war orders in 1916 and 1917, followed by a slump after the United States itself entered the war; and second, the recovery in earnings from 1921 to 1929, the period of the great bull market in Steel and other stocks. This bull market to a large extent appears to have been the belated result of wartime inflation. When, during the years 1916–1920, inflation affected industrial earnings for the first time, stock prices did not rise correspondingly because investors doubted the permanence of these high earnings. But after the depression of 1921, when high earnings appeared once more, the stock market finally proceeded to appraise them as normal. The presence of bonds and preferred stocks in corporate capitalizations made the benefits of inflated earnings converge on their common stocks, and caused a rise in the stock averages far greater than that

---

[2] The upper curve represents earnings before depreciation and taxes, the lower curve the United States Bureau of Labor Statistics index of wholesale commodity prices, and the middle curve the ratio of the former to the latter. This commodity price index will hereafter be called the U. S. B. L. S. index.

CHART V

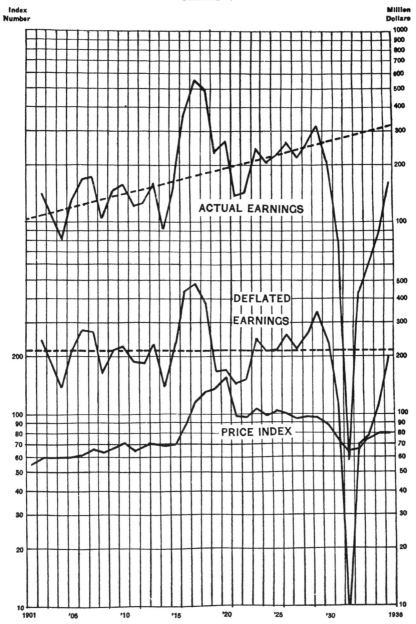

THE HORIZONTAL TREND OF DEFLATED EARNINGS

already registered by the commodity averages. The result, in fact, was the greatest bull market in our history.

During this bull market it was often said that the average corporation grew in earning power with the growth of the country as a whole, and that ownership of a representative list of common stocks automatically let one participate in the expansion of the national wealth and income. Mostly on the record of the last generation, however, a period of wide change in the purchasing power of money, was this belief founded; and another period might later give rise to another belief. Whether the average corporation, even in the past generation, would have shown a rising trend of *deflated* earnings is a question; our study of United States Steel will at least make such a conclusion seem doubtful.

3. EARNINGS AND OUTPUT

The deflated earnings of the United States Steel Corporation have not kept pace with its output of steel, for, as shown by Chart VI, rising output has yielded no more than horizontal deflated profits. Rising output, moreover, has required rising capacity. The chart shows that it has been necessary for the directors of the Steel Corporation to double capacity since 1901 in order to maintain deflated earnings at the level prevailing when the Corporation was first formed.

The presence of idle capacity most of the time in the past is no proof there has been "over-capacity," or over-investment, in the industry, for it is good business policy ordinarily to carry some capacity in excess of usual needs in order to be able to take advantage of the extra demand arising in a boom,[3] when prices and profits are very high.

---

[3] Cf. John B. Canning, "A Certain Erratic Tendency in Accountants' Income Procedure," *Econometrica*, January 1933.

To provide for growth in capacity, new investment paid for out of income has been necessary, and has required the

CHART VI

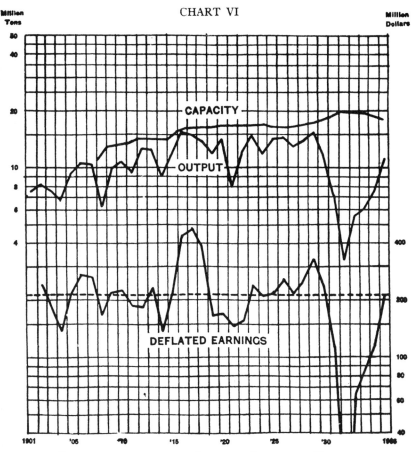

DIVERGENCE BETWEEN THE TRENDS OF OUTPUT AND EARNINGS

withholding from stockholders of large sums that otherwise could have been paid out in dividends. Apparently in the case of this company profits have been plowed back into the business at a rate which has proved just sufficient to maintain the *status quo* of deflated earning power. But the Corporation's reinvestment policy has been only the complement of its dividend policy. Had larger dividends been paid, capacity could not have been increased enough. Had smaller dividends been paid, deflated earnings could have been made actually to grow. As it was, only a horizontal trend of deflated earnings was achieved. If this same reinvestment policy is followed in the future, it should continue to give a horizontal trend of earnings, other things remaining the same.

The War called forth unusually large additions to capacity by the entire industry in the middle of the 1901–1936 period, as shown by Chart VII, and doubtless left behind it some temporary overcapacity that was not taken up until the 1920's. As a consequence, the chart gives the impression that the trend of capacity is flattening out. Much new capacity is now under construction, however, and so in two or three years the chart will give a quite different impression of the trend.

4.   THE FUTURE GROWTH IN THE USE OF STEEL

Since a change in the rate of growth in the use of steel might change the secular trend of the Corporation's earnings, we should inquire into the likelihood of a long-time change in demand, and investigate its probable effect on earnings.

Steel is used in capital goods of all sorts, from steam engines and ships to skyscrapers and bridges. First the railway, in years now past, and then the automobile, have made huge new demands for steel, and have given its production an upward trend, but if nothing more is added to these, will not the trend flatten out? No, for steel has a myriad of uses, and to say that growth in the use of it will subside would be a reckless prophecy. Any relaxation in

CHART VII

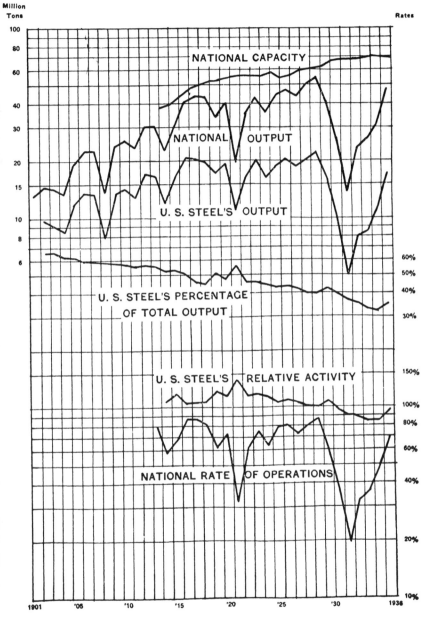

COMPARATIVE RATES OF GROWTH IN THE STEEL INDUSTRY

the need for investing new savings in railways and motor cars would release funds for investment in useful products of some other kind, of which new varieties are constantly being invented and which are likely to be made of steel, our most adaptable material. The steel house in particular seems on the verge of becoming practical, and it may carry on the growth in the demand for steel which the railway and the automobile have sustained till now. A great increase in naval armaments is also a possibility. But whatever it may be, some new use for steel in this industrial age seems likely to arise and maintain the past trend of growth in production. If so, no change in the trend of deflated earnings need be expected, so far as the demand for steel is concerned.

Although a long-range forecast of demand must take account of the slowing-up in the growth of population, this factor is small in comparison with the new inventions that may arise to affect demand in the distant future. Non-rusting steel, or cheap aluminum, would be more likely to upset our forecast of earnings than changes in population growth. The increasing use of alloy steels might likewise have the same effect, for they would permit the same service to be performed by articles of lighter weight, containing less steel. It should be remembered, however, that improvement in the quality of steel is no new influence, but is one of the factors that has been at work in the past, influencing the secular trend that we have already plotted for 1901–1936.

Furthermore, as pointed out in Chapter XVI, § 3, it does not follow as a matter of course that a slackening in the rate of growth of the steel industry need make it less profitable. If the change comes on gradually, so that it takes no one by surprise, steel men can adapt themselves to it by adding new capacity less rapidly, and in this way they can help to preserve the earning power of old capacity. If the steel industry had had no access to outside capital in the past, then its period of fastest growth would have been its period of highest profits, of necessity, as was the case with the automobile industry, but since it has always been able to borrow for expansion, there has always been a tendency for the rate of return in the industry to conform to the general interest rate. That a non-growing industry can be profitable is shown by the meat-packing companies, and that a fast-growing industry can be unprofitable is shown by the radio companies.

5. EARNINGS AND MONOPOLY POWER

If the Steel Corporation is really a monopoly, as has been asserted time and again since it was formed,[4] then its earning power depends only in part on its ability to produce cheaply, and for the rest on its ability to keep prices high. Earnings derived from exorbitant prices are known as monopoly gains, and persist only so long as the monopoly itself lasts; when the monopoly is overthrown, they vanish. Do Steel stockholders need to worry about an eventual loss of monopoly gains, and make allowance for it in forecasting future earnings and dividends?

That either monopoly or monopolistic competition [5] now prevails in the steel industry is suggested by the steadiness of prices in good times and bad.[6] If free competition really prevailed, then prices would equal marginal costs, and

[4] Cf. Frank A. Fetter, *The Masquerade of Monopoly* (New York: Harcourt, Brace and Company, copyright 1931).

[5] Cf. Chamberlin, *Monopolistic Competition*, and Joan Robinson, *The Economics of Imperfect Competition* (London: Macmillan and Company, Ltd., 1933). The term "monopolistic competition" is a purely technical term used by economists and intended to carry no unfavorable connotation.

[6] Cf. the remarks of O. M. W. Sprague on the price policy of the Steel Corporation, quoted in the *Boston Herald*, June 29, 1935.

Denying the charge of monopoly, Mr. Eugene G. Grace, president of the

would be much lower in slack times when only the most efficient mills are running than in boom times when much old and high-cost equipment is brought into use. Diagram 18 illustrates this line of reasoning.[7]

An increasing, rather than a declining, marginal cost curve CC' is shown in the diagram, because the Corporation is known to have some units — mines, furnaces, open-hearths, rolling mills, etc. — which are less efficient to work than others. The units are arranged in order of efficiency, with the lower-cost units being represented by the lower portion of the curve at the left, and the higher-cost by the higher portion at the right. The curve as drawn implies that, when orders are scarce and prices low, the Corporation operates only its best units, which are the ones that can make the most profit under any conditions, but that when business is booming, all units, even the inefficient ones, are put into operation. According to these assumptions, the curve of prime costs, or "increment costs," must necessarily be a rising one. The fact that the *average* cost per ton, as reported by the accountants and as distinguished

Bethlehem Steel Corporation, testified as follows before the Senate Interstate Commerce Committee on April 2, 1936:

"The charge has been made that the basing point method eliminates competition and makes for monopoly in the industry. If that were true a different chapter would have been written in the industry in the last twenty years. The existence of monopolistic conditions would not have permitted the growth of numerous companies, originally small, into the powerful competing units which they have become.

"I believe it has been charged that steel prices are dictated by the American Iron and Steel Institute, or that there are price agreements among steel producers. Such charges do not stand up before the record in the industry of severe price competition and small profits. As a matter of fact the institute has absolutely nothing whatsoever to do with the fixing of steel prices." (*New York Times*, April 3, 1936, p. 37.)

[7] Cf. Chapter XVI, § 2, where cotton goods instead of steel products are discussed.

Diagram 18 assumes that published prices are actual prices. In point of fact this assumption is true only in part, for much secret price cutting takes place during slack times and to that extent indicates that genuine competition, rather than monopolistic price fixing, dominates the steel industry.

from the *increment* cost, actually declines with more active operations, contrary to the diagram, does not disprove our assumption regarding increasing costs. Such figures as are published on average costs per ton exclude neither maintenance on unused equipment nor cash [8] outlays for overhead,

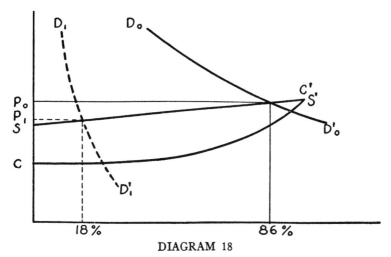

DIAGRAM 18

COSTS AND PRICES IN THE STEEL INDUSTRY

and so do not decline as they should with falling output. The available figures, in fact, are not true prime costs at all.

The common aᴖsertion of accountants that costs are higher in depression than in prosperity is based on the accounting practice of including depreciation in cost, a practice that is quite right in the long run, but a practice, nevertheless, that does not restrain management in the short run from producing at less than "cost" as so defined. Since depreciation goes on whether it is earned or not, and whether the machinery is busy or idle, it offers no motive for shutting a plant down when prices fall too low to cover

[8] As contrasted with bookkeeping entries for overhead, like depreciation and obsolescence.

depreciation in full. Hence depreciation is not a part of what the economist calls prime cost, and it is prime cost that is represented by the line CC' in the diagram.

Clearly the cost curve must have a steep upward slope, or else the *average* margin of profit in the year 1929, when operations were at 86.3 per cent of capacity, could not have been as high as 27.1 per cent of sales.

The curve D_0D_0' in the diagram indicates the position of the marginal revenue curve at the start, with output at 86 per cent of capacity, the 1929 figure, and D_1D_1' its position with output at 18 per cent, the 1932 figure. P_0 is the price at the start, and P_1 with demand curtailed. The decline in price is seen to be small, which implies that the supply curve SS' is not the same as the cost curve CC'. But under pure competition the two curves would really be the same, and prices would follow the marginal cost curve down when volume receded in a depression. Since prices do not in fact behave thus, it would seem that either monopoly or monopolistic competition must prevail in the industry.

Whether outright monopoly, or mere monopolistic competition, best describes the organization of the steel industry is a highly controversial question. Some economists say that the observed behavior of prices indicates outright monopoly under the leadership of the Steel Corporation, others that it shows nothing but monopolistic competition with its usual general reluctance on the part of all producers to cut prices for fear of provoking reprisals. As is well known to economic theorists, price stability through good times and bad is hardly the right policy for a pure monopoly to follow if it wants to maximize its profits; therefore it is doubtful if monopolistic intent on the part of the Steel Corporation is the right explanation of the behavior of steel prices. Rather it would seem that each company, and especially each large company, felt that cutting prices as a means of getting some one order was a policy that did not pay, because if one price was cut, many other prices would be forced down also. Therefore published prices in the steel business are seldom cut sharply, and price declines come only gradually, in response to cheaper methods of production. The exceptions to this rule are in the nature of secret price cuts, and these are usually confined to large orders.[9] With the return of good times, these secret price cuts tend to become smaller and more infrequent, as would be expected from the rising slope of the cost curve CC'.

The price behavior of the steel industry, while not highly competitive in comparison with the price behavior of the textile industry, for instance, is still some distance away from the tactics of a thoroughgoing monopolist. Furthermore, while the steel companies do not seem to compete aggressively for short-run gains by raising and lowering prices with each swing of the business cycle, yet they seem to compete with plenty of vigor for long-run gains by cutting their over-all costs and reducing their stabilized prices with a view to acquiring new customers permanently. Therefore it is very doubtful whether any such degree of monopoly exists within the steel industry as some social reformers would like us to believe. Apparently the best term to apply to the organization of the industry, at least in recent years, is monopolistic competition, which means, not a mixture of monopoly and competition, but a distinct kind of behavior peculiar to markets where sellers are few.

To say that the Steel Corporation has never been a monopoly, however, would be more open to question; for it is true that certain other statistics, while they do not prove conclusively the existence of monopoly, nevertheless are

---

[9] In bidding for large orders, especially from the motor industry, the steel companies sometimes find that whatever monopoly power exists, if such it may be called, resides not in themselves but in their customers.

consistent with truly monopolistic behavior; these statistics are the ones relating to the Corporation's share in the total output year after year. If the Steel Corporation really was a monopoly and had been holding prices too high for years, then it must have restricted its output during this period, for restriction of supply is the principal way in which monopoly power is exerted. Such restriction of output, coupled with high prices, would have induced the independents to expand more rapidly than otherwise, and would have caused the Corporation gradually to lose its share of the market. Chart VII shows that these very things have happened during the last thirty-five years. But since another good explanation,[10] namely, the Corporation's quite liberal dividend policy and its less liberal reinvestment policy, has already been cited for this difference in rates of growth, too much credence should not be given to these statistics as proof of genuine monopoly within the industry.

That expansion by competitors has not been overdone is indicated by Chart VII, which shows that the rate of operations for the industry as a whole, measured as a percentage of capacity, is not tending to decline — if allowance is made for cyclical factors — and implies, therefore, that idle capacity is not increasing.

In conclusion it may be said that, so far as questions of monopoly go, nothing is clearly in sight to make us expect a change in the secular trend of the Steel Corporation's earnings.

6. POSSIBLE UNIONIZATION OF THE INDUSTRY

Should the steel industry be unionized by a successful strike or by labor legislation, the monopoly gains of the Steel Corporation (if any) obtained in the market for steel products would be open to seizure by the labor unions, who

---

[10] Cf. the third paragraph in Section 3 of this chapter.

would be operating their own monopoly in the market for labor. Just what portion of the monopoly gains of the Corporation would be seized by the labor unions it is impossible to say. Although economists have perfected the theory of monopoly enough to deal with the case of one monopoly working inside another, the Steel Corporation does not operate its own monopoly in exactly the way postulated by this theory; hence the theory does not enable us to say whether unionization should result in more pressure on consumers or in a mere sharing of monopoly gains with Labor.

The fraction of the Steel Corporation's earnings that is in the nature of a monopoly gain is small, however, and in any event, unionization of the steel industry would probably not result in any great increase in the wage bill. Such an increase as might occur would probably result in higher prices for steel products, together with a slight decline in sales. Consequently the burden of unionization would fall mostly on the general public rather than on the common stockholders.

7. COMPETITION

Whereas economists usually think of the Steel Corporation as a monopoly, investors usually think of it as a company much beset by competition which it must meet as best it can, like any other manufacturing company. To meet this competition, the Corporation needs good equipment. Critics of the Steel Corporation assert, however, that the company has not kept its mills up to date, and hence is not able to meet this competition effectively.[11] Whether the efficiency of the Corporation's plants, compared with those of its competitors, has remained throughout the entire thirty-five-year period at the same average

---

[11] See the four articles on the Steel Corporation in *Fortune* for March, April, May, and June, 1936. The last article reveals some moderation of the critical comments on plant modernization to be found in the first article.

level the charts do not show, and it is very difficult to get a reliable answer to this question. In the beginning the Corporation took over Carnegie's highly efficient plants, and some years later it built a superb new plant at Gary, Indiana, with the result that during its early years it possessed some of the best plants in the industry. In the 1920's its plants must still have been very efficient, for, as shown in Table 21, its profit per ton in 1929 was higher than that of Bethlehem Steel, its largest competitor, or than Inland Steel, commonly considered a very low-cost producer.

TABLE 21

COMPARISON OF PROFITS AND COSTS

	U. S. Steel	Bethlehem	Inland
Profits per Ton in 1929			
Earnings before depreciation [a] ...	$265,838,000	$67,469,000	$16,717,000
Ingot output in tons	21,868,816	7,343,274	1,734,830
Profit per ton	$12.12	$9.18	$9.64
Costs per Ton in 1929			
Cost of sales [a]	$714,304,000	$275,047,000	$51,869,000
Ingot output in tons	21,868,816	7,343,274	1,734,830
Cost per ton	$32.65	$37.47	$29.86

[a] All figures to the nearest thousand dollars.

The figures in Table 21 are not strictly comparable, of course, because United States Steel had the benefit of earnings on its railroads running from its ore mines to Lake Superior, and from Lake Erie to Pittsburgh, whereas Bethlehem and Inland derived no such earnings, but had to pay freight to outsiders for assembling their raw materials and for distributing their finished products. So far as they go, however, these figures indicate that the United States Steel Corporation reinvested enough money in the 1920's to keep its plants relatively as modern as they were in the beginning.

Table 22 records the outlay made each year on plant

TABLE 22
ANNUAL PLANT OUTLAY OF THE UNITED STATES STEEL CORPORATION [a]

	Cash Spent on Plant	Cash Provided by Depreciation
1901	$16,957,000	$11,959,000
1902	16,587,000	27,814,000
1903	31,042,000	29,293,000
1904	17,958,000	18,207,000
1905	24,395,000	27,405,000
1906	32,155,000	34,707,000
1907	65,996,000	34,053,000
1908	49,423,000	22,474,000
1909	33,759,000	30,222,000
1910	50,091,000	32,451,000
1911	47,815,000	27,793,000
1912	15,387,000	33,379,000
1913	43,212,000	34,762,000
1914	22,746,000	27,467,000
1915	17,562,000	35,296,000
1916	65,711,000	43,036,000
1917	121,119,000	53,500,000
1918	131,836,000	46,545,000
1919	86,704,000	51,583,000
1920	102,112,000	53,014,000
1921	67,013,000	40,073,000
1922	26,844,000	47,089,000
1923	61,878,000	56,885,000
1924	76,549,000	52,547,000
1925	69,573,000	56,087,000
1926	76,366,000	64,221,000
1927	96,500,000	58,906,000
1928	47,746,000	67,237,000
1929	61,043,000	63,274,000
1930	143,491,000	58,550,000
1931	59,602,000	47,318,000
1932	7,169,000	40,320,000
1933	9,639,000	43,584,000
1934	9,778,000	44,579,000
1935	35,313,000	47,634,000
1936	72,713,000	55,467,000
	1,913,784,000	1,518,731,000

[a] Figures to the nearest thousand dollars.

and shows the cash provided therefor by depreciation. The great building program of 1930 was followed by almost no building at all in the three years 1932–1934, and not until 1936 did plant outlay return to normal. Since the company's competitors likewise refrained to a large extent from plant construction during the depression, United States Steel now finds itself little the worse for postponing its own plant outlays.

The fact that United States Steel had a higher profit per ton than Bethlehem or Inland in the boom year 1929, as shown in Table 21, would make it seem unlikely that the big company had done anything so foolish as to let its plant get grossly obsolete. Some modernization, of course, is necessary today just as it has always been, and large expenditures for this purpose were forecast in the Annual Report [12] for 1934, which pointed out especially that mills for the continuous rolling of sheets must be installed. But such an innovation today should prove no more burdensome than did the substitution years ago of the open-hearth for the Bessemer process, or of by-product for beehive coke ovens.[13]

Just because the Corporation during the last few years has not shown as good earnings as Inland Steel or National Steel does not indicate that it has suddenly fallen behind in efficiency; it shows, rather, that the automobile industry, which these independents are best able to serve, has enjoyed the earliest recovery of any large steel-consuming industry.

For want of conclusive evidence to the contrary, then, we shall assume that no serious loss of business to com-

[12] Page 9. See also the Annual Report for 1935, p. 12, and for 1936, pp. 12–13.
[13] For a discussion of the possibility of revolutionary changes in steel-making methods, see the *Iron Age* for November 22, 1934, where the substitution of the "continuous flow" for the "batch" process of manufacture is advocated, and comparison is made with the history of the chemical industry.

petitors because of failure to keep its plants up to date is in sight to change the secular trend of the Steel Corporation's earnings.

8. PLANT LOCATION

Location of plants is quite as much a factor as newness of plants in meeting competition in the steel industry, because the weight and bulk of raw materials and finished products make freight a large item in steel costs. Therefore, if it should be true that the Steel Corporation's plants were not well located, then regardless of their newness they could not compete. There are critics who maintain that Chicago and Detroit are today the best places to make steel in, and that Pittsburgh, where the Steel Corporation has so much capacity, is a "has been" that can sell only at prices low enough to offset the freight handicap under which it operates. These critics say that history shows that the steel industry has been migrating steadily during the past century from the Atlantic seaboard to eastern Pennsylvania, thence to western Pennsylvania, and now to Chicago, as the Middle West has come to be more and more the center of population. Let us see if the implications of this argument are correct, and if, in consequence, the Steel Corporation's investment at Pittsburgh will henceforth prove only a burden to it.

Diagram 19 is a flow sheet of the kind used in chemistry, giving the raw material requirements [14] and the end products of the process of making steel in a completely integrated, ultra-modern steel plant. This flow sheet shows that every two tons, or 4000 pounds, of ore requires 2575 pounds of coking coal and 1500 pounds of limestone for its

[14] See *Fortune*, July 1931, pp. 59–60; and also the May and September issues of the same magazine, for data on the raw material requirements of a modern steel mill.

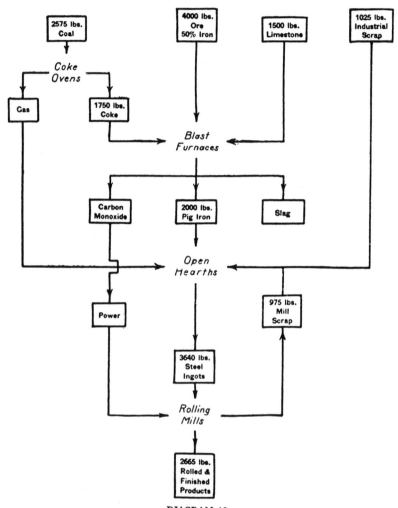

DIAGRAM 19

FLOW SHEET FOR STEEL MAKING

conversion into pig iron. The resulting one ton, or 2000 pounds, of pig iron needs to have 1025 pounds of industrial scrap (as well as 975 pounds of mill scrap) added to it to make the 2665 pounds of rolled and finished products that will emerge. This process of production can be set down in symbols, after the manner of a chemical equation, as follows:

$$2I + 1\tfrac{1}{4}C + \tfrac{3}{4}L + \tfrac{1}{2}S \longrightarrow 1\tfrac{1}{4}P;$$

or

$$8I + 5C + 3L + 2S \longrightarrow 5P;$$

where the coefficients signify the number of tons of each raw material or end product, and where the letters have the following meanings:

> I iron ore
> C coal
> L limestone
> S scrap iron
> P products, rolled and finished

By means of the foregoing production equation, it is possible to tell whether the steel industry is now in geographical equilibrium or whether it is still in process of migrating from Pittsburgh to Chicago, Cleveland, and Buffalo.

Such of the nation's steel-making capacity as uses other sources of raw materials than are used by the Steel Corporation may be omitted from our calculations; thus we may exclude the plants at Birmingham, Alabama; Sparrows Point, Maryland; and Pueblo, Colorado.

Let us assume that the industry does not need to seek its markets, but that its markets settle of their own accord at the natural steel-producing centers. Even though this assumption is true only in part, nevertheless it will be found in the end to introduce no error, because it turns out, as will be shown, that the natural distribution of consumption coincides with the natural distribution of steel making in this country. Therefore we may simplify our analysis by assuming that the location of the markets has nothing to do with the matter.

A further simplification of the argument can be made by assuming that water transportation of materials is so cheap as to be negligible. This assumption introduces no error, because it turns out again that by chance the amount of water transportation is the same regardless of whether the mills are mostly at Pittsburgh, or mostly at Chicago, Cleveland, and Buffalo; for the shape of the Great Lakes is such as to make Conneaut on Lake Erie as close to the ore mines by water as Gary on Lake Michigan.

Let us further assume that limestone and scrap are both obtainable locally, so that only coal and ore have to be assembled by rail.[15] As will be shown, an ordinary market for steel products tends to produce about the right amount of scrap to make the steel it consumes, provided scrap and ore are mixed in their usual proportions.

Once these assumptions are granted, it follows that the essence of the problem is to economize on rail transportation across the state of Ohio from Pittsburgh to the Lake Ports and back again. The way to economize is to get return loads for the freight trains, so that the railroads can operate at full capacity in both directions. By making the tonnage of coal going north approximately equal to the tonnage of ore coming south, the highest efficiency for the railroads and the lowest investment in railway lines can be achieved.[16]

[15] It is further assumed that ample quantities of lake or river water are available for cooling purposes.

[16] In times of recession in general business, when steel production is partly curtailed and the railroads are not forced to operate at capacity, the movement of ore is often suspended during cold weather, because when the ore piles at the Lake are frozen it is hard to load the ore into the freight cars.

While coal, ton for ton, takes up twice as much room as ore, nevertheless a trainload of coal weighs but little less than a trainload of ore, because coal cars are usually loaded to the top, whereas ore cars are usually loaded only half full. Hence a fair ratio of the tonnages in the two directions would seem to be 15 tons of coal going north to 16 tons of ore coming south.

The rail line will have to run between Pittsburgh and Lake Erie, because the best coking coal is mined near Pittsburgh, and Lake Erie is the nearest body of water on the water route to the ore mines at the head of Lake Superior.[17]

If the nation's steel-producing capacity (exclusive of the Alabama, Maryland, and Colorado plants mentioned above) is divided between Chicago, Cleveland, and Buffalo on the one hand and Pittsburgh on the other, in the ratio of 3 to 2, the result would be to provide the Pittsburgh and Lake Erie railroad lines with an ideal traffic distribution. For if 25 tons of coal should be mined near Pittsburgh, and if 15 tons thereof were sent north, then 16 tons of ore could be brought south, with the result that the following operation in the Pittsburgh mills could be carried out with the 10 tons of coal retained for the local blast furnaces:

$$16I + 10C + 6L + 4S \longrightarrow 10P$$

The 4 tons of industrial scrap required would be the normal amount to derive from a market in which 10 tons of finished product were sold. In the steel centers at the water end of the rail lines, on the other hand, the following oper-

---

[17] Although Chicago gets much of its coal by rail, instead of by boat from Lake Erie, this coal still comes from a region fairly near Pittsburgh, namely West Virginia and Kentucky, whence the freight to Chicago is $3.09 a ton, compared with only $1.15 a ton for ore brought down to Pittsburgh from Lake Erie. The coal for the Pittsburgh mills comes from mines close to the Monongahela River and is coked at Connellsville. The coke is then floated downstream to the furnaces, while the gas is piped to the open hearths; the division of the coal in this way into a gas and a light solid saves expense in transportation.

ation could be carried out with the 15 tons of coal received there from Pittsburgh:

$$24I + 15C + 9L + 6S \longrightarrow 15P$$

The total demand for ore would thus be $16 + 24 = 40$ tons, and for coal $10 + 15 = 25$ tons. The lakefront mills would be able to get their own scrap from their own markets, as Pittsburgh did.

Since Youngstown and the Valley are on the route from Pittsburgh to Lake Erie, the steel capacity that is located at these centers does not affect the foregoing analysis much one way or the other.

Pittsburgh's natural market includes Pennsylvania, Delaware, and New Jersey, as well as the territory downstream on the Ohio River and to the south. The natural market for the lakefront mills is Chicago and the territory to the west, Detroit and the automobile centers of Michigan, northern Ohio, and the territory to the east of Buffalo, including New York, Connecticut, and Massachusetts. Should the distribution of the nation's agricultural and mineral resources, and the location of the Mohawk-Hudson corridor to the sea, be such as to create an ultimate distribution of population in about the ratio of 3 to 2 for the lakefront and the Pittsburgh markets, then the distribution of markets would conform exactly with the natural distribution of production. In point of fact, the actual distribution of markets tends to be more in the ratio of 2 to 1 than 3 to 2; but exact conformity is not necessary, because many of the markets for steel are mobile, and are free to move to the spot where steel prices are lowest. Such things as freight cars and ships, for instance, can be made wherever costs are lowest, and then sold wherever needed when finished.

In this country the steel industry seems to be located in the ideal place by nature itself. That the centuries-long shifting of population has now largely run its course would seem to be proved by the fact that the center of population is now in Indiana, close to the great coal and ore route of the steel industry, running between Pittsburgh and Lake Erie.

It is interesting to note that in 1930, the last normal year for the steel industry, production of pig iron was distributed nearly in the proportion of 3 to 2 required for geographical stability by the foregoing analysis. The lakefront states of Illinois, Indiana, Michigan, Ohio, and New York produced 3 tons for every 2 tons produced by the Pittsburgh area, as nearly as can be estimated by the figures in Table 23.[18]

TABLE 23
COMPARATIVE OUTPUT OF THE TWO STEEL REGIONS

Illinois	3,344,674 tons	Pennsylvania	10,304,886 tons
Indiana	3,934,212 tons	West Virginia, etc. ..	864,824 tons
Ohio	6,804,862 tons		
New York, etc.	2,211,434 tons		
	16,295,182 tons		11,169,710 tons

The foregoing calculation of the 3 to 2 ratio is based on the coal and ore requirements of ultra-modern blast furnaces. Older blast furnaces require a larger proportion of coal. To the extent that older furnaces are still in use, they tend to keep the steel industry nearer Pittsburgh. Further improvements in furnaces would permit new savings in coal and allow larger tonnages of ore to be melted with the coal now going north. When that time comes, the Steel Corporation, like the independents, can make its current additions to capacity in its lakefront rather than its Pittsburgh mills. The past growth of Chicago as a steel-producing center at a more rapid rate than Pittsburgh,

[18] Data from p. 4 of the *Annual Statistical Report, 1930* of the American Iron and Steel Institute.

though commonly ascribed to factors affecting demand, has probably been due quite as much to technological changes affecting supply, such as changes in the coal-ore ratio mentioned above. That Pittsburgh is not an inferior location, however, in spite of the more rapid growth of Chicago, is proved by the building of a huge new mill by the Corporation at Clairton, near Pittsburgh, in 1937, when the money could just as easily have been spent for a mill at Chicago.

Unless the lakefront mills of Chicago, Detroit, Cleveland, and Buffalo were built up to the full capacity of their markets, these mills would operate on an "import basis." Under these circumstances, Pittsburgh would export its steel more than half way into competing markets. Years ago, when the lakefront mills were altogether inadequate to supply their natural markets, Pittsburgh did in fact export all the way to Chicago, and prices there were in fact on an "export basis" from Pittsburgh. The price structure that resulted was embodied in the system of "Pittsburgh plus." Such a system was not in strict accord with the Theory of Location, however, because, according to this theory, every mill should get the whole business in the territory nearest it, and the radius of the market for each mill should depend on how low its cost of production was. Diagram 20 indicates the theoretical price structure that should result, assuming that each steel center contained competing mills within itself.

The height of the zigzag line in the diagram is the selling price, freight included, of steel in any place in the market area north of Pittsburgh, largely supplied by the lakefront mills according to our 3 to 2 calculation. The price structure in the market area south and east of Pittsburgh, largely supplied by that center, is not covered by the diagram. Each steel center is shown to have a natural market of its own, represented by one of the "valleys" in the diagram. The distance from the base of the diagram to the bottom of each valley represents the marginal cost of production in each steel center.

The diagram implies that Pittsburgh, even in the absence of the artificial "Pittsburgh plus" system of pricing,

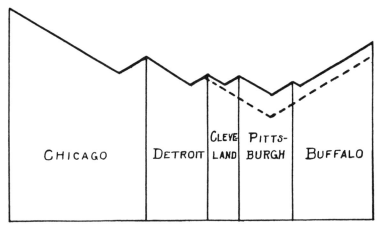

DIAGRAM 20

PRICE STRUCTURE AS GIVEN BY THE THEORY OF LOCATION

can get a small share of the business north of it — as well as all the business south of it. But the truth as regards the Steel Corporation itself is even more favorable, because this company alone of all steel producers is the owner of a railroad (the Bessemer and Lake Erie) running from the coal mines and blast furnaces at Pittsburgh to the ore docks at Conneaut on the Lake. All the profits from this line go into the Steel Corporation's treasury; thus while its competitors must pay full freight on their coal and ore, the Steel Corporation can get its own hauling done at cost. Hence the Corporation can name, in good times when the railroad is running at a profit, prices (represented by the

dotted line) low enough to let it sell far into its competitors' territories; or it can stay within its own natural market, but sell at a better profit than its competitors. Because
its own railroad goes to and from Pittsburgh, its mills in
Pittsburgh can never be called a burden to it. Clearly the
allegation that the Steel Corporation suffers from poorly
located plants is unfounded.

9. THE ORE AND COAL HOLDINGS OF THE CORPORATION

In Minnesota and northern Michigan the Steel Corporation owns by far the largest holdings of high-grade iron
ore of any company in the industry. It also is the owner of
a railroad from the mines to the ore docks. Like other
producers, it has its own lake freighters. Near Pittsburgh
it owns a great acreage of the best coking coal. It has its
own cement mills to use its blast-furnace slag. By all odds
it is the best integrated company in the industry and in
prosperous times such integration results in the lowest
cost of production. During the depression, however, the
normal advantages of integration were lost, because, unlike its less fully integrated competitors, the Steel Corporation could not gain by buying coal, ore, limestone, timber,
gas, freight service, etc., from necessitous sellers at less
than the cost of production.

If the St. Lawrence waterway should ever be put
through, bringing cheap foreign ores into Lake Erie, the
Steel Corporation would suffer a loss on the value of its
great ore reserves; but its investment in Pittsburgh would
in no wise be jeopardized, because the ore would still arrive at the north end, and the coal at the south end, of the
Pittsburgh and Lake Erie route. Consequently no disloca-
tion of the steel industry would result. Likewise the construction of a large canal from Lake Erie to the Ohio River
would produce no more serious result than to force down

the freight rate structure in that territory and rob the Corporation of some of the advantages of owning the Bessemer and Lake Erie Railroad.

10.   DIVIDENDS AND EARNINGS

While earnings rather than dividends have been the subject of our forecasts so far, it has nevertheless been pointed out that in the long run earnings govern dividends, and earnings can be maintained only by restricting dividends and providing funds for investment in new and better equipment. In the past, as shown above, such restriction of dividends and such reinvestment of surplus earnings have proved just sufficient to maintain a horizontal trend of deflated earnings. Hence the particular distribution rate that produced this result is a figure of much interest, worthy of exact measurement. Let us call this distribution rate $\bar{q}$ [19] and define it as the percentage of earnings before taxes and depreciation that can be paid out in taxes, interest, and dividends without impairing the horizontal trend of future earnings. We shall assume that if the Corporation in the past could pay out $\bar{q}$ per cent of its net receipts, retaining only ($100 - \bar{q}$) per cent for reinvestment, then it can do so again in the future.

To compute the past value of $\bar{q}$ per cent, it is necessary to define the distribution rate exactly by taking note of the divers ways in which cash can be distributed to, or contributed by, security holders, as listed below:

I. *Ways of paying out cash;* i.e., *Distributions*
    1. Payment of dividends
    2. Payment of interest
    3. Payment of premiums on bonds

---

[19] This symbol is read "q-bar," and should be distinguished from q simple, which refers to the distribution rate after provision for depreciation.

4. Payment of bonds themselves at maturity
5. Purchase of bonds in open market by the Corporation, as for the sinking fund
6. Purchase of stock in open market
7. Payment of commission to underwriters

II. *Ways of taking in cash;* i.e., *Contributions*
1. Assessment of stockholders, as done by mining companies
2. Sale of stock for cash; i.e., issue of "rights"
3. Sale of bonds for cash
4. Borrowing from the banks

While the distribution rate of the Corporation in the future should be the same as in the past, the participation in this distribution by each of the various classes of security holders should be different, because the financial operations of the Corporation during the past thirty-five years have greatly changed its capital structure. Bonds and preferred stock have been reduced, and earnings have thus been made available for common stockholders. Disbursements which formerly were made on interest, sinking fund, and preferred dividend account, can now be made on common dividend account in large measure. Were it not for the increased tax burden of the Corporation, the common stockholders could receive the whole benefit of the reduction of senior charges that has been achieved since 1901.

11.   DIVIDENDS AND CASH ASSETS

In addition to the benefit of lower senior charges, a further change in dividend-paying power has come about during the last three decades because of the gradual accumulation of huge cash funds. This accumulation is a process which during the next thirty years need not be repeated, for the Corporation, although it started out with a scarcity of working capital and cash assets, has now stored up an ample quantity of these things (save as discussed in section 19 below). The earnings which in the past were set aside to build up bank balances and insurance, contingency, and depreciation funds, can now be paid out directly as dividends, since all these funds are now large enough to provide properly for the volume of business transacted by the company. The depression of 1931–1935 caused a severe drain on cash, to be sure, but this difficulty need not detain us here, as we shall discuss it in detail later. It follows, therefore, that the past average annual gain in cash assets can be included in estimating the future distribution rate, on the theory that a dollar of earnings which in the past went into cash assets can hereafter go into dividends.

The foregoing theory is based on the assumption that cash assets at the start of the 1931–1935 depression were "normal." For this assumption there are good arguments. Is it not reasonable to assume that the directors, when they paid off most of the bonds in 1929, and dipped into cash to do so, left the Corporation with what was thought to be just the right amount of cash for ordinary business needs? If so, 1929 marked the end of the accumulation of cash out of earnings. Furthermore, other items making up net quick assets must likewise have been thought to be at their optimum levels, or else cash would have been diverted into them at that time.

12. THE DISTRIBUTION RATE

The distribution rate for any given year is defined as the ratio of (1) the total disbursements to security holders of all classes, whether bondholders or stockholders, plus the increase in cash assets, plus taxes, to (2) the earnings before depreciation, interest, and taxes.

In Appendix II are to be found the tables used for computing the distribution rate as so defined. These tables [20] show that the average distribution rate for the last thirty-five years has been 70.5 per cent. (See Table VIII in particular.) Let no one say that the precise distribution rate is a trivial matter. It is true enough that a few per cent one way or the other in the fraction of earnings invested in a single year affects total assets only a trifle, but we are not discussing only a single year; we are discussing thirty-five years, during which time the cumulative effect of a high or low distribution rate would be enormous. During this period the amount reinvested by the Steel Corporation has been nearly two billion dollars, or double its original assets, usually thought to have had a fair value of nearly one billion [21] at the start. Since cumulative reinvestment has been so large, the precise reinvestment rate is necessarily a very important figure.

13.   REINVESTED EARNINGS

Inasmuch as the Steel Corporation has distributed only 70.5 per cent of its earnings before taxes and depreciation (according to column 3 of Table VIII in Appendix II), and has reinvested the rest of its quasi-rents and credited at least part of the reinvestment to surplus, while its deflated earnings, by contrast, have shown no better than a

[20] The data for the tables can be obtained most conveniently from the annual "Tabulated History of United States Steel" compiled by the Dow-Jones Co., and published each year in *The Wall Street Journal*. See especially the issue of October 4, 1937, pp. 10 and 11.

It is possible to check most of the totals for the various columns in the tables by reference to the account on page 20 of the *Annual Report* for 1931 entitled "Summary of Net Profits and Undivided Surplus, April 1, 1901 to December 31, 1931." The only difficulty with using this account is that it does not give earnings before depreciation, and so it would have to be adjusted to include total credits to the depreciation reserve for the entire period. It serves, however, as a useful check on many steps in the computation as actually made.

[21] See William Z. Ripley, *Trusts, Pools and Corporations*, revised ed. (Boston: Ginn and Company, 1916), chapter on the Steel Corporation, esp. pp. 242–255.

horizontal trend, it might appear that reinvestment had failed to produce a corresponding increase in earnings and dividend-paying power. It might seem that reinvestment to reduce costs had occurred only in time to take care of lower selling prices and higher wages, and reinvestment to increase volume only in time to provide for lower profits per ton. One must not conclude from all this, however, that reinvestment has been a misguided policy. On the contrary, it has been as wise as self-preservation itself, for without reinvestment, albeit non-profitable, the company could never have continued to meet competition, nor have stayed in business at all.

It would not be fair to assert that the Steel Corporation has not kept its books correctly, nor to say that it has made inadequate charges for depreciation and obsolescence. The company has provided by depreciation for the wearing out of its equipment and by obsolescence for the loss of usefulness thereof. It cannot be maintained that the equipment still in use and partly worn-out should have been completely written off the books just because it no longer has any earning power except in conjunction with additions and betterments that have subsequently been made. We cannot ask the bookkeepers to forecast the loss of earning power and set up reserves to cover that. They have quite enough to do to estimate wear-and-tear and loss of usefulness. It is better for the investor to let accounting conventions stay undisturbed, and then to make his own adjustment of the figures as now reported.

There is no point in trying to estimate the rate of return which the Steel Company earns on its assets at any time, because there is no way of appraising the value of these assets independently of their earning power. Just because they may have such and such a reproduction value does not mean that this reproduction value itself has much significance. If, in the industrial world as actually organized, new steel capacity is seldom built from the ground up but usually arises in the form of additions and betterments to existing plants, then its cost of production is dependent upon the fact that the foundation has already been prepared for it. This very fact may be part of the explanation of why profits per ton decline so persistently. Since the marginal increment of Steel capacity is thus rendered artificially cheap, perhaps it is no wonder the return on old capacity does not hold up.

Whatever the assets of a corporation, and whatever their cost, the benefits to a stockholder are confined to the dividends which the corporation succeeds in paying him. In other words, a stock is worth the present value of its dividends rather than its earnings. A little reflection will show why this is true. The purchase of a stock is merely the well-known exchange of present goods for future goods. The purchase price represents the present goods and the dividends represent the future goods. Whatever reinvestment of earnings or other device the corporation employs as one of its vital processes is no part of the plain exchange of present goods for future goods. Hence the question of finding the intrinsic value of Steel common resolves itself entirely into estimating its future dividends.

14. THE EFFECT OF THE PRICE LEVEL ON DIVIDENDS

The normal dividend-paying power of the Corporation as regards its common stock, once the depression is over and the shrinkage of its quick assets has been made good (as discussed in Section 19), will depend not only on the distribution rate and the amount of senior charges but also on the general price level, because the price level will determine the money value of the normal physical volume of output, and will enter into the cost of raw materials used and into the wages of labor hired. In Chapter XIX on government bonds a full discussion was given to the outlook for commodity prices. In this chapter it is assumed that general prices will return to the 1926 level of 100 when the 1931–1935 depression is completely over. Those readers, however, who expect some other level, may substitute their own estimate without altering the lines of the argument.

Although the use of wholesale rather than retail prices for deflating earnings each year would give exaggerated results in years of extreme prosperity or depression, in an average for a long series of years the exaggerations would be offsetting. In estimating the effect of deflation in 1932, moreover, as is done in Section 22, we have used wholesale rather than retail prices, because at that time the prevailing level of wholesale prices might reasonably have been taken as an indication of the decline to be expected in all prices in due course. Had a cost-of-living index been used in 1932 instead of a wholesale-price index, the resulting estimate of true value would not have been low enough fully to reflect the bearish outlook for the general price level prevailing at that time.

If inflation should occur in the future, a recalculation of the normal dividend computed in the next section will be necessary when the inflation is over. This recalculation should be based on a higher level of commodity prices, which will give a correspondingly higher quasi-rent. Using formula (34b), or Table 28 in Section 22 as a model, the reader should be able to make such a recalculation for himself.

While inflation would increase the paper value of common dividends, it would likewise decrease the purchasing power of these dividends, and so the common stockholder would gain but little from the inflation. Whatever gain he would receive he would get at the expense of the preferred stockholders and the bondholders, whose dividends and coupons would fail to increase at all in paper value, and whose loss in real income, therefore, would make possible a corresponding gain in real income on the part of the common stockholders. This transfer of purchasing power between the various classes of security holders is a familiar injustice common to all relations between debtors and creditors in times of inflation or deflation. If the reader expects inflation, he may calculate for himself, with the aid of formula (8j), how much the present investment value of Steel common would be enhanced by whatever degree of inflation he expects to see.

15. THE NORMAL DIVIDEND ON THE STOCK

The normal quasi-rent to which the distribution rate of 70.5 per cent, computed in Section 12, would apply depends on the general price level, as pointed out in the preceding section. If a return to the 1926 level of prices, with a price index of 100, is expected, the normal quasi-rent according to the computations [22] of Table VII in Appendix II would be $210,700,000. (See bottom of last column.)

Once net quick assets are restored to normal, the tax-paying and interest- and dividend-paying power of the Steel Corporation is, by definition, $\bar{q}$ per cent of normal earnings before taxes and depreciation. In Table VIII of Appendix II, the past value of this distribution rate is computed and found to be

$$\bar{q} = 70.5\%$$

Total distributable income would then be $\bar{q}$ per cent of these normal earnings, or 70.5 per cent of $210,700,000, which amounts to $148,500,000.

---

[22] The figure of $210,700,000 is conservative, because it is an average that is probably weighted too heavily with depression years. As pointed out in Section 2, care should be taken to make all calculations of averages and trends cover a *whole* number of business cycles.

Fixed taxes would require $39,000,000, bond interest $4,900,000, income taxes $26,500,000, and preferred dividends $25,220,000, in a normal year, with the result that the balance remaining for common dividends would be about $52,900,000. Such a balance would mean common dividends of $6.50 a share.[23] The fixed taxes of $39,000,-000 and the income taxes of $26,500,000 just mentioned are discussed in more detail in the next section, and the entire calculation of normal dividend-paying power is summarized in the last column of Table 28 in Section 22 below. In this table, other dividends based on other price levels are also computed, but for the present it is enough to state that a recovery in the price level to the 1926 figure of 100 would mean a normal dividend of $6.50.

16. TAXES

In our calculation of the normal dividend-paying power of the Steel Corporation made in the preceding section, an allowance of $39,000,000 per annum was made for fixed taxes and $26,500,000 for income taxes, but no allowance was made for Social Security taxes.

The allowance of $39,000,000 for fixed taxes in a normal year compares with $37,206,000 in 1936 and with $36,016,000 in 1928. (See Table 24.)

The allowance of $26,500,000 for income taxes in a nor-

[23] The number of shares used in computing dividend-paying power per share is 8,132,840. This is the amount outstanding after the stock dividend in 1927 and the exercise of rights in 1929, but before the purchase of Atlas Portland Cement, Columbia Steel, and Oil Well Supply, and before the sale of newly issued shares to employees, all of which added 554,595 shares to the total capitalization in 1930. The earnings arising from the issue of these shares are included in the 1930-36 figures for Earnings before Depreciation, and are thus included in Table VII of Appendix II in the computation of average Deflated Quasi-Rent for the last thirty-five years, but the error thus introduced is small. Therefore the value of the original 8,132,840 shares is computed as though the additional 554,595 shares had never been issued, and then the worth of the new shares, which were issued for value received, is assumed to be the same per share as that of the original group.

TABLE 24

COMPUTATION OF INCOME TAXES AS AFFECTED BY CHANGING TAX RATES, CHANGING PRICE LEVELS, ETC.

Capitalization Year	Original 1928	New 1928	New 1932	New 1936	New Normal Year
Deflated Quasi-Rent	$210,700	$210,700	$210,700	$210,700	$210,700
Index of Inflation	×96.7%	×96.7%	×64.9%	×80.8%	×100.0%
Inflated Quasi-Rent	$203,700	$203,700	$136,700	$170,200	$210,700
Less Depreciation	−58,900[a]	−58,900[a]	−39,500[d]	−49,300[d]	−60,900[d]
Less Fixed Taxes	−36,000[b]	−36,000[b]	−36,000[e]	−37,500[e]	−39,000[g]
Less Interest	−22,000[f]	−5,600[f]	−5,300	−4,900	−4,900
Net Taxable Income	$86,800	$103,200	$55,900	$78,500	$105,900
Rate of Tax	×12%	×12%	×14½%[h]	×15%	×20%
Federal Income Tax as computed on average rate of operations	$10,400	$12,400	$8,100	$11,800	$21,200
Plus adjustment of one-fourth to allow for difference in accounting rules	+2,600	+3,100	+2,000	+3,000	+5,300
Total Tax	$13,000	$15,500	$10,100	$14,800	$26,500
Actual Federal Income Tax	......	$14,960	$173	$11,608	......
Actual Rate of Operations	......	83.4%	18.3%	59.3%	70%

[a] Since actual charges for depreciation vary with the rate of production, the figure chosen is taken from a year in which output was nearly at an average rate; this year was 1927, when operations were at 78.9% of capacity. Actual depreciation in 1928, when operations were at 83.4% of capacity, was $67,273,000.

[b] Actual fixed taxes in 1928 were $36,016,000.

[c] Actual fixed taxes in 1932 were $32,162,000.

[d] The depreciation charges for 1928, 1932, 1936, and later are proportional to the price levels in these years.

[e] Total of local taxes and federal capital stock tax in 1936 was $37,206,000 with inventories still low.

[f] Interest charges used are those of 1930, the first year after the bond redemption, which were $5,640,000.

[g] Allowing for coming additions to plant.

[h] Consolidated returns taxable at 14½% as contrasted with only 13¾% for unconsolidated returns. Cf. Table 1.

TABLE 25

COMPUTATION OF THE INTEREST RATE TO USE IN CAPITALIZING THE COMMON DIVIDEND

	Original Capitalization		New Capitalization				
	1901	1928	1928	1932	1936	1936	Normal Year
Number of shares	5,083,025 shs.	5,083,025 shs.	8,132,840 shs.	8,132,840 shs.	8,132,840 shs.		8,132,840 shs.
Fixed taxes	$ 2,000,000	$36,000,000	$36,000,000	$36,000,000	$37,500,000		$39,000,000
Bond interest	22,000,000	22,000,000	5,600,000	5,300,000	4,900,000		4,900,000
Preferred dividends	33,700,000	33,700,000	25,200,000	25,200,000	25,200,000		25,200,000
Total fixed charges	$57,700,000	$91,700,000	$66,800,000	$66,500,000	$67,600,000		$69,100,000
Total fixed charges per share	$\hat{\beta} = \$11.35$	$\hat{\beta} = \$18.04$	$\hat{\beta} = \$ 8.21$	$\hat{\beta} = \$ 8.18$	$\hat{\beta} = \$ 8.31$		$\hat{\beta} = \$ 8.50$
Income taxes	none	$13,000,000	$15,500,000	$10,100,000	$14,800,000		$26,500,000
Common dividends[*]	$24,400,000	38,900,000	61,300,000	19,800,000	37,600,000		52,900,000
Total participating payments	$24,400,000	$51,900,000	$76,800,000	$29,900,000	$52,400,000		$79,400,000
Total participating payments per share	$\hat{w} = \$ 4.80$	$\hat{w} = \$10.21$	$\hat{w} = \$ 9.44$	$\hat{w} = \$ 3.68$	$\hat{w} = \$ 6.44$		$\hat{w} = \$ 9.76$
Total fixed and participating payments per share	$\hat{\beta} + \hat{w} = \$16.15$	$\hat{\beta} + \hat{w} = \$28.25$	$\hat{\beta} + \hat{w} = \$17.65$	$\hat{\beta} + \hat{w} = \$11.86$	$\hat{\beta} + \hat{w} = \$14.75$		$\hat{\beta} + \hat{w} = \$18.26$
Capitalization rate for enterprise as a whole	$i_4 = 6\%$	$i_4 = 5\frac{1}{2}\%$	$i_4 = 5\frac{1}{2}\%$	$i_4 = 5\%$	$i_4 = 4\frac{1}{2}\%$	$i_4 = 5\frac{1}{4}\%$	$i_4 = 5\frac{1}{4}\%$
Fair yield for senior securities	$i_3 = 6\frac{1}{2}\%$	$i_3 = 6\%$	$i_3 = 5\frac{1}{4}\%$	$i_3 = 5\frac{1}{2}\%$	$i_3 = 4\frac{1}{4}\%$	$i_3 = 5\%$	$i_3 = 5\%$
$\dfrac{\hat{\beta}+\hat{w}}{i_4}$	$\dfrac{16.15}{6.0\%} = 269.2$	$\dfrac{28.25}{5.5\%} = 513.6$	$\dfrac{17.65}{5.5\%} = 320.9$	$\dfrac{11.86}{5.0\%} = 237.2$	$\dfrac{14.75}{4.5\%} = 327.8$	$\dfrac{14.75}{5.25\%} = 281.0$	$\dfrac{18.26}{5.25\%} = 347.8$
$\dfrac{\hat{\beta}}{i_3}$	$\dfrac{11.35}{6.5\%} = 174.6$	$\dfrac{18.04}{6.0\%} = 300.7$	$\dfrac{8.21}{5.25\%} = 156.4$	$\dfrac{8.18}{5.5\%} = 148.7$	$\dfrac{8.31}{4.25\%} = 195.5$	$\dfrac{8.31}{5.0\%} = 166.2$	$\dfrac{8.50}{5.0\%} = 170.0$
$\dfrac{\hat{\beta}+\hat{w}}{i_4} - \dfrac{\hat{\beta}}{i_3}$	$269.2 - 174.6 = 94.6$	$513.6 - 300.7 = 212.9$	$320.9 - 156.4 = 164.5$	$237.2 - 148.7 = 88.5$	$327.8 - 195.5 = 132.3$	$281.0 - 166.2 = 114.8$	$347.8 - 170.0 = 177.8$
$i_c = \dfrac{\hat{w}}{\dfrac{\hat{\beta}+\hat{w}}{i_4} - \dfrac{\hat{\beta}}{i_3}}$	$\dfrac{4.80}{94.6} = 5.07\%$	$\dfrac{10.21}{212.9} = 4.80\%$	$\dfrac{9.44}{164.5} = 5.74\%$	$\dfrac{3.68}{88.5} = 4.16\%$	$\dfrac{6.44}{132.3} = 4.87\%$	$\dfrac{6.44}{114.8} = 5.61\%$	$\dfrac{9.76}{177.8} = 5.49\%$

[*] The figure for Common Dividends is derived from Table 28 in §22, line entitled "Balance for Common Dividends."

mal year assumes a substantial increase in the present rate of the corporate income tax, namely, an increase from the present rate of 15 per cent to a future rate of 20 per cent. The reason for assuming an increase in the rate is the likelihood, on the one hand, that higher taxes will be needed to balance the federal budget, and the possibility, on the other hand, that certain forms of taxation now in use, such as the pay-roll tax, will be abandoned in whole or in part because they will prove unpopular with too many voters. In view of these probabilities, it seems hardly reasonable to assume the continuance of the present 15 per cent rate of corporate income tax indefinitely. Moreover, as shown in Table 24, a substantial allowance must continue to be made for divergences between the accounting rules followed by the tax collector and those followed by the Corporation itself in reporting to its own stockholders.

No allowance is made for Social Security taxes, because, as explained in the chapter on Taxes and Socialism, the incidence of the Social Security pay-roll tax is deemed to be on wages, either directly through a failure of wages to rise in the future as fast as they otherwise would have done, or indirectly through an increase in the cost of living caused by the addition of these taxes to the former selling prices for manufactured goods.[24]

17. THE PROPER INTEREST RATE TO USE

In order to arrive at the investment value of the stock by capitalizing the normal dividend of $6.50 a share calculated in Section 15, the proper interest rate to use must first be determined. In Chapter XX the question of the future interest rate is discussed in detail. There it is argued that real interest rates will return to the level prevailing before the depression; but, as in the case of our forecast of

[24] Cf. Chapter XVII, § 9.

the price level, every reader is free to substitute his own estimate without altering the lines of the argument. Our estimate, allowing for an interval of low interest rates in the immediate future, specifies a rate of

$$i_a = 5\tfrac{1}{4}\%$$

now for the enterprise as a whole, and

$$i_b = 5\%$$

now for its senior securities.

It should always be remembered that as regards safety the Steel Corporation is if anything a better than average aggregation of capital goods in which to own a share. In considering the question of risk when choosing the interest rate to use one should remember, moreover, that chance can operate in either direction. Unexpected things seem just as likely to happen to raise the dividend-paying power of the Steel Corporation as to lower it from the conservative level at which it has here been estimated.

For capitalizing the common dividend, as distinct from the total distribution of the enterprise as a whole, the right interest rate to use may be found by means of the following formula:

$$(8e) \qquad\qquad i_c = \frac{\hat{\pi}}{\dfrac{\hat{\beta} + \hat{\pi}}{i_a} - \dfrac{\hat{\beta}}{i_b}}$$

For the purposes of this formula, property taxes are grouped with bond interest and preferred dividends, and income taxes are grouped with common dividends,[25] with the result that $\hat{\beta}$ in this case stands for total fixed charges per share, and $\hat{\pi}$ for total participating payments per share.

In Table 25, these values for $\hat{\beta}$ and $\hat{\pi}$ are computed, and,

[25] See line entitled "Balance for Common Dividends" in Table 28 in § 22.

by means of the formula just given, the interest rate i_c, applicable to the common stock, is deduced as

$$i_o = 5.49\%$$

In other words, if the enterprise as a whole should be capitalized at $5\frac{1}{4}$ per cent, and·its senior securities at 5 per cent, then its common stock should sell to yield $5\frac{1}{2}$ per cent on its normal dividend.

Rates of capitalization applicable to other dates in the company's history are also computed in Table 25 and will be made use of later, when the reasons for the rise and fall in the common stock from 1901 to 1929 and from 1929 to 1932 are discussed.

For purposes of comparison, the interest rates applicable to United States Steel at different times are summarized in Table 26. The rate derived in Table 25 for the common stock is shown in the last line of Table 26.

18. THE INVESTMENT VALUE OF THE STOCK AS COMPUTED BY FORMULA

If one considers the interest rate of $5\frac{1}{2}$ per cent, computed in the last column of Table 25 in the preceding section, to be a fair return on such an investment as Steel common, the stock, with a normal dividend of $6.50, would be worth $119.

Should some deduction, however, seem to be necessary to allow for the shrinkage of net quick assets and for the accumulation of unpaid preferred dividends caused by the depression, as discussed in the next two sections, the investment value of the stock would then come to $100 a share instead. The choice between these two values will depend, as will be explained shortly, on whether or not one expects the recent great depression to be followed by an equally great boom.[26]

[26] Concerning the likelihood of such a boom, see Chapter XIX on the prospects for inflation as compared with sound prosperity.

TABLE 26

Interest Rates, Past, Present, and Future, applicable to the United States Steel Corporation

Capitalization	Old	Old	New	New	New	New	New
Year	1901	1928	1928	1932	1936	1936	Normal Times
Character of interest rate	Current	Current	Current	Current	Current	Suitable	Suitable
Riskless yield to perpetuity	3 %	4 %	4 %	3½%	3 %	3½%	4 %
Enterprise as a whole	6 %	5½%	5⅓%	5 %	4½%	5¼%	5¼%
Senior securities	6½%	6 %	5¼%	5½%	4¼%	5 %	5 %
Common stock	5⅛%	4¾%	5¾%	4⅛%	4⅞%	5⅝%	5⅓%

19. THE RECENT SHRINKAGE IN NET QUICK ASSETS

Before dividends can be paid at the full rate indicated by the computed dividend-paying power of the Corporation, any shrinkage in net quick assets caused by the depression must first be made good. At the end of 1936 net working capital had declined to $381,608,000, where it was $59,266,000 under the figure at which the directors had thought fit to leave it after the bond redemption. Insurance and depreciation fund assets, moreover, which stood at $57,582,000 on December 31, 1929, had been almost entirely used up [27] by December 31, 1936, and whatever balance remained had been transferred to the Current Assets. Should business recovery take place in the next few years and bring with it a rise in commodity prices to the 1926 level, some slight increase in the Corporation's working capital would occur from the mere change in prices, but in the main a restoration of working capital and special funds to normal would have to wait on the replenishment of these assets out of earnings.

If the recent long depression in the steel industry should indeed be followed by an equally great boom, as has happened so often before in the industry's history, then a period of super-normal earnings could precede any period of merely normal earnings. The effect of such a boom would be to replenish working capital and pay off preferred dividend accumulations out of earnings, thus returning the Corporation's balance sheet to normal. If no such boom should develop, however, the shortage of working capital and special funds would have to be made up by withholding common dividends to the extent of the shortage, namely

---

[27] Apparently these assets were used to tide the Corporation over the emergency created by the onset of the great depression just when it was in the midst of a great building program originally intended to be financed out of earnings.

to the extent of $15.75 a share on 8,703,252 shares.[28] Should retention of earnings to this degree be prevented by the Undistributed Profits Tax, the same result could be achieved by assessing stockholders $15.75 a share by means of an offer of rights.

20.   PREFERRED DIVIDEND ARREARS

After the payment of the special dividend of $7.00 a share on the preferred stock November 24, 1936, the remaining accumulations on this stock amounted to $9.25 a share, or $33,326,001.75, a sum equivalent to $3.83 a share on 8,703,252 shares of common stock. Since any cash that is used to pay off a non-recurrent obligation like this is cash that could otherwise go out in common dividends, this sum of $3.83 a share must be deducted from the value of the common stock as otherwise determined.

In other words, if the common stock would seem to be worth 119 on the basis of normal dividends, as discussed in Section 18, but if preferred arrears of some $4 must be paid off, then the net value of the stock would be only 119 − 4 or 115. The treatment of preferred dividend accumulations is thus the same as the treatment of a deficiency in cash, or in net quick assets as a whole. If net quick assets, moreover, are short another $15 a share, as pointed out in the preceding section, then a further deduction must be made from the estimated value, bringing it to 115 − 15 = 100. These two deductions need not be made, however, if a boom with super-normal earnings lies ahead, because such a boom would add a special increment to the present worth of the stock, and would offset the effect of the lean years recently endured.

[28] Compare footnote 23 in § 15, where a smaller number of shares is used in computing earnings per share, etc., for the reasons mentioned there.

21. ALTERNATIVE PREMISES

It should be noted that our estimate of investment value is based on a future price level of 100.0, whereas the actual price level in 1936 was only 80.8. The reason for choosing a future price level of 100.0 is the belief that commodity prices will return to the 1926 level when recovery from the 1931–1935 depression is complete, and that such a recovery, bringing with it a return of the national income to the 1929 figure or better, will provide the setting for a normal rate of activity in the steel industry, with operations averaging 70 per cent of capacity once more.

Those readers who question whether such a recovery in the price level will occur, and who prefer not to anticipate it, may recalculate the investment value of Steel on the 1936 price level of 80.8 (as done at the bottom of the next to the last column of Table 28 on the right-hand side) and get an answer of 72 instead of 100. It should be noted, however, that a lower price level would permit the company to get along with lower net quick assets and special funds, and would reduce the deficiency that apparently existed in these items at the end of 1936. Table 27 shows how the deficiency in net quick assets and special funds may be estimated at various price levels.

If the investor's cost of living were to rise during the next few years from 80.8 to 100.0 while wholesale prices were doing likewise, it would be incorrect, as argued in Chapter IX, § 1, for the investor to anticipate this rise in all prices by paying more for common stocks before the advance had taken place. He would gain nothing by paying more in sound dollars now for something that would sell higher in depreciated dollars later, for what he would make on the rise in stocks he would lose on the rise in goods and services. All this is true, however, only if his own cost of living

TABLE 27

DEFICIENCY IN NET CURRENT ASSETS, ETC., AT VARIOUS PRICE LEVELS

	1901	1928	1932	1936
Current Assets	$206,262,000	$562,233,000[b]	$397,486,000	$485,166,000
Less Current Liabilities	− 50,270,000	−121,358,000	− 46,987,000	−103,558,000
Net Current Assets	$155,992,000	$440,874,000	$350,499,000	$381,608,000
Insurance & Depreciation Fund	none	57,882,000	5,648,000	none
Contingent Reserve Fund	none	27,705,000	10,229,000	112,000
Less Employes' Stock Subscription	none	−7,661,000	− 1,510,000	none
Total	$155,992,000	$518,800,000	$364,866,000	$381,720,000
Less Preferred Dividend Arrears	none	none	− 4,504,000	− 33,326,000
Total	$155,992,000	$518,800,000	$360,362,000	$348,394,000
Decreases from 1929	....	....	$158,438,000	$170,406,000
Number of shares	5,083,025 shs	8,132,840 shs	8,703,250 shs	8,703,250 shs
Deficiency in Net Quick and Funds, per share	....	none	$17.68	$15.75
Arrears in Preferred Dividends	....	none	.52	3.83
Total Deficiency Without Adjusting for Change in Price Level			$18.20	$19.58
Total Net Quick Assets & Special Funds in 1929	$544,400,000[a]	$544,400,000[a]	$544,400,000[a]	$544,400,000[a]
U.S.B.L.S. Price Index	×55.3	×95.3	×64.8	×80.8
Deflated Net Quick Properly Required	$301,100,000[c]	$518,800,000[c]	$352,800,000[c]	$440,000,000[c]
Actual Net Quick	−155,992,000	−518,800,000	−364,866,000	−381,720,000
Deficiency	$145,100,000[e]	none[b]	−$12,100,000[ce]	$ 58,300,000[e]
Deficiency in Deflated Net Quick, per share	$28.67	....	−$1.38	$ 6.70
Arrears on Preferred Dividends, per share	none	....	.52	3.83
Total Deflated Deficiency	$28.67	none	−$0.86*	$10.53

* = excess

[a] Computed back from actual 1929 Net Quick Assets.

[b] The Current Assets, etc., as of 1929, are considered normal for the reasons given in the text.

[c] To the nearest hundred thousand dollars.

were to rise as much as wholesale prices. But if the investor's cost of living were to prove more stable than wholesale prices, then it would no longer remain true that he should not anticipate a rise in wholesale prices, and it would no longer remain true that Steel should be appraised on the 1936 price level of 80.8 instead of the expected future price level of 100.0.

Perhaps a better way to view the problem is to consider the price indices of 80.8 and 100.0 as a way of expressing the degree of recovery in the national income that underlies the business of the Steel Corporation at any given time, and to say that a recovery of the national income to normal in terms of physical units would probably be accompanied by a rise in wholesale prices to normal. If so, a rise in the price index to normal would imply a recovery in Steel's own earning power to normal also. But the whole question is so debatable that it cannot be settled here. The best thing to do is to let the reader make his own choice, and use whatever data he thinks best in our formulas. After all, our task is to expound a method, not to hand down a finding.

Just as some readers may not care to anticipate a rise in wholesale prices, so others may not care to anticipate a rise in interest rates. These latter readers, instead of using our rate of $5\frac{1}{4}$ per cent for the enterprise as a whole, may prefer to use a rate of $4\frac{1}{2}$ per cent, equal to the going rate in late 1936 for the best concerns free from debt and not affected by a rising or falling secular trend of earning power. Those who prefer to use the going interest rate as well as the current price level will find the computation of investment value performed for them at the bottom of the next-to-the-last column of Table 28 on the left-hand side. On these premises, the investment value of Steel figures out to be 85 instead of 100.

It should be noted that, in the computation applicable to a normal year and appearing in the last column, the interest rate used is not the full rate of $5\frac{3}{4}$ per cent expected in the future, but is only $5\frac{1}{4}$ per cent. The reason for using the lower rate, as explained before, is to allow for the fact that the future normal rate is not the same as the present yield to perpetuity based on this future rate.[29] Instead, the present yield to perpetuity is an average of a low rate now with a high rate later.

22. CAUSES OF THE RISE AND FALL OF STEEL COMMON

Table 28 shows that the great rise in Steel common from 1901 to 1928 was due mainly to the following causes:

1. A rise in the general price level from 55.3 to 96.7 as measured by the U. S. B. L. S. index of wholesale prices.

2. A decline in senior charges from $55,700,000 to $30,800,000 as a result of the retirement of part of the bonds and preferred stock.[30]

3. The accumulation of ample quick assets and special funds for contingencies.

4. A fall of $1\frac{1}{2}$ per cent in the premium for risk applied to the enterprise as a whole, caused by the reappraisal of the risk factor as the company gradually proved its worth; the premium for risk being 3 per cent in the beginning and $1\frac{1}{2}$ per cent in the end, and the pure interest rate being 3 per cent in the beginning and 4 per cent in the end, with the result that the capitalization rate for the entire enterprise fell from 6 per cent to $5\frac{1}{2}$ per cent.

Offsetting these four bullish influences were two bearish

---

[29] Cf. Chapter X, § 3 and Chapter XX, § 9.

[30] The funds for this retirement were derived largely from the enormous profits made in supplying munitions of war to the British and French before this country entered the War in 1917. The remainder of the funds was provided by assessing the stockholders $20 a share in 1929. This assessment was combined with a stock dividend of one share for seven, whence it was possible to call the entire process by another name, to wit, the right to subscribe to new stock at 140.

TABLE 28

CAUSES OF THE RISE AND FALL OF STEEL COMMON

Influence at Work to Change Value of Stock	Inflation	Bond Redemption	Deflation		Reflation	Reflation		
Capital Structure to Which Calculations Apply	Original	Original	New		New	New		New
Year for Which Price Index is Chosen	1901	1928	1928		1932	1936		Normal Year
Deflated Normal Quasi-Rent	$210,700,000	$210,700,000	$210,700,000		$210,700,000	$210,700,000		$210,700,000
U. S. B. L. S. Index of Prices	×55.3%	×96.7%	×96.7%		×64.9%	×80.8%		×100.0%
Inflated Normal Quasi-Rent	$116,500,000	$203,700,000	$203,700,000		$136,700,000	$170,200,000		$210,700.000
Distribution Rate	×70.5%	×70.5%	×70.5%		×70.5%	×70.5%		×70.5%
Distributable Quasi-Rent	$ 82,100,000	$143,600,000	$143,600,000		$ 96,400,000	$120,000,000		$148,500,000
Fixed Tax Burden	− 2,000,000	−36,000,000	−36,000,000		−36,000,000	−37,500,000		−39,000,000
Balance for Bondholders	$ 80,100,000	$107,600,000	$107,600,000		$ 60,400,000	$ 82,500,000		$109,500,000
Interest Charges	−22,000,000	−22,000,000	− 5,600,000		− 5,300,000	− 4,900,000		− 4,900,000
Balance for Government and Stockholders	$ 58,100,000	$ 85,600,000	$102,000,000		$ 55,100,000	$ 77,600,000		$104,600,000
Federal Income Tax (allowing for depreciation, etc.)	none	−13,000,000	−15,500,000		−10,100,000	−14,800,000		−26,500,000
Balance for Stockholders	$ 58,100,000	$ 72,600,000	$ 86,500,000		$ 45,000,000	$ 62,800,000		$ 78,100,000
Preferred Dividends	−33,700,000	−33,700,000	−25,200,000		−25,200,000	−25,200,000		−25,200,000
Balance for Common Dividends	$ 24,400,000	$ 38.900,000	$ 61,300,000		$ 19,800,000	$ 37,600,000		$ 52,900,000
Number of Shares	5,083,025	5,083,025	5,083,025 or	8,132,840	8,132,840	8,132,840		8,132,840
Capitalization Rate for Entire Enterprise	6 %	5½%	5½%		5 %	4½%	5¼%	5¼%
Fair Yield for Senior Securities in Normal Times [a]	6½%	6 %	5¼%		5½%	4½%	5 %	5 %
Fair Yield for Common Stock, as computed in Table 25	5⅛%	4¾%	5¾%		4⅛%	4⅞%	5⅝%	5½%
Dividend-Paying Power on Normal Output	$4.80	$7.65	$12.06 or	$ 7.54	$2.43	$4.62		$6.50
Fair Yield	5.07%	4.80%	5.74%	5.74%	4.16%	4.87%	5.61%	5.49%
Capitalized Dividend	95	159	210	131	58	95	82	119
Less Any Deficiency in Net Quick Assets, Etc.	−29	none	none	none	+1	−10	−10	−19
Estimated Investment Value	66	159	210	131	59	85	72	100
Actual High	(1901) 55	....	(1929) 395¼ or	261¾	(1932) 67⅛	(1937)	126½	....
Actual Low	(1904) 8⅜	....	(1929)	150	(1932) 21⅛	(1936)	46⅞	....
Actual Dividend	(1902) $4.00	....		$7.00	$0.50		none	....
Normal Dividend (as computed above)	$4.80	....		$7.54	$2.43		$4.62	$6.50

[a] If the coverage of the preferred dividend is scanty, the senior securities are considered more risky than the common stock, and vice versa. Cf. Chapter V, § 9.

influences: a higher pure interest rate and higher taxes. From 1901 to 1928, the pure interest rate rose from 3 per cent to 4 per cent. In the same period, fixed taxes, consisting mainly of ore taxes and local property taxes, increased enormously, and more than absorbed the savings effected by the retirement of most of the bonds and part of the preferred stock. Income taxes, payable to the federal government, were instituted during the same period and reduced the dividend-paying power of the Corporation on its common stock 20 per cent. If it had not been for the increase in taxes of all kinds from 1901 to 1928, the normal dividend on the common stock in 1928 would have been $13.63 instead of $7.54, and the fair value 238 instead of 131. Clearly, it has been not Capital, but the State, that has taken the lion's share of the fruits of progress in the last generation.

The great decline in Steel common from 1928 to 1932 (not counting the speculative rise and fall in 1929) was due mainly to one cause: a fall in the general price level from 96.7 to 64.9 as measured by the U. S. B. L. S. index of wholesale prices. Offsetting this bearish influence was a decline in the capitalization rate for the enterprise as a whole from $5\frac{1}{2}$ per cent to 5 per cent. (Some analysts might argue for a still greater decline in the rate properly applicable in 1932, in view of the period of very easy money that lay immediately ahead.)

In the foregoing explanation of the fall of Steel common from 1928 to 1932, no mention is made of two purely temporary influences that undoubtedly had a great effect on actual market prices as distinct from true investment value; namely, the great decrease in current earnings and dividends and the great change in sentiment from optimism to pessimism. These influences, however, do not properly belong in any appraisal of true investment value; instead, they only explain why the stock sold above and below the best estimates of investment value for 1928 and 1932 respectively that could have been made by an uninspired student who foresaw neither the world-wide deflation that would follow 1928 nor the world-wide abandonment of the gold standard that would follow 1932.

The most important conclusion to be drawn from Table 28 is that the future course of commodity prices in the United States will largely determine the earnings and dividends of the Steel Corporation. If the price level rises, the investment value of the stock will rise also. A rapid inflation might retard earnings temporarily, because it would bankrupt the railroads and utilities, two of the most important customers of the steel industry; but in the end, when the inflation was over, earnings would adjust themselves to the higher price level then prevailing. A slow inflation, spread out over a generation, such as may possibly occur if the government balances its budget within a reasonable time, would have no such deleterious temporary effect on earnings, but it would still produce the same enhancement in the value of Steel common in the end.

Table 28 merely sets down in familiar accounting form the essence of the formula developed in Book I for finding how the value V_c of a stock would change in response to any given change h in the general price level. The formula is as follows:

$$(8\mathrm{j}) \qquad \frac{V'_c}{V_c} = \frac{\dfrac{(1+h)(\beta+\pi)}{i'_a} - \dfrac{\beta'}{i'_b}}{\dfrac{\beta+\pi}{i_a} - \dfrac{\beta}{i_b}}$$

23. TWO GENERAL OBSERVATIONS

Despite its modicum of monopoly power, the Steel Corporation is enough like other companies in its rate of growth, its lack of patent protection, and its reinvestment needs to warrant us in drawing the following general conclusions from its record of earnings during the last thirty-five years.

1. Earnings of the *typical* corporation, after adjustment for changes in the value of money, probably do not keep pace with the growth of the nation. Profits and reserves plowed back into the business usually do no more than maintain the status quo of earning power — unless the dividend policy is unusually niggardly. The large book value that results from the continuous reinvestment of surplus earnings does not usually indicate a correspondingly increased earning power. Rather does it imply that many years have passed since the enterprise was last reorganized or recapitalized. If a corporation does not reinvest a sufficient percentage of its earnings, but pays out too much in cash dividends, it will find itself in the end with its competitive strength severely impaired. In such case, it may resort to borrowing to provide the funds needed for expansion and modernization. This is really borrowing to pay dividends. Those investors who, when such bonds are offered for sale, think they see earnings and assets adequate to support the new issues, deceive themselves, because conventional accounting methods are not so designed as to reveal inherent dividend-paying power. Usually corporations which finance ordinary growth and improvements largely by new capital issues go bankrupt in the end.

2. It is a mistake to say that the investor in utilities is entitled to a "fair return on a fair value," if fair value is defined as *book* value, for the investor in industrials cannot count on such a return. From the social point of view, the real question is this: What portion of the savings of the community should be preëmpted by the public utility industry and thus taken away from private industry? It would seem that the marginal increment of capital employed by the utilities should render the same social service

as the marginal increment employed by private enterprise.[31] Although some such notion may have been vaguely in the minds of those who formulated the fair-return rule, it is probable that justice to investors and customers concerned them more than justice to the rest of the community. Even their concept of justice to investors, however, needs to be revised to take into account the fact that capital in private business really earns no such return as their rule contemplates. The return of 8 per cent on book value allowed by some of the earlier legal decisions was much too high even for those days. Managers should not be permitted, moreover, to run public utilities as interest-compounding machines, nor should they be given a free hand to secure the allowed return on just as much capital as they can stuff into the enterprise. The foregoing study of the Steel Corporation leads to the conviction that such a practice is unfair to the rate-payers of the community and uneconomic in the employment of the productive resources of the nation. For these reasons, the Massachusetts rule of basing return on "prudent investment" — but not reinvestment — seems to be more in harmony with economic theory.

In conclusion, then, it may be said that the significance of the foregoing chapter is not confined to the light it throws on the investment value of United States Steel alone; instead it would seem that the chapter raises the whole question of what capital actually does earn on the average in private business. And until we know what capital really does earn in private business, how can we ask the courts to rule on what it should earn when devoted to public use?

[31] In the very long run the return received, but not the service rendered, will tend to be the same in both fields, because if the return guaranteed to the utilities should be set above the market level at first, the utilities would continually drain savings away from private industry, until such a shortage in private industry would result that the returns there would finally rise to the same level as in the favored field.

CHAPTER XXIII

PHOENIX INSURANCE

The following study of the Phoenix Insurance Company was written in 1936 on the basis of 1935 figures, and has not been revised, because the 1936 figures show nothing that was not forecast in the original analysis. In conformity with our rule of going from the simple to the complex in the use of the mathematical formulas, this case is taken up before the next one on American Telephone; nevertheless some readers may prefer to read the latter case first, because the American Telephone case brings out so clearly the nature of growth and "rights," things which should be well understood before use is made of the more simple formulas which chance to be applicable to this particular insurance stock.

I. PROFITS TO ITS HOLDERS IN THE PAST

The best insurance stocks have been so profitable in the past that many investors think no price for them too high, at least no price that will ever be seen in the actual market. Chronic undervaluation, they say, makes the purchase of insurance stocks the royal road to riches. To prove their point, they show how 200 shares of such a stock as Phoenix, for instance, could have been bought for $32,000 in 1901 and would be worth $540,000 today,[1] assuming that all "rights" had been exercised.

Such a comparison as this, however, by neglecting the factor of compound interest, fails correctly to state the gain from holding Phoenix for a generation. A true version of the facts is given in Table 29, where compound interest at

[1] The price on December 28, 1936 was $90 a share.

TABLE 29

Profit Above Interest from Holding Phoenix for Thirty-Five Years

Year		Outlay Dr.	Receipts[a] Cr.	Compound Interest Dr.	Compound Interest Cr.	Number of Years	Interest Factor[b] $(1 + i)^n - 1$
1901	Original cost of 200 shares @ 160	$32,000	.....	$213,955	......	35	6.6861
1913	Subscription to 100 shares @ 100	10,000	.....	26,035	......	22	2.6035
1923	Subscription to 200 shares @ 100	20,000	.....	20,244	......	12	1.0122
1926	Subscription to 100 shares @ 100	10,000	.....	6,895	......	9	0.6895
1929	Split-up of stocks, 10 for 1, giving 6000 new shares for 600 old held	....					
1901	Dividends declared on 200 shs.	....	$2,800	......	$17,503	34	6.2510
1902	" " " 200 "	....	2,400	......	14,017	33	5.8406
1903	" " " "	....	2,400	......	13,088	32	5.4534
1904	" " " "	....	2,400	......	12,211	31	5.0881
1905	" " " "	....	2,400	......	11,384	30	4.7435
1906	" " " "	....	1,700	......	7,511	29	4.4184
1907	" " " "	....	2,000	......	8,223	28	4.1117
1908	" " " "	....	2,400	......	9,174	27	3.8223
1909	" " " "	....	2,700	......	9,583	26	3.5494
1910	" " " "	....	2,800	......	9,217	25	3.2919
1911	" " " "	....	3,200	......	9,756	24	3.0489
1912	" " " "	....	3,200	......	9,023	23	2.8197
1913	" " " "	....	3,400	......	8,852	22	2.6035
1914	" " " 300 "	....	6,000	......	14,398	21	2.3996
1915	" " " "	....	6,000	......	13,243	20	2.2071
1916	" " " "	....	6,000	......	12,154	19	2.0256
1917	" " " "	....	6,000	......	11,126	18	1.8543
1918	" " " "	....	6,000	......	10,157	17	1.6928
1919	" " " "	....	7,200	......	11,091	16	1.5404
1920	" " " "	....	7,200	......	10,056	15	1.3966

TABLE 29 (Continued)

Year		Outlay Dr.	Receipts[a] Cr.	Compound Interest Dr.	Compound Interest Cr.	n	Interest Factor[b] $(1+i)^n-1$
1921	" " " "	.....	7,200	.....	9,078	14	1.2609
1922	" " " "	.....	7,200	.....	8,157	13	1.1329
1923	" " " "	.....	7,200	.....	7,288	12	1.0122
1924	" " " 500 "	.....	9,300	.....	8,354	11	0.8983
1925	" " " "	.....	10,000	.....	7,908	10	0.7908
1926	" " " "	.....	10,000	.....	6,895	9	0.6895
1927	" " 600 "	.....	11,500	.....	6,829	8	0.5938
1928	" " " "	.....	12,000	.....	6,043	7	0.5036
1929	" " 6,000 "	.....	12,000	.....	5,022	6	0.4185
1930	" " " "	.....	12,000	.....	4,058	5	0.3382
1931	" " " "	.....	12,000	.....	3,150	4	0.2625
1932	" " " "	.....	12,000	.....	2,292	3	0.1910
1933	" " " "	.....	12,000	.....	1,483	2	0.1236
1934	" " " "	.....	15,000	.....	900	1	0.0600
1935	" " " "	.....	15,000	.....	none	0	0.0000
1935	Interest paid	267,129	......	......	267,129	:	.....
1935	Interest earned	......	299,224	299,224	......	:	.....
1935	Value of 6,000 shs. at end, @ 90	......	540,000	......	......	:	.....
	Balance	742,695	......	......	......		.....
		$1,081,824	$1,081,824	$566,353	$566,353		
	Profit	......	$742,695				

[a] Dividends received on January 1 are considered fourth-quarter dividends, and are credited to income for the *previous* year.

[b] Glover's Tables, p. 52.

the conventional rate of 6 per cent is included for every item.

According to the gain and loss account in Table 29, the profit above interest at the end of thirty-five years was $742,695 on an initial investment [2] of $32,000. The reason for this large profit is, on the one hand, the extraordinary growth of the company in the past, and, on the other, the high price of the stock at present. In 1901 the stock sold on its current dividend, today it sells on its future prospects. Paying $14 then, it sold at 160 to yield a full $8\frac{3}{4}$ per cent; paying $2.50 now, it sells at 90 to yield only $2\frac{3}{4}$ per cent. On the face of it, therefore, the stock cannot be as good a buy today as it was then, even if the company should succeed in growing as fast in the future as it grew in the past. Yet the stock may still be cheap today for all that if the present price fails fully to discount the company's reasonable prospects.

But before trying to see how much the 1936 price of Phoenix is discounting in fact, let us pause to appraise the stock by the methods currently employed in Investment Analysis, in order that we may see thereby what is the present state of that art. In its present stage of development, Investment Analysis seldom undertakes to prove that a stock is inherently cheap or dear, regardless of all other stocks; instead it seeks only to show that the given stock is or is not selling "out of line" with other stocks of the same kind; in other words, Investment Analysis usually measures the relative rather than the absolute value of any stock, and leaves to the economist the broad question of whether stocks in general are selling too high or too low. To measure the relative value of an insurance stock, investment analysts give most weight to the following cri-

---

[2] Subsequent outlays for the purpose of taking up rights could have been taken care of with dividends received, and hence may be considered as deductions from dividends rather than as capital outlays.

teria: (1) the ratio of market price to liquidating value, as compared with similar stocks; (2) the ratio of market price to earnings per share, as compared with similar stocks.

2. ITS LIQUIDATING VALUE

The liquidating value referred to above is really a corrected book value, in that it adds the stockholders' equity in reserves to the capital and surplus. An equity in reserves is said to exist because the law requires the companies to set aside in the unearned premium reserve the entire premium received,[3] even though experience shows only part of the premium should be needed for losses, and the rest should be left for expenses and underwriting profit. Since all agents' commissions and some home office expenses must be paid at the start, the cost of acquiring new business must first be charged to income, for these acquisition costs are an intangible item that cannot be entered in the balance sheet as an asset. Paradoxical though it sounds, it is possible, therefore, for a company to grow so fast as to impair its legal solvency, because the amount of the prepaid expenses which cannot be capitalized is equal to some 40 per cent of the original premium.

The theory behind the notion of liquidating value is that the company could normally be sold for that amount at least. Normally, if the stockholders should turn the business over to another large company or group of companies who had their own force of special agents and adjusters to handle the losses that would "come home to roost" in due course — that is if the company should "reinsure" its business — all claims could be paid out of assets and still

[3] The amount of the premium still credited to the Unearned Premium Reserve when the books are closed on December 31 in any year will depend on how long the policy still has to run. Legally the Reserve is kept for reinsuring the liability if it is taken over by another company, or for repaying the insured if the policy is cancelled.

leave a balance equal to the capital plus surplus plus equity in unearned premium reserve — a balance equal, in other words, to the liquidating value as we have defined it. Provided the company's underwriting had been skillful, such a residue on liquidation could reasonably be expected; hence the real worth of the stock must at least equal the so-called liquidating value. Inasmuch as good-will items like trade name and agency connections, requiring years to build up, ought also to be included in any complete estimate of a company's value as a going concern, mere liquidating value should be a safe minimum.

The liquidating value of Phoenix, as defined above, may be computed from the balance sheets [4] for the end of 1935 given in Table 30.

TABLE 30

UNCONSOLIDATED LIQUIDATING VALUE, DECEMBER 31, 1935

Capital		$ 6,000,000
Surplus		24,839,000
Unearned Premiums:	$8,031,000	
Acquisition-cost ratio:	40%	
Stockholders' Equity [a]		3,212,000
		$34,051,000
Number of shares		600,000
Liquidating Value per share		$56.75

[a] Because Phoenix secures such a large underwriting profit, some students would reckon the stockholders' equity in the Unearned Premium Reserve at more than 40 per cent, i.e., at from 45 to 50 per cent.

According to this computation, the liquidating value of Phoenix is only $57, as compared with the actual market price of $90.

But the foregoing computation does not tell the whole

[4] All figures are given, for ease in reading, to the nearest thousand dollars only, in this table and in all other tables to follow. The data are taken from the *Argus Chart, 1936*, p. 73, published by the National Underwriter Company, New York.

truth, as is well known, for the Phoenix Insurance Company is a holding company with a large undisclosed equity in subsidiaries. Until early in 1936 these subsidiaries were owned by an intermediate holding company called the Phoenix ·Securities Company, whose stock stood on the parent company's books at $8,218,080, where it was listed under Miscellaneous Stocks in the investment account. During 1935 the parent company advanced $1,600,000 to the intermediate holding company on a collateral loan secured by shares of some of the operating subsidiaries, with the result that the parent company's ownership of Phoenix Securities was further represented by a note receivable of that amount. Recently this intermediate holding company has been liquidated, and its investments will henceforth

TABLE 31

INVESTMENTS OF THE PHOENIX SECURITIES COMPANY

	Shares Owned	Shares Outstanding	Percentage Owned by Phoenix
Connecticut Fire	19,983	20,000	99.915%
Equitable Fire & Marine	19,790	20,000	98.950%
Minneapolis Fire & Marine	10,000	10,000	100.000%
Central States Fire	9,693	10,000	96.930%
Reliance, Canada	9,640	10,000	96.400%
Great Eastern Fire	18,555	25,000	74.220%
Atlantic Fire	2,434⅜	2,500	97.376%
National Union	677	20,000	minority holding

appear in Phoenix's own list. The exact holdings of the Phoenix Securities Company were as shown in Table 31.[5]

The liquidating value of the subsidiaries held by the Phoenix Securities Company on December 31, 1935, is computed in Table 32. To the extent that the liquidating value of the subsidiary insurance companies (exclusive of minority interests) exceeded the reported value of Phoenix Se-

[5] See *Best's Insurance Reports — Fire and Marine, 1936*, p. 587, col. 1.

TABLE 32
Undisclosed Equity in Subsidiaries, December 31, 1935[a]

	Capital	Surplus	40% Equity in Unearned Premiums[b]	Total	Percentage Owned by Phoenix	Phoenix's Share
Connecticut	$2,000,000	$13,070,000	$1,939,000	$17,009,000	99.915%	$16,995,000
Equitable	1,000,000	4,431,000	388,000	5,819,000	98.950%	5,758,000
Minneapolis	1,000,000	1,083,000	none[c]	2,083,000	100.000%	2,083,000
Central States	1,000,000	1,052,000	none[c]	2,052,000	96.930%	1,989,000
Reliance, Canada	200,000	490,000	17,000[d]	707,000	96.400%	682,000
Great Eastern	250,000	355,000	25,000	630,000	74.220%	468,000
Atlantic	250,000	122,000	none[c]	372,000	97.376%	362,000
Market Value of 677 shares of National Union, held by Phoenix Securities, @ 12 bid					....	8,000
Totals	$5,700,000	$20,603,000	$2,369,000	$28,672,000	....	$28,345,000
Less Phoenix Securities' Stock Held by Parent Company					....	−8,218,000
and Note Receivable Held by Parent Company					....	−1,600,000
Undisclosed Equity in Subsidiaries					....	$18,527,000
Number of Shares					....	600,000
Undisclosed Equity per share, December 31, 1935					....	$30.88

[a] Data from the *Argus Chart, 1936*, pp. 26, 30, 57, 21, 41, and 13, except for Reliance of Canada and National Union.

[b] "Unearned Premiums" are also called "Reinsurance Reserve" in some statistical manuals.

[c] All business reinsured with parent company.

[d] Equity of 25 per cent instead of 40 per cent, because the Reinsurance Reserve required in Canada is only 80 per cent instead of 100 per cent of the premium received.

[e] Taken out to avoid double counting.

curities itself, there existed an undisclosed equity which would need to be included in any calculation of the consolidated liquidating value of the parent company's stock. This undisclosed equity is computed in Table 32. When the undisclosed equity of $31 a share is added to the unconsolidated liquidating value of $57 a share, computed earlier, the consolidated total comes to $88 a share. From the point of view of this book, which is concerned with absolute rather than relative value, this figure of $88 for the liquidating value makes the present market price of 90 seem low, provided the company is to keep on growing.

3. ITS EARNINGS PER SHARE

In estimating relative value by the usual methods of Investment Analysis, consideration would be given not only to liquidating value, as in the preceding section, but also to earnings per share. An obvious way to compute such earnings per share — but one which has a serious disadvantage, as we shall see later — is to find the increase in liquidating value during the year, and to add this figure to the dividends paid in the meantime.

To find the change in the liquidating value of Phoenix during 1935, it is necessary to compute, in the same way as before, the liquidating value as of December 31, 1934, as shown in Table 33.

According to this calculation, the consolidated liquidating value at the end of 1934 was $76.55 a share, as compared with $87.63 a share one year later; evidently the gain during the year 1935 was $11.08 a share. When this gain is added to dividends declared of $2.50 a share, the earnings, as so computed, turn out to be $13.58 a share. If such earnings could be expected to continue, the stock would be very cheap at the current price of 90.

In 1935, however, a good part of the company's earnings

TABLE 33
Consolidated Liquidating Value, December 31, 1934 [a]

	Capital	Surplus	40% Equity in Unearned Premiums[b]	Total	Percentage Owned by Phoenix[b]	Phoenix's Share
Phoenix	$6,000,000	$21,250,000	$3,166,000	$30,416,000	......	$30,416,000
Connecticut	2,000,000	11,014,000	1,910,000	14,924,000	99.915%	14,911,000
Equitable	1,000,000	3,833,000	382,000	5,215,000	98.950%	5,160,000
Minneapolis	1,000,000	159,000	none[c]	1,159,000	100.000%	1,159,000
Central States	800,000	350,000	none[c]	1,150,000	96.163%	1,106,000
Reliance, Canada ...	200,000	457,000	15,000[d]	672,000	96.400%	648,000
Great Eastern	250,000	323,000	24,000	597,000	74.180%	443,000
Atlantic	250,000	58,000	none[c]	308,000	97.168%	299,000
Market Value of 677 shares of National Union, held by Phoenix Securities, @ 9½ bid						6,000
Totals	$11,500,000	$37,444,000	$5,497,000	$54,441,000	....	$54,148,000
Less Phoenix Securities Stock Held by Parent Company						−8,218,000
Consolidated Intrinsic Value						$45,930,000
Number of Shares						600,000
Consolidated Liquidating Value per share, December 31, 1934						$76.55
Consolidated Liquidating Value per share, December 31, 1935, as obtained from Tables 30 and 32						$87.63
Increase in Consolidated Liquidating Value per share during 1935						$11.08

[a] Data from the *Argus Chart, 1936*, pp. 73, 26, 30, 57, 21, 41, and 13, as before.
[b] Percentages owned in 1934 were slightly different from 1935, see *Best's Report, 1935*.
[c] All business reinsured with parent company.
[d] Equity of 25 per cent instead of 40 per cent, because the Reinvestment Reserve required in Canada is 80 per cent instead of 100 per cent of the premium received.

were of a wholly non-recurring sort, being cash or paper profits on its investments, as shown in Table 34. Thus earnings exclusive of appreciation were only $13.58 − $6.39 = $7.19.

TABLE 34

APPRECIATION OF SECURITIES HELD [a]

	Total Appreciation	Percentage Owned by Phoenix	Phoenix's Share
Phoenix	$2,190,000	....	$2,190,000
Connecticut	1,015,000	99.915%	1,014,000
Equitable	363,000	98.950%	359,000
Minneapolis	98,000	100.000%	98,000
Central States	110,000	96.930%	107,000
Reliance, Canada ..	4,000	96.400%	4,000
Great Eastern	19,000	74.220%	14,000
Atlantic	45,000	97.376%	44,000
National Union, 677 shs.			2,000
Total			$3,832,000
Number of Shares of Parent Company			600,000
Appreciation per share			$6.39

[a] Including profits and losses on securities sold, as well as the change in the market value of securities retained. From item 60(b) on p. 11 of the *Annual Report* to the insurance commissioners, the title of the item being, "Gain from investment profit and loss items.") Cf. *Best's Reports, 1936,* "Investment Exhibits," p. 590.

A more straightforward way to measure operating earnings, exclusive of non-recurring profits from appreciation, is by means of Table 35. According to this table, the earnings per share of Phoenix in 1935, exclusive of non-recurring items, were $7.21. At its current market price of 90, therefore, Phoenix would show a price-earnings ratio of 12.5.

Many investment analysts today, if asked whether such a price-earnings ratio made the stock cheap, would probably reply, "Well, that all depends on market conditions." Such an answer, of course, is all right for speculators looking to quick profits, but for investors looking to income over a long period it is no more helpful than the hackneyed comment that "a stock is worth what you can get for it." Neither reply dares squarely to face the question of whether stocks in general are too high or too low, nor of whether a stock would be worth buying for its own sake even if it could never be sold again. Yet stocks do not derive their value from their salability. Their salability, rather, is derived from their value. If so, this value must itself be founded on that thing, whatever it is, that is the essence of stock ownership, which thing is obviously *the right to future dividends*.

4.   THE MOTIVATION OF THE ARGUMENT

Let us now turn from the customary ways of appraising insurance stocks and try to develop a better way of our own, a way that is based on future dividends, and a way that will follow in logic from the economics of the insurance business itself, and that may be epitomized in a suitable formula in which a separate parameter for each and every factor affecting value will appear. The better to show the motivation of the final and correct method of evaluation, let us proceed step by step and try out several tentative methods of appraisal, revising and improving our formula each time. Let us first discuss the banking aspect of the insurance business, next the underwriting aspect, finally the combination of the two.

5.   ITS VALUE AS A BANKING ENTERPRISE

Instead of using either the liquidating value or the earnings per share to find the true worth of an insurance stock, let us follow a more fundamental method of appraisal and view the company as a banking enterprise whose business consists of obtaining "deposits" in the form of unearned

TABLE 35
CONSOLIDATED EARNINGS, 1935 [a]

	Under-writing Gain	Equity in Unearned Premiums	Gross Interest Earned	Less Investment Expense	Less Stockholders' Tax	Less Subsidiary Dividends Declared	Miscellaneous	Total	Percentage Owned by Phoenix	Phoenix's Share
Phoenix	$1,434,000	$47,000	$1,878,000	$ −237,000	$ −142,000	....	$ −34,000	$2,946,000	....	$2,946,000
Connecticut	811,000	28,000	713,000	−118,000	−43,000	$ −300,000	−22,000	1,069,000	99.915%	1,068,000
Equitable	164,000	6,000	206,000	−25,000	....	−100,000	−10,000	241,000	98.950%	238,000
Minneapolis	....	....	49,000	−4,000	....	−20,000	+1,000	26,000	100.000%	26,000
Central States	....	....	44,000	−4,000	....	−48,000	....	−8,000	96.930%	−8,000
Reliance, Canada ...	17,000	2,000	30,000	....	....	−12,000	−6,000	31,000	96.400%	30,000
Great Eastern	5,000	1,000	24,000	....	....	−15,000	−1,000	14,000	74.220%	10,000
Atlantic	−1,000	....	11,000	....	....	....	+9,000	19,000	97.376%	19,000
Totals	$2,430,000	$84,000	$2,955,000	$ −388,000	$ −185,000	$ −495,000	$ −63,000	$4,338,000	....	$4,329,000
Number of Shares										600,000
Consolidated Operating Income per share										$7.21

[a] Data from the "Investment Exhibits" and "Movement of Surplus" in *Best's Reports*, pp. 590, 176, 216, 458, 140, 626, 313, and 66.
If the table at the top of p. 589 of *Best's Reports* had included deductions for the stockholders' tax and for miscellaneous items, it would show earnings per share of $7.21, instead of $7.64, and would agree with our figure shown above.

premiums, and of investing them in stocks and bonds the
income from which the company retains for its own shareholders. If such a business is conducted without underwriting loss, so that all losses and expenses are covered by
underwriting revenues, and if all the assets of the business
are invested in income-yielding securities, then the stockholders can draw off in dividends the entire income from
these invested assets, and their stocks will be worth, therefore, the amount of the company's total assets per share.
Under these circumstances, tentatively assumed to be true,
Phoenix would have a fair value of 109, as computed in
Table 36. According to this view the investment value of

TABLE 36
CONSOLIDATED ASSETS, DECEMBER 31, 1935 [a]

	Total Assets	Percentage Owned by Phoenix	Phoenix's Share
Phoenix	$41,433,000	......	$41,433,000
Connecticut	21,108,000	99.915%	21,090,000
Equitable	6,654,000	98.950%	6,584,000
Minneapolis	2,342,000	100.000%	2,342,000
Central States	2,054,000	96.930%	1,991,000
Reliance of Canada .	794,000	96.400%	765,000
Great Eastern	677,000	74.220%	502,000
Atlantic	458,000	97.376%	446,000
Market Value of 677 shs. of National Union @ 12			8,000
Total Assets			$75,161,000
Less Phoenix Securities Stock Held by Parent Co.			−8,218,000
and Note Receivable Held by Parent Co.			−1,600,000
Consolidated Assets			$65,343,000
Number of Shares			600,000
Net Assets per share, December 31, 1935			$108.91

[a] Data from *Argus Chart, 1936*, loc. cit.

the stock is 109, as compared with the actual market price
of only 90, even without allowing for any underwriting
profits or any future growth.

TABLE 37
Consolidated Earning Assets, December 31, 1935[a]

	Stocks and Bonds, at Market Value	Collateral and Real Estate Loans	Real Estate	Total	Percentage Owned by Phoenix	Phoenix's Share
Phoenix	$33,011,000	$2,202,000	$509,000	$35,722,000	......	$35,722,000
Connecticut	15,587,000	744,000	17,000	16,348,000	99.915%	16,334,000
Equitable	4,704,000	47,000	....	4,751,000	98.950%	4,701,000
Minneapolis	1,117,000	15,000	....	1,132,000	100.000%	1,132,000
Central States	1,147,000	52,000	....	1,199,000	96.930%	1,162,000
Reliance, Canada	657,000	none	....	657,000	96.400%	633,000
Great Eastern	500,000	48,000	....	548,000	74.220%	407,000
Atlantic	345,000	15,000	2,000	362,000	97.376%	353,000
National Union, 677 shs. @ 12						8,000
Totals	$57,068,000	$3,123,000	$528,000	$60,719,000		$60,452,000
Less Phoenix Securities Held by Parent Company						−8,218,000
and Note Receivable Held by Parent Company						−1,600,000
Total Consolidated Earning Assets						$50,634,000
Number of Shares of Parent Company						600,000
Consolidated Earning Assets per share, December 31, 1935						$84.39

[a] Data from *Best's Reports, 1936*, pp. 586, 174, 214, 457, 139, 626, 311, and 65.

6. ITS EARNING ASSETS PER SHARE

The foregoing method of evaluation is in error, however, to the extent that it assumes all assets to be earning assets, for such assets as Cash and Receivables bring in little or no income. Of total assets of $41,433,000 shown on the parent company's Statement to Stockholders, $5,710,000 are non-earning assets of this sort, and only $35,722,000 are listed under Stocks and Bonds or Loans and Real Estate.[6] Evidently earning assets alone would give a better measure of true worth than total assets would give. The consolidated earning assets at the end of 1935 may be found by means of Table 37. According to the calculations in this table, the stock is worth only 84½, as compared with the actual market price of 90.

By coincidence, this method gives nearly the same result as does the use of liquidating value, that is, the earning assets of $84.39 per share turn out to be about equal to the liquidating value of $87.63 per share. For the year 1935, earning assets were slightly less than liquidating value, but for the year 1934, they were slightly more. Nevertheless, similar though the results of the two methods may be for Phoenix at the present stage in its history, the principles of the methods differ, and different values, therefore, could emerge at some other stage in this company's development, or for some other stock than this. In case of disagreement, earning assets per share would seem to be a better measure of true worth than liquidating value per share.

7. INVESTMENT INCOME

What the return on the earning assets themselves will be in the years to come is a question. The reader may guess

[6] Real Estate (meaning the company's home office building) is an earning asset, because the company charges its expenses and credits its earnings with rent on its own property.

TABLE 38
CONNECTICUT FIRE INSURANCE CO.
RATIO OF INTEREST AND RENTS TO ADMITTED ASSETS

	Total Interest and Rents[a]	Total Assets[b]	Ratio
1901	161,988	4,319,000	3.75
1902	170,948	4,735,000	3.61
1903	193,429	5,172,000	3.74
1904	197,617	5,340,000	3.70
1905	206,138	5,814,000	3.55
1906	210,522	5,402,000	3.90
1907	212,937	5,817,000	3.66
1908	231,721	6,366,000	3.64
1909	257,998	6,956,000	3.71
1910	277,596	7,478,000	3.71
1911	296,328	7,521,000	3.94
1912	298,343	7,735,000	3.86
1913	302,723	6,762,000	4.48
1914	223,522	6,769,000	3.30
1915	268,713	6,919,000	3.88
1916	276,552	7,250,000	3.81
1917	282,211	8,415,000	3.35
1918	319,115	9,449,000	3.38
1919	409,026	10,978,000	3.73
1920	469,396	12,142,000	3.87
1921	543,513	12,421,000	4.38
1922	554,952	13,458,000	4.12
1923	582,668	13,795,000	4.22
1924	600,118	14,220,000	4.22
1925	600,248	15,050,000	3.99
1926	639,546	16,125,000	3.97
1927	670,167	17,800,000	3.76
1928	715,046	19,058,000	3.75
1929	787,386	20,132,000	3.91
1930	832,140	20,146,000	4.13
1931	811,792	20,323,000	3.99
1932	829,842	19,272,000	4.31
1933	774,210	17,094,000	4.53
1934	765,964	19,130,000	4.00
1935	723,612	21,108,000	3.43

[a] From Connecticut Insurance Reports.
[b] From Standard Fire Insurance Tables.

for himself, but we shall assume, for the sake of argument, that it will be 4½ per cent. While the present return is now being reduced gradually by the redemption of the higher-yielding issues held by the company, it seems likely that in the future interest rates on new issues will gradually become firmer again.[7] Hence 4½ per cent seems a fair average to expect during the next fifteen or twenty years.[8] In order to avoid the complications caused by fluctuating security prices, a continuation of the present level of stock and bond prices is implied, so far as the market value of the investments held in the company's portfolio is concerned.

For reference purposes, the ratio of interest and rents to admitted assets each year since 1901 is given in Table 38 for one of the company's subsidiaries, chosen instead of the parent company itself because the parent company's own ratio is affected by payments from the Phoenix Securities Company. Since admitted assets exceed "mean invested assets," the ratio computed in Table 38 is not the true rate of return on the company's investments, but only a rough index of changes in this return.

8. UNDERWRITING PROFIT

The trouble with any estimate of true worth that uses simply earning assets per share is its omission of underwriting profit. To take account of underwriting profit, if any, in the case of insurance stocks, one method is to re-

---

[7] See Chapter XIX, § 10, and Chapter XX, § 21.

[8] Those readers who, in forecasting investment income, attach a great deal of importance to the recent fall in coupon rates on new issues will choose a lower figure than 4½ per cent for the future interest rate. But by the same token these particular readers, in forecasting underwriting income, will also choose a rate of underwriting profit that better conforms to recent good showings, and will select a figure higher than we shall choose in the following section. Hence when all is said and done, the points of disagreement in the forecasts will prove largely offsetting. See also § 14 below, entitled "The Investment Value Re-Computed with Alternative Premises."

duce this profit from a percentage of premiums written, the form in which it is usually reported, to a percentage of assets invested. Applied in this way, underwriting profit would serve to raise the investment return by $1\frac{1}{2}$ per cent, let us say, or from $4\frac{1}{2}$ per cent to 6 per cent, depending on the particular company, as will be shown presently.

In the past the underwriting profit of Phoenix has been high for a company writing conservative risks, as the right-hand part of Table 39 shows. The very favorable under-writing record of recent years has been caused by an amazing decline in fire losses for the country as a whole, as shown in Table 40. To count on losses remaining as low as in recent years would not be safe, however, for if losses stay down, premium rates are likely to fall too. Therefore it would be better to take some more conservative figure, rep-resenting the average experience of a long series of years, as the measure of the rate of underwriting profit to expect in the future.

The average underwriting profit of Phoenix for the last fifteen years, according to its Underwriting Exhibits,[9] has been 5.66 per cent. If the same rate can be earned in the future, and if premium income can be raised a little, say by three points to 23 per cent of total assets, then the under-writing profit will become equal to 1.3 per cent of total assets. As earning assets themselves are only seven-eighths of total assets, an underwriting profit of 1.3 per cent of total assets would amount to 1.5 per cent of earning assets. This figure of $1\frac{1}{2}$ per cent may then be added, as explained above, to the figure of $4\frac{1}{2}$ per cent representing the invest-ment return, with the result that the total return will equal 6 per cent of earning assets.

It should be carefully noted that the foregoing analysis

[9] See the *Spectator Fire Index, 1936* (Philadelphia: Chilton Company, Inc.), p. 113, for a summary of this exhibit for 1935, and earlier issues for earlier years.

TABLE 39
THIRTY-FIVE YEAR RECORD OF THE PHOENIX INSURANCE CO.[a]

Year	Total Assets[b]	Capital[b]	Surplus[b]	Re-insurance Reserve[b]	Net Premiums Written[b]	Dividends Declared[b]	Expense Ratio A	Loss Ratio B	Underwriting Profit C	D
1901	5,953	2,000	1,116	2,382	3,238	280	37.1%	59.4%	3.5%	...
1902	6,498	2,000	1,338	2,635	3,414	240	37.4	52.9	9.7	...
1903	6,854	2,000	1,581	2,751	3,552	240	38.0	47.2	14.8	...
1904	7,342	2,000	1,742	3,071	3,950	240	37.1	54.8	8.1	...
1905	8,141	2,006	2,381	3,266	4,058	240	37.9	44.5	17.6	...
1906	7,617	2,000	1,275	3,629	4,449	170	37.4	78.0*	−15.4*	...
1907	7,965	2,000	1,422	3,945	4,726	200	37.5	41.4	21.1	...
1908	8,834	2,000	2,169	3,967	4,551	240	39.0	52.9	8.1	...
1909	9,941	2,000	3,067	4,293	4,889	270	37.4	44.8	17.8	...
1910	10,738	2,000	3,655	4,325	5,027	280	37.9	47.0	15.1	...
1911	11,405	2,000	3,702	4,891	5,532	320	39.1	50.7	10.2	...
1912	11,796	2,000	4,155	4,976	5,176	320	39.9	50.2	9.9	...
1913	14,568	3,000	5,161	5,619	5,800	340	41.2	45.8	13.0	...
1914	14,477	3,000	5,187	5,487	5,400	600	41.6	56.1	2.3	...
1915	15,393	3,000	6,056	5,628	5,440	600	40.5	44.3	15.2	...
1916	16,504	3,000	6,756	5,997	6,220	600	38.7	47.2	14.1	...
1917	18,041	3,000	6,859	6,782	7,782	600	36.6	45.9	17.5	...
1918	19,706	3,000	7,506	7,601	9,237	600	38.5	44.2	17.3	...
1919	21,739	3,000	8,740	6,213	9,601	720	40.6	39.1	20.3	...
1920	23,630	3,000	8,974	9,648	11,529	720	40.9	43.6	15.5	...
1921	24,014	3,000	9,425	9,511	9,825	720	43.5	57.4	− 0.9	− 0.4%
1922	26,008	3,000	11,653	9,462	9,992	720	41.8	48.5	9.7	8.8
1923	29,398	5,000	11,150	11,165	12,922	720	44.3	47.0	8.7	− 6.8
1924	31,567	5,000	13,099	11,233	11,310	930	43.4	55.1	1.5	0.0
1925	33,950	5,000	14,271	12,098	12,678	1,000	41.5	52.5	6.0	− 3.5
1926	36,966	6,000	15,468	12,680	12,774	1,000	42.4	50.2	7.4	0.0
1927	40,712	6,000	18,048	12,704	12,059	1,150	43.7	47.5	8.8	5.4
1928	44,181	6,000	21,121	12,655	12,100	1,200	45.7	45.3	9.0	6.·
1929	45,161	6,000	22,094	12,602	11,977	1,200	47.4	43.9	8.7	8.3
1930	42,738	6,000	20,528	12,042	10,911	1,200	49.5	51.9	− 1.4	4.2
1931	42,337	6,000	19,680	10,928	9,671	1,200	49.3	51.7	− 1.0	10.5
1932	35,410[d]	6,000	12,590[d]	10,228	8,152	1,200	52.5	60.8	−13.3	4.9
1933	34,359	6,000	17,720	8,103	7,221	1,200	52.3	47.4	0.3	14.9
1934	37,779	6,000	21,120	7,914	7,949	1,500	50.0	37.7	12.3	14.6
1935	41,433	6,000	24,732	8,031	8,260	1,500	50.6	34.2	13.2	17.6
Average for last 15 years:							46.5%	48.7%	4.7%	5.7%

[a] From the *Spectator Fire Index*, published yearly.
[b] In thousands of dollars.
[c] For the last fifteen years (1920–1935) an underwriting exhibit has been submitted by the companies to the insurance commissioner and from the yearly exhibits it has been possible to compute a better figure (shown in column D) for the ratio of underwriting profit than the mere balance (shown in column C) obtained by subtracting the ratio in columns A and B from 100 per cent.
[d] Less contingency reserve representing most of the depreciation in market value of stocks and bonds held; figures from Statement to Stockholders.
[e] The great San Francisco fire took place November 13, 1906.

provides for a decided drop in average underwriting profits in the years to come. That such a drop is well-nigh inevitable is indicated by the substantial reduction in premium rates in recent years, and the certainty that these rates cannot be promptly restored to higher levels now that fire losses are beginning to increase again. Fire losses fell so low during the depression, and rates declined so much in consequence, that it is now a serious question as to what will happen to the earnings of the companies for a few years if fire losses should recover to normal. During this expected period when premium rates may lag behind the loss ratio, underwriting profits may become temporarily negative. Even if such an unfortunate thing should happen, however, there is still no reason to think that *average* underwriting profits, over a long series of years in the future, need be depressed below the figure of 5.66 per cent mentioned in the preceding paragraph. Table 41 shows the fall of premium rates in recent years.

9. UNDERWRITERS' ASSOCIATIONS

The premium rates charged by the fire-insurance companies are set by the companies acting in concert through their underwriters' associations, with the result that all companies who are members of the associations charge the same prices. Offhand, this practice of rate-making might seem to smack of conspiracy and monopoly, but on closer analysis it will be seen to be a relatively harmless price-quoting mechanism whose peculiarities result from the nature of the fire-insurance business itself. That all companies should charge the same price for insurance coverage is no stranger than that all chain stores should charge the same price for milk and bread, or all filling stations the same price for gas and oil. When the product is the same, the price is the same, and all who expect to compete for the

TABLE 40
Annual Fire Losses in the United States, 1875–1935[a]

Year	Aggregate Property Loss	Year	Aggregate Property Loss	Year	Aggregate Property Loss	Year	Aggregate Property Loss
1875	$ 78,102,285	1890	$108,993,792	1905	$165,221,650	1920	$447,886,677
1876	64,630,600	1891	143,764,967	1906	518,611,800	1921	495,406,012
1877	68,265,800	1892	151,516,098	1907	215,084,709	1922	506,541,001
1878	64,315,900	1893	167,544,370	1908	217,885,850	1923	535,372,782
1879	77,703,700	1894	140,006,484	1909	188,705,150	1924	549,062,124
1880	74,643,400	1895	142,110,233	1910	214,003,300	1925	559,418,184
1881	81,280,900	1896	118,737,420	1911	217,004,575	1926	561,980,751
1882	84,505,024	1897	116,354,575	1912	206,438,900	1927	472,933,969
1883	100,149,228	1898	130,593,905	1913	203,763,550	1928	464,607,109
1884	110,008,611	1899	153,597,830	1914	221,439,350	1929	459,445,778
1885	102,818,796	1900	160,929,805	1915	172,033,200	1930	501,980,623
1886	104,924,750	1901	165,817,810	1916	258,377,952	1931	451,643,866
1887	120,283,055	1902	161,078,040	1917	289,535,050	1932	400,859,554
1888	110,885,665	1903	145,302,155	1918	353,878,876	1933	271,453,189
1889	123,046,833	1904	229,198,050	1919	320,540,399	1934	201,723,741
						1935	248,763,856

TABLE 40 (Continued)

MONTHLY FIRE LOSSES IN THE UNITED STATES AND CANADA[b]

Months	1930	1931	1932	1933	1934	1935	1936
Jan.	$ 42,344,035	$ 44,090,449	$ 39,224,783	$ 35,547,565	$ 28,002,583	$ 23,430,504	$ 27,729,930
Feb.	43,206,940	41,776,051	39,824,622	36,661,481	31,443,484	25,081,625	30,909,896
Mar.	42,964,392	44,074,362	49,189,124	35,321,248	31,312,359	24,942,703	29,177,406
Apr.	43,550,996	41,423,764	43,822,233	27,825,970	22,028,943	23,267,929	25,786,835
May	38,415,142	37,835,273	39,270,524	24,338,714	25,271,459	21,238,205	21,479,380
June	31,818,266	33,368,378	34,338,670	21,578,609	20,005,692	18,499,675	20,407,485
July	34,847,750	33,024,594	32,982,434	20,004,049	19,484,027	19,293,619	22,357,020
Aug.	36,043,679	31,917,630	31,425,931	23,626,505	19,613,146	18,137,060	21,714,495
Sept.	35,230,456	33,202,986	30,972,318	20,447,571	16,243,870	16,641,882	20,413,537
Oct.	36,838,614	35,501,530	30,734,458	21,465,382	18,236,272	19,785,871	20,439,136
Nov.	35,682,577	35,287,641	31,167,708	22,454,200	20,114,346	20,871,584	22,808,497
Dec.	42,669,915	40,514,368	39,190,506	27,626,439	23,895,879	27,969,288	30,133,628
Totals:	$463,612,762	$452,017,026	$442,143,311	$316,897,733	$275,652,060	$259,159,945	$293,357,245

[a] Source: Journal of Commerce for years 1875 to 1915; National Board of Fire Underwriters for years 1916 to 1935, adding 25 per cent for unreported and uninsured losses.

[b] Source: National Board of Fire Underwriters, Published in the Journal of Commerce.

Both tables are reprinted, by permission, from the *Spectator Fire Index, 1936*, p. 128.

TABLE 41

THE DECLINE IN PREMIUM RATES

Year	Average Premium Rate[a]
1900	1.03
1901	1.07
1902	1.16
1903	1.19
1904	1.18
1905	1.16
1906	1.16
1907	1.18
1908	1.18
1909	1.15
1910	1.11
1911	1.10
1912	1.08
1913	1.06
1914	1.03
1915	1.05
1916	1.02
1917	1.07
1918	1.06
1919	1.07
1920	1.02
1921	1.05
1922	0.99
1923	0.97
1924	0.97
1925	0.97
1926	0.93
1927	0.95
1928	0.92
1929	0.89
1930	0.86
1931	0.81
1932	0.78
1933	0.74
1934	0.72
1935	0.71

[a] Source: *Fire Insurance by States*, 1900–1935, p. 119, and earlier issues, by *The Weekly Underwriter*. (New York: Underwriter Printing & Publishing Co.)

business must trim their hoped-for profits accordingly. What could be more natural?

With hundreds of companies and thousands of types of buildings and contents to be insured, some organized pricing mechanism for publishing quotations is needed to assure buyer and seller alike that the price agreed on is the going rate for the market. If the average transaction in insurance ran into the thousands of dollars, as in wheat and cotton, or stocks and bonds, each transaction could be made the subject of a separate bargain, as on the Board of Trade and the Stock Exchange, but in fact the average premium in fire insurance is far too small to make this worth while. Likewise, if the number of sellers and the classifications of risk were few, and if purchases were made every day, the buyer would find it feasible to shop around for the best price before buying. But as things are, neither the practices of the stock market nor of the gasoline market are suitable to the insurance market, and so some other organization is needed to promulgate prices. This need is now supplied by the Eastern Underwriters' Association, the Southeastern Underwriters' Association, the Western Underwriters' Association, the Board of Fire Underwriters of the Pacific, and other underwriters' organizations.

There is a further question, however, a question harder to answer, which is concerned with whether the established pricing mechanism that is forced on the fire-insurance business by its own peculiarities may not be abused or exploited by the stock companies for their own advantage. Any large measure of extortion, of course, would seem to be prevented by a number of forces, such as competition from the mutual companies, foreign companies, and others not members of the associations, and such as the suspicious eye of the insurance commissioners, the threat of state laws regulating premiums, and the tendency for member companies themselves to evade their own rules [10] if a particular class of business becomes too profitable. Consequently the result seems to be that for the *average* risk the premium rate is not too high, and certainly not as high as one would expect if the companies conspired together to get a monopoly price.

Even for particular classes of risks, the workings of competition seem to be quite effective in producing premium rates that are closely in accord with actuarial experience, with the result that a company can gain but little by picking and choosing between various kinds of *buildings* to be insured. But between various *persons* to be insured no such indifference of choice is to be found, for some persons are honest and others quite the reverse in making out their claims for damage after a fire. Hence the essence of successful underwriting is to minimize the moral hazard, as it is called; no other underwriting problem is half so important as this. Because the local agent is better qualified than anyone else to know which customers are honest and which are not, which are careful and which are irresponsible, which are prosperous and which would like to "sell out to the insurance company," the selection of good local agents is the most effective way of keeping losses down. In the long run, the best company is the one that has the best agency system.

10. THE ECONOMICS OF THE INSURANCE BUSINESS

If it is true that gambling is irrational, and that the loss of a dollar hurts more than the gain of a dollar helps, then a fee for risk-bearing should reasonably be expected wherever risks are borne in the economic world. Thus, if the stockholder in a fire insurance company runs the risk of losing all his investment because of a conflagration, he should expect to be specially compensated for submitting

---

[10] One form of such evasion is the payment by the companies of certain expenses of their agents in lieu of the payment of higher commissions to them.

to this risk. Insurance commissioners and company executives recognize that the social disutility of a series of underwriting losses such as might eventually impair the solvency of the insurance companies far exceeds the social disutility of a series of underwriting profits that might come from slightly overcharging the public. Hence enlightened regulatory authorities usually err on the side of safety, and make sure that the premiums will be adequate to pay both expenses and losses. This attitude accounts for some measure of underwriting profit in the business.

Underwriting profits as reported, however, are greater than can be accounted for in this way. The explanation is probably that what is labeled underwriting profit and reckoned a reward for risk-taking is really in the nature of interest on a certain invisible asset not shown on the balance sheet but commonly known as "good will." If good will is defined as the expense of organizing a company, training its personnel, and building up its agency connections, then good will is a costly asset, and no one will set out to acquire it without some reason to hope for a fair return on his investment once made. By the very nature of the insurance business, the return on an investment in good will must come from profits on underwriting.

How much the good will of Phoenix in particular has cost over the years gone by would be hard to estimate, but if a return of 5 per cent on the investment was fair, and if the company made 5 per cent likewise from underwriting, on the average, then the implied value of the good will would be nearly the same as the annual premium income, or from eight to ten million dollars. Such a sum is not absurdly high, for an insurance company sells a service, not a ware, and produces with men, not machines; hence its assets, aside from securities (which "pay their own keep") must of necessity consist of the intangible items that are known as good will but never are shown on the balance sheet.

To the extent, however, that the stockholders in financing the organization and growth of an insurance company must sink their capital not only in good will but also in demand deposits and receivables on which no interest can be obtained, the underwriting profit actually received represents a return on other outlays besides good will. But to the extent that the stockholders gain by receiving premiums before paying losses and by investing these revenues in stocks and bonds during the interval, they should expect to suffer a compensating reduction in underwriting profits, if their return is to be fixed strictly in accord with economic theory. As regards the balance between non-interest-bearing assets, like cash and receivables, on the one hand, and non-interest-bearing liabilities, like unearned premiums and unpaid losses, on the other hand, the liabilities outweigh the assets, and the stockholders tend to gain on balance from interest items; hence on balance that part of the underwriting profit ascribable to the visible peculiarities of the balance sheet ought to be negative, and the total underwriting profit ought to be correspondingly reduced.

The amount by which in theory the total underwriting profit should be so reduced is large, as appears in the calculation in Table 42. The excess of liabilities shown in this table represents money not belonging to the stockholders, but entrusted to them in the ordinary course of business, and available for investment by them in earning assets. Let us call the earning assets so obtained "free money," because no interest has to be paid on it to its real owners. Since this free money can be invested at the same rate as other money, namely, $4\frac{1}{2}$ per cent, it should bring in "free income" of some $220,000. Under competition this free income would tend to be returned to the public in the form of lower premium rates.

If the normal underwriting profit is 5.66 per cent of premiums written, or $1\frac{1}{2}$ per cent of invested assets, as computed in Section 9, it would have amounted to $468,000 in the year 1935, while the free income for the same year, according to the computations above, would have amounted to $220,000. Had there been no free income, however, it would seem reasonable to believe that normal underwriting profit would have been $220,000 larger, or $688,000 in all. This latter figure represents the underwriting profit which

TABLE 42

FROM STATEMENT FOR STOCKHOLDERS, JANUARY 1, 1936

Cash on hand and in Banks	$ 4,028,000
Cash in hands of Agents, etc.	1,488,000
Re-Insurance due on Paid Losses	7,000
Interest and Rents due and accrued	188,000
Non-Interest-Bearing Assets	$ 5,711,000
Reserve for Unadjusted Losses	$ 1,049,000
Reserve for Re-Insurance	8,031,000
Reserve for Taxes and Miscellaneous Items	913,000
Dividend Payable January 2, 1936	600,000
Non-Interest-Bearing Liabilities	$10,593,000
Excess of Liabilities	$ 4,882,000

the company's good will might theoretically be expected to bring in if there were no "free money" to augment its earnings.

By showing average underwriting profit of 5.66 per cent of premiums written, Phoenix has made a very fine record for itself.[11] Apparently the fire-insurance business, like most others, has its intra-marginal and its marginal firms so far as managerial skill is concerned. Phoenix today is

[11] Phoenix has escaped casualty underwriting losses, because the Phoenix fleet is unusual in that it contains no casualty companies. In contrast to *fire* underwriting, which has been generally profitable, *casualty* underwriting, in spite of its rapid growth, has been distinctly unprofitable at times. Usually a fast-growing business, because it must attract new capital, or because it must finance its growth out of earnings, is more profitable than a slow-growing business, but such has not been the case recently with casualty as compared with fire underwriting. During the depression Phoenix also escaped without serious *investment* losses, because its investment policies were shrewd and conservative during the preceding stock market boom.

clearly an intra-marginal company, and seems likely to stay so as long as good management within the company can train new good management, or recruit it from without, to replace itself when it is gone.[12]

II.   THE INVESTMENT VALUE WITH GROWTH COMPLETED

For convenience in exposition, let us assume in the present section that the growth of the Phoenix Insurance Company has been completed; later we can remove this restriction in our reasoning.

[12] Although life insurance is not the subject of this chapter, some comment on the economics of the life-insurance business may be of interest at this point. In contrast to fire insurance, with its modest but positive underwriting profit, life insurance has exhibited a profit both large and persistent, at least until recently. Little trace of this profit, to be sure, is visible in the published reports of the life-insurance companies, because the accounting methods required by law are only designed to show if the companies could be liquidated without loss to policy-holders, and fail to reveal the investment made in the acquisition of new business. Acquisition costs, according to the law, must be charged to expense, not to assets; hence the larger these outlays, the less the apparent earnings now, but the more the potential earnings later. Yet regardless of the apparent earnings, the real earnings of the life-insurance companies are large, and large by force of economic causes arising from the very nature of the business and the way the industry is organized. The business itself has enjoyed a long and rapid growth. During a period stretching over the seventy years preceding the depression, life insurance first grew rapidly in popularity, and then took on a whole new lease of life when the rise in the cost of living caused by the War forced policy-holders to make a corresponding increase in the amount of life insurance carried. The industry during much of this period has been dominated by the mutuals, who have had to finance their growth out of earnings, because they had no stockholders from whom they could secure new capital by the offer of rights. Hence the profit-margin in the business has had to be large enough to make the growth of the business self-financing. Because the public has insisted on insuring mainly in mutual companies, the public has been obliged to pay the price of its prejudices in the form of higher premiums (even after allowing for dividends returned to policy-holders). It has been as though the consumers of electricity had insisted on forming their own clubs for generating electric power, and had shunned the capital market, thus placing on themselves the necessity of paying rates high enough to finance the growth of their business wholly out of earnings and without recourse to the bond market at all. Under such circumstances the rate of profit in the utility business would have been, perforce, far higher than it need have been, and under similar circumstances the rate of profit in the life insurance business has likewise been higher than it need have been if the preferences of the public had been

Should investment income [13] be 4½ per cent and underwriting profit 1½ per cent of earning assets,[14] as estimated in Sections 7 and 8, total earnings would be 6 per cent thereof. Earnings per share would then be 6 per cent of $87¾, or $5.27. From these earnings, what dividend could be paid?

If the assets of the company consisted of bricks and mortar, subject to obsolescence, some portion of its earnings, in addition to depreciation, would need to be reinvested in plant to maintain the *status quo* of earning power, a fact made all too plain by the past experience of industrial enterprises.[15] But since the company is not an industrial company and owns no physical plant save its own office building, and since the cost of keeping its organization up to date is charged not to assets but to expenses, the company would not need to make any provision for reinvestment, nor pass any of its earnings to surplus, once it had ceased to grow. Instead, all of its earnings could be distributed as dividends. Earnings of $5.27 a share, therefore, would mean dividends of $5.27 a share, and the investment value of the stock could then be found simply by capitalizing these earnings and this dividend.

Let us assume, for the sake of argument, that interest rates in general will return to the level of the 1920's as soon as general business recovery carries business activity and commodity prices back to the level of 1926 or thereabouts. Under these circumstances the stocks of non-growing companies free from bonded debt and from most of the hazards

different. The high profit has made the shares of the stock companies very profitable as long-pull investments, and has enabled the mutuals to sink large sums in expanding their membership.

[13] For a discussion of the effect on investment value of assuming an interest rate lower than 4½ per cent, see § 14 below.

[14] Earning assets are here assumed to be equal to liquidating value, for the reason given in § 13, where the value of l is computed.

[15] See Chapter VI, § 3, and Chapter XXII on U. S. Steel.

of obsolescence should yield about 5 per cent.[16] To those stockholders who considered 5 per cent a fair return on their money, an annual dividend of $5.27 would be worth 105, and to them the investment value of Phoenix would be 105, as compared with the current market price of 90. Let us call the investment value as so computed the static investment value. As we have seen, its formula is

(8a) $$V = \frac{\gamma}{i} = \frac{\pi}{i}$$

where

V = investment value

γ = earnings per share   = $5.27

π = "pure dividend" per share = $5.27

i = interest rate   = 5%

with the result that

$$V = \frac{\$5.27}{5\%} = \$105$$

12. THE GROWTH OF THE PHOENIX INSURANCE COMPANY

Ever since the Phoenix Insurance Company was organized in 1854 it has been growing steadily, and to say that its growth is now completed would be foolhardy unless supported by good reasons.

Mainly because the insurance business as a whole has grown, Phoenix itself has grown. Although the company and its two main subsidiaries, the Connecticut Fire and the Equitable Fire and Marine, have done somewhat better than the industry as a whole, their growth has been by no means largely at the expense of competitors, as Table 43 shows.

[16] The rate of 5 per cent chosen for Phoenix is less than that of 5¼ per cent chosen for U. S. Steel and General Motors because fire insurance companies have a better record of longevity than manufacturing companies.

TABLE 43

RANKING OF THE THREE LEADING MEMBERS OF THE PHOENIX FLEET[a]

Year	Phoenix Assets	Phoenix Premiums[b]	Connecticut Assets	Connecticut Premiums[b]	Equitable F. & M. Assets
1901	11	12	20	19	..
1902	10	13	19	19	..
1903	10	13	19	19	..
1904	10	13	20	20	..
1905	10	11	21	20	..
1906	10	13	19	18	..
1907	10	12	20	19	..
1908	10	13	20	18	..
1909	10	12	20	19	..
1910	11	12	20	20	..
1911	11	12	21	21	..
1912	11	14	20	23	..
1913	9	11	25	21	..
1914	9	13	25	23	..
1915	9	13	27	23	..
1916	9	13	27	25	..
1917	9	14	24	23	..
1918	10	13	24	23	..
1919	10	14	24	23	..
1920	10	15	24	24	77
1921	10	13	23	24	79
1922	10	14	24	25	77
1923	10	13	25	24	..
1924	10	16	28	27	78
1925	10	17	29	29	76
1926	10	15	30	32	78
1927	10	16	29	31	76
1928	11	16	29	..	78
1929	11	16	30	30	75
1930	11	17	28	31	75
1931	11	16	27	28	71
1932	11	18	27	34	71
1933	10	18	25	33	..
1934	9	18	21	31	71
1935	9	17	24	32	70

[a] Source: *Standard Fire Insurance Tables* for 1935, 1925, 1915, and 1905, published by Standard Publishing Co., Oliver Building, Boston, Mass.

[b] Premiums on fire risks only.

The past growth of the fire-insurance business as a whole has resulted from two factors: (1) the increase in the number and size of insurable buildings and contents, attendant upon the rise in the country's population and its per capita wealth; (2) the increase in the percentage of insurable property that is protected by insurance, attendant upon the spread of the conviction that insurance is a necessity for protecting business and personal credit. Offsetting these two factors has been a decline in the average premium rate, attendant upon the development of fire-resistant ways of constructing buildings and more effective methods of fire fighting. Lower premium rates have meant less income from the same amount of insured property.

Phoenix itself has actually grown, in terms of premium income, after adjustment for the change in the purchasing power of money, at the rate of only 1½ per cent per annum during the period 1910–1935. The national income, on the other hand, has grown at the rate of 3 per cent per annum during this same period,[17] while population has grown at the slower rate [18] of 1½ per cent.

The assets of the companies themselves have grown faster than their volume of business written, if Phoenix is a fair example, for a much larger capital and surplus are employed today in relation to premium income than was the custom a generation ago. But have not the companies by now attained all the financial strength that can be used to advantage?

An examination of the two factors causing growth in the past would suggest that only one will be operative in the future. The companies will continue to benefit from the increase in the national wealth, but they can hardly hope

[17] Cf. Willford I. King, *The National Income and Its Purchasing Power* (New York: National Bureau of Economic Research, 1933), Table IX, p. 77.
[18] *Ibid.*, Table I, p. 47.

to make the use of fire insurance more general than at present, when at least 75 per cent of the potential business is already being written, and the market, therefore, may be considered 75 per cent saturated — a figure high in comparison with other industries. Should another rise in the general price level occur, insurance values and premiums written should respond again, as they did during and after the War, but after the rise was over the money received and the dividends paid would have less purchasing power than now, with the result that the insurance stockholder would receive no real benefit from the inflation. Thus in the last analysis only one factor, the growth of the country as a whole, seems still to be at work to induce the growth of the fire-insurance business.

Offsetting this favorable factor are the recent great technological innovations in fire fighting, represented by telephones, motorized apparatus, and paved highways. The introduction of these improvements is only now being completed, as witnessed by the increasing speed of fire engines within the last few years. Since it usually takes many years for important inventions to produce all their results, it would seem that the effect of these innovations on premium rates is still to be felt in full.

Yet so persistent has been the growth of Phoenix in the past, and what is more important for our purposes, so impressive was its growth during the decade of the 1920's, when conditions were much the same as at present, that the possibility of some further growth should not be too quickly dismissed. In particular, since Phoenix does such a small fraction [19] of the total business (less than ¼ per cent), con-

[19] Even the largest company in the industry, the Home Insurance Company, does scarcely 1 per cent of the total business. It is indeed remarkable that the industry should harbor such a multiplicity of relatively small producers, and in this respect it differs notably from most other businesses transacted on a nation-wide scale.

ceivably it could achieve its growth in the future by slowly taking a little, business away from each of a good many competitors, without disturbing the peace of the industry.

13. THE INVESTMENT VALUE WITH GROWTH EXPECTED

Without some allowance for future growth, therefore, no appraisal of this insurance stock would be complete. To allow for growth, one should use the same formulas as would be applied to a public utility,[20] where growth in the future is likewise a dominating consideration. Just as public utilities can be evaluated by assuming "a fair return on a fair- value," so too may insurance stocks by assuming a known return on their known assets. Bank stocks may also be evaluated on the same assumption and by the same formulas. And whatever the rate of growth or duration of growth, allowance for this growth may be made by specific parameters in the formulas — something we have never been able to do heretofore. Growth having been a main source of profit in the holding of bank and insurance stocks in the past, the new method represents a great advance in the art of Investment Analysis.

Suitable formulas to use are (67a), (75a), (79a), and (90a). Since in the special case where the variable w in these formulas equals unity these formulas take on the simpler aspect of (67b), (75b), (75c), (79b), (79c), (90b), (90c), and (90d), we should first look to see what the value of w will turn out to be. To begin with,

(15) $w = uv$, by definition

where

(14a) $u = 1 + g$, by definition

(2) $v = \dfrac{1}{1 + i}$, by definition

g = yearly growth in assets

i = interest rate on money

[20] Chapter XI, § 1.

We have already assumed, in our earlier calculations, that

$$i = 5\%$$

with the result that

$$v = \frac{1}{1.05}$$

If we now assume, for reasons to be given shortly, that

$$g = 5\%$$

with the result that

$$u = 1 + g = 1.05$$

we may apply the simplified formulas mentioned above, for then

(15) $$w = uv = \frac{1.05}{1.05} = 1$$

and the condition that w shall be unity is fulfilled.

To assume that growth will equal 5 per cent per annum is reasonable enough, for the parent company has already shown itself capable of growing at the average rate of 5.55 per cent year after year for twenty-five years, during the period from 1910 [21] to 1935. If the assets for the two dates are deflated by the wholesale price index of the United States Bureau of Labor Statistics,[22] the net growth for the period turns out to have been exactly 5 per cent a year, compounded annually. Even if the company's portfolio were selling at a somewhat higher price today than twenty-five years ago, no important part of the company's annual growth could be accounted for in this way, because the total appreciation for the period would have to be divided by 25. Moreover, most of the investments in the portfolio are bonds, the average prices for which have advanced but little during this period if both good and bad issues are considered.

[21] The calculation is made to begin with the year 1910 so as to avoid the complications caused by the absence of subsidiaries prior to that date.
[22] Given in Appendix II, Table VII.

The book value of the stock today, as required by our formulas, is the total equity of the stockholders, and is thus the same as the "consolidated liquidating value" already computed; therefore we may write

$$C_o = 87\tfrac{3}{4}$$

A bank or insurance company, like a public utility, benefits from the factor of leverage to the extent that its earning assets exceed its stockholders' equity. If earning assets should be less than book value, however, leverage would work in the opposite way, and reduce, rather than increase the stockholders' gains. Let us see what is the value for the leverage l in the case of Phoenix. With a book value, including equities, of $C_o = 87\tfrac{3}{4}$, and earning assets of $A_o = 84\tfrac{1}{2}$, the stock enjoys a leverage of only

(40a) $$l = \frac{A_o}{C_o} = \frac{84\tfrac{1}{2}}{87\tfrac{3}{4}} = 0.963, \text{ for 1935.}$$

This low leverage is based on 1935 figures; 1934 figures would have shown a leverage of

$$l = \frac{78.39}{76.13} = 1.030, \text{ for 1934.}$$

Apparently the leverage varies slightly from year to year, and some approximate figure like

$$l = 1, \text{ on the average,}$$

would be the best choice.

The pure dividend rate, as a percentage of book value, may be computed by means of the following formula:

(46a) $$p = c - r$$
where
(52b) $$c = l\left(a - b + \frac{b}{l} \right)$$

and
$$l = 1$$
with the result
$$c = a$$
Hence in this particular case

(46b) $p = a - r$, when $c = a$

We have already assumed that the interest and dividend income of Phoenix in the years to come, plus its underwriting profits, expressed as a percentage of earning assets, will be
$$a = 4\tfrac{1}{2}\% + 1\tfrac{1}{2}\% = 6\%$$
Returning to the formulas

(46a) $p = c - r$

and

(46b) $p = a - r$, if $c = a$

we must assume that the company will keep the same relative financial structure as it grows, with the result that

(54) $r = g$

as proved in Chapter XI, § 1. Therefore formula (46b) becomes

(46c) $p = a - g$
$$= 6\% - 5\%$$
$$= 1\%$$

Accordingly, the pure dividend which the company can now pay without obliging itself to assess its stockholders later in the guise of offering them rights [23] is

(28b) $\pi_0 = pC_0$
$$= (1\%)\,(\$87\tfrac{3}{4})$$
$$= 88\cancel{c}$$

[23] For a discussion of the true nature of rights, see Chapter V, § 5.

Incidentally, the present dividend rate of $2.00 regular plus 50¢ extra, or $2.50 in all, is nearly three times the pure dividend of 88¢ just computed. Evidently the company cannot continue to pay the present dividend for long without getting some of its outlay back through the issuance of rights if it is to maintain exactly the present leverage. Once the company's growth is completed, however, dividends can be increased to the full rate indicated by the then-attained earnings per share, for then no reinvestment of earnings will be required any longer, as pointed out in Section 11.

Let us assume that the stock, at the end of the period for which it is to be held, when growth is supposed to have ended, can be sold at a price to yield 5 per cent. In that event, the proper formula to use would be

(90e) $$V_o = n\pi_0 + \frac{\gamma_0}{i}$$

This last formula is easy to interpret, because it says that if, taking compound interest into account, dividends π_t and static investment value $\frac{\gamma_t}{i}$ both increase just fast enough each year for n years to offset their lower present worth, then the factor of interest can be neglected, and the investment value of the stock with growth expected becomes just equal to n times the present dividend, plus the investment value of the stock in the absence of growth.

The pure dividend π_n that is to be expected at the end of n years, when growth will have been completed, is

$$\pi_n = \gamma_n = \gamma_0 u^n$$

If one thinks that growth at the rate of 5 per cent will persist for four years, he will write

$$n = 4$$

Such an assumption would require the parent company's total assets to go from \$41,433,000 reported at the end of 1935 to a total of \$50,362,000 at the end of 1939. The latter sum would be only 11 per cent greater than the peak assets of \$45,161,000 in 1929. It is implied, of course, that the subsidiaries will grow in proportion. With the likelihood of business recovery and rising commodity prices during the next four years, such an estimate of the company's future growth is not extravagant. Let us see what investment value the stock would have in this case:

Summarizing our data, we have

$$n = 4$$

$$\pi_0 = 88\cent$$

$$\frac{\gamma_0}{i} = 105 \qquad \text{(See § 11)}$$

If these data are inserted in the formula

(90e) $$V_0 = n\pi_0 + \frac{\gamma_0}{i}$$

we get

$$V_0 = (4)\ (88\cent) + 105$$
$$= 3\tfrac{1}{2} + 105$$
$$= 108\tfrac{1}{2}$$

Were one to discount the future ten years ahead, instead of only four, the estimated investment value would be increased to

(90e) $$V_0 = n\pi_0 + \frac{\gamma_0}{i}$$

$$= (10)\ (88\cent) + 105$$
$$= 9 + 105$$
$$= 114;$$

while if one were to discount the future not at all, the estimated investment value would be

$$V = (0) \ (88\cent) + 105$$
$$= 105$$

Thus the present market price of 90 for the stock, failing to discount the future at all, is too low, providing our assumptions are correct. Some price between $108\frac{1}{2}$ and 114, such as 110 let us say, would seem to represent the best estimate of the true worth of Phoenix, and this is our final choice for the investment value of that stock.

It should be carefully noted, however, that for simplicity in exposition, all considerations relating to the cyclical character of the loss ratio and the bond market are pushed to one side in the foregoing discussion. In practice, of course, the buyer of an insurance stock today should give full weight to these considerations, and should allow for the possibility of (1) a temporary period of reduced underwriting profits,[24] and (2) lower bond prices some years hence.[25] So great, in fact, is the likelihood of lower bond prices a few years from now, that a depreciation in the portfolios of insurance companies should definitely be counted upon by the buyer of insurance stocks today.

14. INVESTMENT VALUE RECOMPUTED WITH ALTERNATIVE PREMISES

Some of the premises in the foregoing calculation are uncertain enough to warrant recomputation of the value of the stock on alternative premises, in order that we may see if any wide margin of error lies hidden in our final estimate.

First let us see what difference it would make to assume a slower rate of growth and a lower rate of interest. Should growth for the company at 4 per cent a year instead of 5

<hr>

[24] Cf. § 8 above.   [25] Cf. Chapter XX, §§ 10 and 22.

per cent, and interest for the stockholder at 4 per cent instead of 5 per cent, both be postulated, the rate of growth and the rate of interest would still remain equal, and the simplified formulas (75d) and (90e) could still be used. The lower rate of interest assumed as a fair return on the stock would imply a lower return also on the company's own invested assets, a return of $3\frac{1}{2}$ per cent, let us say, instead of $4\frac{1}{2}$ per cent, making the ratio of investment income plus underwriting income to invested assets 5 per cent, instead of 6 per cent as in our original assumptions. This lower total return, however, would not change the net or pure dividend, π_0, from the figure of 88¢ already computed, as the following calculation shows:

(46c)
$$p = a - g$$
$$= 5\% - 4\%$$
$$= 1\%, \text{ as before}$$
$$\pi_0 = pC_0$$
$$= (1\%)(87\tfrac{3}{4})$$
$$= 88\phi, \text{ as before}$$

Evidently in formula

(90e)
$$V_0 = n\pi_0 + \frac{\gamma_0}{i}$$

the first term, $n\pi_0$, would remain the same in spite of those altered assumptions. Likewise the second term, $\dfrac{\gamma_0}{i}$, would remain substantially the same, its new value being

$$\frac{\gamma_0}{i} = \frac{cC_0}{i} = \frac{aC_0}{i} = \frac{5\%C_0}{4\%} = 1.25C_0$$

compared with its former value of

$$\frac{\gamma_0}{i} = \frac{cC_0}{i} = \frac{aC_0}{i} = \frac{6\%C_0}{5\%} = 1.20C_0$$

The increase in the second term would thus be only $4\frac{1}{6}$ per cent, with the result that the increase in the *total* of the first and second terms would be less than 4 per cent. Clearly these particular changes in the assumptions, namely a 1 per cent slower rate of growth and a 1 per cent lower return on invested assets, together with a 1 per cent lower yield on the stock, would cause almost no change in the investment value of the stock; whatever change did occur would be in the direction of making the stock worth slightly more.

Second, let us see what difference it would make to change the basis of the terminal value, and use a different formula, with a different assumption concerning the selling price at the end of the period of expected growth. Having chosen heretofore a terminal value equal to "investment value with growth completed," we have implied thereby that the ending of growth would not reduce the profitableness of the fire insurance business. Such an assumption is dangerous. There exists a strong tendency in the fire insurance business for competition to drive the underwriting profits down to zero, or even make them slightly negative, and this tendency might become overpowering if the cessation of growth relieved the need for further outlays on good will. Should the underwriting profits of Phoenix disappear, total earnings would drop from 6 per cent to $4\frac{1}{2}$ per cent of invested assets, according to our previous assumptions (see §§ 7 and 8). In this event, the terminal value, or selling price at the end, required by our formulas, should not exceed the liquidating value at the end, and in this case, therefore, the proper formula to use would be

(75d) $$V_0 = n\pi_0 + C_0$$

where

$$C_0 = \text{liquidating value now} = 87\tfrac{3}{4}$$

Assuming a four-year period of growth, the stock would be worth today

$$V_o = (4)\ (88\cent) + 87\tfrac{3}{4}$$
$$= 91\tfrac{1}{4}$$

or, assuming a ten-year period

$$V_o = (10)\ (88\cent) + 87\tfrac{3}{4}$$
$$= 96\tfrac{1}{2}$$

If the more modest assumptions concerning future growth and interest rates, mentioned earlier, are combined with the more modest assumption, just mentioned, concerning terminal value, no further reduction in investment value results, for our last formula

(75d) $$V_o = n\pi_o + C_o$$

is such that the 1 per cent reduction in rates of growth and interest are offsetting as regards the first term, and irrelevant as regards the second.

Evidently the foregoing two changes in the premises do not give rise to a sufficient difference in the results to cast serious doubt on the figure of 110 selected earlier as our best estimate for the investment value of the stock.

The reason why, in the case of Phoenix, the new methods of appraisal using our formulas and the old methods of appraisal using liquidating value give much the same results, and no striking difference in estimated value appears in spite of the highly-refined character of our new formulas, will be brought out in the section to follow.

15. THE EARLIER IMPORTANCE OF GROWTH

The effect of future growth in adding to the investment value of Phoenix today turns out to be surprisingly small, as pointed out in the preceding section. The reason is that today this company's ratio of earnings to invested assets is low. Back in the years 1901–1910, when underwriting yielded a profit of 10 per cent of premiums written, and premiums themselves amounted to 50 per cent of total assets, there could be shown an underwriting profit equal to 5 per cent of total assets, or $7\frac{1}{2}$ per cent of the stock-holders' own equity. Even though at that time interest rates were low, being only $3\frac{1}{2}$ per cent, nevertheless the total return on invested assets in those days reached 11 per cent, i.e., $7\frac{1}{2}$ per cent + $3\frac{1}{2}$ per cent, instead of only 6 per cent as now. Hence the pure dividend rate [26] p was much higher, as shown by formula

(46a)
$$p = c - r$$
$$= 11\% - 5\%$$
$$= 6\% \text{ of liquidating value (not par value)}$$

If the company's growth at the beginning of that period had been discounted ahead for a period of ten years, with the result that

$$n = 10$$

and if the stock had a liquidating value then of

$$C_0 = 203\tfrac{1}{2},$$

then the revised investment value for the stock at that time would have been estimated to be

(75d)
$$V_0 = n\pi_0 + C_0$$
$$= npC_0 + C_0$$
$$= (np + 1)C_0$$
$$= [(10)(6\%) + 100\%]C_0$$
$$= (160\%)C_0$$
$$= (160\%)(203\tfrac{1}{2})$$
$$= 326$$

[26] The *actual* dividend in 1901 was $14 a share, as compared with the "pure dividend" of $\pi_0 = pC_0 = (6\%)(203\tfrac{1}{2}) = \$12.20$.

Evidently a generation ago [27] the company was able to do business in such a way as to make growth a much more important factor in appraising its stock than it is now, for then [28] Phoenix, according to our formulas, was really worth 160 per cent of its liquidating value, whereas now it is worth only 125 per cent of this value.

Other stocks than Phoenix would show other results than Phoenix today. Many bank stocks, for instance, if appraised by means of formulas (75d) or (90e) above, which take account of future growth, would show much higher values than if appraised by some more common method that neglected future growth altogether. Hence we must still conclude that the only correct way to appraise a stock like Phoenix is by means of the new formulas which this chapter has been designed to illustrate.

[27] The actual market price at that time was less than 80 per cent of the liquidating value $C_o = 203\frac{1}{2}$.

[28] The value of 326 per share computed for this date is higher than the present value per share, of course, because the number of shares has been increased by rights and a split-up since then.

PART II

POST MORTEMS

CHAPTER XXIV

AMERICAN TELEPHONE IN 1930

I. LEARNING BY ONE'S MISTAKES

The old saying that "experience keeps a dear school, but fools will learn in no other" is untrue. Fools will not learn from experience; only wise men will, and rare is the man so wise as to go back and study experience carefully and in detail. Yet post-mortem examinations afford one of the best ways of learning how to avoid mistakes and do better in the future. Just as army strategists study military history with great care, and refight in imagination the campaigns of famous generals, so should the thoughtful investor study financial history with great care and remake in imagination the transactions of former markets.

To students of Investment Value, a reëxamination of the prices of public utility stocks in the spring of 1930 will prove most instructive. At that time stocks were at the top of their rally after the collapse from the 1929 boom. The Dow-Jones industrial average was making a peak of 294 on April 17, after having fallen from 381 on September 3, 1929, to 199 on November 13, 1929. Annual reports for the year 1929 were at hand, and with their aid the "New Era" enthusiast could plot the supposed trend of growth of his favorite companies. President Hoover had induced many big corporations to make unusually large outlays on plant, with the aim of supporting the capital-goods industries. The sales and earnings of the General Electric Company, the leading maker of equipment for the utilities and their customers, were running almost as high as in the previous year, and its stock, after a 4-for-1 split-up, at 95 was climbing up to where it bade fair to pass the 1929 high of 403. Many investment experts at this time considered the 1929 collapse a "technical reaction," because business was thought to be "fundamentally sound." Even among professional economists there were few indeed who understood the forces then at work to deflate the general price level and produce one of the worst depressions in history. Hence it would hardly have been fair to expect the investment analysts themselves to reckon on a substantial change in trend when forecasting future earnings. A level-headed extrapolation of past trends, however, might reasonably have been expected of them. Let us see what such an uninspired view of the future would have led to in the way of estimated fair prices for certain well-known utility stocks, of which we shall first consider American Telephone.

2. THE NET DIVIDEND ON THE STOCK

Although the stock of the American Telephone and Telegraph Company had not had such a phenomenal rise in the boom as some others, the 1929 peak being only $310\frac{1}{4}$ as compared with the 1918 low of $90\frac{5}{8}$, the stock was a favorite with investors. With 469,801 stockholders on its books,[1] the company had a wider distribution for its shares than any other corporation in the country. Although the stock, with a dividend of $9.00, yielded only $3\frac{1}{4}$ per cent at its 1930 high of $274\frac{1}{4}$, investors considered its periodic offerings of rights as equivalent to additional cash dividends. Such a table as Table 44 was often to be seen in newspaper articles and investors' manuals, and clearly implies how investors were accustomed to think of rights.

In 1930 the erroneous view that rights were income was still almost universal, and almost no one looked on them as

[1] See the *Annual Report of the American Telephone and Telegraph Company, for the Year 1929*, p. 19.

an assessment plus a stock dividend. In truth, the net dividend that could have been paid by the company, with the rate of growth and percentage of funded debt of those years, was only 80¢ a share, as will be shown by the calculations to follow; but few people realized then how the

TABLE 44

RIGHTS TO AMERICAN TELEPHONE AND TELEGRAPH STOCKHOLDERS [a]

Accruing to Stock of Record	Terms of Offering	Value of Rights High	Value of Rights Low
June 12, 1901	1 for 3	18	15 1/8
June 30, 1902	1 for 4	15 3/4	14 1/2
June 30, 1903	1 for 5	6 1/2	4 15/16
June 15, 1907	1 for 6	76¢	25¢
June 30, 1911	1 for 5	7 1/4	5 1/4
Dec. 11, 1916	1 for 10	2 1/8	1 7/8
May 20, 1921	1 for 5	7/8	1/8
Sept. 8, 1922	1 for 5	4 5/8	2 7/8
June 10, 1924	1 for 5	4 7/16	2 15/16
June 8, 1926	1 for 6	6 11/16	5 3/4
June 1, 1928	1 for 6	16 1/8	11 3/8
May 10, 1929	1 for 6	8	3
May 23, 1930	1 for 6	23 1/8	16

[a] All of these offerings were of new stock at par except in 1929, when bonds convertible at 180 the next year were offered.

company's practice of taking back with one hand what it doled out with the other concealed a serious dearth of present dividend-paying power. Had people known this, doubtless the stock would never have sold so high, because these same people would surely have failed to understand that low dividend-paying power now reflected only the hunger of a profitable business for more capital, and was really an augury of higher dividends to come.

3. THE RATE OF GROWTH OF THE COMPANY

When people looked at earnings per share and rate of growth, they came nearer to making a sound appraisal of the stock than when they looked at dividends. Consolidated

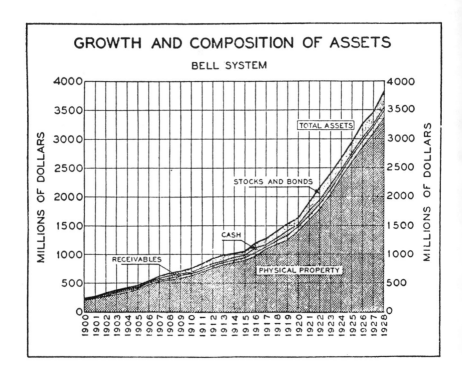

GROWTH AND COMPOSITION OF ASSETS

BELL SYSTEM

TOTAL ASSETS

STOCKS AND BONDS

CASH

RECEIVABLES

PHYSICAL PROPERTY

MILLIONS OF DOLLARS

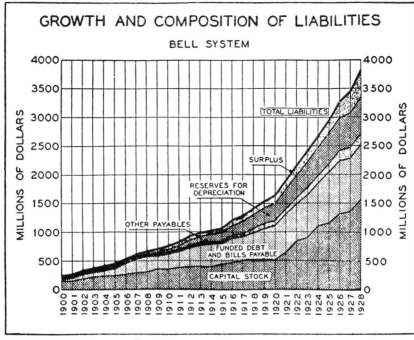

GROWTH AND COMPOSITION OF LIABILITIES

BELL SYSTEM

TOTAL LIABILITIES

SURPLUS

RESERVES FOR DEPRECIATION

OTHER PAYABLES

FUNDED DEBT AND BILLS PAYABLE

CAPITAL STOCK

MILLIONS OF DOLLARS

GROWTH OF THE BELL SYSTEM

earnings [2] per share in 1929 were $13.96 on the basis of the number of shares outstanding at the end of the year, and growth had been fast and steady, as shown by Chart VIII, taken from the company's own manual describing its securities.[3]

CHART IX

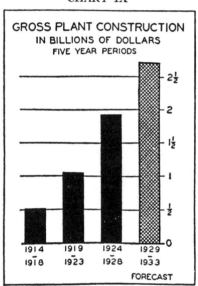

FORECAST OF GROWTH OF THE BELL
SYSTEM

The company's *Annual Report* for 1928 contained a chart [4] (reproduced as Chart IX) showing plant construction for 1914–1918, 1919–1923, and 1924–1928, and gave

[2] See the table in Section 6 below, where earnings at the rate of 10.61 per cent on the book value of $131.70, or $13.96 in all, are shown. To this figure of $13.96 a share should be added the undistributed equity in Western Electric of $3,495,246, or 25¢ a share on the 13,944,945 shares of the parent company's stock outstanding or being paid for in installments.

[3] *Bell Telephone Securities, 1929,* p. 16. Issued by Bell Telephone Securities Company, New York.

[4] See p. 27 of the *Report.*

a forecast for 1929–1933 that showed the management itself to be expecting a continuation of the past trend. Speculators in the 1929 boom had become excited about the inventions of the Western Electric Company, the wholly-owned subsidiary which manufactured most of the equipment used by the company, because in connection with its scientific researches on sound this subsidiary had perfected an apparatus for making sound motion pictures. Sober investors realized, however, that the profits from such incidental inventions of Western Electric would be only of minor importance in comparison with the earnings from American Telephone's regular business.

4. THE RETURN ON INVESTED ASSETS

Although the company handled most of the telephone business of the country, the enterprise was not run as a high-handed monopoly for the benefit of its owners; instead, the rates charged by its subsidiaries were regulated by state commissions so as to keep earnings down to a "fair return on a fair value." In the prosperous year 1929 these earnings reached 9.04 per cent on net assets, after deducting depreciation reserves and current liabilities, but in view of the success of this company in defending its rate cases, such a return in a very good year did not seem precariously high.

All of the foregoing facts about Telephone being common knowledge in 1930, opinions differed only as to their interpretation. Starting from the same data, different investment analysts reached different appraisals of the stock. The 1930 high of 274¼ indicates what the majority of experts apparently thought the stock was really worth at that time. Let us see if the new methods which have been developed in this book would have confirmed their appraisal.

5. ASSUMPTIONS IN 1930 REGARDING THE COMPANY'S
FUTURE

A simple extrapolation of past trends for ten years ahead
would have made the following assumptions about the
future of the company and its stock seem fair and reasonable in 1930:

1. The return on invested assets will remain as at
present.[5]
2. The ratio of stock to bonds will remain as at present.
3. The rate of growth will continue as at present.
4. At the end of ten years growth will end.
5. At that time, ten years hence, the stock will sell at
book value.
6. During the ten-year period, the investor shall receive
6 per cent on his purchase price, as either dividends or appreciation.

The foregoing assumptions are clearly most optimistic;
therefore if they should yield a price lower than the actual
market, one could be sure that the actual market was too
high and the stock was not a good buy. Certainly it is
optimistic to think that a return of 9 per cent on invested assets can always be earned for a decade more, even
through slack times if any. It is even more optimistic to
say that growth will continue at 10 per cent compounded
annually for ten years more; in this case this assumption
would have required the company to grow to more than
$2\frac{1}{2}$ times its 1929 size. With 19,000,000 telephones already
in use in the United States,[6] how could any such growth

---

[5] A further assumption was that book figures for invested assets and depreciation reserves would be allowed to stand, and that no change would be
made in the depreciation policy.
[6] *Bell Telephone Securities, 1929*, table, p. 19.

have been achieved, even if the dial system had been widely installed so that machine switching replaced manual switching in most central stations and absorbed a great deal of new capital in the process? A return to the investor of 6 per cent on the purchase price of his stock was not considered high, however, in 1930, when people still remembered the huge gains made in the 1920's from common-stock purchases. But the assumption that market price should equal book value after growth ceased was moderately optimistic, because experience with the railroads showed that dividends usually failed to keep pace with book value after growth ceased. When the need for new capital is over, politicians and even the courts seem to lose their solicitude for the investor.

6. FORMULA AND DATA FOR COMPUTING INVESTMENT VALUE

The formula for evaluating the stock according to the foregoing assumptions is as follows:

$$(75a) \qquad V_0 = C_0 \left(pw \frac{w^n - 1}{w - 1} + m_n w^n \right)$$

The knowns for insertion in this formula are derived from the data given in Table 45.

Other knowns, including some not needed in this particular formula, but useful if the reader wishes to apply other formulas to the problem, are as follows:

Bonded debt, etc., per share:	$B = \$\ 69.31$
Common equity per share:	$C =\ \ 131.70$
Depreciation, etc., per share:	$D =\ \ \ \ 66.10$
Total Assets per share:	$\$267.11$

$$\text{Leverage: } l_0 = \frac{B_0 + C_0}{C_0} = \frac{\$201.01}{\$131.70} = 1.526$$

TABLE 45

AMERICAN TELEPHONE & TELEGRAPH COMPANY

CONSOLIDATED FINANCIAL STATEMENT FOR 1929 [a]

	Liabilities	Payments	Computed Variables
Senior Securities:			
Funded debt[b]	$ 929,587,484	$ 54,655,367[c]	
Preferred stock	110,824,447	7,326,523	
	$1,040,411,931	$ 61,981,890	$b =$ 5.96%
Common Stockholders' Equity:			
Minority stock	$ 106,542,393	$ 8,518,541	
Common stock	1,394,495,412	116,378,771	
Surplus	475,864,827	84,881,037	
	$1,976,902,632	$209,778,349[d]	$c =$ 10.61%
Allowances:			
Reserves	$ 780,662,823		
Current Liabilities	211,500,502		
	$ 992,163,325		
Gross Liabilities:	$4,009,477,888		
Net Liabilities:	$3,017,314,563	$271,760,239	$i =$ 9.01%
Number of shares:		15,010,378 shares	
Minority stock and installments[e]		$ 106,542,393	
Parent Co. stock and installments		1,394,495,412	
		$1,501,037,805	

[a] *Annual Report, 1929*, pp. 21 and 23.

[b] Exclusive of $218,952,200 of convertible 4½'s of '39, which, as argued in § 8 below, were in reality an issue of new stock being sold in two installments at $180, and issued a year later.

[c] Exclusive of a half-year's interest of $4,926,425 on the foregoing convertible bonds.

[d] No important adjustment need be made in net income because of the foregoing bonds, as the interest earned on the proceeds of the bonds about offsets the interest paid on the bonds themselves for the half-year.

[e] Strictly speaking, the minority stock does not share in the growth of the company in exactly the same way as parent-company stock does, but no convenient way is known for separating the participation of each, and so as a good approximation they are treated alike. The amount of the minority issues is small in any event.

The rate of growth is shown by Table 46, which yields the following data:

| Estimated future rate of growth: | | $g = 10\%$ |
| Reinvestment ratio: | In this case, | $r = g = 10\%$ |

Since the leverage l is expected to remain constant throughout the period of growth, it is correct to set $r = g$ as done above, for the reasons given in Chapter XI, Section 1, item (vii).

TABLE 46

GROWTH OF ASSETS OF BELL SYSTEM

Year	Total Assets	Increase
1924	$2,664,000,000	11.0%
1925	2,938,000,000	10.3%
1926	3,257,000,000	10.9%
1927	3,457,000,000	6.1%
1928	3,827,000,000	10.7%
1929	4,228,000,000	10.5%
Average		9.9 %

The foregoing high rate of growth, g, and high reinvestment ratio, r, imply the very low *net* dividend or "pure dividend," π, of 80¢ a share during the years of growth, as the following computation shows:

$$(28b, 46a) \qquad \pi = pC = (c - r)C$$
$$= (10.61\% - 10.00\%) (\$131.70)$$
$$= \$.803 = 80¢$$

The pure dividend rate, as a per cent of *book* value (not par value) of the common stock, is thus seen to be

$$p = c - r = .61\% = .0061$$

If the investor is to receive a return of 6 per cent on the fair purchase price, whatever it turns out to be, then we must set

$$i = 6\%$$

and get

(2) $$v = \frac{1}{1 + i} = 0.9434$$

Likewise if the reinvestment ratio, as a per cent of the stockholders' equity, is

$$r = 10\%$$

then by

(14a) and (54) $u = 1 + g = 1 + r = 1.10$

Hence

(15) $w = uv = (1.10)\ (0.9434) = 1.0377$

If growth is to continue for ten years, then

$$n = 10$$

and

$$w^n = 1.448$$

If the stock is to sell exactly at book value at the end of the ten-year period, then we must set the constant of market price

$$m_n = 1$$

The values of the variables to be inserted in the formula may now be summarized as follows:

$$C_o = 131.7$$
$$p = .0061$$
$$w = 1.0377$$
$$w^n = 1.448$$
$$m_n = 1$$

7.   THE INVESTMENT VALUE OF THE STOCK

Solution of the formula, using these values for the variables, gives a fair market price for the stock of

$$V_o = 200\tfrac{1}{2}$$

8.   ADJUSTMENT FOR CONVERTIBLE BONDS

This fair price as just estimated must be adjusted, however, for the convertible bonds offered to stockholders of record May 10, 1929, because these bonds were in reality a postponed and disguised issue of new stock at 180 in 1930, in the ratio of one such share for each six already held. Since the conversion price was made to rise from time to time, the effect of the option involved was to force conversion in the first year, 1930.

According to formula (4b) in Chapter V, Section 7, the price of the stock ex-rights would be

$$(4b) \qquad \hat{V}_0 = \frac{NV_0 + S}{N + 1}$$

The data for this equation are as follows:

$$V_0 = 200\tfrac{1}{2}$$
$$N = 6$$
$$S = 180$$

The subscription price S of $180 a share was actually paid in two installments, one of $100 on July 1, 1929, when the convertible bonds were sold, and one of $80 on or before December 31, 1930, when the bonds were converted into stock.

The resulting value ex-rights figures out to be

$$\hat{V} = 197\tfrac{1}{2}$$

It is this estimated fair price of $197\tfrac{1}{2}$ that should be compared with the actual high price of $274\tfrac{1}{4}$ in 1930 when one is judging the excesses of the late bull market in Telephone.

9.   THE DEGREE OF OVERVALUATION IN THE 1930 PRICE

Even a change in assumptions so as to make the company's period of uninterrupted growth twenty years instead of ten, which would require it to grow to *six and three quarters* times its 1929 size, would not have sufficed to give its stock an investment value in excess of the all-time high of $310\frac{1}{4}$ ex-rights in 1929. Twenty years of steady growth would only have warranted a price rights-on of $V_o = 300$, or a price ex-rights of $\hat{V}_o = 283$.

If the assumptions regarding the company's future which we have made are fair, in the light of what was common knowledge at the time, then actual prices are seen to have gone far above all reasonable expectations. Had investment analysts at that time generally known how to translate prospects into prices, and bridge the gap in their reasoning so as to go from financial data to fair value, so great an over-bidding of market prices could hardly have taken place. If the correct methods of evaluation had been known by all professional financial advisers in the 1920's, and had been available in the standard treatises on investments, so that a headstrong public could have been confronted with convincing arguments by recognized authorities, then some of the boom and some of the subsequent losses might have been avoided. Investment analysts at the time, though, were as helpless before the public mania for stocks as physicians a hundred years ago were before a smallpox epidemic, and many of the analysts themselves succumbed to the mania. Now that the proper methods of evaluation are known, however, there remains no excuse for another boom so severe any more than for a smallpox epidemic now that vaccination is almost universally practiced. Yet when the next emergency comes, even the doctors may be hard to convert to the more advanced practice of their art, and to make matters worse, the disease of over-valuation will doubtless display new and confusing symptoms.

CHAPTER XXV

CONSOLIDATED GAS [1] AND UNITED CORPORATION IN 1930

I. THE FORMER ENTHUSIASM FOR UTILITY STOCKS

When people speak of the "utilities" in discussing the stock market, they usually mean in particular the power and light companies or their stocks. It is to these stocks that we shall turn now. We shall show that these eagles once soared so high as to make American Telephone look like a barnyard rooster. It is easy enough to say this now, but even in 1930, after the boom had passed its peak, many people were still very bullish on the utilities. They said that we were in an "electrical age" when new uses for electricity were being found every day. Electric refrigeration, electric cooking, washing, ironing, water heating, and perhaps even house heating were coming with a rush, and promised to increase the domestic consumption of current many-fold. In industry, the arc-welding of the steel frames of sky-scrapers and the electrification of railways — to mention only two examples — were cited as proof of the rapidly growing use of electricity. Much of this was true, and still more would have been true if no business depression had intervened to blight the thriving shoots of electrical progress. Nevertheless it does not follow from these splendid prospects for the industry that such high prices for the shares were warranted.

The chain of logic by which the utilities were evaluated in those days contr̄ ̄ed two weak links: first, in reasoning from output in kilowatt-hours to earnings per share; and

---

[1] Name since changed to Consolidated Edison.

second, in reasoning from earnings per share to intrinsic value. Weakness in the first link was inexcusable because it resulted from a blindness to facts that were common knowledge at the time, but weakness in the second was pardonable, because it resulted from a hiatus in the technique of investment analysis itself, and reflected only the bewilderment of those who were struggling with the problem and trying to solve the theoretical questions involved.

2. THE PROSPECTS FOR THE RESIDENTIAL DEMAND FOR ELECTRICITY

As regards the first error, it should have been obvious to any level-headed student that neither energy sold nor gross revenues collected, but only assets invested, formed the true measure of growth. No amount of increase in "k.w.h." would benefit the stockholder if rates were cut to offset it, as they would have to be unless assets kept pace with output. Part of the demand was peculiar, moreover, in that it could be satisfied without proportionate increase in plant. The distributing system being already complete in outline, it needed only moderate further outlays to permit it to carry two or three times as much load, for many parts of it had excess capacity as originally constructed. To send into homes the extra current for the new refrigerators, stoves, etc., that were being sold would require no more meters in the houses nor poles in the streets, but only some larger transformers on the line and another generator in the power plant. Hence, as far as the residential market was concerned, the brilliant prospects for increased sales there implied no such brilliant prospects for new capital investment by the companies. The best that could be said was that the high returns per unit of new investment obtainable with the companies' present rates for energy left a cushion for absorbing new taxes if necessary, or for subsidizing below-cost sales of current to non-residential users in that portion of the utilities' market that was competitive.

Even in the residential market, the prospects for growth were over-estimated in the boom, because people looked at electrical energy as a simple instead of a complementary good — to use the terminology of the economist. A moment's thought, however, would have shown that electricity could no more be consumed without appliances than gasoline without an automobile. And it was the cost of appliances, not current, that was keeping the use of electricity from going ahead still faster. People could buy refrigerators and mangles only as fast as they could save money from what was left over after paying the grocer and landlord. In general it was true, moreover, that the early increments of consumption required only small and inexpensive appliances, whereas the later increments required large and costly ones, so that from the companies' point of view the law of diminishing returns applied to consumer investment in appliances. The small user of current, to add to his consumption, needed to spend only a few dollars to buy a flatiron and a toaster, but the large user had to spend hundreds of dollars to buy a refrigerator and an electrically driven oil burner. Since a good many people had already bought the smaller appliances, they could not increase their consumption further without buying the larger ones, but this they would find it hard to do. Some of the costly things which they wanted to buy, moreover, were no gluttons for current. Washing machines, for instance, drew no more power than a reading lamp, but they cost many times as much and ran only an hour or so a week. The same was true of sewing machines and electric fans. A few more such inventions, so desirable in the eyes of the housewife but so lacking in profit for the power companies, would have arrested the growth of domestic consumption to a serious degree, for every dollar spent for one of these sparing users of current was a dollar less for a lavish user like an electric stove.

In conclusion, then, it may be said that even if the housewife was eager to make electricity her maid-servant, her investment in appliances need not have led to a proportionate increase in her use of electrical energy, and even if the residential consumption of current did shoot ahead, it would not have led to a proportionate increase in the invested assets of the companies themselves.

3. THE PROSPECTS FOR THE INDUSTRIAL DEMAND FOR
ELECTRICITY

In the industrial field, an equally sober view of the future of the power companies was needed in 1930. The forces which had caused the enormous growth in the past were mostly spent and could not produce an equal growth in the future, especially as measured on a ratio chart. Just as electricity had already displaced gas for illumination in the domestic field by 1930, and could not hope to do so all over again, so the central station had likewise displaced the private power plant in the industrial field by 1930, to a large degree, and could not hope to do so all over again. For every potential customer who had not yet been persuaded to shut down his own steam plant and use public power, there existed a present customer who might decide to install a Diesel engine and develop his own power — unless his power company would cut its rates enough to dissuade him. This competitive situation in the industrial field, where growth by substitution had largely run its course, was known to thousands of factory managers, and was in no sense a secret; consequently utility investors had only themselves to blame if they extrapolated into the future the compound interest trend of growth in the past, with no inflection point shown on the curve, even years ahead.

Hence, while continued growth in "k.w.h." was to be expected, continued growth in assets, at the same rapid rate, was certainly not to be expected.

4. THE INTERCONNECTION OF GENERATING PLANTS

Another influence which had made for past growth, but could not make for future growth forever, and whose approaching termination was less obvious, was the holding company movement. This movement had performed the great service of uniting the many small local companies into a few enormous interconnected systems, and had absorbed great quantities of new capital in the process. The new capital had been spent for long-distance transmission lines and big, modern power plants. The economies obtainable by the investment of the new capital were so great that it paid to close down most of the small local power stations, and to install new generators to duplicate the capacity of those closed down, even though the old plants were in no sense worn out. No wonder the invested assets of the industry piled up! But once this modernization program had been completed, it could not be done over again with the same speed in the near future. No new technical innovation arose to warrant the virtual scrapping of existing plants all over again. On the contrary, the new inventions tended in the opposite direction so far as their hunger for more capital was concerned. The thyratron, designed to transform energy from A.C. to D.C. and back again, raised hopes of sending 30 per cent more power over the present high-tension lines without any large new capital outlays. The improved steam stations were turning out current at costs so low as to make further hydroelectric developments — always enormous users of capital — uneconomical in the future as a rule. In almost every direction, therefore, the growth of invested assets was getting ready to slow down. And yet it was invested assets, and not "k.w.h." or "gross," which formed the rate base for any company; and it was growth of assets, and nothing else, that would send future earnings up.

5. "A FAIR RETURN ON A FAIR VALUE"

If investors studied the operating ratios of their companies and hoped to gain when these ratios were lowered by economies, they were barking up the wrong tree, because no economies could be claimed by stockholders but all must be passed on to customers, unless these economies were obtained by the investment of new capital, which even then was entitled to no more than "a fair return on a fair value."

In some respects this legal formula — "a fair return on a fair value" — was vicious. It afforded no incentive for economy in operation, but every incentive for waste in investment. It is really a great tribute to the utility managers' sense of public responsibility that they did not shamelessly exploit this weakness in the laws regulating them. They had a monopoly and could have made the most of it by overinvestment. They could have built hydro stations instead of steam, if they had wanted to serve their stockholders instead of the public. Such was not the ethics of the industry, however, for its operating men took too much pride in a good job well done. Fraud and extortion in the financing of holding companies there may have been in some cases, but not in the management of operating companies as a rule. Rate bases may have been padded by under-depreciation, and holding-company earnings may have been swollen by paper profits, all at the behest of speculators and financiers, but steam and hydro capacities were not wrongly proportioned nor generating and transmission equipment improperly balanced at the request of operators and engineers. The first abuses were but passing and curable, but the last would have been permanent and costly.

6. THE HAZARD OF POLITICAL PERSECUTION

Even the financial abuses in the utility industry were common knowledge during the boom. Every broker's clerk knew, and anyone who bothered to look in an investor's manual could have found out, that Insull's Middle West Utilities Company, for instance, got most of its earnings by showing paper profits on inter-company sales of securities. But investors in sound utility stocks considered these manipulative practices by others irrelevant to the intrinsic value of their own holdings, and thought they could afford to let over-speculation elsewhere bring its own punishment in due course to those who indulged in it. To assume that investors should have had the foresight at that time to see how innocent and guilty would all be chastised alike a few years later when anger blazed up over the wrongs done by a few would be to ask for more skill in political prophecy than we have assumed for investment analysts in other respects so far, and so we shall not list future political persecution among the things which a level-headed investor in 1930 ought to have counted on. All we shall ask of him is that he should have reckoned on a flattening out of growth in assets within a few years. With the evidence then available to every well-educated and reflective person, a slackening of growth in terms of invested assets should have been possible to foresee, if a person had put his mind on the question, and had had the courage to trust his own common sense.

It is interesting to see, when one studies the markets of former days, how much the right decision depends, not on inside information nor on economic subtleties, but on paying attention to the right questions and having confidence enough to believe in the common-sense answer to them. When people make mistakes, it is usually because they do not have experience enough to sense what are the right questions to ask or time enough to think out the answers, and so they rely on popular opinion in making their decisions. People could decide most questions correctly if they could only find their way to the heart of the problem in time. Eventually most people do reach it, but those who do not arrive early find that the market has already responded to the facts, and it is too late then for them to buy or sell to advantage.

7. THE RATE OF RETURN

Besides doubting the continued *growth* of assets at the past rate, the investor should also have doubted the continued *return* on assets at the past rate. Even though the courts had ruled that 8 per cent was a fair return, and even though the notion was common that private business yielded 10 per cent or more, a little reflection would have shown that 8 per cent guaranteed by the courts was better than 10 per cent at the mercy of competitors. Moreover, was 8 per cent really a considered judicial opinion? Had not the Interstate Commerce Commission, in setting the return for the railroads, decided on the much more conservative rate of $5\frac{3}{4}$ per cent, and might not the fair return allowed the utilities be expected to settle down towards some such minimum as this eventually?

8. THE PRICE-EARNINGS RATIO FOR THE STOCK

A level-headed investor during the boom ought to have considered all that has been said above about rate of growth and rate of return, even if he was not inspired with enough economic prescience (and how many of us were?) to foresee the impending depression. If he was so fortunate during the boom as to own utility stocks, he would have found himself wondering, therefore, whether their prices were getting too high, and would have wished for some way to test the fairness of prices. Without access to any method for making such a test, he could only accept with grave misgivings the dictum of the market place that there was "nothing to worry about until the utilities reach twenty times earnings," and then when this figure was reached, see it revised to thirty, forty, and fifty times earnings, with the "reasonable limit" always above any price yet attained.

9. SPECIFIC ASSUMPTIONS REGARDING THE COMPANY'S FUTURE

Let us suppose that our investor is the owner, in the 1920's, of Consolidated Gas [2] of New York, the Number One favorite of the investment trusts according to the analyses of their portfolios published in the newspapers. Let us further suppose that in the spring of 1930 our skeptical investor obtains access to the new methods of evaluation proposed herein. Then his first step will be to draw up, for the sake of argument, some sort of forecast of the company's future. For this purpose, six assumptions like those used earlier for American Telephone will serve, thus:

1. The return on invested assets will remain as at present.
2. The ratio of stocks to bonds will remain as at present.
3. The rate of growth will continue as at present.
4. At the end of ten years growth will end.
5. At that time, ten years hence, the stock will sell at book value.
6. During the ten-year period, the investor shall receive 6 per cent on his purchase price, either as dividends or appreciation.

[2] This company, though called a gas company, was primarily an electric utility.

10. COMPUTATION OF THE INVESTMENT VALUE OF THE
STOCK IN 1930

To apply these assumptions, the same formula as for
Telephone will be required, thus:

(75a) $$V_o = C_o \left(pw \frac{w^n - 1}{w - 1} + m_n w^n \right)$$

The variables for insertion in this formula are derived
from the balance sheet and income account of the company,
given in Table 47.

TABLE 47

CONSOLIDATED GAS COMPANY OF NEW YORK
CONSOLIDATED FINANCIAL STATEMENT FOR 1929

	Liabilities	Payments	Computed Variables
Senior Securities:			
Funded debt	$240,832,790	$14,969,505	
Unfunded debt	22,070,285		
Preferred stock	189,985,796	10,397,903	
	$452,888,871	$25,367,408	$b = 5.60\%$
Common Stockholders' Equity			
Minority interests	$ 2,180,421	$ 205,086	
Common stock	$391,513,174[a]	34,850,507	
Surplus	213,056,848	19,551,912	
	$606,750,443	$54,607,505	$c = 9.00\%$
Allowances:			
Reserves	$ 79,301,292		
Current Liabilities	32,597,613		
	$111,898,905		
Gross Liabilities	$1,171,538,219		
Net Liabilities	$1,059,639,314	$79,974,913	$a = 7.55\%$
Number of shares:	11,456,981 shares[b]		

[a] Including premium on capital stock.
[b] The minority interest was very small, and so it need not be considered
when working with the number of shares outstanding.

Other variables of computation are as follows:

Bonded debt, etc., per share	$B =$	$ 39.53
Common equity per share	$C =$	52.96
Depreciation, etc., per share	$D =$	9.77
Total Assets per share		$102.26

$$\text{Leverage: } l_0 = \frac{B_0 + C_0}{C_0} = \frac{\$92.49}{\$52.96} = 1.75$$

Since consolidated statements for the company, drawn up so as to show the effect of its merger with Brooklyn Edison, do not go back behind 1927, one cannot study its trend of growth over as long a period as was possible for American Telephone. For the short period in question, however, the growth appears to have been at the rate of $7\frac{1}{2}$ per cent per annum, compounded, inasmuch as total assets increased from $1,013,767,665 on December 31, 1927 to $1,171,538,219 two years later. Hence we may write

$$h = 7.5\%$$

Since in cases to which the formula we are here using applies

$$r = g$$

we may write also

$$r = 7.5\%$$

as proved in Chapter XI, Section 1, item (vii).

Like Telephone, "Con Gas" issued rights which enabled it to hold up its gross dividend. The gross dividend was increased to $4.00 a share in 1929, as compared with $5.00 a share before the 2-for-1 split-up in 1928. The net or "pure" dividend which could have been paid without recourse to the sale of either stocks or bonds is given by the usual formula:

(28b, 46a) $\pi = pC = (c - r)C$

$= (9.0\% - 7.5\%) (\$52.96)$

$= \$.794 = 79\cancel{c}$

The pure dividend rate, in terms of the *book* value of the common stock, is

(46a) $p = c - r$

$= (9.0\% - 7.5\%) = 1.5\% = .015$

If our investor is to receive a return of 6 per cent on the investment value, whatever it turns out to be, then we must set, as before

$i = 6\%$

and get

(2) $v = \dfrac{1}{1.06} = 0.9434$

Likewise if the reinvestment ratio is

$r = 7.5\%$

then

(14a) and (54) $u = 1 + g = 1 + r = 1.075$

Hence

(15) $w = uv = (1.075)(0.9434) = 1.01415$

If growth is to continue for ten years, then

$n = 10$

and

$w^n = 1.1509$

If the stock is to sell exactly at book value at the end of the ten-year period, then we must set the constant of market price

$m_n = 1$

The values of the variables to be inserted in the formula may now be summarized as follows:

$$C_0 = \$52.96$$
$$p = .015$$
$$w = 1.01415$$
$$w^n = 1.1509$$
$$m_n = 1$$

Solution of the formula, using these values for the variables, gives

$$V_0 = \$69.54$$

If this fair market price of $69\frac{1}{2}$ is compared with the actual market price of $136\frac{7}{8}$ at the top of the spring rally in 1930, it will be seen that these new methods of evaluation would have provided our skeptical investor with a convincing reason for selling then.[3]

Any of our other standard formulas of evaluation would have indicated about the same degree of over-valuation for Consolidated Gas, as we shall show in the three computations to follow.

First, if terminal value is defined in terms of the price-earnings ratio at the end, instead of the book value then, the proper formula to use is as follows:

(79a)
$$V_0 = C_0 \left(pw \frac{w^n - 1}{w - 1} + e_n w^n c \right)$$

If a suitable price-earnings ratio seems to be 10, the same as was considered right for an industrial stock before the boom, then we may set

$$e_n = 10$$

---

[3] The same formula, with the period of steady growth increased to $n = 20$ years, will give the somewhat larger value of $V_0 = \$88.62$, but even this seems low in comparison with the actual market prices.

As shown above, the leverage, return on invested assets, and interest rate on bonds etc., are as follows:

$$l = 175\% = 1.75$$

$$a = 7.55\% = .0755$$

$$b = 5.60\% = .0560$$

$$c = 9.00\% = .0900$$

It will be noted that the first term in formula (79a) above is the same as in our previous formula, (75a), and so part of the computation need not be repeated. When the variables of computation given above are inserted in the new formula, (79a), the investment value, based on the final price-earnings ratio,[4] turns out to be

$$V_o = \$63.45$$

Second, if terminal value is defined in terms of the yield at the end, the proper formula to use is as follows:

$$(90a) \quad V_o = C_o \left\{ pw \, \frac{w^n - 1}{w - 1} + \frac{w^n}{y_n} \left[(q_n - 1)(l - 1) b + q_n c \right] \right\}$$

If a suitable yield seems to be 5 per cent, then

$$y_n = 5\% = .05$$

In the foregoing formula, q_n stands for the distribution rate in the year n. It is defined thus:

$$(82, 83a) \quad q_n = \frac{\beta_n + \pi_n}{a_n} = \frac{\beta_n + \pi_n}{\beta_n + \gamma_n}$$

This definition implies the assumption that at the end of the period of growth the enterprise becomes a mature company capable of paying out in interest and dividends in the year n a certain proportion, q_n, of its earnings after depre-

---

[4] A price-earnings ratio of 11 instead of 10 would have given a price of $68.95, which figure is very close to the price of $69.54 obtained by the previous formula.

ciation.[5] A fair value [6] to assign to q_n might have been 70 per cent. Insertion of the foregoing variables of computation in the formula given above leads to an investment value, based on final yield, of

$$V_o = \$70.03$$

Third, if no terminal value at all is assigned, but if the company's growth is assumed to follow a logistic curve, then the proper formula to use is

$$(67a) \qquad V_o = C_o \left[pw \cdot \frac{w^n - 1}{w - 1} + \left(\frac{2c}{i} - \frac{c + g}{u(1 + i) - 1} \right) w^n \right]$$

If the point of inflection in the foregoing curve is assumed to occur ten years hence, then

$$n = 10$$

Such an assumption implies, of course, that substantial growth, though at a diminishing rate, continues even after ten years have passed, and, what is far more important, that no decline occurs in a, the return on investment, even though the utility companies should no longer be able to plead in the courts that earnings must be maintained in order to attract new capital as freely as ever. From a strictly legal point of view, of course, it ought not to be necessary for them to seek protection in this argument, for the Constitution is supposed to protect their property from confiscation. Strictly speaking, a "fair return" should be whatever return is usual in competitive enterprise, and should be in no wise dependent on the company's rate of growth. Unfortunately for the stockholder, however, the

[5] Cf. Chapter VI, § 3.

[6] Since the utilities seem to have been in the habit of under-depreciation, a distribution rate of 70 per cent would seem ample for them. But if the same distribution rate were to be used for the utilities as was used for General Motors in Chapter XXI, namely, $q_n = 83\frac{1}{3}\%$, this higher rate would give a value for Consolidated Gas of $V_0 = \$91.48$.

courts cannot be counted on to be so consistent in their judgments. Nevertheless, we shall overlook this point now for the sake of argument, and assume that return on investment will stay up forever, so that a will remain constant.

In applying the formula above, it should be remembered that g is the rate of growth before the point of inflection, and has already been estimated to be as follows:

$$g = 7.5\%$$

When all the knowns are inserted in our formula, the investment value, based on a logistic curve of growth, turns out to be

$$V_0 = \$119.35$$

To summarize our results so far, the following comparison of estimated and actual values for Consolidated Gas in 1930 is given:

Investment value, based on:

Book value at end	69½
Price-earnings ratio at end	63½
Yield at end	70
Logistic curve of growth	119½
Actual market price:	
High in 1929	182
High in 1930	136⅞

Clearly the stock had been grossly over-valued in the bull market, and was still a good sale in the spring of 1930.

One fact, however, the foregoing calculations overlook, namely, the conservative financial structure of the company, whose ratio of stock to bonds was low in comparison with many other utilities, so that for this company

$$l_0 = 1.75 \text{ only}$$

Heretofore we have assumed that the company has already settled down into the maintenance of the optimum capital structure and found the happy medium between a small funded debt bearing low interest charges and a large funded debt giving a favorable leverage for stockholders. Let us now drop this assumption and see how much would be added to the fair value of Consolidated Gas if it were to finance all of its future growth with bonds and pay out all of its earnings in dividends, but still keep its bond rate down, so that we could continue to write

$$b = 5.60\%$$

Pursuance of this changed dividend and borrowing policy for ten years would not have been out of the question, moreover, for it would have reduced the leverage only to

$$l_{10} = 3.60$$

In this case, the proper formulas to use for various assumptions about the basis of selling prices in the end would be as follows:

Book Value:

$$(93) \qquad V_0 = C_0 \left\{ (a - b) \left(\frac{w^n - 1}{w - 1} \right) w l_0 \right.$$
$$\left. + \frac{b}{i} (1 - v^n) + m_n v^n \right\}$$

Price-Earnings Ratio:

$$(97) \qquad V_0 = C_0 \left\{ (a - b) \left(\frac{w^n - 1}{w - 1} \right) w l_0 \right.$$
$$\left. + \frac{b}{i} (1 - v^n) + e_n w^n l_0 \left[a - b + \frac{b}{l_0 u^n} \right] \right\}$$

Yield at End:

$$(99) \qquad V_0 = C_0 \left\{ (a - b) \left(\frac{w^n - 1}{w - 1} \right) w l_0 + \frac{b}{i} (1 - v^n) \right.$$
$$\left. + \frac{w^n l_0}{y_n} \left[a q_n - b \left(1 - \frac{1}{l_0 u^n} \right) \right] \right\}$$

The data being the same as for the previous formulas, the investment value, based on the three different terminal values, works out as follows:

Book Value:	$V_o = \$70.95$
Price-Earnings Ratio:	$V_o = \$78.74$
Yield:	$V_o = \$67.78$

Thus we see that by assuming an immediate change in financial policies — of which there was then no sign — it would have been possible to justify slightly higher prices for Consolidated Gas, but the actual highs of 1929 and 1930 would still have seemed wholly unwarranted.

11. VIRTUAL RECAPITALIZATION BY MEANS OF HOLDING COMPANIES

Some intimations of a *virtual* change in Consolidated Gas's policy might have been deduced from the formation of the United Corporation, which was linking up a great super-power system in the industrial East, had already acquired 107,000 shares of Consolidated Gas,[7] and was planning apparently to make an offer for more. The House of Morgan in our generation seemed bent on a consolidation in the utility field to rival the United States Steel Corporation created by the elder Morgan in the industrial field. Should an offer of both preferred and common stock be made by the United Corporation for Consolidated Gas common, it would be tantamount to a recapitalization of the latter company, from the point of view of one who sold the preferred stock received in exchange and retained only the common. That the plan might be to offer a certain amount of United Corporation first preferred stock was shown by the provision for 1,000,000 shares of such stock in the latter company's authorized capitalization. None

[7] *Boston News Bureau,* evening edition, April 22, 1930.

of this class of stock had yet been issued, and no restrictions as to its dividend rate existed. Since the stock was evidently intended to be a high-grade investment like General Motors $5 preferred, recently underwritten by Morgan, it too might well have carried a $5 rate. What the ratio of preferred to common in the exchange offer would be, no outsiders knew. A reasonable guess would be $50 in United Corporation preferred and the rest in common for each share of Consolidated Gas. This would permit the holding company to pay a dividend of $5.00 a share on the one-half share of preferred issued, and $1.00 or so a share on the common shares issued, out of the proceeds of dividends received from Consolidated Gas itself.

Such an offer as this would effect a virtual change in Consolidated Gas's own capitalization as shown below:

	Senior Securities		Equity	
At start:	$B_0 =$	$39.53	$C_0 =$	$52.96
Change:	$\Delta B =$	$+50.00$	$\Delta C =$	-50.00
At end:	$\hat{B}_0 =$	$89.53	$\hat{C}_0 =$	$ 2.96

In this way [8] the leverage could virtually have been changed from

$$l = 1.75 \text{ to } \hat{l} = 31.3$$

Such a narrow equity for the holding-company common would have seemed no more extreme than that for Steel common when it was first issued nearly thirty years earlier.

The promoters could not hope to stick to this unbalanced capitalization forever, but if they could do so for ten years, and still have their stock sell at the conventional ten times earnings at the end of that period, then they

---

[8] The symbol $\hat{B}$ is read "B-cap," and means B after recapitalization in the manner specified. Likewise for $\hat{C}$ and $\hat{l}$. The symbol ΔB is read "delta B," and means "increase or decrease in B."

could justify a higher price now. The new present worth would be given by the usual formula:[9]

$$(79a) \qquad V_o = \hat{C}_o \left(\hat{p}w \cdot \frac{w^n - 1}{w - 1} + e_n \hat{c} w^n \right) + \Delta B$$

Here

$$(46a) \qquad \hat{p} = \hat{c} - r$$

$$(54) \qquad r = g = 7.5\%$$

$$(52b) \qquad \hat{c} = l \left(a - \hat{b} + \frac{\hat{b}}{l} \right)$$

where

$$l = 31.3$$

Recapitalization would affect the "bond rate," b, which would need to be recomputed in the following way:

	Liability	Payment	Rate
At start:	$B_o = \$39.53$	$\beta_o = \$2.214$	$b_o = 5.60\%$
Change:	$\Delta B = 50.00$	$\Delta\beta = 2.500$	$\Delta b = 5.00\%$
At end:	$\hat{B} = \$89.53$	$\hat{\beta} = \$4.714$	$\hat{b} = 5.27\%$

The new value for the rate of earnings on common equity, as given by formula (52b), would then be

$$\hat{c} = 76.7\%$$

and the pure dividend rate would be

$$\hat{p} = \hat{c} - r = 76.7\% - 7.5\% = 69.2\%$$

The knowns for insertion in formula (79a) above may now be summarized as follows:

$$\hat{C}_o = \$2.96$$
$$\hat{p} = .692$$
$$w = 1.01415, \text{ as before}$$

[9] The $50 of preferred received in the exchange of shares must be included, of course, in the newly computed value.

$$w^n = 1.1509, \text{ as before}$$
$$e_n = 10.00$$
$$\hat{c} = .767$$

If these quantities are put into formula (79a), they make the apparent value for Consolidated Gas rise 40 or 50 per cent to

$$V_o = \$48.28 + \$50.00 = \$98.28$$

Highly instructive is this calculation; it shows how the devices of "high finance" seem able to create riches out of thin air by a mere stroke of the pen. As the Law of the Conservation of Investment Value admits of no exceptions, however, the gain to the common stockholders must be at the expense of some other group of security holders. Those who pay par for the holding company's $5 preferred stock, therefore, even though it is junior to so many bonds and preferred stocks issued by the operating company, are evidently the losers.

It is now clear why the power stocks as a class went so much higher than Telephone in the boom. The explanation is to be found in the scheme that was afoot to recapitalize the industry by means of the United Corporation and other such "super holding companies." [10]

12. UNITED CORPORATION WARRANTS

The promoters made money out of the holding companies in two ways. First, they bought the stocks of the operating companies before news of the consolidation was published, and sold them afterwards at a profit. Second, they obtained a promoter's fee in the form of option warrants, whose market value, at little apparent cost to the issuing company, usually turned out to be large. These warrants gave the holder the right to buy new stock when-

[10] As one of the most extreme cases of such holding companies, the American Superpower Corporation might be mentioned.

ever he chose at some specified price, often above the present market. This option was expected to prove of value at some future time if the company should prosper greatly and eventually pay a dividend large enough to justify, and more than justify, the outlay involved in exercising the warrant.

Such warrants as these were issued to the promoters of the United Corporation, who thereby obtained the perpetual right to subscribe to new shares of United Corporation common stock at $27.50 a share. Since the actual market price of its shares reached a high of $75\frac{1}{2}$ in 1929, these warrants must have been worth at their peak not less than

$$\$75.50 - \$27.50 = \$48.00$$

If an investor insisted on receiving 6 per cent interest or more on all of his holdings, he would not pay out the subscription price of $27.50 to convert his warrant into a common share unless the dividend paid on the common stock was at least 6 per cent of $27.50, or $1.65 per annum. With the actual dividend never going above 56¼¢ a share, even in the year of highest payments, few investors ever wanted to make the subscription. As a result, the inherent absurdity of the option warrants was never revealed so that all the world might look and laugh. It is interesting to conjecture, however, as to what might have happened. Suppose there had been no depression. Suppose that the United Corporation had grown rapidly, the dividend had risen, and one day the directors had established a rate of $1.80 a share, where the yield on $27.50 would have been 6½ per cent. Then the next day the company would have been deluged with one hundred million dollars of new money forced upon it by the holders of 3,732,059 option warrants. What use would the new money have been to the company? Since no well-managed company would

have been going on for years with a deficiency of $100,000,-
000 in its current assets, $100,000,000 suddenly shoved
down its throat would only have had to be disgorged again.
None of these well-fed directors would have let their own
cooks wake them up in the middle of the night and force
them to eat a dozen plank steaks; why should they have
granted their stockholders the right to stuff their company
with a hundred million dollars just at the time when the
cash account was so full that the dividend had to be raised?

Be that as it may, the warrants were there, and their
price needs explanation. On December 31, 1929, these war-
rants closed at $14\frac{7}{8}$, even though the stock sold at $32\frac{1}{4}$, or
only $17\frac{3}{8}$ points higher. To the plain man it must have
been a mystery to see people buy warrants and pay the
equivalent of $42\frac{3}{8}$, i.e., $14\frac{7}{8} + 27\frac{1}{2}$, for a stock that could
be bought in the open market for $32\frac{1}{4}$, at an apparent sav-
ing of $10\frac{1}{8}$ points. The explanation lay in the fact that the
warrants tied up less money than the stock. If the stock
were to continue to pay no dividend — and none had been
paid up to December 31, 1929 — then the saving in interest
on the warrants would make up in a reasonable time for
their relatively higher price in the beginning. The following calculation shows how many years n with no dividends
would need to elapse to make the warrants and the common equally attractive at their going prices:

(128e) $$n = \frac{\log(M_c - M_w) - \log S}{\log v}$$

The knowns for insertion in the foregoing equation are as
follows:

$$S = 27\frac{1}{2}$$
$$M_c = 32\frac{1}{4}$$
$$M_w = 14\frac{7}{8}$$
$$v = \frac{1}{1.06} = 0.9434$$

If the equation is solved for n, using these data, it shows that a period of

$$n = 7.88 \text{ years}$$

or slightly less than eight years, would need to elapse without dividends to justify the spread of only $17\frac{3}{8}$ points, instead of $27\frac{1}{2}$, between the warrants and the stock [11] of the United Corporation.

13. MOTIVES FOR PROMOTING HOLDING COMPANIES

The promoters, in their desire to make money out of the stocks of the operating companies and the warrants of the holding companies, were assisted in their schemes by other people who liked holding companies for other reasons. The managers in seeking new capital, the engineers in handling the interchange of power, and the lawyers in meeting state regulation, all found the holding company helpful; but most of all the investment bankers seemed to see in the holding company an effective device for obtaining a monopoly in the sale of the bonds of the holding company and its subsidiaries. Just as years ago all the great banking houses had established their connections in the railroad field, and each had acquired an exclusive right to float the securities of its own particular clients, so now these same houses were seeking similar connections in the utility field, and each was trying by means of holding companies promoted by itself to acquire an exclusive right to

[11] At a later time (April 20, 1935) the warrants at $\frac{1}{2}$ were selling for only $2\frac{1}{4}$ points less than the stock at $2\frac{3}{4}$. A calculation like that above would indicate that the market looked for forty-three years to elapse before dividends were resumed at a rate of $1.80 a share. The matter is probably not as simple as this, however, for considerations of probability seem to be involved when the stock itself is selling below the subscription price of $27\frac{1}{2}$. In this case it is a question not only of *when* ($n = ?$) the subscription should be made, but also of *whether* it should be made. If the spread of only $2\frac{1}{2}$ points occurred with the stock at $32\frac{1}{2}$ and the warrants at 30, for instance, then this latter question would not arise, and it would simply be a matter of computing $n = 42.95$.

the banking business of its own particular companies. With these companies always needing new capital, or requiring the refunding of old obligations, and with their securities ever in demand by investors, the underwriting profits to the bankers over a period of years promised to be handsome indeed. No wonder that J. P. Morgan & Company, intent on keeping their position as the leading underwriters in the country,[12] and anxious to find an ample supply of sound investments for their customers, should have sought a prominent place in the sponsorship of the United Corporation. It was altogether legitimate for them to do so.

At the time when the virtual recapitalization of the operating companies was under way, it was all a mystery as to just how much of a rise in their stocks would be warranted by any given exchange offer made by a holding company. The public then had no access to the methods of calculation which we are using here. Hence it is no wonder that prices went soaring, for speculation has ever fed on mystery.

This particular holding company was especially calculated to dazzle the imagination of the public. Designed to join the electric and gas services of all the East into one gigantic system, it was to take over the following important properties: the United Gas Improvement Company, the Public Service Corporation of New Jersey, the Consolidated Gas Company (of New York), the Niagara Hudson Power Corporation, the Commonwealth and Southern Corporation, and the Columbia Gas and Electric Corporation. Water power from Niagara and the Adirondacks was to

---

[12] Under the terms of recent legislation, by which bankers have been obliged to divorce their underwriting operations from their commercial lending, J. P. Morgan & Co. have elected to abandon investment banking and confine themselves to deposit banking, and most of their underwriting connections have gone to the newly organized firm of Morgan, Stanley & Co.

be made available in New York City by a tie-up with Niagara Hudson. Natural gas for Baltimore, Philadelphia, and even New York, was to be obtained from fields owned by Columbia Gas and Electric. The Pennsylvania Railroad was to electrify its line from Philadelphia to Pittsburgh.[13] Maybe other properties, in adjacent cities like Baltimore, Boston, Cleveland, and Detroit, might also be taken over one day — who knew? Certainly there was everything to hope for, and speculators did not hesitate to include it in the price.

These hopes were well founded. Many of them have been realized during the years of the depression, but the price of "Con Gas" has not stayed up. Not the hopes, but the deductions from them, were wrong, as we have been to such pains to show by our calculations above.

14. THE POLITICAL ATTACK ON CONSOLIDATED GAS

The entire drop in price undergone by "Con Gas" during the bear market of 1929–1932 was not due merely to over-valuation in the boom. Part of it, from 70 down, was due to the depression and to politics. The depression caused a slight loss in gross revenues and a somewhat greater loss in net, because of inflexible overhead costs, but still the company showed itself to be nearly as "depression proof" as its most ardent admirers claimed. Not so as regards its vulnerability to politics, however. Here the law of compensation seems to have taken its toll, for the politicians reasoned that any business which did not feel the depression directly deserved to be made to feel it indirectly in its tax bill. After all, said they, what could be more logical than to lay new taxes on those who could pay them most easily?

[13] For an exhaustive engineering survey of the project see the report prepared for the U. S. Geological Survey by W. S. Murray entitled *Superpower System for the Region between Boston and Washington* (Washington, 1921).

"Con Gas" itself was a special target for the politicians. The new administration in New York City was less friendly than the old, and made a special drive to take the "water" out of the company's rate base, and cut its fair return down. Undoubtedly the most effective way to hurt the company was to set up city-owned plants to skim the cream off its business.[14] The threat of public competition, therefore, did more in a few months to extort rate reductions than litigation would have done in years. Whether this was fair treatment of the company's owners is a question that must be left for each observer to answer in accordance with his own social and economic prejudices.

Regardless of the right or wrong of this political attack, its effect can be measured by our formulas as soon as the necessary data for the calculation are given. When once the new rate base, $\hat{A}$, the new fair return, $\hat{a}$, and the new bond rate, $\hat{b}$, are specified, then the resulting value for the stock can be computed. For the sake of argument, let us assume on the one hand that "water" to the extent of 25 per cent is squeezed out, and that the fair return is pushed down to 6 per cent, while on the other hand the debt [15] is refunded at $4\frac{1}{2}$ per cent, and growth continues as before. The new knowns will be as follows:

$$\hat{A}_o = 75\%A_o = (75\%)\,(B_o + C_o)$$
$$= (75\%)\,(\$39.53 + \$52.96) = \$69.37$$
$$\hat{C}_o = \hat{A}_o - B_o = \$69.37 - \$39.53 = \$29.84$$
$$\hat{a} = 6\% = .060$$
$$\hat{b} = 4\frac{1}{2}\% = .045$$

[14] Cf. the *New York Times*, December 20, 1934, p. 1.

[15] These figures are only by way of example, and represent the average carrying charge for all the senior securities taken together. Certain first mortgage bonds of the company have recently been sold to give a much lower return than $4\frac{1}{2}$ per cent, however; the New York Edison $3\frac{1}{4}$'s of 1966, for instance, were offered on July 20, 1936, to yield 3.15 per cent.

$$r = 7\tfrac{1}{2}\% = .075$$

$$l = 232\% = 2.32$$

$$\hat{c} = l\left(\hat{a} - \hat{b} + \frac{\hat{b}}{l} \right) = 7.89\% = .0789$$

$$\hat{p} = \hat{c} - r = 7.89\% - 7.50\% = .39\% = .0039$$

$$w = 1.01415 \quad \text{if} \quad v = \frac{1}{1.06} = 0.9434$$

$$\text{and } u = 1.076$$

$$w^n = 1.1509 \quad \text{for } n = 10$$

If the stock is to sell at book value at the end of a period of ten years, then

$$m_n = 1$$

and

$$n = 10$$

The usual formula applies, thus:

$$(75a) \qquad V_0 = C_0\left(pw \cdot \frac{w^n - 1}{w - 1} + m_n w^n \right)$$

When the variables above are inserted in this formula, they give a fair market price under the new assumptions of

$$V_0 = \$35.60$$

This last calculation shows that Consolidated Gas of New York, on the basis of the foregoing assumptions regarding its future, was unduly depressed at its 1935 low of $15\tfrac{7}{8}$.

CHAPTER XXVI

AMERICAN AND FOREIGN POWER IN 1930

I. CONTROL BY ELECTRIC BOND AND SHARE

An appraisal of the *investment* value of so speculative a stock as American and Foreign Power may at first sight seem incongruous, but the reason for including it in our case studies on investment value is not far to seek. In 1925 this stock indirectly found its way into the portfolios of many bona fide investors, because in that year the General Electric Company declared a special dividend consisting of stock in the Electric Bond and Share Securities Corporation, one of whose subsidiaries was the American and Foreign Power Company, Inc. As General Electric itself had long been a favorite with thousands of bona fide investors, including universities, hospitals, insurance companies, and conservative individuals both rich and poor, and as most of these investors believed General Electric was an ideal stock to hold permanently, Electric Bond and Share, and thus American and Foreign Power, came into the hands of these same conservative investors and remained generally in their portfolios, unsuited though it was to their needs.

During the great bull market of 1921–1929, Electric Bond and Share remained dormant for a long time, but in 1928 it started a spectacular advance which made it one of the outstanding speculative favorites at the end of the boom. As it rose, many conservative investors were tempted to sell it, and would have done so if they only could have been sure that it was really too high. Too high to them meant so high that permanent investment was no longer justified, because future dividends could not give a fair return on the then attained price. The investment policies of these conservative investors forbade them to speculate on the ups and downs of ordinary bull and bear markets, but required them to consider the *long-run* merits of their holdings, and to sell if the price got too high as judged by that standard.

2. GROWTH BY THE REHABILITATION OF COMPANIES PURCHASED

In the case of Electric Bond and Share, it was exceedingly difficult to put this policy into effect, because no method was available at that time for making an estimate of the investment value of the stock. That Electric Bond and Share by 1929 consisted mostly of American and Foreign Power was clear enough, for an analysis of its holdings showed that three fourths of its "break-up" value came from this subsidiary,[1] but this subsidiary itself seemed well-nigh impossible to appraise. What with the new properties that American and Foreign Power bought every few months, and what with the new securities that it issued to pay for them, the investment analyst found it a task to keep track of assets and capitalization alone. Apparent growth in earnings was amazing, but this growth seemed to be offset by a like growth in shares outstanding. Whether the original owners of the enterprise stood to gain anything by letting in so many new shareholders was impossible for the outsider to tell by a study of the annual reports alone. He could only take the management's word for it.

[1] Other subsidiaries were American Gas and Electric, American Power and Light, National Power and Light, Electric Power and Light, and its subsidiary United Gas. For a full list of the holdings of the Electric Bond and Share Co., see its *Annual Report for 1929*. For an itemized table giving the value of each holding, at that time, see the *Boston News Bureau* (evening edition), June 13, 1929.

The record of growth as such was dazzling indeed, as shown in Table 48.

But even this table did not tell the full story of growth attained. The Annual Report for 1929 stated that "gross

TABLE 48
The Growth of American & Foreign Power

Year ending	Gross Revenues	Net Income	Shares Outstanding [a] Common	Warrants
Dec. 31, 1923	$4,467,000	....	920,000	480,000
Dec. 31, 1924	6,648,873	$2,752,695	936,688	463,312
Dec. 31, 1925	8,847,971	3,594,977	943,988	456,012
Dec. 31, 1926	10,183,775	3,893,468	1,243,988	456,012
Dec. 31, 1927	19,976,172	4,940,184	1,244,388	2,594,420
Dec. 31, 1928	30,112,578	13,091,207	1,248,930	3,256,954
Dec. 31, 1929	63,709,000	24,756,305	1,624,357	3,434,000

[a] The company's preferred. stock issues, which also increased steadily, are omitted from this table because they were not equity issues.

earnings for the entire twelve months ended December 31, 1929, of all companies controlled by your Company, including companies acquired since January 1, 1930, were in excess of $80,000,000." [2]

American and Foreign Power achieved this growth by acquiring operating properties in the following places:

1923	Panama, Guatemala, eastern Cuba
1924	Cuba
1925	Ecuador
1926	Cuba, especially Havana
1927	Brazil, Colombia, Venezuela
1928	Havana, Mexico, Chile, Argentina, Costa Rica
1929	Shanghai, Bombay, Mexico, Brazil, Argentina

In continually buying new properties like this, American and Foreign Power was doing something quite different from anything American Telephone or Consolidated Gas

[2] Page 3.

had done. Neither of these had done more than grow like a tree, rooted to one spot; and 10 per cent a year had been as fast as these stay-at-homes could expand. Not so with American and Foreign Power. Always seeking more properties, buying them when cheap, rehabilitating them, and refunding their debt, this company was more a dealer or trader in utilities than a mere manager of them. Like any other trader, moreover, whether in horses, mines, or real estate, its success depended on driving shrewd bargains over and over again. This very bargaining power, and the future trading gains expected from it, formed the basis of the price of its stock. No mere appraisal of properties already bought would satisfy the stock market; full credit must also be taken for future properties yet to be bought. The reasoning was like the familiar argument to the effect that investment trust stocks should sell above liquidating value because of the trading gains to be made by their expert managers. If, and only if, the trading gains never fail to be made is this argument sound.

The trading gains which American and Foreign Power could make might roughly be measured in terms of the amount of new property to be bought; provided, however, that the management, with its long experience, refrained from buying at all unless the price was right. By assuming (1) that the company would find a given amount of new property to buy cheaply during a certain period, and (2) that it would so rehabilitate all its holdings, including those to be bought, as to raise its return-on-investment to a given rate by the end of the period in question, one could reach some consistent estimate of the present worth of its stock. A slightly different way of handling the same question would be to ask *how much* the company would need to buy, and buy cheaply, to justify the current price for its stock, as given by the market at the time. In Chapter

XIII, the formula to use for answering this latter question is derived and shown to be as follows:

$$(121) \quad z = \frac{A_n}{A_0} = \frac{l_n}{A_0} \cdot \frac{M_0(1+i)^n - \left(\tfrac{1}{2}c_0 + \dfrac{1}{n}\right) s_{\overline{n}|}\, C_0}{e_n c_{n'} + \left(\tfrac{1}{2}c_{n'} - \dfrac{1}{n}\right) s_{\overline{n}|}}$$

In this formula, z is the amount of growth required to justify the actual price M_0, on the basis of the conditions implied by the other data. Since a company growing as fast as this one would probably need to assess its stockholders, under the guise of rights, for more money than it paid out in dividends, its pure dividend, π, would be negative, and would appear as a net assessment, which would have to be compounded by means of the factor [8] $s_{\overline{n}|}$. The price-earnings ratio expected at the end is e_n, and all the other symbols retain their usual meaning.

3. DATA AND ASSUMPTIONS NEEDED IN THE FORMULA OF EVALUATION

Values for some of the data can be computed from the assets and earnings given in Table 49.

Table 49 yields the following knowns:

$$a_0 = 6.60\%$$
$$b_0 = 6.33\%$$
$$c_0 = 7.02\%$$
$$B_0 = \$45.47$$
$$C_0 = \$28.66$$
$$\overline{A_0 = \$74.13}$$

$$(50a) \quad l_0 = \frac{B_0 + C_0}{C_0} = \frac{A_0}{C_0} = \frac{\$74.13}{\$28.66} = 2.59$$

---

[8] For the mathematical definition of this symbol, $s_{\overline{n}|}$, see Chapter XIII, § 2, equation (103). The value of $s_{\overline{n}|}$ is conveniently available in mathematical handbooks under the title "Amount of an Annuity." Cf. Glover's *Tables*, pp. 104 ff., or Huntington, *Mathematics for Engineers*, p. 65.

TABLE 49

AMERICAN & FOREIGN POWER CO., INC.

ADJUSTED [a] FINANCIAL STATEMENT FOR 1929

	Liabilities	Payments	Computed Variables
Senior Securities:			
Bonds of subsidiaries	$ 95,830,000	$ 5,750,000	
Bonds of parent company .	50,000,000	2,500,000	
Preferred stock of subs. ...	39,350,000	2,750,000	
Preferred stock of par. comp.	163,640,000	11,460,000	
Contractual liabilities	14,170,000	850,000	
Contracts payable	15,270,000	910,000	
Minority interests	18,460,000	900,000	
	$396,720,000	$25,120,000	$b = 6.33\%$
Common Stockholders' Equity:			
Common stock	$218,140,000		
Surplus	31,920,000		
	$250,060,000	$17,550,000	$c = 7.02\%$
Allowances:			
Current liabilities	$20,600,000		
Miscellaneous credits	3,670,000		
Gen'l & replacement res. ..	50,670,000		
Other reserves	14,670,000		
	$89,610,000		
Gross liabilities	$736,390,000		
Net liabilities	$646,780,000	$42,670,000	$a = 6.60\%$
Number of shares:			
Outstanding	1,624,357.0		
Held against paid-up warrants	3,433,999.8		
Held against part-paid warrants	3,667,376.0		
Total	8,725,732.8		

[a] The financial statement given in this table is called an *adjusted* financial statement, because it is not an exact copy of the figures published in the *Annual Report*, but shows instead what the company's capitalization and income account *would have been* if the warrants had all been exercised. The warrants are assumed to have been converted into common stock by the surrender of 1 share of second preferred stock, series "A," plus 4 warrants, in exchange for each new share of common issued. No warrants are assumed to have been exercised with cash, as it would have been cheaper to use the second preferred stock, quoted slightly below 100. Since not all of the outstanding second preferred stock would have been

Let us imagine ourselves to be back in the spring of 1930, and assume that the company, in the course of its growth during the next few years, will reshape its capitalization by selling enough bonds to make the ratio of bonds to stocks much more favorable to stockholders, and change its leverage from

$$l_0 = 2.59 \text{ to } l_n = 4.00$$

The rate of earnings on common will then be given by the usual formula

$$(520)\qquad c_{n'} = l_n \left(a_{n'} - b_{n'} + \frac{b_{n'}}{l_n} \right)$$

If the company should so rehabilitate its properties as to raise its return on invested assets from

$$a_0 = 6.60\% \text{ to } a_{n'} = 7.5\%$$

and should so refinance its debt as to lower its bond rate from

$$b_0 = 6.33\% \text{ to } b_{n'} = 6.0\%$$

then its earnings-on-common would rise from

$$c_0 = 7.02\% \text{ to } c_{n'} = 12.0\%,$$

a consequence which can be deduced from the foregoing formula.

Let us further assume that the expected growth, rehabilitation, and refinancing will be completed in five years, so that

$$n = 5$$

---

used up in this way, because more was outstanding than was required to satisfy the warrant holders, the unconverted balance is shown included in the item "Preferred Stock of Parent Company." The items in the income account are estimated when necessary to fit the adjusted items in the capitalization. The table shows contracts payable and notes payable reduced to the figures reported for May 20, 1930 (in the *Boston News Bureau*, evening edition, June 8, 1930). The two bond issues of $20,000,000 and $50,000,000 sold in the spring of 1930 to reduce floating debt are shown in the adjusted figures, under Bonds of Subsidiaries, and Bonds of Parent Company.

Figures of first two columns are rounded off to the nearest $10,000.

If the rate of interest sought by the investor is 6 per cent, then

(2) $$v = \frac{1}{1+i} = \frac{1}{1.06} = 0.9434$$

and

$$s_{\overline{n}} = 5.6371, \text{ when } n = 5$$

The book value at the start is given by the table above as

$$C_o = \$28.66$$

A liberal price-earnings ratio five years thence would seem to be

$$e_n = 15$$

For the actual market price, the high for 1930 may be used, which would give

$$M_o = 101\tfrac{3}{4}$$

This price was equal to *fifty* times 1929 earnings of $2.01, on the capitalization as it would have been if the option warrants were exercised with preferred stock. Even this price was far exceeded at the very peak of the bull market, when the stock sold at $199\tfrac{1}{4}$, or at a *hundred* times earnings! Nothing like these prices were seen for operating companies like Consolidated Gas, or for ordinary holding companies. If these prices had the slightest justification, it was because this company was growing in a manner all its own. To see what justification there was, we must resort to our formula above.

The knowns for insertion in this formula may now be summarized as follows:

$$M_o = \$101.75$$
$$n = 5$$
$$(1+i) = 1.06, \text{ whence } (1+i)^n = 1.3382$$
$$s_{\overline{n}} = 5.6371$$

$$C_o = \$28.66$$
$$c_o = 7.02\%$$
$$l_n = 4.00$$
$$A_o = \$74.13$$
$$c_{n'} = 12.0\%$$
$$e_n = 15$$

When these knowns are put into formula (121), they give a value of

$$z = 5.24$$

4. IMPLICATIONS OF THE MARKET PRICE IN 1930

This value for z means that, to justify the price of its stock in 1930, the company would have had to quintuple its assets in five years. Having doubled its assets in 1929, it would have had to buy twice as many properties in 1930 as in 1929, and would have had to continue buying at this rate in every year thereafter for five years. Could it have been done? Were there enough properties available? Could they have been bought at any such speed without driving up their prices to a point where there would have been no gain to the company from purchasing them?

Level-headed people would hardly have answered yes to these questions in 1930. The stock sold at $101\frac{3}{4}$, however, just because people did not know how to pose these questions; and utility men themselves, from meter-readers to sales managers, and from sales managers to presidents, were deceived by a tip, a pool, and a paper profit, even as you and I. They had high hopes for their business, but no logical evaluation of these hopes in terms of stock prices. The very fact that American and Foreign Power was one of the hardest of all stocks to appraise rationally was the reason why it sold at the most extravagant prices, for speculation ever feeds on mystery, as we have seen before.

5. THE COLLAPSE OF THE STOCK IN THE BEAR MARKET OF
1929–1932

In the great bear market, through no fault of the company's, its stock turned out to be well-nigh the perfect short sale. From a high of 199¼ on September 21, 1929, the stock fell to 2 on May 31, 1932, a drop of 99 per cent. In its fall, it carried down the stock of the parent company, Electric Bond & Share, from 189 to the equivalent [4] of 1⅔.

Unlike American Telephone and Consolidated Gas, American and Foreign Power found that its business was anything but "depression-proof." Its stock came down for two reasons — over-valuation at the start, and financial troubles at the end. The financial troubles arose from the economic difficulties of the countries in which it did business, difficulties of the kind that every economist today feels he should have foretold in 1929. In Cuba the price of sugar fell very low because of post-war over-expansion and because of tariffs by European nations seeking to expand their beet-sugar acreage — and in the end came revolution. In Mexico the price of silver declined greatly, partly because of Indian abandonment of the silver standard, and many mines were closed. In Brazil the price of coffee collapsed when the government's scheme to hold prices up went amiss. In Argentina the price of wheat fell. In Chile the price of nitrate collapsed, and exports almost ceased because of competition from synthetic nitrates and lack of demand from farmers in distress. Copper also added to the distress of Chile. All of these South American countries were further embarrassed by the suspension of the gold standard in England and the fall of sterling. Small wonder that American and Foreign Power saw its gross revenues

[4] The stock of the Electric Bond & Share Co. was "de-split" 1 for 3 on March 22, 1932, when one new share of $5 par stock was issued in exchange for each three shares of old no-par stock. The low on the new stock was 5.

decline and often found it impossible to transfer earnings from where they were made to where they were needed to meet its obligations. Among its obligations on December 31, 1930 were $50,000,000 of bank loans incurred to pay for some of its new acquisitions. Had all gone as planned in the beginning, these loans would have been replaced soon with bonds or preferred stock, but as it was, the company was caught unprotected, and was faced with the threat that its bankers, instead of renewing its loans at maturity, would call them instead in order to seize its valuable properties at panic prices. Although nothing so ruthless was done in fact, investors who knew of "squeezes" in the past naturally felt no desire to buy into such a situation in 1932. Earnings for that year, moreover, amounted to *minus* $12.93 a share outstanding. Optimistic indeed would have been the investor who would have picked this stock to buy in 1932, and yet it is quite possible to believe now, in 1937, that the company will weather the depression and come through with an equity for the common stockholders well in excess of current market prices for its stock.

It is much to be hoped that this venture of American capital into foreign countries will not come utterly to grief, for capital exports from the United States are greatly needed to help these countries and sustain our own trade. Since many a year must pass before capital exports can resume their usual form of loans to foreign governments, it is all the more important to have these exports take place in the meantime in the form of investments by large corporations in fixed assets abroad.

CHAPTER XXVII

CONCLUSION

The foregoing case studies are intended to be suggestive rather than exhaustive. They are designed to show how the buyer of stocks and bonds should go about it to find out if he is getting his money's worth. The last word on the true worth of any security will never be said by anyone, but men who have devoted their whole lives to a particular industry should be able to make a better appraisal of its securities than the outsider can. If the foregoing studies provoke these experts to publish studies about their own stocks and bonds that are more detailed and more profound than anything this book has offered, then the writing of this book will have been justified, for its real purpose has been to propound a consistent Theory of Investment Value, a theory whose usefulness will become the more apparent, it is firmly believed, the better the facts it has to work with.

The time seems to be ripe for the publication of elaborate monographs on the investment value of all the well-known stocks and bonds listed on the exchanges. These articles should be as detailed as those now appearing in the magazine *Fortune*, for instance, but should be more statistical and mathematical, being addressed to the professional investment analyst rather than to the general reader. They should be technical monographs like those appearing in the economic journals, and by means of them investment analysts should debate the value of various securities year after year, continually bringing their appraisals up to date as conditions change. Such a literature as this, giving each investigator the benefit of his predecessors' findings, would help the art of Investment Analysis to grow with the same avoidance of duplicated effort as physics, chemistry, and medicine now pride themselves upon. And with the coming of better professional appraisals of the leading issues on the Stock Exchange should come fairer, steadier prices for the investing public.

APPENDIX I

BOOKINGS AND STOCK PRICES FOR UNITED STATES STEEL

TABLE I
No. 1 Heavy Melting Steel Scrap Composite Price [a]
(Average of Pittsburgh, Chicago, and Philadelphia Quotations, Gross Ton)

Year	Jan.	Feb.	Mar.	Apr.	May	June	July	Aug.	Sept.	Oct.	Nov.	Dec.
1918 ...	$29.93	$29.92	$29.58	$28.47	$28.79	$28.87	$29.00	$29.00	$29.00	$29.00	$28.50	$25.00
1919 ...	17.77	14.75	14.52	15.79	15.06	16.54	19.13	20.25	18.87	18.67	20.50	22.77
1920 ...	25.13	26.00	25.50	24.42	23.71	23.47	24.21	25.88	26.53	23.73	20.00	15.92
1921 ...	14.04	15.21	13.17	11.63	12.20	11.47	11.00	11.57	12.15	12.88	12.73	12.29
1922 ...	12.45	12.46	13.46	14.71	15.67	15.52	15.92	16.30	18.33	19.20	18.02	17.94
1923 ...	20.22	21.46	24.79	24.00	20.77	18.94	17.23	16.58	16.98	15.15	15.13	17.37
1924 ...	19.15	19.21	17.56	15.20	14.71	14.88	16.00	16.58	17.20	17.08	18.17	20.08
1925 ...	20.10	18.27	16.92	15.48	15.46	16.09	16.46	17.23	17.42	17.08	17.63	17.37
1926 ...	16.97	15.50	15.83	15.27	14.35	14.40	15.42	15.88	16.25	15.58	15.25	15.08
1927 ...	15.17	14.58	14.65	14.71	13.95	13.60	13.48	13.80	13.92	13.48	13.18	13.48
1928 ...	13.70	13.71	13.65	13.81	13.90	13.52	13.13	13.75	14.75	15.85	15.97	15.97
1929 ...	17.02	16.96	16.71	17.18	16.54	16.39	16.60	16.86	16.60	15.78	14.15	14.15
1930 ...	14.65	14.92	14.88	14.30	13.71	13.31	13.08	13.29	13.70	12.77	11.28	11.28
1931 ...	11.30	11.15	11.10	10.83	9.94	9.39	9.25	9.25	9.12	8.78	8.61	8.61
1932 ...	8.41	8.27	8.23	8.12	7.48	6.89	6.46	6.93	7.69	7.62	7.45	6.92
1933 ...	6.77	6.83	6.96	7.73	9.70	9.97	11.27	12.08	11.35	10.56	9.94	10.50
1934 ...	11.73	12.25	12.82	12.54	11.57	10.67	10.53	10.15	9.63	9.54	10.04	11.40
1935 ...	12.18	11.98	11.06	10.46	10.70	10.74	10.96	12.25	12.71	12.67	12.90	13.33
1936 ...	13.48	14.12	14.75	14.59	13.39	12.81	13.29	15.04	16.45	16.63	16.31	16.94
1937 ...	18.33	19.30	21.25	21.02	18.09	17.16	18.79	21.00	19.02	....	....	....

[a] Source: Annual Review Number, *The Iron Age*, January, 1937. Most recent figures obtained by averaging the weekly figures in various issues during 1937.

TABLE II

UNITED STATES STEEL CORPORATION

MARKET PRICES OF COMMON STOCK MONTHLY [a]

	High	Low	Last	High	Low	Last
		1918			*1919*	
Jan.	98	88⅝	97⅞	96¾	88¾	89⅞
Feb.	98½	92⅞	96	95¾	88¼	92
Mar.	92⅝	86½	89⅞	100⅝	91¾	98⅝
Apr.	96⅜	88¾	94⅝	103	97⅛	97½
May	113¾	95⅜	97⅝	109½	96½	108⅜
June	110⅜	96¼	108	111⅞	103⅛	107½
July	109¼	101½	108½	115½	107⅜	109⅛
Aug.	116½	107⅜	111¾	110¼	98⅜	103¼
Sept.	116	107⅛	112½	108⅛	100¼	107¼
Oct.	114⅝	100⅞	102⅞	112¼	104¼	109⅜
Nov.	104⅛	94	95¼	112⅜	101¾	102½
Dec.	99¾	92½	95	107⅜	100⅝	106⅝
		1920			*1921*	
Jan.	109	104⅜	105¼	84¾	80½	82⅝
Feb.	105⅝	92¼	93⅝	85	81¼	81⅜
Mar.	106	93	104	82⅞	77¾	81
Apr.	107½	93⅝	94⅞	85	79⅛	83⅜
May	97⅛	89⅝	94⅛	86½	79½	79⅝
June	95	91¼	92⅝	80½	70¼	74⅞
July	95⅝	87¼	88	76¼	71⅜	74⅞
Aug.	91¼	83⅞	88¼	76¼	72⅜	74¼
Sept.	91½	85⅞	86	80½	73⅞	79½
Oct.	89⅞	85¼	88⅛	81⅝	74¼	80⅞
Nov.	88⅞	80	81¾	84¾	80⅛	82¾
Dec.	83¼	76¼	81	85	82⅝	84¼
		1922			*1923*	
Jan.	88	82	85	108¾	104	104½
Feb.	96½	84¾	94⅝	108¾	104¼	107⅜
Mar.	96½	93⅛	95½	109⅝	105⅜	107½
Apr.	100⅛	95⅛	98⅛	108¼	103¼	103⅛
May	102½	96⅝	100⅝	103⅞	95	97¾
June	103¼	96¾	99⅛	97¾	89⅝	90¼

[a] Sources: monthly *Bank and Quotation Record* of the *Commercial and Financial Chronicle*, and the *New York Times*.

TABLE II (Continued)

	High	Low	Last	High	Low	Last
July	102½	98⅛	101½	92⅝	85½	85⅝
Aug.	105½	100	104	94	86	93⅛
Sept.	106⅜	100⅞	100⅞	93¾	85⅞	86⅞
Oct.	111½	101½	104⅞	91½	87⅞	91½
Nov.	110⅞	99⅞	100⅞	96½	90⅞	94½
Dec.	108⅛	101	106⅞	100⅛	93⅞	99⅝
		1924			*1925*	
Jan.	107	98⅛	107	129⅝	119¾	126¼
Feb.	109	101⅜	103⅝	128¼	122⅛	122⅝
Mar	104¼	97	98⅝	125⅜	112⅜	115⅜
Apr.	101	95½	98	118⅛	112⅞	113⅞
May	100	94⅞	95½	120¼	113⅜	116⅛
June	100⅛	94¼	99½	117¼	113⅜	115¾
July	107⅞	99⅛	107⅞	120⅜	114⅝	117⅝
Aug.	111¾	105¾	109¾	125⅞	117½	120⅜
Sept.	110¼	105⅜	108½	125⅝	118¼	119⅞
Oct.	109⅝	104¾	109⅜	130¼	120⅛	128
Nov.	119⅛	109	117¾	139¼	124⅞	128½
Dec.	121	116	119¾	137⅜	128⅝	135⅞
		1926			*1927*	
Jan.	138½	131¾	133⅞	159¼	153½	157
Feb.	134	123¾	125	162⅜	155⅞	159⅞
Mar.	128⅛	117⅝	121	167¼	156½	167
Apr.	124⅝	117	123⅛	172¾	165½	165⅞
May	125	118¼	125	176	164⅝	174½
June	144	122½	143⅜	125⅞	118⅞	119⅜
July	149¼	137⅞	146½	137⅝	119½	136
Aug.	159⅝	146⅝	150½	148⅜	129¼	143⅛
Sept.	152¾	142¼	150	160½	143⅜	149⅝
Oct.	154¾	133⅞	138½	154⅝	128⅝	129⅞
Nov.	153⅜	137¾	146⅛	147⅝	130⅛	146½
Dec.	160½	146½	157⅜	155	138	151⅞
		1928			*1929*	
Jan.	152¾	143⅝	146¼	192¾	157⅛	183½
Feb.	147	138⅛	139⅜	192¼	168¼	191½
Mar.	152	137⅜	147⅜	193⅞	171½	183¾

TABLE II (Continued)

	High	Low	Last	High	Low	Last
Apr.	154	143¾	145½	191⅞	176¼	188⅞
May	150⅜	142½	146¾	186	163	165⅝
June	147⅜	132⅜	137⅜	191⅜	165½	190¾
July	145⅜	134⅛	142⅝	210¾	189½	209⅝
Aug.	155⅝	139¼	154½	260½	209⅛	256½
Sept.	161⅝	152	159¼	261¾	221⅛	222¾
Oct.	166½	156	159⅞	234	166½	193¼
Nov.	172½	160⅛	167⅜	190¾	150	162⅛
Dec.	167	149¾	161¼	189	156⅝	171
		1930			*1931*	
Jan.	184⅝	166	184⅝	145	137⅞	139¼
Feb.	189¼	176⅞	183⅛	147½	137⅞	147½
Mar.	195	177¾	193⅞	150⅜	139⅛	139⅞
Apr.	198¾	180¼	184	140¼	115	120
May	183¾	165¾	173⅝	121	89⅞	91
June	173¾	151⅝	159⅝	104¾	83⅛	100¾
July	170	153¼	165¼	105¾	83½	85⅜
Aug.	172¼	155½	171¼	93¼	83¾	87½
Sept.	173¾	154¾	155½	88½	71	71⅜
Oct.	160⅜	143¼	144	73¼	62¼	67½
Nov.	149¾	138	145½	74⅞	53	56¾
Dec.	147½	134⅜	139⅛	55¼	36	38⅝
		1932			*1933*	
Jan.	46⅞	35½	37⅜	32	26⅝	28¼
Feb.	52⅝	37⅜	46	29¼	23½	24¼
Mar.	51¼	38¾	39	33¾	23⅜	27⅜
Apr.	40½	27¾	28¼	46⅞	27⅛	46⅝
May	31⅜	25½	25¾	53⅝	43⅜	51⅞
June	30⅜	21¼	22	60	51	58
July	29⅜	21⅜	28⅞	67½	49	52
Aug.	49⅜	27⅝	46⅛	58½	49¼	54⅝
Sept.	52½	35⅝	43	56⅞	43¾	45⅝
Oct.	44	33⅛	35⅝	48½	34¾	36¾
Nov.	39¾	31⅛	31¾	46	35⅜	43⅞
Dec.	34	25	27½	48⅝	44⅜	47¾

TABLE II (Continued)

	High	Low	Last	High	Low	Last
		1934			*1935*	
Jan.	58⅜	46	56⅛	40⅛	35⅝	37
Feb.	59⅞	54¼	54½	38⅝	31½	32½
Mar.	56¾	48¾	52⅜	33	27½	28¾
Apr.	53⅜	46½	46⅝	33⅞	28⅛	32¼
May	47⅝	39	39	35½	30⅝	31½
June	43¼	37⅜	38⅝	34⅜	30⅝	33⅜
July	41⅜	33½	34⅜	43⅞	33¼	43¾
Aug.	36¼	31⅞	33⅞	46¼	41⅛	43¾
Sept.	34⅞	29⅜	33⅞	48¾	42½	45
Oct.	35	31¼	31⅞	47⅞	41⅜	46¼
Nov.	39⅛	31½	38⅞	50⅝	45⅞	47⅛
Dec.	39½	36⅛	39	49	44⅛	48½
		1936			*1937*	
Jan.	50⅜	46⅜	50⅜	97¼	75	96¾
Feb.	65	49⅝	63⅛	114½	95⅜	111¼
Mar.	67⅞	60¼	64⅞	126½	110⅜	121⅝
Apr.	72⅜	55	57¾	120½	98¾	101¼
May	61⅝	54⅛	61⅛	105½	91⅝	100¾
June	64¾	58½	60⅛	102¾	92½	99⅜
July	68¼	56¾	64¾	119½	99	118½
Aug.	71¼	64½	70⅜	121¼	107⅝	108⅜
Sept.	73⅛	69⅜	70	107⅝	78¼	80¾
Oct.	79¾	69⅝	76¼			
Nov.	79⅜	72	76⅛			
Dec.	79⅞	73⅝	78			

APPENDIX I

TABLE III

Derivation of Bookings from Unfilled Orders and Production[a]

	Unfilled Orders	Pro- duction	Book- ings	Unfilled Orders	Pro- duction	Book- ings	Unfilled Orders	Pro- duction	Book- ings
		1919			*1920*			*1921*	
Dec. '18	547								
Jan.	495	87	35	686	84	158	550	90	48
Feb.	489	86	80	701	90	105	504	75	29
Mar.	402	82	−5	729	96	124	457	51	4
Apr.	355	70	23	762	60	93	425	42	10
May	317	58	20	804	68	110	398	38	11
June	362	68	113	805	70	71	372	32	6
July	413	74	125	814	75	84	351	25	4
Aug.	452	81	120	790	80	56	329	30	8
Sept.	465	70	83	758	85	53	331	34	36
Oct.	479	50	64	717	87	46	311	44	24
Nov.	528	62	111	657	89	29	309	52	50
Dec.	612	73	157	592	94	29	310	48	49
		1922			*1923*			*1924*	
Jan.	308	47	45	499	86	98	344	82	107
Feb.	300	57	49	526	88	115	352	92	100
Mar.	326	65	91	534	89	97	342	95	85
Apr.	369	70	113	525	93	84	301	80	39
May	381	75	87	503	93	71	259	71	29
June	408	75	102	460	92	49	233	61	35
July	418	75	85	425	89	54	227	45	39
Aug	431	67	80	389	87	51	234	52	59
Sept.	484	67	120	362	87	60	247	65	78
Oct.	499	76	91	336	90	64	250	66	69
Nov.	494	81	76	314	82	60	286	70	106
Dec.	487	80	73	319	78	83	342	77	133
		1925			*1926*			*1927*	
Jan.	358	90	106	360	92	81	276	86	74
Feb.	377	93	112	340	92	72	261	91	76
Mar.	348	94	65	322	95	77	258	96	93
Apr.	319	85	56	285	93	56	250	92	84
May	292	76	49	267	90	72	220	90	60
June	268	72	48	255	89	77	220	77	77
July	257	68	57	263	85	93	226	74	80
Aug.	256	70	69	259	88	84	230	71	75
Sept	271	75	90	262	88	91	226	68	64
Oct.	301	80	110	268	87	93	239	68	81
Nov.	337	85	121	277	78	87	247	68	76
Dec.	371	85	119	288	74	85	284	67	104

[a] The method of derivation is explained in Chapter II, § 2, footnote 3. All figures are expressed as a percentage of monthly capacity. For want of published figures on shipments themselves, figures on production are used, since both sets of figures move very closely together. Unfilled orders used to be published monthly, being announced at noon on the tenth of each month, and printed in the financial newspapers the next morning.

TABLE III (Continued)

	Unfilled Orders	Pro- duction	Book- ings	Unfilled Orders	Pro- duction	Book- ings	Unfilled Orders	Pro- duction	Book- ings
		1928			*1929*			*1930*	
Jan.	306	83	105	288	86	96	303	74	77
Feb.	313	89	96	287	91	90	303	85	85
Mar.	308	91	86	307	95	115	308	84	89
Apr.	275	92	59	307	97	97	292	81	65
May	242	88	55	298	100	91	272	76	56
June	257	77	92	294	98	94	265	70	63
July	252	74	69	281	97	84	268	57	60
Aug.	255	76	79	251	94	64	238	60	30
Sept.	260	84	89	267	87	103	226	56	44
Oct.	263	89	92	279	84	96	230	54	58
Nov.	257	85	79	281	73	75	239	47	56
Dec.	278	80	101	300	64	83	258	43	62
		1931			*1932*			*1933*	
Jan.	270	47	59	162	26	20	116	16	12
Feb.	257	52	39	156	27	21	113	19	16
Mar.	258	57	58	151	25	20	112	15	14
Apr.	250	53	45	142	23	14	114	21	23
May	231	47	28	133	21	12	118	30	34
June	221	39	29	124	16	7	129	42	53
July	215	35	29	120	15	11	123	53	47
Aug.	199	32	16	120	13	13	116	49	42
Sept.	196	29	26	121	16	17	108	36	28
Oct.	194	28	26	122	19	20	...	34	..
Nov.	181	31	18	120	18	16	...	24	..
Dec.	168	24	11	120	15	15	...	28	..
		1934			*1935*			*1936*	
Jan.	...	29	..	...	41	..	...	42	..
Feb.	...	37	..	...	47	..	...	47	..
Mar.	...	42	..	...	45	..	...	50	..
Apr.	...	41	..	...	43	..	...	62	..
May	...	45	..	...	40	..	...	63	..
June	...	48	..	...	36	..	...	66	..
July	...	29	..	...	36	..	...	63	..
Aug.	...	23	..	...	40	..	...	68	..
Sept.	...	20	..	...	41	..	...	69	..
Oct.	...	22	..	...	42	..	...	70	..
Nov.	...	24	..	...	43	..	...	67	..
Dec.	...	29	..	...	45	..	...	67	..
		1937							
Jan.	...	74							
Feb.	...	80							
Mar.	...	83							
Apr.	...	87							
May	...	88							
June	...	87							
July	...	81							
Aug.	...	82							
Sept.	...	77							

TABLE IV

Seasonal Variation of Bookings

Link Relatives in Chronological Order

Year	J/D	F/J	M/F	A/M	M/A	J/M	J/J	A/J	S/A	O/S	N/O	D/N
1919	...	2.29	...	...	0.87	5.65	1.11	0.96	0.69	0.77	1.73	1.42
1920	1.01	0.67	1.18	0.75	1.18	0.64	1.18	0.67	0.95	0.87	0.63	1.00
1921	1.66	0.60	0.14	2.50	1.10	0.55	0.67	2.00	4.50	0.67	2.08	0.98
1922	0.92	1.09	1.86	1.24	0.77	1.17	0.83	0.94	1.50	0.76	0.84	0.96
1923	1.34	1.17	0.84	0.87	0.84	0.69	1.10	0.94	1.18	1.07	0.94	1.38
1924	1.29	0.93	0.85	0.46	0.74	1.20	1.11	1.51	1.32	0.88	1.54	1.25
1925	0.80	1.06	0.58	0.86	0.87	0.98	1.19	1.21	1.31	1.22	1.10	0.98
1926	0.68	0.89	1.07	0.73	1.29	1.07	1.21	0.90	1.08	1.02	0.93	0.98
1927	0.87	1.03	1.22	0.90	0.71	1.28	1.03	0.94	0.85	1.27	0.94	1.37
1928	1.01	0.91	0.90	0.69	0.93	1.67	0.75	1.15	1.13	1.03	0.86	1.28
1929	0.95	0.94	1.28	0.84	0.94	1.03	0.89	0.76	1.61	0.93	0.78	1.11
1930	0.93	1.10	1.05	0.73	0.86	1.13	0.95	0.50	1.47	1.32	0.97	1.11
1931	0.95	0.66	1.49	0.78	0.62	1.04	1.00	0.55	1.62	1.00	0.69	0.61
1932	1.82	1.05	0.95	0.70	0.86	0.58	1.57	1.18	1.31	1.18	0.80	0.94
1933	0.80	1.33	0.88	1.64	1.48	1.56	0.89	0.88	0.67	...	...	...

TABLE V
Seasonal Variation of Bookings
Link Relatives Arrayed

	J/D	F/J	M/F	A/M	M/A	J/M	J/J	A/J	S/A	O/S	N/O	D/N
1	0.68	0.60	0.14	0.46	0.62	0.55	0.67	0.50	0.67	0.67	0.63	0.61
2	0.80	0.66	0.58	0.69	0.71	0.58	0.75	0.55	0.69	0.76	0.69	0.94
3	0.80	0.67	0.84	0.70	0.74	0.64	0.83	0.67	0.85	0.77	0.78	0.96
4	0.87	0.89	0.85	0.73	0.77	0.69	0.89	0.76	0.95	0.87	0.80	0.98
5	0.92	0.91	0.88	0.73	0.84	0.98	0.89	0.88	1.08	0.88	0.84	0.98
6	0.93	0.93	0.90	0.75	0.86	1.03	0.95	0.90	1.13	0.93	0.86	0.98
7	0.95	0.94	0.95	0.78	0.86	1.04	1.00	0.94	1.18	1.00	0.93	1.00
8	0.95	1.03	1.05	0.84	0.87	1.07	1.03	0.94	1.31	1.02	0.94	1.11
9	1.01	1.05	1.07	0.86	0.87	1.13	1.10	0.94	1.31	1.03	0.94	1.11
10	1.01	1.06	1.18	0.87	0.93	1.17	1.11	0.96	1.32	1.07	0.97	1.25
11	1.29	1.09	1.22	0.90	0.94	1.20	1.11	1.15	1.47	1.18	1.10	1.28
12	1.34	1.10	1.28	1.24	1.10	1.28	1.18	1.18	1.50	1.22	1.54	1.37
13	1.66	1.17	1.49	1.64	1.18	1.56	1.19	1.21	1.61	1.27	1.73	1.38
14	1.82	1.33	1.86	2.50	1.29	1.67	1.21	1.51	1.62	1.32	2.08	1.42
15	⋮	2.29	⋮	⋮	1.48	5.65	1.57	2.00	4.50	⋮	⋮	⋮
Median	0.95	1.03	1.05	0.84	0.87	1.07	1.04	0.94	1.31	1.02	0.94	1.11
Arith. mean of middle 7 terms:	1.01	1.00	1.04	0.82	0.88	1.09	1.02	0.96	1.26	1.02	0.94	1.10

TABLE VI

INDEX OF SEASONAL VARIATION OF BOOKINGS

Months to which average link applies	Average of middle 7 links for each pair of months	Logs. of links	Log. of correction factor	Logs. of corrected links	Months between which ratio applies	Logs. of these ratios [a]	Unadjusted index of seasonal variation	Adjusted index of seasonal variation	Month to which it applies
....	....	....	....	....	J/J	.0000	100.0	110.0	Jan.
F/J	1.00	0.0000	− .0026 =	.9974	F/J	.9974	99.4	109.4	Feb.
M/F	1.04	0.0170	− .0026 =	.0144	M/J	.0118	102.8	112.8	Mar.
A/M	0.82	9.9138	− .0026 =	.9112	A/J	.9230	83.8	93.8	Apr.
M/A	0.88	9.9445	− .0026 =	.9419	M/J	.8649	73.3	83.3	May
J/M	1.09	0.0374	− .0026 =	.0348	J/J	.8997	79.4	89.4	June
J/J	1.02	0.0086	− .0026 =	.0060	J/J	.9057	80.5	90.5	July
A/J	0.96	9.9822	− .0026 =	.9796	A/J	.8853	76.8	86.8	Aug.
S/A	1.26	0.1004	− .0026 =	.0978	S/J	.9831	96.2	106.2	Sept.
O/S	1.02	0.0086	− .0026 =	.0060	O/J	.9891	97.5	107.5	Oct.
N/O	0.94	9.9731	− .0026 =	.9705	N/J	.9596	91.1	101.1	Nov.
D/N	1.10	0.0414	− .0026 =	.0388	D/J	.9984	99.6	109.6	Dec.
J/D	1.01	0.0043	− .0026 =	.0017	J/J	.0001	...	...	
				.0001			12)1080.4	12)1200.4	
		40.0313 − 40				Average unadjusted index	90.0	100.03	
		+ 80 − 80				Adjustment needed	10.0		
		12)120.0313 − 120					100.0		
						Average adjusted index			

Average log. 10.0026 − 10
Adjustment needed −.0026
Average adjusted log. 10.0000 − 10

[a] Or of the chain relation.

TABLE VII

BOOKINGS ADJUSTED FOR SEASONAL VARIATION

	Raw Bookings[a]	Adjusted Bookings	Raw Bookings	Adjusted Bookings	Raw Bookings	Adjusted Bookings	Index of Seasonal Variation[b]
	1919		1920		1921		
Jan. ...	35	32	158	144	48	44	110
Feb. ...	80	73	105	96	29	27	109.4
Mar. ...	−5	−4	124	109	4	3	112.8
Apr. ...	23	25	93	99	10	11	93.8
May ...	20	24	110	132	11	13	83.3
June ...	113	126	71	79	6	7	89.4
July ...	125	137	84	93	4	4	90.5
Aug. ...	120	138	56	65	8	9	86.8
Sept. ...	83	78	53	50	36	34	106.2
Oct. ...	64	59	46	43	24	22	107.5
Nov. ...	111	110	29	29	50	50	101.1
Dec. ...	157	144	29	26	49	45	109.6
	1922		1923		1924		
Jan. ...	45	41	98	89	107	97	110
Feb. ...	49	45	115	105	100	92	109.4
Mar. ...	91	80	97	86	85	75	112.8
Apr. ...	113	120	84	90	39	42	93.8
May ...	87	104	71	85	29	35	83.3
June ...	102	114	49	55	35	39	89.4
July ...	85	94	54	60	39	43	90.5
Aug. ...	80	92	51	59	59	68	86.8
Sept. ...	120	113	60	56	78	73	106.2
Oct. ...	91	84	64	60	69	64	107.5
Nov. ...	76	75	60	59	106	104	101.1
Dec. ...	73	67	83	76	133	121	109.6
	1925		1926		1927		
Jan. ...	106	96	81	74	74	67	110
Feb. ...	112	102	72	66	76	70	109.4
Mar. ...	65	57	77	68	93	82	112.8
Apr. ...	56	60	56	60	84	89	93.8
May ...	49	59	72	87	60	72	83.3
June ...	48	54	77	86	77	86	89.4
July ...	57	63	93	102	80	88	90.5
Aug. ...	69	79	84	97	75	87	86.8
Sept. ...	90	84	91	85	64	60	106.2
Oct. ...	110	102	93	86	81	75	107.5
Nov. ...	121	120	87	86	76	75	101.1
Dec. ...	119	109	85	78	104	95	109.6

[a] From Table III.
[b] From Table VI, last column.

TABLE VII (Continued)

	Raw Bookings	Adjusted Bookings	Raw Bookings	Adjusted Bookings	Raw Bookings	Adjusted Bookings	Index of Seasonal Variation
	1928		1929		1930		
Jan. ...	105	96	96	87	77	70	110
Feb. ...	96	88	90	82	85	78	109.4
Mar. ...	86	76	115	101	89	78	112.8
Apr. ...	59	63	97	103	65	69	93.8
May ...	55	66	91	109	56	67	83.3
June ...	92	102	94	105	63	71	89.4
July ...	69	76	84	93	60	66	90.5
Aug. ...	79	91	64	74	30	35	86.8
Sept. ...	89	84	103	97	44	41	106.2
Oct. ...	92	86	96	89	58	54	107.5
Nov. ...	79	78	75	74	56	55	101.1
Dec. ...	101	93	83	76	62	56	109.6
	1931		1932		1933		
Jan. ...	59	54	20	18	12	11	110
Feb. ...	39	36	21	19	16	15	109.4
Mar. ...	58	52	20	18	14	12	112.8
Apr. ...	45	48	14	15	23	25	93.8
May ...	28	33	12	14	34	41	83.3
June ...	29	32	7	8	53	59	89.4
July ...	29	32	11	12	47	52	90.5
Aug. ...	16	18	13	15	42	48	86.8
Sept. ...	26	24	17	16	28	26	106.2
Oct. ...	26	24	20	19	..	..	107.5
Nov. ...	18	18	16	16	..	..	101.1
Dec. ...	11	10	15	14	..	..	109.6

APPENDIX II

THE DIVIDEND–PAYING POWER OF UNITED STATES STEEL

TABLE I

The Steel Corporation's Capacity, Output, and Rate of Operations

Year	Capacity (in thousands of tons)	Output	Computed Ratio	Annual Report Figure
	Rolled and Finished Products		Rate of Operations	
1901	7,719[a]	7,426	96.2%	....
1902	not avail.	8,197	not avail.	....
1903	not avail.	7,459	not avail.	....
1904	not avail.	6,793	not avail.	....
1905	not avail.	9,226	not avail.	....
1906	not avail.	10,578	not avail.	....
1907	10,600[b]	10,565	not avail.	....
1908	12,900[c]	6,207	48.1	....
1909	13,146[d]	9,860	not avail.	75.0%[*]
1910	13,418[d]	10,734	not avail.	80.0%[*]
1911	14,143[d]	9,476	not avail.	67.0%[*]
1912	13,897[d]	12,507	not avail.	90.0%[*]
1913	14,063[d]	12,375	not avail.	88.0%[*]
1914	14,155[d]	9,015	63.7%	62.0%[*]
1915	15,350	11,763	76.5%	85.0%
1916	16,080	15,461	96.2%	100.0%
1917	16,125	14,943	92.7%	war
1918	16,200	13,849	85.5%	war
1919	16,200	11,998	74.0%	74.5%
1920	16,500	14,229	86.2%	88.3%
1921	16,500	7,860	47.6%	47.5%
1922	16,600	11,785	71.0%	71.3%
1923	16,700	14,721	88.2%	88.3%
1924	16,900	11,723	69.4%	69.0%
1925	16,252	13,271	81.7%	78.4%
1926	16,472	14,334	87.1%	88.0%
1927	16,750	12,979	77.4%	78.9%[f]
1928	17,159	13,972	81.5%	83.4%
1929	17,705	15,303	86.3%	89.2%[f]
1930	18,371	11,609	63.2%	65.6%[f]
1931	19,647	7,196	36.6%	38.0%
1932	19,270	3,591	18.6%	18.3%
1933	19,271	5,536	28.7%	29.0%
1934	19,262	6,005	31.2%	31.0%
1935	18,613	7,474	40.2%	38.8%
1936	17,929	11,030	61.5%	59.3%

[a] Capacity as of April 1, 1901.
[b] Capacity as of July 1, 1907, according to Annual Report for 1908, p. 28, and before purchase of Tennessee Coal and Iron Co. and completion of Gary plant.
[c] Capacity as of Jan. 1, 1909, according to Annual Report for 1908, p. 28.
[d] Computed from rate of operations and output.
[*] Rate of Output as given in annual reports under "General."
[f] Based on capacity at end of previous year, apparently.

TABLE II

NATIONAL CAPACITY, OUTPUT, AND RATE OF OPERATIONS

Year	National Capacity[a] (in 1000 tons of ingots)	National Output[a]	National Rate of Operations[b]	U. S. Steel's Rate of Operations[c]	Ratio of Steel's to Nation's Rate of Operations[d]
1901	.....	13,156	...	...	....
1902	.....	14,556	...	...	....
1903	.....	14,105	...	...	....
1904	.....	13,530	...	...	....
1905	.....	19,463	...	...	....
1906	.....	22,624	...	...	....
1907	.....	22,559	...	...	....
1908	.....	13,677	...	...	....
1909	.....	23,299	...	...	....
1910	.....	25,154	...	...	....
1911	.....	23,029	...	...	....
1912	.....	30,285	...	...	....
1913	37,905	30,280	80.0%	...	....
1914	39,524	22,820	57.8%	61.6%	106.6%
1915	43,823	31,284	71.4%	79.6%	111.6%
1916	47,586	41,401	87.0%	95.1%	109.3%
1917	50,455	43,619	86.5%	91.4%	105.7%
1918	52,348	43,051	82.3%	87.7%	106.6%
1919	53,194	33,695	63.3%	77.0%	121.6%
1920	54,802	40,881	74.6%	84.9%	113.8%
1921	55,818	19,224	34.4%	48.3%	140.4%
1922	56,061	34,568	61.7%	70.5%	114.3%
1923	56,760	43,486	76.5%	89.2%	116.6%
1924	58,438	36,811	63.0%	71.3%	113.2%
1925	55,844	44,141	79.0%	83.1%	105.2%
1926	57,999	46,936	80.9%	87.6%	108.3%
1927	59,436	43,777	73.7%	77.8%	105.6%
1928	61,759	50,325	81.5%	83.0%	101.8%
1929	63,068	54,850	87.0%	87.0%	100.0%
1930	66,897	39,739	59.3%	64.1%	108.0%
1931	68,299	25,429	37.2%	36.2%	97.3%
1932	68,199	13,464	19.7%	18.0%	91.4%
1933	69,391	22,894	33.0%	29.4%	89.1%
1934	69,735	25,949	37.2%	31.7%	85.2%
1935	69,429	33,940	48.9%	41.8%	85.5%
1936	69,245	47,513	68.6%	65.6%	95.6%

[a] Source: *Annual Statistical Report of the American Iron and Steel Institute* for 1936, p. 16, col. 2, and p. 14, lowest table.

[b] Computed from two preceding columns.

[c] Rate of operations in terms of ingot capacity and output, not in terms of rolled and finished products. Computed from data in Annual Reports.

[d] Computed from two preceding columns.

TABLE III
The Steel Corporation's Declining Share in the Total Output

Year	National Output[a] (1000 tons of ingots)	U. S. Steel's Output[b] (1000 tons of ingots)	U. S. Steel's Share[c]
1901	13,156	not available	not available
1902	14,556	9,744	66.9%[d]
1903	14,105	9,168	65.0%
1904	13,530	8,406	62.0%
1905	19,463	11,995	61.5%[d]
1906	22,624	13,511	59.7%
1907	22,559	13,343	59.1%
1908	13,677	7,839	57.5%
1909	23,299	13,355	57.3%
1910	25,154	14,179	56.5%
1911	23,029	12,753	55.3%
1912	30,285	16,901	55.9%
1913	30,280	16,656	55.0%
1914	22,820	11,826	51.8%
1915	31,284	16,376	52.3%
1916	41,404	20,911	50.5%
1917	43,619	20,285	46.4%
1918	43,051	19,583	45.5%
1919	33,695	17,200	51.0%
1920	40,881	19,278	47.2%
1921	19,224	10,966	57.0%
1922	34,568	16,082	46.6%
1923	43,486	20,330	46.8%
1924	36,811	16,479	44.7%
1925	44,141	18,899	42.8%
1926	46,936	20,307	43.3%
1927	43,777	18,486	42.3%
1928	50,325	20,106	40.0%
1929	54,850	21,869	39.9%
1930	39,739	16,726	42.1%
1931	25,429	10,082	39.6%
1932	13,464	4,929	36.6%
1933	22,894	8,047	35.1%
1934	25,949	8,660	33.4%
1935	33,940	11,131	32.8%
1936	47,513	16,910	35.6%

[a] Source: *Annual Statistical Report of the American Iron and Steel Institute.*
[b] Source: *Wall St. Journal* table, mentioned in § 12.
[c] Computed from two preceding columns.
[d] Also see U. S. Steel's Annual Report for 1905, p. 25.

TABLE IV
CHANGES IN CAPITALIZATION

Year	Bonds	Preferred Stock	Common Stock	Changes in Bonds and Preferred Stock[a]
1901	$364,735,900	$510,281,100	$508,302,500	....
1902	360,713,900	510,281,100	508,302,500	$— 4,022,000
1903	551,000,677	360,281,100	508,302,500	+ 40,287,000[b]
1904	571,752,666	360,281,100	508,302,500	+ 20,752,000
1905	567,858,690	360,281,100	508,302,500	— 3,894,000
1906	562,121,180	360,281,100	508,302,500	— 5,738,000
1907	600,150,904	360,281,100	508,302,500	+ 38,030,000
1908	593,196,842	360,281,100	508,302,500	— 6,954,000
1909	606,349,752	360.281,100	508,302,500	+ 13,153,000
1910	596,320,161	360,281,100	508,302,500	— 10,030,000
1911	620,469,941	360,281,100	508,302,500	+ 24,150,000
1912	643,098,672	360,281,100	508,302,500	+ 22,629,000
1913	627,083,403	360,281,100	508,302,500	— 16,015,000
1914	627,031,724	360,281,100	508,302,500	— 52,000
1915	616,432,706	360,281,100	508,302,500	— 10,599,000
1916	603,471,027	360,281,100	508,302,500	— 12,962,000
1917	586,786,347	360,281,100	508,302,500	— 16,685,000
1918	582,646,169	360,281,100	508,302,500	— 4,140,000
1919	568,727,932	360,281,100	508,302,500	— 13,918,000
1920	554,828,231	360,281,100	508,302,500	— 13,900,000
1921	540,706,561	360,281,100	508,302,500	— 14,122,000
1922	539,582,061	360,281,100	508,302,500	— 1,125,000
1923	527,034,900	360,281,100	508,302,500	— 12,547,000
1924	511,272,930	360,281,100	508,302,500	— 15,762,000
1925	509,479,578	360,281,100	508,302,500	— 1,793,000
1926	492,689,353	360,281,100	503,302,500	— 16,790,000
1927	475,174,529	360,281,100	711,623,500	— 17,515,000
1928	456,602,415	360,281,100	711,623,500	— 18,572,000
1929	112,257,978	360,281,100	813,284,000	—344,344,000
1930	101,820,111	360,281,100	868,743,500	— 10,438,000
1931	98,887,294	360,281,100	870,325,200	— 2,933,000
1932	95,950,255	360,281,100	870,325,200	— 2,937,000
1933	93,179,824	360,281,100	870,325,200	— 2,770,000
1934	90,923,289[c]	360,281,100	870,325,200	— 2,257,000
1935	88,811,490[c]	360,281,100	870,325,200	— 2,112,000
1936	93,511,074[c]	360,281,100	870,325,200	+ 4,700,000

[a] To nearest $1000.
[b] Preferred stock was reduced $150,000,000 this year.
[c] Exclusive of $4,740,000 of bonds of Pittsburg, Bessemer and Lake Erie R.R. included in consolidated statement for the first time in 1934. See p. 7 of Annual Report for 1934.

TABLE V
YEARLY INCREASES IN CASH AND FUNDS
(in thousands of dollars)

	Marketable Securities	Time Deposits	Cash[a]	Insurance & Depreciation Fund Assets	Contingent Reserve Fund	Total	Change
1901	7,251	none	55,316	none	none	62,567	......
1902	6,091	none	50,163	930	none	57,184	— 5,383
1903	5,986	12,823[b]	50,200	3,111	none	72,120	14,936
1904	7,142	none	60,646	5,799	617	74,204	2,084
1905	6,588	none	58,956	15,716	641	81,901	7,697
1906	7,702	7,600[b]	67,637	25,504	1,542	109,985	28,084
1907	8,831	6,000[b]	53,964	30,783	1,216	100,794	— 9,191
1908	4,824	50[b]	49,548	20,817	1,903	77,142	— 23,652
1909	4,764	none	58,521	19,053	1,986	84,324	7,182
1910	4,411	none	56,954	11,916	3,295	76,576	— 7,748
1911	2,047	none	43,499	8,524	3,651	57,721	— 18,855
1912	1,836	none	67,154	14,131	3,568	86,689	28,968
1913	2,241	none	66,951	15,615	3,847	88,654	1,965
1914	2,012	none	61,963	9,412	4,717	78,104	— 10,550
1915	7,748	none	94,084	13,563	4,844	120,239	42,135
1916	40,338	40,870	148,395	48,206	5,804	283,613	163,374
1917	233,047	48,528	184,795	54,741	8,204	529,315	245,702
1918	277,746	15,870	173,806	49,723	10,711	527,856	— 1,459
1919	159,070	870	166,727	42,025	10,983	379,675	—148,181
1920	150,351	870	123,661	38,393	10,730	324,005	— 55,670

[a] Exclusive of Agents' Balances or Cash Working Funds.
[b] Collateral loan.
[c] Less employees' stock subscriptions.

TABLE V (Continued)

	Marketable Securities	Time Deposits	Cash[a]	Insurance & Depreciation Fund Assets	Contingent Reserve Fund	Total	Change
1921	131,463	6,924	116,857	34,006	16,189	305,439	— 18,566
1922	59,605	9,506	126,700	108,347	13,242	317,400	11,961
1923	64,086	7,038	143,500	106,816	9,882	331,322	13,922
1924	46,675	3,993	131,357	102,532	6,416	290,973	— 40,349
1925	50,612	6,457	125,529	112,747	875	299,220	8,247
1926	72,615	8,073	132,537	104,709	3,857	321,791	22,571
1927	59,589	8,478	112,867	95,897	3,835	280,666	— 41,125
1928	57,367	10,173	152,108	133,207	4,007	356,862	76,196
1929	60,544	4,279	130,674	57,582	20,044[c]	272,123	— 83,739
1930	71,066	9,537	117,203	41,070	— 1,418[c]	237,458	— 35,665
1931	69,358	6,208	75,240	4,332	2,713[c]	157,851	— 79,607
1932	46,139	5,602	60,224	5,648	8,719[c]	126,332	— 31,519
1933	49,405	2,816	55,324	5,468	none	113,013	— 13,319
1934	54,626	2,866	67,687	5,650	none	130,829	17,816
1935	55,321	1,248	79,134	5,172	none	140,875	10,046
1936	39,905	2,548	81,393	none	none	123,846	— 17,029

[a] Exclusive of Agents' Balances or Cash Working Funds.
[b] Collateral loan.
[c] Less employees' stock subscriptions.

TABLE VI
Adjusted Distributions to Security Holders and Taxing Agencies
(in thousands of dollars)

Year	Reduction in Senior Securities[a]	Premium on Bonds	Interest Payments	Preferred Dividends	Common Dividends	Increase in Cash and Funds[b]	Adjusted Distribution to Security-Holders[c]	Taxes Paid[b]	Total: Adjusted Distribution[d]
1901	......	......	......	......	......	......	......	......	......
1902	4,022	none	22,034	35,720	20,333	− 5,383	76,726	2,391	79,117
1903	−40,287e	6,800f	25,637	30,404	12,708	14,936	50,198	2,973	53,171
1904	−20,752	none	30,091	25,220	none	2,084	36,643	3,053	39,696
1905	3,894	none	29,766	25,220	none	7,697	66,577	3,646	70,223
1906	5,738	none	29,401	25,220	10,166	28,084	98,609	4,356	102,965
1907	−38,030	none	29,352	25,220	10,166	− 9,191	17,517	5,384	22,901
1908	6,954	none	31,264	25,220	10,166	− 23,652	49,952	5,361	55,313
1909	−13,153	none	31,504	25,220	20,332	7,182	71,085	8,704	79,789
1910	10,030	none	30,630	25,220	25,415	− 7,748	83,547	9,161	92,708
1911	−24,150	none	31,145	25,220	25,415	− 18,855	38,775	9,622	48,397
1912	−22,629	none	32,569	25,220	25,415	28,968	89,543	9,840	99,383
1913	16,015	783	32,518	25,220	25,415	1,965	101,916	13,226	115,142
1914	52	910	32,322	25,220	15,249	− 10,550	63,203	12,646	75,849
1915	10,599	971	31,783	25,220	6,354	42,135	117,062	13,640	130,702
1916	12,962	1,017	31,026	25,220	44,476	163,374	278,075	26,600	304,675
1917	16,685	864	30,125	25,220	91,494	245,702	410,090	252,265	662,355
1918	4,140	830	29,821	25,220	71,162	− 1,459	129,714	297,645	427,359
1919	13,918	933	29,211	25,220	25,415	−148,181	− 53,484	81,594	28,110
1920	13,900	835	28,514	25,220	25,415	− 55,670	38,214	76,224	114,438

a From Table IV, last column.
b From Table V, last column.
c Total of columns 1-6.
d Total of columns 7 and 8.
e 1903 — $20,000,000 received from J. P. Morgan Co. for same amount of bonds.
f 1903 — $6,800,000 paid to J. P. Morgan Co. as 4% underwriting commission.
g 1929 — $143,697,624 received on stock subscription for 1,016,605 shares at 140, which should have netted only $142,324,700; but because the Corporation itself sold some unused rights, these shares actually netted $372,924 more, thus making the negative dividend that much greater for the year 1929.
h Cf. Table 1, p. 224.

TABLE VI (Continued)

Year	Reduction in Senior Securities[a]	Premium on Bonds	Interest Payments	Preferred Dividends	Common Dividends	Increase in Cash and Funds[b]	Adjusted Distribution to Security-Holders[c]	Taxes Paid[h]	Total: Adjusted Distribution[d]
1921	14,122	747	27,745	25,220	25,415	— 18,566	74,683	37,684	112,367
1922	1,125	875	27,492	25,220	25,415	11,961	92,088	35,798	127,886
1923	12,547	940	27,072	25,220	29,227	13,922	108,928	55,083	164,011
1924	15,762	968	26,343	25,220	35,581	— 40,349	63,525	45,277	108,802
1925	1,793	1,103	26,006	25,220	35,581	8,247	97,950	50,923	148,873
1926	16,790	1,243	25,515	25,220	35,581	22,571	126,920	52,400	179,320
1927	17,515	1,398	24,665	25,220	49,814	— 41,125	77,487	46,291	123,778
1928	18,572	1,958	23,788	25,220	49,814	76,196	195,548	50,976	246,524
1929	344,344	40,627	14,944	25,220	—78,849g	— 83,739	262,547	54,972	317,519
1930	10,438	87	5,640	25,220	60,366	— 35,665	66,086	48,052	114,138
1931	2,933	64	5,469	25,220	36,984	— 79,607	— 8,937	34,248	25,311
1932	2,937	62	5,313	20,716	none	— 31,519	— 2,491	32,305	29,814
1933	2,770	3	5,164	7,206	none	— 13,319	1,824	31,710	33,534
1934	2,257	none	5,051	7,206	none	17,816	32,330	35,780	68,110
1935	2,112	none	4,960	7,206	none	10,046	24,324	38,377	62,701
1936	— 4,700	none	4,918	50,439	none	— 17,029	33,628	48,814	82,442

a From Table IV, last column.
b From Table V, last column.
c 1903 — $20,000,000 received from J. P. Morgan Co. for same amount of bonds.
f 1903 — $6,800,000 paid to J. P. Morgan Co. as 4% underwriting commission.
g 1929 — $143,697,624 received on stock subscription for 1,016,605 shares at 140, which should have netted only $142,324,700; but because the Corporation itself sold some unused rights, these shares actually netted $372,924 more, thus making the negative dividend that much greater for the year 1929.
h Cf. Table 1, p. 224.

c Total of columns 1-6.
d Total of columns 7 and 8.

TABLE VII
ACTUAL AND DEFLATED QUASI-RENTS OR EARNINGS

Year	Earnings before Depreciation and after Taxes[a]	Taxes[b]	Actual Quasi-Rents[c]	U.S.B.L.S. Price Index[d]	Deflated Quasi-Rents[e]
1901	......	....	......	55.3	......
1902	140,155[f]	2,391[f]	142,546[f]	58.9	242,000[f]
1903	106,725	2,973	109,698	59.6	184,100
1904	79,750	3,053	82,803	59.7	138,700
1905	126,498	3,646	130,144	60.1	216,500
1906	163,185	4,356	167,541	61.8	271,100
1907	167,457	5,384	172,841	65.2	265,100
1908	99,249	5,361	104,610	62.9	166,300
1909	139,378	8,704	148,082	67.6	219,100
1910	148,318	9,161	157,479	70.4	223,700
1911	112,343	9,622	121,965	64.9	187,900
1912	117,927	9,840	127,767	69.1	184,900
1913	147,166	13,226	160,392	69.8	229,800
1914	81,747	12,646	94,393	68.1	138,600
1915	140,250	13,640	153,890	69.5	221,400
1916	342,997	26,600	369,597	85.5	432,300
1917	304,161	252,265	556,426	117.5	473,600
1918	196,066	297,645	493,711	131.3	376,000
1919	152,291	81,594	233,885	138.6	168,700
1920	185,095	76,224	261,319	154.4	169,200
1921	100,791	37,684	138,475	97.6	141,900
1922	109,789	35,798	145,587	96.7	150,600
1923	187,954	55,083	243,037	100.6	241,600
1924	161,184	45,277	206,461	98.1	210,500
1925	173,783	50,923	224,706	103.5	217,100
1926	207,345	52,400	259,745	100.0	259,700
1927	172,315	46,291	218,606	95.4[g]	229,100
1928	200,986	50,976	251,962	96.7[g]	260,600
1929	265,839	54,972	320,811	95.3[g]	336,600
1930	157,710	48,052	205,762	86.4[g]	238,200
1931	46,484[h]	34,248	80,732	73.0[g]	110,600
1932	−26,665[i]	32,305	5,640	64.8[g]	8,700
1933	10,523[i]	31,710	42,233	65.9[g]	64,100
1934	27,412[i]	35,780	63,192	74.9[g]	84,400
1935	52,818[i]	38,377	91,195	80.0[g]	114,000
1936	112,320	48,814	161,134	80.8	199,400
	4,911,346	1,537,021	6,448,367		35)7,376,100
					Average: 210,700

[a] Item 1 of Income Account on p. 1 of *Annual Report* for 1936, and from similar accounts in earlier reports.   [b] See p. 2 of *Annual Report* for 1936, and other reports for earlier years.   [c] Total of first two columns.   [d] *Survey of Current Business.* U. S. Dept. of Commerce.   [e] Computed from columns 3 and 4.   [f] In thousands of dollars.   [g] Revised Index: 1926 = 100.   [h] Exclusive of extraordinary income from sale of utility plant.   [i] After taxes, etc., on iron ore properties.

TABLE VIII
THE DISTRIBUTION RATE

Year	Total Quasi-Rent[a]	Adjusted Distribution Thereof[b]	Total Distribution Rate[c]	Tax Rate[d]	Investors' Rate[e]	Five-year averages	
						Tax Rate[f]	Investors' Rate[f]
1901	......	......	...	...	...	...	...
1902	142,546	79,117	55.5%	1.7%	53.8%	...	...
1903	109,698	53,171	48.5	2.7	45.8	...	...
1904	82,803	39,696	47.9	3.7	44.2	...	...
1905	130,144	70,223	54.0	2.8	51.2	2.6%	49.5%
1906	167,541	102,965	61.5	2.6	58.9	...	...
1907	172,841	22,901	13.2	3.1	10.1	...	...
1908	104,610	55,313	52.9	5.1	47.8	...	...
1909	148,082	79,789	53.9	5.9	48.0	...	...
1910	157,479	92,708	58.8	5.8	53.0	4.4%	42.8%
1911	121,965	48,397	39.7	7.9	31.8	...	...
1912	127,767	99,383	77.8	7.7	70.1	...	...
1913	160,392	115,142	71.8	8.2	63.6	...	...
1914	94,393	75,849	80.4	13.4	67.0	...	...
1915	153,890	130,702	84.9	8.9	76.0	9.0%	62.4%
1916	369,597	304,675	82.4	7.2	75.2	...	...
1917	556,426	662,355	119.0	45.3	73.7	...	...
1918	493,711	427,359	86.6	60.3	26.3	...	...
1919	233,885	28,110	12.0	34.9	-22.9	...	...
1920	261,319	114,438	43.8	29.2	14.6	38.3%	41.9%

Year	a	b	c	d	e	f	g
1921	138,475	112,367	81.1	27.2	53.9	...	...
1922	145,587	127,886	87.8	24.6	63.2	...	...
1923	243,037	164,011	67.5	22.7	44.8	...	...
1924	206,461	108,802	52.7	21.9	30.8	...	...
1925	224,706	148,873	66.3	22.7	43.6	23.5%	45.6%
1926	259,745	179,320	69.0	20.2	48.8	...	...
1927	218,606	123,778	56.6	21.2	35.4	...	...
1928	251,962	246,524	97.8	20.2	77.6	...	...
1929	320,811	317,519	99.1	17.1	82.0	...	...
1930	205,762	11<,138	55.5	23.4	32.1	20.1%	58.0%
1931	80,732	25,311	31.4	42.5	−11.1	...	...
1932	5,640	29,814	528.6	572.8	−44.2	...	...
1933	42,233	33,534	79.4	75.1	4.3	...	...
1934	63,192	68,110	107.8	56.6	51.2	...	...
1935	91,195	62,701	68.8	42.1	26.7	60.9%	16.6%
1936	161,134	82,442	51.2	30.3	20.9	...	...
	6,448,367	4,547,424	70.5% h	23.8% h	46.7% h	23.8% h	46.7% h

a From Table VII, column 3. (In thousands of dollars.)

b From Table VI, last column. (In thousands of dollars.)

c Ratio of the two preceding columns.

d Ratio of column 8 in Table VI to first column in this table.

e Difference between the two preceding columns.

f Ratio of five-year total of taxes to five-year total of rents.

g Ratio of five-year total of dividends, etc., to five-year total of rents.

h Ratio of thirty-five-year totals.

INDEX

INDEX

United Gas Corporation, 553n
United Gas Improvement Company, 548
United States Bureau of Labor Statistics price index, 412n, 413, 458, 459, 497, 589
United States Government Securities, 270n
United States Steel Corporation, 409-62, 541
arrears on preferred, 453-54
bonds, 584
bookings, 572-73
seasonal variation, 574-78
affected by boom, 454
capacity, 581
capitalization changes, 584
capitalization rate, 449-51, 452, 459
senior issues, 450
Carnegie plants, 426
cash assests, 440-41, 585-86
coal holdings, 438
competition, 422-23, 425-29
common, causes of rise and fall, 458-60
common stock, 584
contributions, 440
cost curve, 420-21
costs,
compared with prices, 421-22
compared with profits, 426
increment, 420-21
prime, 420
debt retirement, 270n
depreciation, 421-22, 443
depreciation fund assets, 453
distribution rate, 440, 441-42, 590-91
distributions, 439-40
dividend-paying power, 415-16, 439-47
normal, 446-47
uncertainty, 450
dividends, common, paid, 587-88
dividends, preferred, arrears, 453-54
earnings,
compared with output, 414-16
deflated, 412-14
derived from monopoly power, 419-24
reinvested, 238, 415-16

source of dividends, 439-40
trend, 412-14
flow sheet, 429-31
forecasters of price of common, 9
Gary plant, 426, 432
growth in future production, 416-19
investment value, 451
labor unions, 424-25
marginal revenue curve, 422
market prices of common, monthly, 568-71
monopoly gains, 424-25
monopoly power, 419-24
net quick assets, shrinkage, 453-54, 456
obsolescence, 443
operations rate, 581
compared with national, 417, 582
ore holdings, 407n, 438
output compared with earnings, 414-16
output, ingots, 583
percentage of national, 417, 583
output, rolled and finished products, 581
"over-capacity" refuted, 414-16
overhead, 421
plant, 425-38
preferred stock, 584
dividend arrears, 453-54
price level, effect on dividends, 444-46, 455, 459-60
prices compared with costs, 421-22
production, 572-73
profits compared with costs, 426
quasi-rent, 197
actual, 589-91
deflated, 589
railroad holdings, 407n, 426
reinvestment of earnings, 238, 415-16, 442-44
return earned on assets, 443
rights, 440, 454, 458n
risk, 450
senior and junior issues, 70-71
stock,
common, 584
preferred, 584
tax rate, 223-26, 252, 447-49, 450
taxes paid, 224-25, 587-89